The PC-SIG Library

"PC-SIG provides a much needed service, organizing and distributing the vast amount of public domain and user-supported software available for the IBM PC. We are happy to have our user-supported software included in the library; many of our registered users obtained their first copy of PC-Write from PC-SIG."

—Bob Wallace
President
Quicksoft

"...one of the best organized, most professionally run sources of free software in the entire public domain. ... it may well become the source of free IBM software. ... Get the catalog. You'll think you've died and gone to free software heaven."

—*"Whole Earth Software Catalog 1984"*

"There is no better way for an IBM, Compaq or IBM compatible owner to tap the incredible riches of FREE public domain and user-supported software than through PC Software Interest Group (PC-SIG) and this catalog. Well run and well organized, PC-SIG is rapidly becoming the defacto "master library" of the IBM public domain. Unconditionally recommended."

—Alfred Glossbrenner
Author of *"How To Get FREE Software"*

The *PC-SIG* Library

A Directory of Public Domain
and User Supported Software for
the IBM-PC, PC jr., and Compatibles

Compiled by:

Richard Petersen
Hazel Gray
Richard Watson
Elvin Bollet
Marion Horton

Published by:

PC Software Interest Group (PC-SIG)
1030 E. Duane Ave. Suite J
Sunnyvale, CA 94086

May 1985

Trademarks:

"Freeware" is a trademark of Headlands Press
"1-2-3" and "Symphony" are trademarks of Lotus Corporation
"Easywriter" is a trademark of IUS
"Wordstar" is a trademark of MicroPro
"Volkswriter" is a trademark of Lifetree Software
"Multiplan" is a trademark of Microsoft

ISBN 0-915835-02-9

Dedicated to the authors of public domain and user-supported programs without whose effort this book could not exist.

CONTENTS

1.0 INTRODUCTION

PC-SIG (PC Software Interest Group) has created this directory to its organized library of public domain and directly-marketed user-supported software for the IBM-PC, PC-compatibles, and the PCjr. We offer a low-cost, simple way to obtain a large variety of useful software for your PC or compatible—from short, specialized sub-routines that may solve a particular problem to fully formed and supported word processor, spreadsheet, and database packages.

Public Domain Software

Books, publications, screenplays, music, and now software, can be divided into two categories: copyrighted and public domain. Copyrighted material is restricted by law as to who can make copies of a work and distribute or modify it. Public domain material is the opposite: The originator chose not to seek formal rights or royalties to the work, and has made it available to the public to use or alter under fewer or no restrictions. This directory (and the PC-SIG library) contains hundreds of programs written for the IBM-PC that are in the public domain.

Direct-Market, User-Supported Software

An alternative to retail marketing is direct marketing. In direct marketing, you are dealing directly with the originator of the product, rather than supporting a hierarchy of manufacturer, distributor, wholesaler, and retailer. Although the direct-marketed, user-supported software in this directory is copyrighted, the cost is dramatically lower than for equivalent retail-marketed software. Direct marketing makes it possible to present mature, supported software for 10 to 30% of the cost of retailed software, or approximately the equivalent of the programmer's royalty were the work to be distributed through a software manufacturer and publisher. Most of the user-supported software in this directory is distributed in about the same way as the public domain software; that is, you may get copies from a friend, user group, PC-SIG, or in some cases directly from the author. The difference is that the software authors request that the user send them a suggested donation once he or she has found the software useful and satisfactory. The donation in most cases enables the author to provide software support for the product, and to continue to improve and expand the products and services available under this low-cost, alternative method of software distribution.

How this Software Came About

In the relatively short time the IBM-PC and compatibles have been on the market, how could so much software become available for little more than the cost of the diskettes that contain the programs? Actually, the software contained in our library has come from several sources, including the following:

- Government Grants
  Government-sponsored projects require that the results be placed in the public domain. Your tax dollars paid for the development of some of our programs, and the authors received their compensation from the government contract.

- Specialization
  Many programs are very specific in application and lack the mass appeal to copyright, publish, distribute, and support.

- Alternate Marketing
  The user-supported software represents a departure from conventional production and distribution of micro-based software. The software generally equals or exceeds the quality and documentation level of "store-bought" programs, but allows less restrictive distribution of the software and gives the author more direct contact with his/her customer base.

- Idealism
  Yes, it's still alive. Strange as it may seem to some people, there are many capable programmers who believe their programs should be available hassle-free to anyone who truly wants them.

How Useful are the Programs?

Very. The direct-marketed—and many public domain—packages are documented, user-oriented fully supported applications that rival their retail-distributed counterparts in every aspect but price. The selection includes word processors, spreadsheets, database management systems, and other applications.

There are public domain games with full animation and high-resolution color graphics that could make you forget about trips to the arcade.

Then there are all the specialized routines and programs that make your computer easier to use—printer spoolers to enable you to print while running another program, programs and subroutines that help you develop music or graphics. These programs range from "as is" routines to debugged, fully documented and supported applications programs. They all have run on a PC somewhere, sometime. In short, the great bulk of selections provide ways to get your PC to do something that you may lack the expertise, time, or inclination to provide yourself. At $6 per diskette, however, you probably won't lack the funds.

Notice also, that it does not cost $6 per program; it's $6 per 'diskette', and each diskette is loaded with programs of a particular category, so if one routine isn't exactly what you were looking for, the next one might be.

The PC-SIG Library

The PC-SIG software library represented by this directory is the collection of many hundreds of public domain and user-supported programs distributed onto over three hundred diskettes. We are constantly improving our library by enlarging the selection and making it more accessible through better organization and categorization. The disks in the library were generated sequentually so the latest programs tend to be on the higher number disks.

This updated version of the PC-SIG library directory features many new and enhanced diskettes. The purpose of this book is to acquaint all levels of computer users—from novice to expert—with the availability of public domain and direct-marketed programs for the IBM-PC, PCjr, and compatible computers.

We have enhanced this new version in several ways. In Section 2.0, "Getting Started", we provide a simple tutorial for the new user. In Section 3.0, "Program Descriptions", there are descriptions of the major and more popular programs in the library. File descriptions for each of the diskettes can be found in Section 4.0, "Disk Contents". The last two sections of the book are comprised of the glossary, index, and how to get copies of the diskettes and how to contribute to the library.

About the PC Software Interest Group

We are dedicated to making quality, low cost software available to users of IBM PC's and compatibles. Pursuant to this goal, we provide the following services in addition to this directory:

- Organize the software topically and onto diskettes
- Maintain contact with program authors
- Maintain the latest versions of the software
- Fix bugs
- Update users with the latest versions for a nominal charge

Disclaimer

PC-SIG distributes its software directly to subscribers from the address listed below. We have no regional or local distributors or subsidiaries. Only by dealing directly with PC-SIG or the author of a program can you be assured that you receive the most up-to-date version of a program. We cannot be responsible for or support public domain software obtained from other sources.

PC-SIG is located at:

PC Software Interest Group (PC-SIG)
1030 East Duane Ave, Suite J
Sunnyvale, CA 94086
(408) 730-9291

2.0 GETTING STARTED

This section is written to give a brief introduction to the commands necessary to run programs on your PC. If you are already familiar with DOS commands and running programs you may wish to skip this section.

Now that you have purchased your PC, you are considered a "user". Usually, the new user is in awe of his PC and may feel some apprehension about "using" it. You will not "damage" your PC by typing on the keyboard. As long as you make backup copies of your software, especially your DOS disk, feel free to experiment and learn at your own pace. The PC is a tool and virtually helpless without you the "user". You're in charge (at least most of the time). The PC does not evaluate what you type, everything is taken literally. So watch for those periods and spaces in the wrong places.

DOS

DOS stands for "Disk Operating System" and contains the commands necessary to operate your computer. Simply stated, DOS allows your computer to understand the commands you type in to retrieve information from a diskette, or hard disk, and to use that data. You must start with DOS before using any program in this library. How to use DOS is covered in the DOS manual which comes with your computer, however, many people do not take the time to go through it. We will describe the following basic DOS commands in this section:

DIR	(DIRectory) To view the names of files on the disk
DISKCOPY	To make copies of an entire disk
FORMAT	Prepares a blank disk for use by your computer
COPY	To copy files from one disk to another or to the printer
TYPE	Allows you to display the contents of a text file on the screen

Using DOS

Insert your DOS disk in the disk drive and turn on your computer. A prompt "A>" appears followed by a blinking cursor. After this prompt you may enter DOS commands and start programs. Commands can be typed in upper case, lower case or a mixture of the two.

With the DOS prompt "A>" on the screen, type:

```
DIR
```

followed by the "Enter" or "Return" key (all DOS commands require you to depress the Enter key to activate the command). You should see a table of names and numbers similiar to the following on your screen:

```
 Volume in drive A has no label
 Directory of A: \

COMMAND    COM  17664    3-08-83  12:00p
ANSI       SYS  1664     3-08-83  12:00p
FORMAT     COM  6016     3-08-83  12:00p
CHKDSK     COM  6400     3-08-83  12:00p
SYS        COM  1408     3-08-83  12:00p
DISKCOPY   COM  2444     3-08-83  12:00p
DISKCOMP   COM  2074     3-08-83  12:00p
BASIC      COM  16256    3-08-83  12:00p
BASICA     COM  25984    3-08-83  12:00p
           9 File(s)     282098 bytes free
```

This table is a list of the files on your disk. The first column lists the name of the file followed by its three character extension. The following columns list the size, creation date and time of the file respectively. You may use the "DIR" command to list only certain files, if you wish. The "*" which is called a wildcard may be used with many DOS commands to refer to several files at one time. For example you may list only the files with the extension "EXE" by typing:

```
DIR *.EXE
```

or only those files beginning with the letters "DISK" by typing:

```
DIR DISK*.*
```

Filenames

All programs and data on your diskettes are addressed by filename. This makes it important to understand what a filename is. A filename consists of 1 to 8 characters followed by an optional extension of 1 to 3 characters which often follows the name. The extension is always preceeded by a ".". The following are examples of filenames:

```
DISKCOMP.COM
MENU.BAS
README.TXT
DATA
```

The file extension is used to give some idea of the type of file. For example the extension ".BAS" indicates that the file is a BASIC program, ".TXT" indicates that the file contains text or written material. A list of the generally used file extensions is presented in a later part of this section.

Making a Copy of a Disk

The DISKCOPY command is used to make a copy of an entire disk. Making a backup copy of a disk protects you if your original disk is damaged, lost or erased. To make a copy of a disk put your DOS disk in Drive A, assuming you are at the "A>" prompt, (if not, type A: <RET>) and type:

```
DISKCOPY A: B:
```

Depress the Enter key. You will be prompted to put your "Source" (original) disk in Drive A: and and your "Target" (blank) disk in Drive B:. Those with a single disk drive will get prompts alternately for Drive A: and Drive B:.

Formatting a Disk

Formatting a blank disk is required before you can copy files to it. To format a disk, put your DOS disk in Drive A: (assuming you are at the "A>" prompt) and type:

```
FORMAT B:
```

Depress the Enter key. You will be prompted to put the disk you want to format in Drive B:. When you are asked if you want to "format another?" you may either format another disk or return to DOS.

Copying Files

Sometimes it is useful to add files to a disk (such as BASICA.COM to a public domain program disk so you can more easily run BASIC programs). Or, you can create disks with selected files on them. To copy BASICA.COM from the disk in Drive A: to the disk in Drive B: type:

```
COPY A:BASICA.COM B:
```

The "*" wildcard may be used to copy mutliple files. For example typing:

```
COPY A:*.COM B:
```

would copy all files with the extension .COM from the disk in Drive A: to the disk in Drive B:.

Listing a Text File on the Screen

The TYPE command may be used to list a text file to your screen. Type "TYPE" and the name of a file you wish to display. For example:

```
TYPE B:README.TXT
```

would list on your monitor screen the file "README.TXT" from the disk in Drive B:

Running Programs

Most programs on the library disks are either written in BASIC or have been compiled into .EXE or .COM files. BASIC programs can be distinguished by the file extension .BAS after the filename.

Running BASIC Programs

Programs with the extension ".BAS" require you to load BASIC to run the program. On a PC this can be done by typing "BASIC" or "BASICA" and the filename of the program you wish to run. On the PCjr you will need the BASIC ROM cartridge.

For example to run the program "Wombat" on Disk #1 you would put your DOS disk in Drive A: and library Disk #1 in Drive B:. Following the DOS prompt "A>" type:

```
BASIC  B:WOMBAT
```

then press the Enter key.

A disk sometimes contains programs which work with (or "chain" to) other programs on a disk. In order for this to work, the disk must be in the same drive as the prompt displayed when you started the program. On some disks there is a program called "MENU.BAS" which may be used to call other programs.

To run a disk of BASIC programs with a "MENU" program put your DOS disk in Drive A:. After the "A>" prompt enter:

```
BASICA
```

When the computer displays an "Ok" prompt, remove your DOS disk and place the program disk in Drive A:. Now, enter:

```
RUN"MENU
```

Depress the Enter key and you will be off and running. This method should work on all computers, although your computer may have a more efficient way of accomplishing the same thing. Because of the variations between computers, it is impossible to list the most efficient method of running chain programs on the various types of computers. Sometimes all that is required is to copy BASICA.COM to your program disk.

Running Compiled Programs

Compiled programs (ones with file extensions .EXE and .COM) can be executed directly from DOS. After the DOS prompt, A >, B >or C > just type the name of the program and any options that the program requires. Example, for the program named PC-FILE.COM:

PC-FILE (the file extension is optional)

then press the Enter key.

Program Documentation

Many programs have documentation files with the extension .DOC which explain how to use them. These files may usually be listed on a printer for reference. For example:

```
COPY A:XYZ.DOC LPT1:
```

will print out the contents of the file XYZ.DOC. Some authors have provided special procedures for listing the documentation for their programs. It is a good idea to follow their instructions as some documentation is not listable using the copy command or looks better if you use their procedures.

It is a good idea to make a printed copy of the document file before trying to run the programs as there may be things you must know before you can run the program. Some of the disks have "README" files. These should be displayed or printed before using the disk.

Filename extension conventions

Certain filename extensions have been adopted for specific types of files. This tells users what kind of material is in a file from its extension.

The following file naming conventions are generally used (though there may be exceptions). "Listable" means that they are text files which may be typed using the DOS "TYPE" command, copied to a printer or viewed using a text editor.

.ABS	Abstracts - brief program descriptions (listable)
.APL	APL source files
.ASC	ASCII text files (listable)
.ASM	Assembly language source files (listable)
.BAS	BASIC source files (may be listed from BASIC by typing "LLIST")
.BAT	Batch file (listable)
.C	"C" language source files (listable)
.COM	COM files - are directly executed by typing filename from DOS
.DAT	Data files
.DBF	dBASE II data files (require dBASE II)
.DOC	Document files (listable)
.EWF	Easywriter text file
.EXE	Execute files - are directly executed by typing filename from DOS
.FOR	Fortran source files (listable)
.NDX	dBASE II index files
.OBJ	Object files (used by Linker)
.PAS	Pascal source files (listable)
.PIC	Color graphic screen images
.PRG	dBASE II Program files (listable) require dBASE II
.TXT	Text files (listable)
.UNP	Text files describing how to "unprotect" commercial programs
.VC	Visicalc templates
.WKS	Lotus 1-2-3 worksheets (Require Lotus 1-2-3)
.WS	Wordstar text file

Compatibility

There are many considerations which affect whether a program in the library can be run on your system. These include the type of computer, options installed, amount of memory, requirement for another program to run with it and the version of DOS you are using.

Computers from many manufacturers will run many of the programs written for the IBM PC. Some machines such as the Compaq, Corona, AT&T and Tandy 1000 and 1200 are very close to the IBM PC and should run nearly every program in this library. Other machines such as the Sanyo 550, and the TI are significantly different from the PC and will not run all programs. Even machines with a low level of compatibility will still be able to read PC formatted disks allowing knowledgeable users to modify the source code for their particular machine.

Even the PC will not run all programs. Some programs were written to use the color graphics card and will not run without it. These programs are identified in the disk directory with a "+" after the filename extension.

The amount of memory in your system may affect whether or not you can use a program. Some programs require more than 128K of memory. This was more of a consideration when only 64K of memory was available on the motherboard of a PC. Most users now have 256K or more of memory which is enough to run nearly all programs in this library.

Some programs require another program to operate. Lotus 1-2-3 worksheet files (with filename extension .WKS) require Lotus 1-2-3. Source code programs for BASIC, dBASE II, Pascal, C and other languages require a compiler or interpreter for that language.

Finally, the version of DOS you are using may affect whether a program will operate. Some programs require DOS 1.1, others require DOS 2.0 or later. DOS compatibility affects mostly programs which access the file directory. How DOS accesses the directory, changed between the two versions. Disk descriptions noted with a "DS2", after the version number in the disk title line, require DOS 2.0 or later to be read, even though some of the programs may run under DOS 1.1.

The PCjr

The PCjr is very close in design to the PC. However there are a few differences that jr owners should be aware of. Most of the software in the PC-SIG library works well on the jr. All of the programs can be copied or have their directories listed on the jr.

Some programs require an 80 column display. When the jr is first turned on the display is 40 columns wide with fairly large type. To convert the jr to a 80 column display put your DOS disk in the drive and after the 'A>" prompt type:

```
MODE CO80
```

Another difficulty jr owners may encounter is with modem communications. If you are planning on using a modem with your jr you should be aware that the jr has different internal communication circuitry from the standard PC. Because of this, communication packages written for the PC do not work with the jr. It is important that your communications program was written for the jr.

Graphics programs that were written before the popularity of the jr may not make the necessary adjustments for the jr to work properly. More recent graphics programs do not seem to have the difficulties of earlier programs. PC-SIG library disks with higher disk numbers are more likely to run on the jr.

3.0 PROGRAM DESCRIPTIONS

Following are descriptions of some of the major public domain and user-supported programs for the PC. They were provided either by the authors of the programs or were extracted from the documentation (with some minor editing). In most cases it will be necessary to read the on-disk documentation which accompanies each program.

There are also many other high quality programs in the library, not described here, which should be tried.

Working with words (word processing)

Word processors allow you to write, modify and print documents.

There are several very good user-supported word processing programs available. In some cases they are better than commercial programs costing several hundred dollars. PC-WRITE is probably the most popular although you may want to try others to see which you prefer.

PC-WRITE 2.4, (#78) u-s $75

PC-WRITE by Quicksoft is a powerful word processing program. It comes with a complete 118 page manual including tutorial and index, on diskette. It supports most printers and/ 46 printer control files are included. Notable features include nine help screens, very fast edit and save functions, split screen editing, and user configuration of keyboard, display, and printer. PC-WRITE uses standard DOS files, and makes a good program editor as well. It also works well on PCjr and supports paths on hard disk systems. Page breaks and fonts such as boldface, are visible on the screen.

As of January 1985, Quicksoft had over 2,400 registered users of PC- WRITE plus 12,000 diskette and bulk account users. Registered users receive a full printed manual in a binder, a quick reference card, telephone support, a newsletter, and two free update (or source) diskettes. You will also get a $25 sales commission when someone you have supplied a copy registers with Quicksoft. Quicksoft has a full time staff of four devoted entirely to PC-WRITE.

PC-WRITE Version 2.4 Summary of Features

CURSOR MOVEMENT:
By character, word, line, paragraph, tab, to start or end of line or of text, to top or bottom of screen. Scroll by line, page up or down; horizontal scroll; bookmark.

SEARCH AND REPLACE:
Search forward or backward, six wild card matches, lower case matches upper. Replace once, global replace to end of text, unreplace; replace matching case.

EDITING ACTIONS:
Insert or overwrite mode. Decimal tab mode to align numbers. Delete character or word to left or right, delete to end of line, un-delete. Automatic wordwrap option, margin release. Enter aligned with line above. Insert or delete space, slide block right/left. Transpose, change case, center a line of text.

BLOCK OPERATIONS:
Move, copy, delete selected and highlighted text of any length, partial lines OK. Copy selected text to another file, insert file. Undelete.

MARGINS:
Left, right, paragraph, bell margins. Temporary left and right margins. Optional Ruler line on screen has shadow cursor, can be edited like text. Margins (and options) in separate Ruler file, set automatically or manually. Reformat paragraph or all text to right margin, slide all text right/left. Reformat modes: ragged right, justify (flush right), un-justify.

FILE OPERATIONS:
Save text, switch files, rename text, cancel a save, exit (all very fast). Ruler line can split screen to edit in two places or edit two files at once. Uses DOS 2.00 pathnames and PATH= names. DOS 2.00 shell command

PAGE BREAKS:
Show current and maximum line on page, page in text, line in file, column. Hard (user inserted) and soft page breaks. Repage command to reset soft page breaks.

FONTS:
Underline, boldface, subscript, superscript; pica and elite pitch in correspondence and craft quality; seven more (depending on printer).
LAYOUT:
Footnote text to end of page or to other file. Block text kept on same page. Set multiple line spacing and lines per inch. Set/clear current fonts. Set printed page length and margins. Define multiline headers and footers flush left, right, center, or mixed for left/right pages, page number option.
PRINT:
Print single sheets, print to file, chain print, include user commands/text. Translate characters to printer commands for custom, foreign, or scientific text.
KEYBOARD:
Redefine key to be a sequence or phrase, sticky shift for one-finger typing, record/playback keystrokes, Ctrl key option, insert any code.
DISPLAY:
Monochrome, single color, or multi-color mode; can customize attributes. Has status line and 24 editing lines, font character visible/invisible mode.
HELP SCREENS:
Keyboard summary screen and optional eight tutorial screens. Can be customized.
FILES:
ASCII standard DOS files, Ctrl Z option, 60K max file size (47K on PCjr).
COMPUTERS:
IBM PC/XT/AT/JR, COMPAQ, etc. One or two double sided drives, 128K or more RAM prefered.
PRINTERS:
IBM, Epson, Okidata, Diablo, NEC, HP, Toshiba, many others. (Can customize.)

Quicksoft
219 First St. N #224
Seattle, WA 98109

WORDFLEX 1.60, (#68)

WORDFLEX is a basic word processing program. It was written specifically for the IBM PC and it utilizes all cursor and scroll control keys. It also runs on compatibles like Compaq (and similar).

All standard word processing utilities are included; automatic word wrap with paragraph reformatting, insertion or overwrite mode, deletion by character, line or block of lines, search and/or replace from the beginning of the document or from the current cursor position, block text moves (from one section of the document to another or from one document to another) as well as block text copy with original block unchanged. Right justification of text is one of the editing or printing options which can be easily enabled or disabled. All critical word processing functions have been optimized for speed: screen display, search and replace, scanning through a document.

WORDFLEX comes with a set of default settings of editing and printing features. These defaults can be changed temporarily or permanently according to the user's preference. The following features distinguish WORDFLEX from other low cost (user supported) word processing programs:

- WORDFLEX is a single program allowing both text editing and formatted printing with no need to exit from the main program and to use another.
- WORDFLEX utilizes all installed (and available) memory of the PC. Consequently, very large documents can be edited.
- Up to five documents can be edited simultaneously with virtually instantaneous transfers of blocks of text between them.
- Virtually all 255 characters of the IBM PC set can be entered into text files, including the Esc character.
- WORDFLEX will run on an IBM or non-IBM monochrome monitor or, with a Color Adapter Card, on an RGB color monitor. The colors used for display can be changed by a program included on the diskette.
- WORDFLEX has the following universal printer output controlling features: underline and/or boldface; adjustable left margin; multiple line spacing. All other features (changes of font, subscripts, superscripts) are entered using command (escape) sequences specific to each printer.

WORDFLEX generates standard ASCII text files fully compatible with most other word processing or proofreading programs. The files are also fully compatible with IBM PC compilers and assemblers.

WORDFLEX diskette contains three programs, five part on screen tutorial, and a three part detailed manual.

Start using your WORDFLEX packages by displaying file 'read_me'. (issue DOS command 'type read_me' without the quotes, of course). This file contains further instructions on how to proceed. You should follow the instructions leading to creation of a WORDFLEX working diskette (or copy WORDFLEX onto your fixed disk). The program will not run from the distribution diskette unless you explicitly instruct it to do so.

The diskette distributed by PC-SIG contains an 'Evaluation' version of WORDFLEX with a five part on screen tutorial, and a three part detailed manual. It is identical to the full version with the exception of a file utility module allowing display of directories, file rename, delete, hide and unhide. The full version can be obtained exclusively from NEMCO, 9 Walnut Street, Rutherford NJ 07070 for $35.00, postage and handling included.

EDIT V1.11, (#294) u-s $25

EDIT is a text editor and word processing program for the IBM PC family of computers. It is very simple to use. To create or edit a file called "text", you simply type:

```
EDIT TEXT
```

in response to the DOS prompt. To exit EDIT and return to DOS, you press the function key F1, which selects EDIT's Quit command, and then press E.

EDIT supports a wide array of editing operations, including powerful commands that are often not available even in very expensive word processors. EDIT gives you a wide range of control over the final layout of your printed file, including headers and footers, page size, tab stops, margins, right justification, spacing, etc. It supports not just "word wrapping", but full automatic paragraph reformatting. Under versions 2.0 or later of DOS, EDIT even allows you to execute DOS commands, or start another program without leaving EDIT.

There are a few things EDIT leaves out. It doesn't allow you to edit files much bigger than about 50,000 characters (25 single spaced pages of text). It doesn't include a spelling checker (although it stores files as normal text, so that most spelling checking programs work with files created by EDIT). It doesn't support footnotes, or automatic table of contents generation. EDIT doesn't try to do everything, but it does do everything that most people need from a text editor or word processor, and it does those things very well.

Screen editors

Screen editors are similiar to word processors but usually lack extensive print formatting controls. They are primarily used to edit programs and for word processing which do not require formatted printouts.

SCREEN, (#86) u-s $35

SCREEN is a powerful text editor made for use on the IBM PC. It is not intended as word processor, but could be used as one if used in conjunction with a text formatting program. This editor has all of the advanced editing features of a high priced word processor, and is ideal for program editing.

Some of the many features supported are:

- full screen cursor movement.
- line lengths up to 240 characters.
- full insert and delete capabilities.
- block operations (move,copy,delete).
- upper & lower case conversions of text.
- split a line in two.
- concatenate two lines.
- center a line.
- exchange two lines of text.
- repeat a line of text.
- send text to the printer.
- go to absolute or relative page numbers.
- file length may exceed memory.
- external files may be written to or read from.
- search, replace & global replace.
- all function keys utilizied.
- two page help menu.
- supports the MICROSOFT MOUSE.
- works with DOS 1.1 or DOS 2.0.

The user's manual shows you how to set up the computer and the software for ease of use. All capabilities of the SCREEN editor are explained in detail. A help menu is included in the editor which shows all commands available. A printout of a function key overlay has also been included to help you quickly use the function keys without refering to in the manual.

FRED, (#83) u-s $20

FRED stands for FRee EDitor. It is a full screen editor for the IBM- PC. It displays files of up to 1500 lines and with lines up to 254 characters long on a monochrome display or on an 80 column graphics display. The screen is a window onto the file. The window can move up, down, left and right. Lines which are longer than the screen are partly displayed. If you insert data, characters seem to be lost off of the end of the line; they are not lost but are just no longer displayed. Move the cursor off of the screen to the right and they will reappear as the window moves.

FRED updates the display buffer directly so that screen updates appear instantaneously. It is fully possible to scroll through a file at typamatic speeds. FRED is written in about 590 lines of compiled BASIC and about 30 lines of assembler. FRED is similar to the IBM Personal Editor, most of its keys are the same and its approach to handling the screen is about the same.

Text processing tools

Text processing tools help in the preparation of text or written material. They are not word processors or editors but perform specialized tasks not usually built into a word processor.

PC-READ, (#194) u-s $35

PC-READ is a compiled Pascal program that accepts a text file and grades it on a slightly modified Gunning Fog Index. The Gunning Fog Index measures the complexity of writing. It represents the complexity as an average grade level (elementary, high school, college) at which the text could be easily read. For instance, a Fog Index of 9 means 9th grade reading level. Most successful popular writing grades below a 13 on a Fog Index scale.

As the Fog Index rises, people will find the text more and more difficult to read. Government and business writing often has a very high Fog Index. This means that people will have trouble reading and understanding the writing. The input text file should be an ASCII file; it shouldn't have any special control codes imbedded in the text (printer controls are okay). PC-READ will process a file with special codes (e.g a WordStar file), but the resulting Fog Index may not be accurate.

PC-READ will give you a running tally of words and sentences as it is processing. PC-READ will continue processing until either: A) It reaches the end of the file, or B) It has processed 50 sentences. The 50 sentence limit allows you to process a sample from a long text file and is more than enough to generate a representative Fog Index.

After processing your text, PC-READ displays a Fog Index table, a graphic showing your sample's Fog Index range, and your actual Fog Index. You will have the option to process another file or to terminate the program.

REFLIST, (#231) u-s $25

REFLIST aids the authors of scientific and technical manuscripts by allowing them to easily extract and change the format references to conform to the standards of a particular publication.

- REFLIST reads the manuscript and compiles a list of the citations to other publications.
- It draws the full reference out of a Master File and formats the reference list according to the style requiements of almost any journal.
- It can return to the text file and replace the citations with the appropriate numbers.

Citations may be made within the text, (Smith and Jones, 1985) or numbered (7). REFLIST was written to be easy to use, and operates by selecting choices from a menu on the screen. This means that the details of how it works need not concern the user. One program is used to read through your text file and format the reference list, and another helps you to enter new references into a master catalog. Other files act as examples of reference formats for the formatting program to copy. You can change these example formats or add new ones to the collection.

Requirements are: any computer running MS DOS, with a minimum of 64K of memory and one disc drive. It will handle text written with any word processing program.

Start by copying the 18 page manual in file "REFLIST.DOC" to your printer, and practice on the text supplied in file "EXAMPLE.MSS".

UTIL 1.2 (#60) u-s $3

UTIL allows an experienced user to easily manipulate ASCII data files using PC-DOS 2.0. Some functions will operate in DOS 1.1 if buffered I/O prefixes are used.

Command Syntax:

UTIL [prefix] subcommand [operand[operand[...]]] [<infile] [>outfile]

subcommands:

HELP or ?—Writes the help file to standard output
COPY or CPY—Moves ASCII text standard input to standard output selectively, see description below.
WCS or OUTC or SAY—Writes each operand value to standard output as an ASCII text line.

** FMODE=n—Changes the mode of each filename operand value to the decimal value given as "n" (1=read only, 2=hidden, 4=system, 32=changed, 0=normal no change, etc)
** DIR or FILES—Writes a batch file image to standard output which contains a line for each file found.
** SYSDIR—as above except only system and hidden files are included.
** CHGDIR—only normal files which have been flagged as changed are included in dir output.
** ENV—Writes SET commands to standard output which represent the current DOS environment.
HEX or UNPACK—Converts a standard input file to an ASCII text standard output containing printable hex representation of each input byte (suitable for transmission over an ASCII net).
PACK—Converts a standard input file of ASCII text lines which contain only printable hex characters into a satandard output where each pair of input characters is packed into an output byte.
PASTE—Lines from a paste file (required operand) and added to the end of lines read from standard nput starting at input line FROM=nnn (optional).
PASTE PAGE=nn—Converts standard input to a two column page format of nn lines per page.

(note ** indicates DOS 2.0 only)

See the documentation which accompanies the program for more details.

John R. Hind
4100 Pickwick Dr.
Raleigh, NC. 27612

UNWS, (#81)

UNWS (UNWordStar) strips the high order bits from WordStar files. This makes WordStar files compatible with many other word processors, communications programs and printers.

To use copy UNWS to your WordStar disk then enter the command UNWS and the program comes back and asks for names of input and output files. It is very fast.

ROFF, (#50,#194)

ROFF is a text formatter. Using ROFF, you can make nice printouts of a file with as little or as much help from the program as you want, depending on the commands. There are default values for all parameters, so if you don't put any commands in at all, your file will come out with filled, right-justified lines. The default line-length is 80 characters and the default page-length is 66 lines per page. "Filled lines" means that as many input words as possible are packed onto a line before it is printed and "non-filled" lines go through the formatter w/o rearrangement. "Right-justified" simply means that spaces are added between words to make all the right margins line up nicely.

This version of ROFF, based on the formatter in Kernighan and Plauger's book SOFTWARE TOOLS, is written in BDS C, and employs the directed I/O functions that go along with that package.

All commands have the form of a period followed by two letters. A command line should have nothing on it but the command and its arguments (if any); any text would be lost.

Table of Commands

Command	Break?	Default	Function
.bp n	yes	n = +1	begin page numbered n
.br	yes		cause a break
.ce n	yes	n = 1	center next n lines
.fi	yes		start filling lines
.fo string	no	empty	sets footer to string
.he string	no	empty	sets header to string
.in n	no	n = 0	sets indent value to n
.ls n	no	n = 1	sets line spacing to n
.m1	no	n = 2	sets topmost margin to n
.m2	no	n = 2	sets 2nd top margin to n lines
.m3	no	n = 2	1st bottom margin to n lines
.nf	yes		stop filling lines
.pl n	no	n = 66	sets page length to n

.rm n	no	n = 80	sets right margin to n
.sp n	yes	n = 1	space down n lines
.ti n	yes	n = 0	sets temporary indent of n
.ul n	no	n = 1	underline next n lines

This version of ROFF, based on the formatter in Kernighan and Plauger's book SOFTWARE TOOLS, is written in BDS C, and employs the directed i/o functions that go along with that package.

Pascal tools, (#130-#132)

Presented here are some useful tools, which were originally presented in the book "Software Tools in Pascal" by Brian W. Kernighan and P. J. Plauger.

Program	What it does
ARCHIVE	File archiving program
CHANGE	Changes patterns in text
CHARCNT	Count characters in input
ECHOARG	Echo arguments to output
FINDP	Find patterns in text
FMT	Produce formatted output
KWIC	Produce lines for KWIC index
LINECNT	Counts number of lines in a text file
MACRO	Expands string definitions
PRINTF	Print files with headings
SORTF	Sort lines in text file
TED	Line editor for text files
TRANSLIT	Transliterate characters
UNIQUE	Deletes adjacent duplicate lines
UNROTATE	Formats lines for a KWIC index
WORDCNT	Counts words in standard inputs

Database programs

Database programs allow you to maintain lists of information such as mailing lists, telephone lists—even an entire accounting system if properly set up. They range from simple single one-file-at-a-time systems to complicated relational database systems.

PC-FILE III, (#5) u-s $49

PC-File III is a general purpose database manager program. It is menu-driven, features superb power and speed, and is very easy to use. Designed for business, professional and home users, PC-File III allows you to quickly retrieve data, change it, resequence it, perform queries, and prepare reports for display, printing or subsequent retrieval by your word processing program. Reports can be designed in many different layouts.

FEATURES include:

- Full screen editing and cursor control
- Optional security (encryption)
- Global update and delete
- A "browse" mode
- User defined macros ("smart keys")
- User defined data types
- Sort on any field, mixed ascending and descending
- Report columns can be "calculated" from fields in the database
- Mailing labels can be produced in single or "multiple across" format
- An instant ("snapshot") mailing label
- Exchange data with 1-2-3, Visicalc, WORD, MailMerge, and many other programs
- All fields are indexed; search types are generic, embedded, soundex and wildcard
- Select (for printing) on any fields, with boolean "and/or" comparisons
- Automatic input of date and time

- Automatically uses all available RAM memory for super fast performance
- Three proprietary disk writing techniques are used to ensure against accidental loss of data

FUNCTIONAL SPECIFICATIONS:

- Database type: Indexed on all fields
- Hard Disk Support: Program and/or data files may reside on hard disk
- Electronic Disk Support: Program and/or data files may reside on electronic disk
- Correctly handles "scientific" numbers
- Databases can be re-structured. Existing data will transfer from old database to newly created database.
- Program is not copy protected
- Maximum Records per Database: 32,767
- Maximum Fields per Database: 42
- Maximum Field length: 1665 characters (varies depending on number of fields)
- Maximum Record length: 1665 characters
- Maximum number of Sort Control fields: 10
- Maximum number of Comparisons for print selection: 10
- Maximum number of "calculated fields" in a report: 20

SYSTEM REQUIREMENTS:

- A computer which runs MS-DOS
- 128K of RAM memory
- A double sided diskette drive
- Printer is optional

DATABASE OF STEEL 3.1, (#214,215,266,267) u-s $20-30

The Database of Steel consists of the following 3 applications:

1. DATABASE MANAGEMENT SYSTEM

Includes Accounting, Payroll, Inventory and A/R Applications Programmable, Relational.

• Manual is on disk • Report Generator • Customizable Screens • ASCII Output • Written in Basic for easy modification • Tax Tables • Creates Subfiles • Sort on 3 Fields • Recalculate Files • Over 15,000 lines of Source Code Given • 3 Files Open Simultaneously • Global Field Changes • Key Strings to Numbers • Realtime Transfers Between Files • Retrieve on conditions for each field • Form Generator • Subrecords • Numeric Ranges • Subtotals • 14 Ways to Calculate Fields • Transfer Data Between Files.

2. SPREADSHEET

• 21 ways to calculate numbers or write your own subroutine • Written in Basic for easy modification • Compiled Version Provided (192K) • Sample Checkbook Application • Numbers and Text may be placed anywhere on the screens • Automatic Recalculation • Source Code Given • Bar Charts • Full Cursor Control.

3. EXPERT SYSTEM

• Inference Engine • Design your own expert systems • Diagnosis multiple solutions • Assigns Probability with Rules • Intellignet Search Pattern with Manual Override • Logic Path through subcategories displayed • Detects Contradictory Evidence • Explaination of Reasoning • Accepts Unknown Input • Source Code and Compiled Versions (192K) • Written in Basic for easy modification • Sample Application • No Royalties on Applications

You get the source code in Basic. We wrote the program in Basic because most users already know how to program in Basic. With the source code you can modify the system to do anything that can be done in Basic.

You do not have to be a software engineer to use the system. The entire system is menu driven. You do not have to learn hundreds of commands. You do not have to keep reading the manual since all the options are displayed on the screen.

If you write any application programs in basic you can reduce your programming time by 50% or more. You probably waste 50% to 80% of your time coding the inputting of data, storage of data in the files, retrieval of data, correction of data, screen design and other repetitous tasks. By using the database or spreadsheet to handle your repetitous tasks you will reduce your programming time by 50% or more. There are no royalties on applications.

- for IBM PC, XT or AT with 128K
- PC JR with 128K and Cartridge Basic
- Compatibles with 192K and Microsoft Basic

$20 on 4 DSDD disks, postpaid
$30 on 8 SSDD disks, postpaid

POTOMAC PACIFIC ENGINEERING INC.
Post Office Box 2027
Gaithersburg, Maryland 20879

NEWBASE, (#233) u-s $39

NewBase is a data management system that makes it easy to organize and manage information so it can be ordered, changed or retrieved and then printed to suit a variety of circumstances. NewBase is suitable for both the first-time computer user and the expert.

From phone lists through complex sales reports, NewBase helps you put it all together. Files on just about anything can be designed by NewBase. Also, NewBase interfaces with many of the most popular word processing systems. Ease of use by non-technical personnel has been the primary design consideration. Absolutely no programming expertise is required. Completely menu driven, there is no special syntax or computerese to learn.

The easy to use design of NewBase has not limited its power or flexibility. The report generator can print-user specified fields in titled columnar format, automatically generating column headings and paging. Reports may contain statistical summaries including totals, subtotals, running totals and averages. The form generator allows printing on any paper in any format with text included. Mailing labels may be printed up to three across with auto reversal of first and last names.

Other features include:

- Multi-key sorting
- Searching for Less Than, Greater Than, Equal, Included, Not, or Or.
- Global update/edit multiple records with a single entry.
- Audit trail.
- Multi-level file password protection.
- Lookup tables.
- Macro keys.
- Single keystroke entry of repetitive data.
- Protected fields.
- Date fields.
- Calculated equation fields.
- Numeric accuracy to 16 digits.
- Report library.
- Form library.

System requirements are 128K memory with two floppy disk drives or fixed disk and an 80 column monitor.

NewBase can handle up to 32,000 records with the proper hardware.

Start by copying the file "READ_ME.DOC" to your printer.

File Express, (#287, #288) u-s $40

File Express is an information management program written for the IBM Personal Computer and other compatible computers using PC-DOS. This allows easy manipulation of small and medium sized databases using menu driven commands. File Express allows you to create and maintain files of facts, figures, names, mailing lists, patient records or what have you.

With file express you can:

- Define new databases, specifying the type and length of information allowed into each field.
- Easily Add, Delete, Edit and Display information from your files.
- Generate Reports from your files, complete with subtotals, totals, multiplication, division, and subtraction on any numeric fields.
- Sort records on up to ten fields, with each separate field able to be sorted into descending or ascending order. The sort criterion may consist of any subset at any location within a field.
- Search or Sort for specific information within a record, irregardless of upper and lower case letters.
- Designate certain fields for automatic entry of time and date in several different formats when inputting data. Some of these are also updated upon any modification of a field within a record.
- Define fields within a record to be self-calculating. Calculation can be between numeric fields or between numeric fields and constants. All calculated fields are recalculated after any modification of a record.
- Print Mailing Labels, up to three across. This will be the easiest label printer that you have ever used.
- Create new databases from existing ones, adding new fields within the record and discarding unneeded ones, changing the field lengths and rearranging the order.
- Create Mailmerge type files from your databases.

LISTMATE 1.0, (#252) u-s $25

ListMate 1.0 is a mailing list manager that produces data 100% compatible with MultiMate(tm) secondary document data formats. Lists created in ListMate can be entered, manipulated, printed, and exported to MultiMate directly without conversion. It is important to note, however, that MultiMate uses non-standard file formats. This fact makes ListMate data exclusively compatible with MultiMate. ListMate lists can be merged directly with MultiMate "boiler plate" documents in MultiMate.

A general understanding of MultiMate and the Merge process is helpful in order to take full advantage of ListMate lists and their data format. Once the MultiMate merge process is understood, ListMate's advantages will become clear and it will prove to be a real time saver.

Features of the product include:

- A Three Level Sort
- Data Extraction Routines
- Virtual Memory Caching of data
- "Smart Sorting"
- Page format for records
- Runtime Palette selection
- Word selection within fields for Sort/Extraction
- Support for 66 printers

ListMate operates on a record format of up to 10 user-named fields. Operations, such as the Sort and Extract, may be initiated on individual words and numbers within these fields. This feature makes ListMate's 10 fields into up to 180 relational database fields. Another noteworthy feature is ListMate's "Smart Sorting". A sort may be specified using words and/or numbers and ListMate will sort a list into numerical/alphabetical order without any other information beyond which number word in the fields are to be used as keys. Full on-line help, runtime color or monochrome "palette" selection and network considerations via user defined memory limitiations complete this abbreviated list of features.

To receive further instructions, simply load the system. Help is provided every step of the way. To start ListMate: load DOS; at the DOS prompt (A>) type 'LISTMATE' (do not include the quotes) and press the Enter key. The first screen will provided all the instructions and information you will need to use ListMate without ever seeing the documentation.

Beyond all of its features, ListMate was created for secretarial use: it requires minimal training for experienced MultiMate users, operates in a straightforward manner, and is geared for rapid data entry and review. Coupled with MultiMate's Merge feature, ListMate is a worthwhile investment for anyone who has ever encountered the procedure of creating a secondary merge document manually in MultiMate.

ListMate is being distributed on a FairWare(tm) basis: the product can be copied and distributed freely. Anyone finding the product useful is requested to send the suggested contribution of $25 to SWFTE, Inc. Disks may be purchased from SWFTE, Inc. for $25, plus $5 for postage and handling. We are proud of ListMate and hope that you will enjoy it as much as we do.

We encourage you to send any questions, comments, suggestions or contributions directly to:

SWFTE, Inc.
P.O. Box 219
Rockland, DE 19732

ABC-FILE 1.1, (#119) — u-s $30

ABC-FILE is a data filing system that accepts up to 1500 records with up to 12 fields in each record.

When you define your DataFile you will be asked not only to Name the Fields for each Record, but also to specify the length of each field. (The computer must be told how much space to allocate in your file for each field and each record.) The maximum field length allowed in ABC- File is 50 characters and the minimum length is 2 characters.

Capabilities:

- Max number of records — 1500
- Max number of fields — 12
- Max characters per field — 50
- Max number of index files = # of fields

ABC-File is not intended to be all things for all people. It is not intended to be used to maintain a 65000 plus (+) record file for some Fortune 500 company.

It is, however, designed to be easy to use, user friendly throughout and will adequately maintain a reasonable size file for most any purpose. Customer files or mailing lists of 100-1000 records are handled very well. Other ideas include daily schedules, technical article cross references (with the first field used for a keyword(s), at 50 characters per field you can enter 550 characters of text about the article), recipe files, sales records, parts inventory, student grades, etc.

This version includes the abilty to specify fields to be character or numeric, and if numeric, the number of default decimal places for each field. Also included are simple calculations on fields. You can define any field to be the result of a calculation on any two other fields in the record. Numeric operators include +, -, * and /. You will not be prompted to enter data into calculated fields while in the add record function. ABC will update the field automatically. Reports containing numeric fields will be totaled and averaged for each numeric field.

SYSTEM REQUIREMENTS: • IBM PC/XT • 128K Memory • At least 1 disk drive or hard disk • Epson FX/MX-80 or equivelant • Color or Monochrome monitor.

3by5 1.0, (#253)

3by5 is an information management program that offers speed, simplicity and versatility in entering, indexing and retrieving free- text and structured data. It is as simple to use as a 3x5 card file. Entering information is simple. You may use 3by5's integrated word processor or any other word processor, text editor or computer program to enter data in any format: words, phrases, sentences, paragraphs or fixed files.

Searching files is fast, thanks to 3by5's unique indexing method (signature screening). Just enter a SEARCH key (any combination of 3 to 60 characters) and 3by5 will find the first and all subsequent occurences of the key in your file. Moreover, when the key is found, it is displayed in the context of the sentence or record in which it appears. As each occurrence is found, you have the option of continuing the search, editing the record, printing the information, transferring records from one file to another, or ending the search.

You may search for partial keys, i.e. an incomplete word or phrase. For example, the search key "CDONA" will locate the name "McDonald" and "MacDonald". You may also search for combinations of key terms which appear in the same sentence or record (up to 1024 characters long) by using the conjunctions "and" (symbol = "&") or "or" (symbol = "|"). For example, "basic&cobol&ibm|pascal&compaq" will locate records which contain the words "Basic", "Cobol" and "IBM" or the words "Pascal" and "Compaq".

3by5 allows you to search and edit up to three files at a time in addition to one ASCII output file. 3by5 also allows you to search standard ASCII files, and WordStar and WordPerfect Document files. The ability to search and edit multiple files is aided by 3by5's multiple windows. For example, while editing in one window, you may search in another.

ADDRESS LABEL SYSTEM, (#261) u-s $30

High speed name/address data entry system for producing and maintaining customer files, address labels, and mailing lists. Especially useful for capturing large volumes of names and addresses for direct mail advertising.

Databases

Databases are predefined files which may be used with a database program. The databases included here include lists of references and a recipe file.

LETUS A-B-C, (#121-#123) u-s $30

Letus A-B-C is a database of articles and letters from magazines about IBM Personal Computers. It was created using Jim Buttons's PC-File III, another user-supported program (see disk #5). Together with PC-File III the Letus A-B-C database provides the IBM PC user with a tool for easily performing literature searches at a very nominal cost in one's office or home.

The initial release of Letus A-B-C covers the period 1982 through 1983 for the following five magazines devoted to the IBM PC: Softalk (SOFT), Personal Computer Age (PCAGE), PC Magazine (PCMAG), PC World (PCW), and PC Tech Journal (PCTEC). The database normally comes on three double-sided, double density diskettes, with all of 1982 on a single diskette and with 1983 distributed on the other two.

An attempt was made to include every article of each magazine, even when the authorship at times was unclear (e.g., magazine editorials, promotionals, etc.). Generally each magazine provides its own index on a periodic basis, most typically at the end of the year or end of the volume, with articles categorized by Subject, Author, and Title. The Letus A-B-C database extends this index table method by providing a "keyword" field that can quickly be searched with PC-File. For example, one can search for all of the articles that make reference to a particular product or idea (e.g., PC-File, User-Supported Software, etc.). Letus A-B-C also contains many "Letters to the Editor", "Questions and Answers", "Helpful Hints", etc...........those things that are so hard to find when you really need them!

BOBCAT, (#247)

BOBCAT is for anyone using micro-computers in business who needs specific information quickly without having to read through hundreds of publications.

BOBCAT is a computerized INDEX, a data base. It will tell you where to quickly find the product reviews, tutorials, general articles, buying guides, ads on new or special products, etc., that are published in leading magazines, news letters, newspapers and research reports.

If you do not have access to the publications where the information is, and need it immediately, for personal study or research, phone the publisher for SAME DAY PHOTO COPY SERVICE.

Actually, most of the listings are useful to anyone, it's just that they don't index information on games, educational or lab applications, and "heavy hacking or programming".

BOBCAT is on a DD DS 5.25 disk, compatible with MS-DOS and Jim Buttons' PC FILE III.

Start by copying the file BOBCAT.TXT to your printer.

NAEPIRS, (#266)

The National Assessment of Educational Progress (NAEP) is the first effort to improve American education by providing continual, comprehensive and dependable national achievement data. NAEP data have been collected since 1969 on 9-, 13-, and 17-year-olds in ten different learning areas. These are: art, career and occupational development, citizenship, literature, mathematics, music, reading, science, social studies and writing. Different learning areas are periodically reassessed in order to measure possible changes in educational achievement over time. Since 1969, the National Assessment has interviewed and tested more than one million young Americans.

This computer program, the National Assessment of Educational Progress Information Retrieval System (NAEPIRS), provides immediate and easy access to NAEP findings and trends. You may obtain information responsive to your needs by selecting the appropriate descriptors and having NAEPIRS search the database for relevant findings. These findings will apppear on the screen and can easily be printed.

Here are some examples of the findings NAEPIRS contains: "About 10 percent of the surveyed students at each age group do not read at all in their spare time." "Nine-year-olds who indicated that they watched television daily for up to three or four hours performed 14 percentage points above the nation on the reading and comprehension exercises."

The National Assessment is funded by the National Institute of Education, USDE.

To start the program type:

NAEPIRS

Select items from menu as desired. The program will display or print all documentation by running the program. This program is an example of a quality human interface.

microGOURMET 1.10, (#116,#117) u-s $30

MicroGOURMET is a software package which was designed to help those of you who spend lots of time looking through cookbooks and rummaging through scraps of paper to find recipes. It will help reduce the time spent choosing recipes to prepare for both family and guest meals. It is also an aid to menu planning. You can select recipes for whatever time period you wish (a week, for instance), print the recipes (as a reference), and prepare and print a shopping list to take to the store.

You can also add recipes of your own at any time. You can change the recipes supplied if your taste dictates a change in ingredient proportions, or you want to modify the instructions to suit your cooking style. You can also delete any recipe that you don't like (we hope that doesn't happen often).

microGOURMET uses a hierarchy of menus. When you select an option from the main menu, another menu may then be displayed, offering a further refinement to your choice of actions. This process continues until you have focused on exactly what you want to do and then, for example, recipes are retrieved and displayed or printed and if you like, added to a shopping list file.

With microGOURMET you can retrieve recipes by category alone, or by category and one other criterion, such as recipe name or ingredients or preparation time.

If you are using GOURMET.HI, you can examine the ingredient index before proceeding, to see whether the ingredients you have in mind are in a recipe somewhere. You can also see how the ingredient is specified, and whether there are several alternatives (i.e., variations) for your ingredients.

MicroGOURMET requires dBASE II.

Spreadsheets

Spreadsheets are useful whenever you take out a columnar pad to add up a column of numbers, plan a forcast or other numbers-based analysis. Spreadsheets are great for "what if" type questions because an entire forcast may be quickly generated from changes in a few numbers. The spreadsheets listed here do not have the capacity of a program such as Lotus 1-2-3 but they may be used to perform similar functions.

PC-CALC, (#199) u-s $48

PC-Calc is a general purpose spreadsheet program by the author of PC-FILE.

FEATURES include:

- Individually adjustable column widths
- Zero column width for "hidden" columns
- Sheet-to-sheet linkage allows data to be retrieved into a spreadsheet from another spreadsheet, providing a "3-dimensional" capability
- Data in PC-File III databases can be retrieved into a spreadsheet cell. No limit to the number of databases or spreadsheets that can be accessed by another spreadsheet
- Powerful formatting options, including: left-, right-, and center-justify; specify fixed number of decimal places, or integer; commas in numbers (optional); floating dollar sign; trailing percent sign; negatives in parentheses or with minus sign; horizontal bar graphs using *****
- Title locking - vertical, horizontal or both
- If...Then function (nesting permitted)
- Replicate command greatly reduces keystrokes, while producing sophisticated spreadsheets
- Text may overlap into adjacent cells
- Row-wise or column-wise recalculation
- Uses all the IBM PC keyboard special keys: HOME, END, Arrows, PG UP, PG DN, TAB, BACKTAB
- Flexible print options include: print all or part of a spreadsheet; output to printer or disk; dot commands for page breaks, conditional page breaks, characters per inch; adjustable left margin; double- or single-space; optional pause between pages for form change; optionally print spreadsheet border;

printer setup strings; optionally print cell contents

- Unique configuration command: monochrome or color display; choose your own colors to highlight five areas of the screen; specify screen width from 40 to 80 characters wide; as few as eight lines per screen, for small screen portables; six selectable screen layouts; configure special keyboard keys; configure for popular brands of printers; temporary or permanent configuration
- Math functions: Absolute value, Arctangent, Cosine, e to the power of x, Integer, True integer, Natural log, Sign, Sine, Square root, Sum and Tangent
- Statistical functions: Average, Count, Minimum, Maximum
- Net present value function

FUNCTIONAL SPECIFICATIONS:

- 26 columns by 255 lines
- 64 characters per cell
- Numeric precision to 14 decimals
- Column width from 0 to 75
- Hard disk compatible
- Electronic disk compatible
- On-screen prompts
- Formulas may contain cell references, constants, math functions or If...Then functions, seperated by +,-,*,/
- Commands: Blank, Configure, Delete, Edit, Format, Global, Insert, Load, Print, Quit, Replicate, Title, Xternal, Zap
- Program not copy protected

SYSTEM REQUIREMENTS:

- A computer which runs MSDOS
- 128K or more of RAM memory
- Double sided diskette drive
- Monochrome or color display, 40- to 80-columns, 8 to 25 lines
- Printer is optional

PC-CALC (Guy Gordon's), (#224) u-s $25

PC-CALC is laid out similarly to classic spreadsheet programs. It is not intended to completely replace these programs, but will allow you to learn what a spreadsheet is all about. Written in BASIC, PC-Calc has many limitations. First, interpretive Basic is slow. Second, it must pause once in a while to free more space for variables. (When this happens PC-Calc will not respond for up to 2 minutes). If you are running the compiled version of PC-Calc these may not be problems. Third, Basic limits your space to about 1000 cells.

If you start using PC-Calc and find that it serves a useful purpose in your home or at work, then it may be time to start looking at the full priced spreadsheets, which are bigger, faster, have more features, (and cost a whole lot more). Your experience with PC-Calc will be of great value to you in evaluating the many commercially available spreadsheets.

The PC-Calc user's manual is intended to accommodate a large number of people with a wide range of computer experience. It is organized into three main sections.

Section 1 is an introduction to PC-Calc and includes information about starting PC-Calc and what the user will see. You should read this section before trying anything with the PC-Calc program.

Section 2 is an instructional section, containing lessons which have been structured to foresee some of the problems and questions that will arise. These lessons will lead you from initiating a PC-Calc session through various exercises which illustrate how PC-Calc can assist in solving problems and increasing your efficiency. The exercises should be run with the terminal in front of you, as they are designed to lead you through the features of PC-Calc. With usage, you will become familiar with some of the more advanced features of PC-Calc.

Section 3 is the command reference. This section contains a description of each of the commands available to the user. As you use the advanced features of PC-Calc, and become more familiar with them, you will find yourself spending more time in this section. The best way to learn PC-Calc is to use it. Do not be afraid of making mistakes and experimenting. No matter what you type at the keyboard, you cannot hurt the computer or the PC-Calc program, although it is always a good idea to have a backup of all programs.

PC-PAD 1.3, (#170) u-s $20

PC-PAD is a word processing/spreadsheet (or "wordsheet") program designed around the MS-BASIC full-screen line-editor to provide textediting, spreadsheet computation, and printing capabilities with minimum complication. Its design is based on the thought that many users of such software would prefer a simple set of useful functions (with option to expand to meet special needs) instead of the general capability (and hence complexity) built into bigger programs. It uses the programmable function keys on the IBM keyboard to build on capabilities of the resident editor. This approach economizes on program size (around 9K bytes) while providing full support of the familiar BASIC editing protocols. Commands, especially at the character and word level, once mastered for either PC/PAD or the BASIC editor, are thus automatically mastered for both.

Along with the user's guide (file PC/PAD.DOC), PC/PAD provides an on-line "help file" to aid users in implementing these functions. PC/PAD as written is set up for an IBM PC with 64K of memory (48K should work), a single disk drive, and an 80-column minotir. A printer is optional, although probably desirable. As indicated above, it also requires IBM's disk BASIC (or BASICA) to run. The BASIC workspace has room for nearly 30K characters of text with a 64K system, probably around 14K with 48K.

FREECALC V.1, (#170) u-s $35

FREECALC has been designed to give particular attention to the needs of the first time spreadsheet user. For example, you can create a useful spreadsheet without any knowledge of how to write a formula in FREECALC. This is made possible by providing the user with cretain basic formulas and allowing the user to point (by use of the cursor), to the cells to be included in the formula. FREECALC is not just for beginners. The progrm also has an area for you to enter your own formulas. These formulas can be as complex as you like. They may contain any number of expressions, and parentheses may be nested as deeply as you wish.

FREECALC comes with three samples spreadsheets, and a tutorial. FREECALC requires 128K if using DOS 1.1 and 192K if using 2.0 or later. The program will run in the IBM PC, PC-XT, PC-AT, and the PC-jr. You can use either a color or monochrome monitor. The program will work with a hard disk. FREECALC comes with 35 pages of documentation on the diskette which you can print at your printer.

Financial applications

FINANCE MANAGER 3.0B, (#151) u-s $40

FINANCE MANAGER is a general purpose "GENERAL LEDGER" program suitable for small business and home finance uses. It is designed specifically for ease of use with minimal bookeeping experience.

FINANCE MANAGER will keep track of all your Assets (things you own), Liabilities (who you owe), Net Worth, Income and Expenses. This program is completely menu driven and simple to use.

Double entry (debits & credits) bookeeping is used in this program. Although the user is not expected to be an expert in accounting, some basic knowledge of bookeeping fundamentals is needed in order to set up your chart of accounts and to enter transactions. Two demonstration accounts (one personal, one business) are included on the program disk in order to assist you in getting started. Many people can use FINANCE MANAGER without training or instructions.

Some of its features include the following:

- Up to 399 accounts
- Trended reports
- Multiple sets of books
- Profit & loss statement
- Three subtotal levels
- Customized configuration
- Save reports to disk file
- Automated closing entries
- Monthly, quarterly or yearly report
- Account history statement
- General journal statement
- Balance sheet statement
- Sources & Uses of funds statement
- Up to 4,000 transactions per year
- Unlimited transactions on a PC/XT
- Ability to sort transactions

- Beginning balances automatically set each year
- Defaults for input fields to minimize data entry
- Ability to correct & delete transactions
- Multiple debits & credits per transaction

- Graphics display for account balances
- Variable fiscal year capability

MINIMUM SYSTEM CONFIGURATION: • IBM PC or XT (or compatibles) • Either a monocrome or color board • 80 column display • 256K memory • 1 disk drive • 1 Formatted data diskette for each accounting system • 1 Formatted program disk • IBM DOS (Version 1.1 through 2.1)

All documentation for using Finance Manager is on the disk.

PC-CHECK MANAGER, (#250) u-s $25

PC-CHECK MANAGER is a full function checkbook register which allows the user to track all checks and deposits for multiple checkbooks.

- PC-CHECK MANAGER is menu drive for easy use.
- PC-CHECK MANAGER allows entry of checks and deposits returned on the monthly statement to balance the checkbook and identifies differences.
- PC-CHECK MANAGER utilizes user defined ledger accounts for summarizing checks and deposits by category. This is especially useful for income tax preparation.
- PC-CHECK MANAGER has an automatic check and deposit payee entry function which allows the user to predefine commonly used payees for one key payee and account entry.
- PC-CHECK MANAGER has a report for account balance, outstanding checks and deposits, all checks and deposits, and ledger accounts.

PC-CHECK MANAGER requires 128k, DOS 1.1 or later, one disk drive, an optional printer. Start by copying the manual in file "CK.DOC" by typing "DOC", or retrieve the ASCII data with your favorite word processor. The latest update may be obtained by sending $25 to:

Charles Little
807 Lipton Drive
Newport News, VA

Personal Finance Manager 4.5, (#164) u-s $24

The Personal Finance Manager (PFM-4), Version 4.5 is an IBM PC/XT/Jr program intended for use by the household budget manager to keep track of all household money matters from checking accounts to investments. All functions are menu driven requiring no knowledge of commands, however, data input and search functions automatically repeat, providing rapid data entry.

PFM-4 provides four major and several minor functions useful for controlling home finances, including:

- A checking account program to keep track of all checks, deposits, withdrawals, interest, and major cash purchases. PFM-4 will operate 5 separate checking accounts on one disk, and permits as many separate data disks as the user requires.
- An investment and savings account program to track where money is invested and how well those investments are performing. Up to 99 separate accounts may be tracked on one disk.
- Budget reports to show how much was spent in any of 99 user defined budget areas such as food, movies, computer equipment, within any specified time period. Each of the 5 checking accounts may have up to 99 separate budget areas.
- The following detailed and summary reports are available on the screen or on paper, covering any desired time frame:
  - Check Register (For each of 5 accounts)
  - Detail of purchases in each budget area (99 areas for each checking account)
  - Summary of purchases in all 99 budget areas for each of the 5 checking accounts, by area, with grand total
  - Tax deductible purchases
  - Checking account deposit report
  - Investment account detailed report, with transaction summary at end (for each of 99 accounts)
  - Investment summary of all accounts, with grand total
- Checkbook balancing routine
- Built in sort routine for each data file provides three level sorting of data by date, type of entry, and by check number for checking accounts.

- Checking account minimum balance warning flags for each account.
- All entries are immediately retrievable for changing or deletion via a record search routine.

HARDWARE REQUIREMENTS: • IBM PC, XT, Jr or compatible with at least 192 Kb RAM. The program will not run on some compatibles such as the Zenith 150. • 1 double sided, Double density floppy disk drive. • Monochrome or color graphics monitor.

PC-CHECK MANAGER, (#275) u-s $25

PC-CHECK MANAGER is menu driven and simple to use. It can handle multiple checkbooks by assigning different names to each file. The drive on which the data is located can be selected both at program startup and when a new checkbook data file is selected. The user can assign unlimited Payees to which checks are regularly written and unlimited Ledger Accounts, so as to speed data entry. The program will automatically assign the Ledger Account Number when a pre-assigned Payee is selected.

CDB, (#282) u-s $20

The CheckBook Distribution Program provides a quick & easy way to group check or credit card data into expense categories. For example, check data may be abbreviated to just the $-Amount and a short expense Code for speedy data entry. However, more complete entries, including dates and check descriptions, may also be used when desired. This flexibility provides fast results for tax, business, or budget purposes.

The program is designed to be simple and easy to use. One may start entering check data immediately, and convenient editing features are available for correction of mistakes. In addition, the program keeps a running check ledger balance to assist in data verification and checkbook balancing.

PC-CHECK, (#282) u-s $40

This checking program has been designed to efficiently and easily allow anyone to keep track of one or more home or office checking accounts. With this program, checking information (including check numbers, check dates, comments, amounts, balances, and descriptive codes) can be stored on disks where it can be easily accessed for reference, revision or addition.

Check files may be searched to find any specific entry with any of the above specified fields and files can be manipulated easily through the program with options like merging files, backing up files, deleting and renaming files. The year-end processing option will allow the operator to create a separate, finalized file of all the checking transactions for a specified period of time.

HOME FINANCE ANALYST, (#282) u-s $15

The HOME FINANCING ANALYST is a comprehensive real estate evaluation program written from the perspective of homeowners, potential homeowners, or renters. It is destined to assist these people as well as real estate agents, brokers and developers in forecasting and allocating the costs of home ownership and in comparing ownership versus rental alternatives. It is also useful in determining if mortgage refinancing is worthwhile. The program, however, cannot be used to evaluate real estate purchased for investment purposes, as it does not take into account depreciation charges and rental income.

The program works with the IBM-PC, compatible systems, and both versions 1.1 and 2.0 of PC-DOS/MS-DOS. Only one disk drive is necessary. The compiled version requires at least 128 Kb memory, while the non-compiled version needs 64 Kb. The latter is less efficient and does not have the same degree of precision as the compiled version (0.01% error detected). Should you run out of memory in the non-compiled version, the screen will warn you and prompt you to save your work under a file name. The program will then continue as usual. This problem does not occur in the compiled version.

Personal General Ledger 1.3, (#165) u-s $50

The Personal General Ledger is a complete set of Journals and General Ledger to be used as a template with Lotus 1-2-3 (tm) and the IBM PC (tm). This set of books can be used by any individual to keep his personal records plus some minor business records. The ledger balances have a full audit trail back through the journals.

Contributors will be kept informed of possible new developments such as a Personal Financial Statement template and/or a Federal/State tax calculation template. Also, questions will also be answered from contributors, only.

FEDERAL INCOME TAX FORMS,(#290) u-s $35

FITT84 is a Lotus 1-2-3 worksheet for the 1984 Federal Income Tax Return. The following forms and schedules are provided:

Form 1040	U.S. Individual Income Tax Return
Schedule A	Itemized Deductions
Schedule B	Interest and Dividend Income
Schedule D	Capital Gains and Losses
Schedule E	Supplemental Income Schedule
Schedule W	Deduction for a Married Couple When Both Work
Schedule G	Income Averaging
Schedule C	Profit or (Loss) From Business
Form 2441	Credit for Child and Dependent Care Expen.

TAX FILE DBS, (#295) u-s $15

The TAX-FILE software is a very complete TAX RECORD KEEPING system. It enables a person with very little effort to collect records of income and expenses and to assemble them in quick fashion in order to prepare yearly income tax forms.

The TAX-FILE requires that the user have available a copy of dBASE II (copyrighted by Ashton-Tate). At the "." prompt simply enter DO MENU <RETURN>. You will be taken directly into TAX-FILE. It is best to use this version of TAX-FILE with a hard disk. The files grow large and data and programs won't fit on one diskette after a while.

SAGE TRADER (#242) u-s $50

Sage Trader is useful to an agricultural producer or commodity trader who needs to store, analyze and display commodity price information on an IBM monochrome screen. It permits the commodities trader to concentrate on trends instead of details.

The data entry and review process is speeded by the use of an automatic response file. This feature allows you to update files at the rate of more than two files per minute or summarize the day's activity with one key stroke.

The program can be easily adapted to make good use of your printer's special features. A permanent file of printer control codes can be created to meet your special needs.

It offers menu driven convenience with command driven speed. A brief description of each menu selection appears under each menu. More detailed information is provided by the Help option.

Your data is automatically saved to disk file when you change files or end the program. This protects your data from careless errors.

The graphics are "typewriter" graphics. Only the turning points are plotted. These points are represented by letters or numbers. This makes the program compatible with most parallel printers and the monochrome display. You may use dot matrix, daisy wheel or thimble printers.

The program requires an IBM PC with 128 K of memory and one disk drive. It will work with the monochrome or graphics screen and most printers. Version 2 requires DOS 2.X and supports the advanced features of DOS 2.X. A parallel printer is recommended.

Stock Charting System 1.5, (#246) u-s $25

The purpose of this system is to draw and/or print volume-high-low- close charts for any stock. Bonds, commodities, or other securities that have high-low-close prices, can also be charted. Short- and long-term moving average lines can optionally be included on each chart.

Whenever a new stock is added to the system, the user may specify daily or weekly updating of price and volume data, and may also specify the number (up to 90) of days or weeks of data to be retained for that individual stock. A double-sided diskette can hold data for each of up to 110 different stocks.

Volume and high, low and closing prices are typed in by the user from data published in Barrons (for weekly updating) or the Wall Street Journal or other daily paper. Short- and/or long-term moving average periods can optionally be specified or changed at will for each individual stock. Moving averages can be computed and charted temporarily on a "what-if" basis, or stored permanently on diskette.

The system does not make buy/hold/sell recommendations.

Per-share annual earnings and dividends are maintained to permit computation of the price/earnings ratio and yield for each stock. Also, high and low estimated 5-year prices can be entered, to permit computation of total annual return. This information may be obtained from Value Line or another advisory service.

The stock charting system, which contains several programs and associated text files, is menu-driven, allowing the user to easily select all options without memorizing commands. All menus have a "Help" function; when invoked by pressing the letter "H", the instructions applicable to that part of the system will appear on the screen.

Stock charts may be printed on an Epson FX-80 or equivalent graphics printer. The program modules are written in interpreted BASIC with embedded machine-language subroutines.

The hardware requirements are an IBM Personal Computer with at least 64K of memory and two disk drives (programs on A:, data on B:). The stock charting system will operate with either the IBM monochrome or graphics adapter, or both, but the graphics adapter is required for drawing charts. The system has been tested with DOS 1.1 and 2.0, and also on the Compaq computer.

CASH 1.0, (#261)

This is a simple general ledger that provides a convenient method for a small business to record their cash transactions. The program structure is very straight forward and is therefore easy to customize to individual needs.

PORTSWORTH PACKAGE, (#101) u-s $15

The PORTSWORTH package is a set of application programs that you can use for monitoring and evaluating your stock portfolios. Portfolios of up to 25 stocks can be processed.

The package consists of four main programs (PORTCOST, PORTMRKT, DLTAPRNT, and DLTAPLOT). Each have an input file that is read from a diskette. You use one input file for both the PORTCOST and the PORTMRKT programs, and another input file for the DLTAPRNT and DLTAPLOT programs.

You may create the two input files (HOLDLIST.DTA and DLTAFILE.DTA) with the PC DOS EDLIN utility or with a suitable word processing program that produces comma-delimited files. Sample HOLDLIST and DLTAFILE files are included on the diskette.

You may use the PORTCOST.BAS program to produce an item listing for a stock portfolio of up to 25 stocks.

Similarly, you may use the PORTMRKT.BAS program to produce a current value item listing for a portfolio of up to 25 stocks. During use, the program solicits data from you on current stock prices and on the price changes since the previous valuation. You are able to correct mistakes you make during input. Online corrections of keyboard input are processed.

You will be using the DLTAPRNT.BAS program to produce a bar chart of dollar changes for each cycle of portfolio valuation input data. The program also produces a chart depicting the percent change in value for each cycle. Since the program operates in text mode, data that cannot be effectively displayed in one screen can be produced as one continuous chart.

The DLTAPLOT.BAS program is provided to enable you to produce a line chart for display on the monitor. The chart shows the cumulative changes in value of the portfolio over the number of cycles processed. This program operates in high resolution graphics mode.

Business

FINANCE, (#227) u-s $30

FINANCE will help anybody who wishes to do (or to learn to do) basic financial analysis such as mortgage and loan analysis, bond analysis, compound interest problems, and capital budgeting analysis. The program is NOT a "black box" and will provide you with the setup and solution procedure for each problem. It was originally developed at a university for teaching basic finance.

Loans—Monthly payment, unpaid balance at the end of N periods, and the interest paid and amortisation schedule for Nth year. In addition, the loan payment can be calculated for any type of repayment schedule (monthly, weekly, semiannual, etc.).

Bonds—Calculation of bond price, annual bond yield to maturity, realized yield with different reinvestment rates, duration and elasticity.

Compound Interest Problems—One deposit, future value; Periodic fixed deposits, future value; Desired final value, required initial deposit; Desired final value, required periodic deposits.

Capital Budgeting—With some imagination this spreadsheet can handle replacement equipment, lease-purchase, mortgage refinancing and new equipment decisions. If you are interested in these applications, contact Computer Handholders, Inc. for additional documentation.

FINANCE uses single-key menu selection, all problem setups are done by answering a series of questions, and the F1 key is used to change mistaken entries. FINANCE requires an IBM PC with 128K (FINANCE takes 78K of memory), a single disk drive, an 80 column display and PC DOS 1.1, 2.0 or 2.1. A documentation file FINANCE.DOC is provided on the disk.

PC-GENERAL LEDGER 1.2, (#237) u-s $50

PC-GENERAL LEDGER is a simple, easy to use, fool proof, complete general ledger system. Some of its features are:

- Cash receipts, cash disbursements, and general journals.
- Write checks on a printer or enter data from check stubs.
- Maintains a file of 100 names and addresses for easy check writing.
- Month and year to date trial balances for each account.
- Balance sheet and income statement.
- Recurring journal entries.
- Add new accounts to the chart of accounts in the middle of an accounting entry.
- While making entries, find accounts using either the account number or a few letters from the account name.
- Send account numbers, account names, month and year to date amounts to a file that Lotus 1-2-3 can read.
- Complete and detailed audit trails.
- Manual included.

PC-GENERAL LEDGER was written by a financial executive with over 25 years of accounting, finance, tax, and general management experience combined with eight years experience programming personal computers. The programs have been developed, written, and updated over the last year and a half.

The program will run on the IBM PC, XT, or AT, Compaq, Columbia, Eagle, Tandy 1000 and 1200, Leading Edge, and other compatible machines. Requires two double sided drives (or a hard drive), 128K memory, and an 80 or 132 column printer.

The user-supported donation requested by the author is $ 50.00. If you are not happy with the program or cannot use it after making the donation write for a full refund, no questions asked. You can keep the program.

Gerry Fricke
CHARTER SOFTWARE
P.O. Box 70
Monticello, IL 61856
217-762-7143

POWER WKS, (#289) (Evaluation disk)

This disk is an evaluation disk that shows off some of the capabilities of these POWER worksheets for LOTUS 1-2-3. The cost of the complete software is $49 and may be purchased from the distributor listed on the disk. The following are descriptions of the individual worksheets on this disk.

AGENDA allows you to go from one worksheet to another while remaining entirely under menu control.

BSTAT accepts from one to six sets of data and performs two major analytical tasks. First, BSTAT provides a basic statistical summary for each data set. Second, it allows visual comparison of the data with over 40 graphs.

Loaded with graph options, DEPREC is a comprehensive worksheet which performs straight line, sum-of-years-digits, declining balance and ACRS depreciation calculations. Also provided is a crossover depreciation schedule which automatically converts from declining balance to straight line depreciation when appropriate.

NPV Calculates the Net Present Value of a cash flow at a number of discount rates, and plots Net Present Value against the discount rates.

PROFIT is a comprehensive profitability and breakeven analysis worksheet. PROFIT can produce a wide variety of graphs showing the sensitivity of one factor against another.

ROR calculates the Rate of Return of a cash flow using three methods, (1) the Internal Rate of Return, (2) the Modified Internal Rate of Return and (3) the Financial Management Rate of Return.

SREGR (for Simple Linear Regression) provides both tabular and graphical linear regression analysis. In addition to calculating intercept and slope, this Power-Worksheet also calculates the correlation coefficient and the value of Student's t.

INVENT (#235) u-s $50

INVENT—"Parts Inventory Control" can be used by small retail businesses to manage inventory. This program supports the additional needs of businesses that deal in parts and services, such as motorcycle and recreational vehicle dealers; auto repair, TV service, plumbing and heating shops; sporting goods, paint, clothing, camera, furniture, hardware, music, shoe, appliance stores, etc.

The advantages of this program over other inventory programs is its execution speed (written in 8088 assembler), its data compaction on diskettes (8191 records which expand to 150 characters each), its emphasis on data entry (skip fields, save last used records in memory, foreground data entry, background diskette and printer operation), its sort time (about 20 seconds for 5000 records) and its search speed (index in memory). It is menu driven, provides on line help, takes advantage of the function keys and except for monthly history updates, requires no diskette swapping.

The program provides the following options:

1. Diskette option to format (five 1024 byte sectors per track) or backup diskettes.
2. Record option to save supplier and manufacture names, create default, and miscellaneous (printer, and financial) data; enter inventory data records; and create a sorted index (description or part number for each record).
3. File option to count, order (optional, can just use receive), receive, sell, return from customer, or return to supplier. Printed audit trail, option for estimates, allows function keys adjustment of selling price, optional sales tax.
4. History option to periodically save sales and financial data. Can update daily (optional), monthly, and yearly. Edit programs for sale and tax history diskettes. Program to calculate reorder point and quantity.
5. Print option for master list, orders, under stock, over stock, count/order, sales history, and tax information (LIFO and FIFO). Qualified by class, supplier, dates, etc.

6. Utility option to transfer data to DOS format and to adjust all selling prices, by class and manufacture.

System requirements: IBM PC with 256KB memory and two double sided diskette drives, 132 column printer, 80 column display, and DOS 1.1 or 2.0.

Start by reading the dataset README.DOC which will explain how to print the 47 page Tutorial and User's Guide, how to copy the program to a DOS diskette, and how to run the program.

TASKPLAN, (#155) u-s $20

TASKPLAN is handy for the business person in evaluating the costs associated with each individual time period of a planned project.

Given the irregular time periods and costs of overlapping tasks, TASKPLAN solves for each period's incremental and cumulative costs. TASKPLAN's simple approach gets you to the answer without all the complicated efforts required by those big-and-expensive computer programs.

TASKPLAN'S INPUT: number of tasks (up to 50) • number of time periods (up to 60) • project name • task data - name - start time - end time -cost • cost multipliers - M1 = constant or variable - M2 = constant • rounding method - normal - conservative

TASKPLAN'S OUTPUT: Tabulation of the costs • incremental (sum for each task occurring during the time period) • cumulative (running total through the current time period)

TASKPLAN'S FEATURES/OPTIONS: • diskette storage/retrieval of task data • revising task data • histogram of results • hardcopy (printer) of results * sample project is provided

SYSTEM REQUIREMENTS: IBM PC or XT • 96K memory • DOS 1.1, 2.0, or 2.1 • 1 disk drive • monitor (mono. or color) • System Options • printer (dot matrix or letter quality)

TIME AND MONEY, (#251) u-s $50

This program manages all aspects of home finance. It allows you to track the use of your money, create and use budgets, and project how certain financial plans will work out for you in the future. It has built-in analyses to help with common financial decisions such as buying vs. renting a house or fixing the old car vs. getting a new one.

Careful use of a program like TIME AND MONEY can frequently save the user from 1 to 5 percent of his gross annual income. This is sometimes enough to pay for the whole cost of a computer system.

The program was designed to be very easy to use. All functions are accessed out of a series of menus. The highest level menu, listing all available functions, appears automatically when the user turns on his machine. Start the program by inserting your disk and turning the machine on.

The program includes a manual on the disk. This manual can be displayed from the main menu or printed out by following the menu directions.

TIME AND MONEY will work with any IBM personal computer, including the junior, if the computer has 128K of memory, and at least one double- sided floppy disk. It is compatible with DOS 1.1, 2.0, or 2.1. It will work equally well in color or black and white.

BUDGETRK 3.3, (#155) u-s $25

BUDGETRK is written to keep track of budgeted disbursements. BUDGETRK.BAS and BUDGETRK.MOD are both written in IBM DISK BASIC and are menu driven. Since each budget item is filed as a separate file on a disk, using a subdirectory allows for creation of an infinite number of budget items.

Both BUDGETRK.BAS and BUDGETRK.MOD track individual budget disbursements by charging them against a budgeted amount that is entered when the budget item is initiated.

In BUDGETRK.BAS, budget item budgeted amounts and budget item disbursements are added to a project budget and disbursement record, thus allowing budget items to be accounted for both individually and corporately. A total of 30 projects are supported.

In BUDGETRK.MOD, budget item budget amounts are encumbered against a predetermined project budget amount. A total of 80 projects are supported. Example: You are going to remodel an office complex.

Using BUDGETRK.BAS you would initiate a project called "Remodel Offices". Then you would initiate a budget item of $20,000 for the president's office, a budget item of $15,000 for the vice president's office, etc., assigning each budget item to project "Remodel Offices". As each budget item is initiated, the budget amount is added to the project budget amount (which started at zero). Then, as money is disbursed, that disbursement is recorded in the budget item record and added to the project disbursement total.

Using BUDGETRK.MOD you would initiate a project called "Remodel Offices" and you would also be prompted to enter a project budget amount. Then you would initiate budget items just as you would in BUDGETRK.BAS. As each budget item is initiated, the budget amount for that item is encumbered against the project budget amount reducing the project budget balance. Then, as money is disbursed, that disbursement is recorded in the budget item record but is not charged against the project budget since the project budget was encumbered when the budget item was initiated.

Talking to other computers (communications)

PC-DIAL, (#129) u-s $29

PC-Dial is a general purpose asynchronous communications program. It employs a simple and straightfoward approach to communica tions. Its wide range of capabilities surpass those of many of the more expensive communications programs on the market today. PC-Dial is easy to understand, easy to use, powerful, and small in size.

FEATURES include:

- Communicates at speeds from 110 bps up to 9600 bps
- Upload & download text files. While sending you may dynamically send or bypass selected records
- Upload & download binary files. The error checking "X-Modem" protocol can be used
- Can utilize non "intelligent" modems
- Can utilize intelligent modems. This includes a wide variety of modems which utilize commands to Auto-Dial a phone number
- Can automatically redial a phone number repeatedly until connection is made
- Saves a snapshot image of your screen to disk upon command
- Captures all or portions of incoming data in a disk file
- Employs user defined filters to remove or change undesirable characters in the incoming data
- You can dynamically slow down the transmission speed, so as not to overrun the other computer
- Communication paramters (parity, speed, stop bits, data bits, etc.) can be dynamically altered
- You can build automatic sign on sequences of any length, to enable logging on to a variety of remote computers without having to remember phone numbers, passwords, and access codes
- Allows user specification of screen colors
- You can move among different subdirectories on a hard disk (while communicating) for retrieving and sending data

- Can communicate properly with computers which use "XON/XOFF" characters

FUNCTIONAL SPECIFICATIONS:

- Communications protocols supported: Asynchronous
- Hard disk support: Program and/or data files may reside on hard disk, supports subdirectories (DOS 2.0 or later)
- Electronic disk support: Program and/or data files may reside on electronic disk
- Program capacities: Speeds from 110 bps to 9600 bps
- Program is not copy protected

SYSTEM REQUIREMENTS:

- An IBM PC or compatible
- A serial communications port and modem
- PC-DOS or MS-DOS version 1.1, 2.0 or later
- 96K of RAM memory

PC-TALK III, (not in library) u-s $35

PC-TALK III is a full-feature communications program for the IBM PC and compatibles. The program uploads and downloads files and has a 60 entry auto-dial directory. Optional parameters in the Dialing Directory allow selective character stripping/converting and for storing pacing instructions for each entry. Transmit options allow for transmitting binary files, line pacing files, and transmitting files using XMODEM error-checking protocol at 300 to 1200 baud. There are forty programmable permanent logon/input strings. A 70 page User's Guide is supplied on disk.

SYSTEM REQUIREMENTS: Minimum 64K, one disk drive, Asynchronous communications port, Modem - preferrably direct connect with auto-dial feature (such as Hayes Smartmodem). PC- TALK III can be used with acoustic modems. 300 and 1200 baud modems are supported. Printer optional, other than initially required to print the User's Guide.

Send $35 for a production copy to:

FREEWARE
The Headlands Press,
Inc. P.O. Box 862
Tiburon, CA 94920

PC-VT, (#286) u-s $35

PC-VT is a software emulator which makes the IBM PC function as a DEC VT102 or a VT100 Video Terminal. Selection of terminal type is made in the SETUP B display (Chapter 6). PC-VT defaults to VT102 emulation. PC-VT also supports VT52 compatibility mode.

Here is a brief list of the functions handled by PC-VT.

- Emulates both VT100 and VT102 Terminals. Emulates VT52 compatibility Mode of the VT100.
- Communication over an RS232 port configured as either COM1 or COM2 selectable from the SETUP display.
- Communications support for all of the popular baud rate and data bit/parity bit combinations.
- Full Duplex with no EIA modem control. Only data leads have to be connected (FDX A mode). Suitable for use with a null modem (direct) connection to the host computer or with a modem which does not require modem control signals.
- VT52 Compatibility Mode.
- Support for Hayes dialing commands and includes a Dialing Directory with 10 entries.
- ALT F1 thru ALT F10 as Macro keys.
- Full receive parity checking can be enabled.
- Both Numeric and Application Keypad modes.
- Full cursor control.
- Full feature Upload and Download file capability. Both ASCII and XMODEM (CRC capable) are supported. Path name support is included if you are using DOS 2 or later. ASCII file upload includes a "handshake" capability to compensate for slow host systems.
- Capability to transmit a sustained Break.

- NO SCROLL key XON/XOFF support.
- Connection of a printer as LPT1 or LPT2 including local print screen operations.
- Capability to echo all displayed characters to LPT1 or LPT2 as hardcopy record of a terminal session.
- Using special ALT key keystrokes, access to several special function procedures.
- SETUP A and SETUP B displays.
- Full XON/XOFF support for both transmit and receive.

RBBS, (#212)

This is a package of software which lets your PC act as a bulletin board. It will act as the host computer, allowing others to log on and down load files to their own system. With the excellent menu and help systems installed in this package even novice users have little trouble logging onto the system and using it.

LU (#190)

Library utility for packing and unpacking several files so they may be uploaded or download as one file to a bulletin board system.

UNSQ (#120, #212)

UNSQ -UNSQueeze- is used when a program has been compressed in order to stuff more information on a disk or shorten the time required to download a program from a bulletin board. To use this program type:

```
UNSQ filename
```

For a listing of the two options enter UNSQ with no filename.

Mathematics and Statistics

EPISTAT 3.1, (#88) u-s $20

EPISTAT is a statistical package written in Advanced BASIC for the IBM PC or other compatible microcomputer. It is designed to allow rapid analysis of small data sets (under 2000 data items). It requires at least 64K RAM, one disk drive, a monochrome or color monitor, and PC-DOS or MS-DOS. To make use of the graphics features of EPISTAT, you will also need a color/graphics adapter card, a high resolution monitor, and a dot matrix printer with graphics capability. EPISTAT supports Epson, IBM, Okidata and C.Itoh Prowriter printers in 10 or 15 inch widths.

The 25 programs in EPISTAT provide for data entry, editing, sorting, selecting records, crosstabs and both histogram and scattergram graphs. Statistical tests or functions include: analysis of variance, Bayes' theorem, binomial distribution, Chi-square test, correlation coefficients, Fisher's exact test, linear regression, Mantel-Haenszel Chi-square tests, McNemar's test, normal distribution, Poisson distribution, rank sum and signed rank tests, Student's T-test, and of course mean, median and standard deviation. Other features include data transformations, sample size determination, and random assignment of cases and controls.

Data can be printed in input order or sorted by any variable. A utility is provided to transfer data from a standard card-image datafile (like a Lotus 1-2-3 Printfile) into EPISTAT format. A ten page user's guide with references and an example data set is included on the disk to aid in gaining familiarity with program operation and the proper interpretation of results.

SPPC System Demo, (#232) u-s $25 up

SPPC stands for "A Statistical Package for the Personal Computer" which is designed for use with the IBM PC and compatible computers. Although SPPC contains only a few programs at present, they are quite powerful and more will be added in the near future.

You can test SPPC programs by use of two data files on the diskette. A raw data file has the name LONGLEYR.DAT and a summary data file has the name LONGLEYS.DAT—or you can test the programs by using your own data.

Longley data is included because it constitutes a severe test for any multiple regression program as described by Peter Lachenbruch in his article which appeared in the November 1983 issue of BYTE Magazine. We are pleased to tell you that SPPC Multiple Regression program produced a completely accurate solution to the Longley data. None of the programs that were reviewed by Lachenbruch would do that.

Registrants will be placed on a mailing list and notified of additions to SPPC and provided updates for Version 1.0 for the cost of postage and handling.

The author is interested in what additional procedures you would like to see included in SPPC. Since he is in the process of developing the entire package you can tell him exactly what you would like to see. He promises to do everything he can to accomodate your needs and interests.

WALMYR Publishing Company
PO Box 3554, Leon Station
Tallahassee, FL 32315

COMPLEX.LIB 1.2, (#248) u-s $45

COMPLEX.LIB is a complete library of complex functions to be used with IBM's Pascal and FORTRAN compilers 2.X. Pascal and FORTRAN programs that use the complex functions from the complex function library need only make the proper call in the program and then use the complex function.

There are single and double precision complex functions for arithmetic, transcendental and trigonometric functions.

ARITHMETIC FUNCTIONS INCLUDE:
addition • subtraction • multiplication • division • 1/X where X is complex.

TRANSCENDENTAL FUNCTIONS INCLUDE: square root of complex X • raise complex X to integer power • take integer root of complex X • raise e to complex X • Ln of complex X • log of complex X to complex base Y • raise complex Y to complex X.

TRIGONOMETRIC FUNCTIONS INCLUDE: sine of complex X • cosine of complex X • tangent of complex X • arc sine of complex X • arc cosine of complex X • arc tangent of complex X.

Everything needed to understand how to use the complex function library is found in the four files that make up the complex function library.

All registered owners will receive 40 pages of documentation that covers all of the complex functions.

The complex function library should work with a number of other Pascal and FORTRAN compliers, such as the MicroSoft compilers. As the information about which compilers are compatible with the complex function library is obtained it will be distributed to all registered owners.

Simulation Rule is willing to try and create a version of the complex function library for the earlier versions of the IBM Pascal and FORTRAN compilers. This is a special request, and there is an additional $12 fee for this service. The source code of the complex function library is available with a non-disclosure agreement and for a fee of $750.00.

EIGHTCRV, (#261)

EIGHTCRV.BAS is a program that fits 8 different curves to a set of data. The program is written in GWBasic. The program uses a printer for most output. The printer control codes written into the program are Star Delta 10 codes, which should be compatible with Star Gemini and Epson codes. Most output is in condensed type. This allows the scatter diagram, drawn in character graphics, to be as large as possible.

To use the program, the data set containing the dependent, Y, and predictor, X, variables must be saved in SDA (space delimited ASCII) format on disk. SDA format is simple and easy to use. Variables are in columns and cases are in rows. In each row of the data file, numbers are separated by spaces in free format. EIGHTCRV assumes all variables it reads are numeric, so any character data in the file should appear after all numeric variables. SDA format was chosen because it is easy to create with any text editor, like DVED, FULLEDIT, or RV-EDIT and is readable by GWBasic, Turbo Pascal, Minitab and SPSS, among others. It is also very compact, taking only about 25% of the disk space that .DIF files take. The file EIGHTCRV.SDA is an example of an SDA file.

This version of the EIGHTCRV program is adapted from the program 8CURVS in the book Basic Programs for Production and Operations Management by Pantumsinchai, Hassan and Gupta, Prentice—Hall, 1983. Some users may find the original version more to their liking. The entire package of programs in this book has been extensively modified and converted to run on the IBM PC. More information about this package may be obtained from MicroPack, Inc., 223 W. Jackson Blvd, Suite 1110, Chicago, Illinois, 60606.

EIGHTCRV.BAS was adapted by Joseph C. Hudson, 4198 Warbler Dr., Flint, MI 48504. Other than receiving the generous permission of the authors to submit this program to PC-SIG, the adaptor has no connection with any of the firms mentioned above.

Languages

CHASM 2.13, (#10) u-s $30

CHASM is a full featured assembler for the IBM PC. Substantially simpler than the IBM Macro assembler, CHASM is ideal for those learning assembly language. Despite this simplicity, CHASM is powerful enough for production coding, and several commercial software packages have been written at least partially in CHASM.

Using CHASM you can:

- Learn assembly language, and explore the internal workings of the IBM PC.
- Write lightning fast stand-alone programs.
- Produce external machine language procedures and functions for Turbo Pascal. Write optimized code for critical functions, and add capabilities not offered by Turbo.
- Produce machine language subroutines for BASIC programs, both interpreted and compiled.

CHASM comes in two versions. A simple version which runs under the BASIC interpreter is available for free trial as User- Supported software. Those who make the suggested $30 payment receive a free upgrade to an advanced compiled version. The compiled version runs substantially faster, and supports many advanced features not found in the interpreted version.

SYSTEM REQUIREMENTS: • Interpreted version, under DOS 1.x: 64K • Interpreted version, under DOS 2.x with 96K RAM • Compiled version, either DOS with 128K RAM • All versions require at least one disk drive, and an 80 column monitor.

LADYBUG 1.0c, (#94) u-s $35

LADYBUG is a graphics language based on LOGO Turtle Graphics. It contains most of the graphics commands, procedure making commands, and control commands from the Apple II(2) implementation of LOGO done by Terrapin, Inc. This version is described in the book LOGO FOR THE APPLE II, by Harold Abelson, published by McGraw-Hill in 1982. It is very similar to other versions for the Apple II, IBM PC, Texas Instruments, and TRS-80(3) computers. Words from other LOGO implementations are included for compatibility.

In addition it has:

- Commands and words from various other LOGO implementations.
- Commands with the same names as IBM LOGO commands are mainly compatible with IBM LOGO.
- A library of procedures adapted from a variety of sources.
- Painting of areas.
- Clipping of drawings (as well as wraparound).
- A fast full screen editor.
- Support for using both displays if both are present.
- Sounds -- PLAY statement like Basic.

The major features missing are:

- List manipulation.
- Variable numbers of parameters to primitives.
- Saving screen images.

LADYBUG REQUIREMENTS: • 128K of memory. • One single sided disk drive. • A graphics adaptor. • A graphics display of any kind. Color is supported only on a color display; 80 column editing is supported only on a high resolution monitor. A color TV set will work but colors will not be accurate. • DOS 1.1, 2.0, or 2.1. (DOS 1.0 has not been tested.) • An IBM PC, PCjr, or compatible machine. • The IBM Monochrome display is also supported, if present, for editing and when in text mode. References in this document to "the Monochrome display" refer to the IBM Monochrome display and not to a black and white graphics monitor.

XLISP 1.4, (#148)

XLISP is an experimental programming language combining some of the features of LISP with an object oriented extension capability. It was implemented to allow experimentation with object oriented programming on small computers. There are currently implementations running on the PDP-11 under UNIX V7, on the VAX-11 under VAX/VMS and Berkeley VAX/UNIX, and on the 8088/8086 under CP/M-86 or MS-DOS. It is completely written in the programming language 'C' and is easily extended with user written built-in functions and classes. It is available in source form free of charge to non-commercial users. Prospective commercial users should contact the author for permission to use XLISP.

Many traditional LISP functions are built into XLISP. In addition, XLISP defines the objects 'Object' and 'Class' as primitives. 'Object' is the only class that has no superclass and hence is the root of the class heirarchy tree. 'Class' is the class of which all classes are instances (it is the only object that is an instance of itself).

The manual is intended to be a brief description of XLISP. It assumes some knowledge of LISP and some understanding of the concepts of object oriented programming.

Laxon & Perry FORTH 2.0.0, (#263,264)

This is a public domain FORTH system. This Forth uses the files of the host operating system. Although this reduces performance, it is much more portable and more convenient.

BATCH FILE UTILITIES, (#82) u-s $10

The Batch file utilities are a helpful set of programs that show the power and useful nature of batch files. There is a fine tutorial on the disk that uses the utilities to display its own text and give helpful examples along the way. Options in the tutorial allow the novice to read every sentence and the old pro to skip ahead.

These utilities will get an operator started in the right direction to use batch files to save a lot of time and keyboard pounding. Batch file utilities for yes/no prompting, character input, locating files,& determining system configuration are included.

Programmer's utilities

PROGRAMMER'S CALCULATOR, (#87) u-s $15

Programmer's Calculator is divided into two programs, Calculator and Conversion. After the initial screen the first screen displayed is the calculator program. To access the Conversion program screen use the function key (F10). This key is used to toggle between the two programs. When switching between programs, the program you leave is frozen at the point you pressed (F10). This allows you to return to the program where you left off.

The Calculator Program is a powerful RPN (Reverse Polish Notation) calculator. It displays on screen the four stack registers, six memory registers and a display register thereby making it unnecessary to write down the contents of the registers when making complex calculations. In addition to the general functions found on most calculators the Programmer's Calculator has six logical functions (and, or, not, etc.). Numbers used in the general calculations may be up to 16 digits in accuracy.

The Conversion Program provides a fast and efficient way to convert numbers between decimal, hexadecimal, binary, and octal. Numbers up to 20 bits binary may be converted and the two's complement may be calculated on numbers up to 15 bits in length.

SPRITE, (#238) u-s $20

SPRITE lets you conveniently create Sprite characters. A Sprite character is a graphics figure made from a set of colored pixels. Instead of displaying this figure pixel by pixel, BASIC lets you display the figure in one step with the graphics form of the PUT statement. This is similar to the Sprite graphics available on other microcomputers.

The graphics PUT statement displays a figure that is stored in an array in a coded form. Trying to encode a figure in an array is very tedious; the manual is very vague and confusing. This is where SPRITE comes in.

SPRITE lets you design your Sprite figure and sample it with different palettes and background colors. Your Sprite figure can be as large as 160 X pixels by 100 Y pixels (32 X 20 is default). This is as large as one fourth of the display screen. You can even save and restore works in progress. When you are ready, SPRITE will create a file of BASIC statements. These BASIC statements (an array declaration and a set of DATA statements) can be merged into a BASIC program and used with a PUT statement.

Joey Robichaux
1036 Brookhollow Drive
Baton Rouge, La. 70810

User-supported DOS utilities

BACK SCROLL v6.4, (#129) u-s $20

Back Scroll! is a bi-directional scrolling utility. Once activated, Back Scroll! will buffer the screen scrolling so that the user may recall, with a few simple keystrokes, data that has previously been scrolled off the screen. The user may either scroll by line or by page through Back Scroll!'s buffer. In addition, Back Scroll!'s printer commands allow the user to select and print any data that is currently in the buffer.

When Back Scroll! is loaded, it becomes an extension to DOS and from then on will be transparent to the user and most programs. The activation of Back Scroll!, once loaded, can be done at any time without any danger to the current operation. When entering and exiting Back Scroll!, the current display screen will be saved and restored so that the user may continue without any interference.

Note: Back Scroll! will only support the eighty column text display mode of either the color or monochrome display card. Unpredictable results may occur when Back Scroll! is toggled while in either the forty column mode or in any graphics mode.

Installation and operational instructions may be found on disk in the file: BACKSCRL.DOC.

The Kampro Group
Post Office Box 90654
Honolulu, Hawaii 96835

DB Screen, (#128) u-s $10

Dbscreen (DBS) allows you to use your IBM Personal Computer to easily create dBASEII screens. Instead of entering row and number designations into a format file for your screen fields, you simply 'paint' your screen on the terminal in a full screen edit mode. You can see exactly what your screen is going to look like. Dbscreen will also let you modify print dBASEII screen formats. Equipment requirements are minimal: 64K of RAM, one disk drive and an 80 column display. Start by printing, and reading, the 13 page manual. Type COPY DBS.PRT PRN (or LPT1).

DISKCAT 4.0, (#106) u-s $30

DISKCAT is a file cataloging program that keeps track of all of your disk files -no more ticking disk after disk into a drive to see if the file you need is on it. Various programs included on the disk will sort by name, extension, date, etc. and print the catalog file. You can search the catalog for location of a particular program, and perform other gymnastics, too many to list here. As your library of disks and programs grows you will find DISKCAT more and more useful.

Maximum number of file name entries: up to 3000, depending on memory.

HARDWARE REQUIREMENTS: Minimum: 128K (192K on Compaq), one disk drive, 80-column monitor. • Recommended: a RAM disk-emulator or hard disk (to hold DC4.DTA), a printer, and a graphics board. DOS: 1.0, 1.1, 2.0 or 2.1.

Start by printing the 15 page documentation. Type "COPY DC4.DOC PRN".

FREECOPY, (#226) u-s $25

FREECOPY is a disk utility that is functionally equivalent to DISKCOPY which is distributed with IBM PC DOS. I am releasing this software into the public domain because I believe that the time has come for users to see and criticize professional quality source code. I welcome all comments on FREECOPY, particularly about any bugs you discover in the code. In developing FREECOPY, I reversed engineered DISKCOPY and made sure that I did not violate the proprietary rights of either IBM or Microsoft. In fact, I took great pains to ensure that FREECOPY is better than DISKCOPY.

The executable code is a binary .COM file that comes in machine readable format. The source code is structured assembly language with lots of comments.

Squire Buresh Associates, Inc.
P.O. Box 112
Millbury, MA 01527

GINACO, (#66) u-s $15

GINACO UTILITIES, marketed commercially as 'Big Blue'berry Pie a La Mode, is an array of 56 files and basic programs of wide diversity and great utility. Each program is self-documented by an initial full screen text display. The user is provided an opportunity to continue with the program or return to the MENU. The array includes more than 100 easily-extractable routines and sub-routines of highly practical use for either the serious or week-end programmer.

Included are many print routines, special forms, input/output routines, file management and word processing programs, and label-print routines of varying complexity and utility. These utilities have been enthusiastically used by thousands of IBM-PC owners. A recommended User-Supported-Software donation is $15, and a DOS 1.1 to 2.1 formatted disk and mailer. $20 if no disk or mailer is provided.

G I N A C O
10708 Santa Fe Drive
Sun City AZ 85351

QUICKREF, (#59) u-s $10

QUICKREF helps you create templates for your function keys. All of the 40 possible function keys may be included in a template. This program will create new templates, update or revise old ones, etc. The templates may be reviewed on the monitor and then printed out on the printer. There are several pages of user guide to help you, named QUICKREF.DOC.

ULTRA-UTILITIES 4.0, (#133,245) u-s $40

The Ultra-Utilities are an excellent set of programs to help with the housekeeping and problem solving of computer operations. There are several programs in the set, some of them are described below.

U-Zap, U-File, and U-Format:

These files are a powerful tool set that may be used to inspect or modify information on floppy disks. Please use these with caution and only on a copy of the disk you wish to modify. These programs are designed to be used by programmers or others with an understanding of diskette drive operation and file structure. The programs are easy to use with help screens and menus to guide the way. Enter one of the above commands at system level and follow the menus advice.

U-Mind:

"At FreeSoft, we do quite a lot of database work, both for ourselves and for clients. After writing about the seven millionth database manager, we came to a startling conclusion: very little was actually changing from program to program. We admittedly are experts when it comes to reinventing the wheel, but this time a thought struck us, 'Why not write a database program generator?' (TA-DA! Sound of trumpets...). Well, that was several years ago, and Ultra-Mind is the end result. Basically what it does is allow you to set up your unique database needs, and then actually writes a dedicated database program in BASIC while you watch."

What we found was that we were doing in a few minutes what used to take hours or days. Here's a brief outline of Ultra-Mind's capabilities and features:

1) This program allows you to set up a customized data entry system and then writes a dedicated BASIC database manager program.
2) The data entry can be divided into multiple screens, called "pages".
3) Several different types of input fields are supported: Numeric, Alphanumeric, Formatted Numeric, Calculated, Automatic Date, and Automatic Time. In addition, the user can specify any keys that are restricted from entry for each individual field (No Z's allowed, for instance).
4) Non-field symbols, such as titles or borders, can be placed anywhere on the data entry screens for a truly professional appearance.
5) Generated program is documented with remarks for easy customization.
6) Sophisticated hashing algorithm nullifies BASIC's slow execution. Typical record access (no matter how many records in the system) when the key field is known is under 1/2 second.
7) Knowledge of BASIC, data-file input/output routines, or other special functions is not required. A small amount of BASIC formula format is helpful for using calculation fields.
8) All generated programs can be compiled for added speed under the Search and List functions.

9) Number of fields and total field characters is dependent only on available memory (total field characters per record must be less than 65,536 characters not counting program size).

We hope you'll enjoy this package and will choose to support The FreeSoft Company in our endeavor to bring you the most interesting software at the best price. We place this product in your hands at no cost in order for you to truly judge its appropriatness for your applications.

PC-COMPARE 1.24, (#113)

PC-COMPARE is a utility for comparing ASCII/text files. These files may be BASIC programs saved with the ",A" option, source code in any of the programming languages, any text file such as a letter or manuscript written with a text editor, or Wordstar(tm) files saved in the non-document mode.

A system with at least 128K of RAM, one disk drive, any version of PC- DOS or MS-DOS and IBM-PC compatibility is needed to run the program.

NOTE: this version of PC-COMPARE is not a "FREEWARE(tm)" type of program and no donation for user-support is necessary or suggested.

Features:

- Clear single menu of choices from the user for file names and options.
- The two files, up to 64K each in size, are read entirely into memory for a quick compare.
- In one of the two full versions explained below, files of either 1000 lines or 2000 lines each can be compared. The 1000 line version uses less memory, for those with under 256K of RAM.
- Any mismatches are saved, with the output showing current system time and date, DIRectory information about each of the files being compared, as well as line numbers and listings of the mismatches for each file.
- Resynchronization of lines after a rematch.

PC-COMPARE is a full-feature version of a commercial product—AUTOCOMP -except that this is limited to comparing files of up to 100 lines each. AUTOCOMP, as well as other utilities such as a BASIC precompiler, BASIC trace and BASIC REMark programs, are available from:

TIMESHARE ASSOCIATES, INC.
10202 Robinson
Overland Park, KS 66212
(913) 642-7564

For the PC-COMPARE version, type RUN to execute a batch file tutorial of the program. PRINTDOC will print out the complete documentaton text file.

DEFKEY, (#113)

The purpose of this program is to allow the user to customize almost all of the keys of the PC's keyboard, provided that PC-DOS Version 2.0 is being used. Using this utility, it is possible to assign almost any string to almost any key or combination of keys (such as ALT-A, etc), thus significantly decreasing the amount of typing that the user will have to do. For example, it is possible to assign the DOS command 'DIR' to the ALT-D sequence so that whenever these keys were pressed, 'DIR' would be printed out.

QSYS 3.0, (#118) u-s $50

QSYS is an operating environment, a menu system, an appointment calendar and message system. It provides password access for up to 24 users to your programs with up to 10 levels of security. It provides a tree-structured menu system for your software library, allowing you to define as many menus as desired. It provides extended batch file capabilities, including re-execution of previous tasks, cancellation of the current task or the entire batch file, and return to the DOS command line to execute any other task while batch file execution is temporarily suspended.

QSYS comes with its own configurable emulated disk, allowing extremely fast program loading, batch file execution, and the freedom to switch diskettes as desired during execution of a batch file. It incorporates a message system which allows each user to maintain private messages for an appointment calendar, and to send a message to up to 5 other users at once, at up to 5 different times, if desired. The QSYS message system will give audible notification of a pending message even while the system is executing another program.

QSYS defaults to a full screen clock/calendar display during periods of inactivity. The calendar includes functions for entering the month and year to display, as well as single step and continuous forward or reverse scrolling throughout the range of the DOS calendar. The clock can be configured to display 12 or 24 hour format, HH:MM or HH:MM:SS.

QSYS has many other features which will ease and enhance the use of your system. It comes complete with extensive documentation in the ASCII format, which can be printed on most any printer. Also included is an installation aid program that will configure QSYS to your system with minimal effort.

SYSTEM REQUIREMENTS: • IBM PC or PC-XT • DOS 2.X • 192K of Memory • IBM Compatible Color/Graphics Monitor Adapter • Two Double-sided, Double-density Diskette Drives or • A Winchester Disk and One Double-sided Diskette Drive.

A user-supported contribution of $50 is suggested.

Dennis Lee
906 Greenbriar Loop
Round Rock, TX 78664
CompuServe # 70376,452

EASYRITE/LABELFILE, (#146) u-s $10

LablFile and EasyRite are a pair of programs developed by GINACO for the IBM PC and compatible machines. They both function with the PC Jr. EasyRite is a unique word processor and editor which makes the computer perform like a typewriter. It is enthusiastically accepted by those individuals who are dismayed and/or discouraged with all the complicated commands of many high priced word processors. Editing is straight forward and simple. There are no search and replace provisions. The program is self documented with screen displayed instructions which may be recalled by the easily accessible CONTROL MENU at any time during program execution. A FACT file is provided for practice edit and print use.

LablFile is a self documented, highly flexible file management and label print program which compliments EasyRite. Thousands of PC owners use it in a multitude of ways. Both of the programs are provided in expanded ASCII BASIC and compiled form. The recommended User-Supported software donation is $10, along with a DOS 1.1 to 2.1 formatted disc.

GINACO
10708 Santa Fe Drive
Sun City AZ 85351

SYSMENU, (#250)

SYSMENU is appropriate for all PCs with a hard disc. It provides a convenient way to move between DOS directories while executing programs and performing other DOS tasks. Instead of entering DOS commands, the user selects menu items.

The menu items and their corresponding DOS commands are contained in a textfile. Each disc directory and subdirectory may contain a SYSMENU textfile. These textfiles are created by the user using any available text editor.

SYSMENU reads the textfile, displays the menu as entered in the textfile, allows the user to make a selection, creates a batch file with the corresponding DOS commands and runs the batch file. The menu system can be made as simple or complex as desired, however knowledge of the everyday DOS commands is required.

There are no special system requirements. The program could be used on a floppy disc machine as it will facilitate any repetitive entry of DOS commands. A monochrome screen is assumed.

Start by copying the file "SYSMENU.DOC" to your printer.

Diskjockey, (#284) u-s $35

Diskjockey is a utility program that opens up individual sectors and tracks for inspection and change. Diskjockey can also tell you how a disk is formatted. It is an easy program to use with no documentation necesary. Enter "DJ" to start the program and menu screens guide you from there.

AUTOMENU v2.0, (#284) u-s $25

AUTOMENU is the solution to the problem of learning all the DOS commands required to access many different application programs. No longer will the user be required to type in a list of commands to find the program they are looking for; with a single press of a key, almost any application program can be made available. AUTOMENU provides the user with an easy to read and understand menu of options to choose from, then automatically executes the commands required to bring that menu option selected to the user's fingertips. AUTOMENU provides the user with the capability to set up their own customized menu systems. The user can define the menu titles, the menu options displayed, and DOS compatible commands required to carry out each of these menu options.

To use this software for the first time requires knowledge of DOS and a text editor. The AUTOMENU.DAT file contains all the information needed for the menu. Before starting, determine what you plan to title your menus, what menu options you wish to have, and the DOS commands required to execute those options.

Load-us, (#284) u-s $10

Load-US (tm) is a utility developed by SWFTE, Inc. which allows you to run Lotus 123 (tm) and Symphony (tm) directly from a hard disk without the system disk in Drive A. This utility is NOT a copy program; it is a technological breakthrough that allows authorized users to use 123 and Symphony on a hard disk system. Load-US saves you the aggravation of locating your System disk each time you need to run 123 or Symphony.

To start Load-US: load DOS, copy Load-US onto your hard disk (into your Lotus subdirectory, if you have made one), type 'Load-US' and press Return to start Load-US. Follow the instructions on the Load-US system screens to install the system. Once installed, Load-US permits you to run Lotus 123 or Symphony normally without your Sytem disk.

ColLst, (#276)

ColLst allows you to get the listings of your column-oriented material in the style that you prefer. Among ColLst's features are:

- Page layout controls—controlling width, length, column positions, and number of columns.
- Optional headers—giving you time and date stamps as well as title, subtitles, and page numbers.
- Optional internal commands—indicators in the file to turn the listing on or off, start a new column or page, insert another file, or change the headers.
- Retains user settings—parameter settings specified by the user become the values for all future uses until reset.
- Batch commands—easy to use commands to print several files without user supervision.
- Default values—used to minimize keyboard entries.

To use ColLst type: START

FindFile v2.0, (#277) u-s $5

FINDFILE is a utility which searches through the files in your sub-directories. FINDFILE provides you with the ability to find those lost files and the means to better manage your files.

With DOS 2.x and a hard disk drive you can easily keep hundreds of files in dozens of directories. As they accumulate, keeping track of them becomes increasingly difficult. The only tools which are provided with DOS 2.x are at best insufficient.

To start the program use the TYPE command to read TYPE.ME

TYPE TYPE.ME

FindFile requires a single sided floppy, 96K of RAM and DOS 2.x at a minimum. FindFile has an easy to learn and use interactive interface. FindFile runs on the IBM PC, XT, Jr, AT and most compatibles.

FindFile is easily installed, just follow the instructions in file COVER. For a listing, use the included program LISTER to print COVER.

ALIGN 1.6, (#217) u-s $20

ALIGN assists technical hobbyists and service technicians who service PC diskette drives. 40 track single or double-sided drives are supported.

- ALIGN is intended for use with a DYSAN analog alignment disk for 40 track drives, 224/2A #800180, an oscilloscope and the drive manufacturer's alignment and service procedures. Suggested sources are included in ALIGN's documentation.
- ALIGN operates a diskette drive while you make drive checks and adjustments.
- You can move the diskette drive head to absolute track locations and run the drive under test while checking and adjusting:
  - Radial head alignment
  - Head azimuth
  - Head positioner hysteresis (backlash)
  - Instantaneous speed variation
  - Index timing
  - Track 0 stop
  - Track 0 switch
- Commands are provided to select the drive, head, track and run time. Special commands and function keys make it easy to start and stop the drive, seek the alignment tracks, adjust the track 0 switch and reset the diskette controller.

ALIGN differs from the many disk diagnostic programs on the market in that it is used to actually fix and service diskette drives, not just diagnose them.

ALIGN runs under IBM PC-DOS on a PC, PC-XT, PC-AT or compatibles with at least 64K and an 80 column display, either monochrome or color. It does not yet support the PC-AT's High Capacity drive, nor does it run on a PCjr. The diskette drives to be adjusted are connected to the PC in the normal manner, although signal and power extension cables are helpful.

Start by copying the 9 page manual in file "ALIGN.DOC" to your printer.

Public domain DOS utilities

VDEL, (#28,#273)

VDEL.COM is a type of safety net that is used in place of the normal delete command. Use VDEL just as you would use DEL and a wildcard option:

```
VDEL B:*.*
```

VDEL will now display the files on the B: drive one at a time and ask if you want to delete it or save it. This allows you to choose the files to be deleted without having to continue listing the directory and going back to delete another file. Also in its safety net roll it prevents you from deleting something that you didn't know was on that particular disk.

MOVE, (#80,#183,#273)

MOVE is a cross between COPY and VDEL. PC DOS version 2.00 or greater is required. Options may be preceded by "/" or by " -".

Syntax: MOVE [SourceDir]FileSpec [TargetDir] [OptionList]

OptionsList:
/Erase -Erase Erase each file after successful copy.
/Terse -Terse Suppress version message, instructions.
/Yes -Yes Automatic "Yes" response to each query.

Examples:

1. Copy using full directory specifications.

```
C>MOVE C:\DIRA\*.* C:\DIRB:
```

2. Copy from A: to current disk and directory. Delete each file after it's moved.

```
C>MOVE A:*.* /E
```

WHEREIS, (#110,#273)

WHEREIS Searches for specified file(s) through all DOS 2.0 directories listing matching files with their appropriate directories and sub- directories.

Format: WHEREIS [filename[.ext]] Wildcard (*) can be used.

ST, (#111,#273)

This program provides three significant enhancements to the "type" command:

1) the display is paged, not scrolled, and thus is much easier to read.
2) Previously displayed pages are saved and can be accessed by use of the PgUp and PgDn keys.
3) Wordstar's 'funny' characters are converted to normal display characters. As all WordStar users know, 'type'ing a WordStar file creates a strange display.

Directions: Type ST for directions and to be prompted for a filename to be listed. Type ST <filename> to list a file. PgUp and PgDn move through the display pages in the file. The '+' toggles the display of page number in each page. This display is convenient for keeping your place in big files—especially files that are bigger than memory and only part of the file can be kept in memory. This display is normally off, it is toggled on when "buffer wrap-around" occurs. If it bugs you, hit the '+' key and turn it off.

SDIR24C, (#185,#273)

This command produces a sorted list of files on your screen. It may be used instead of the DOS "DIR" command. Format:

SDIR [d:][path][filename[.ext]] [options]

[filespec] same as for DIR command

[options] * /A—List hidden files.
* /E—Without screen erase.
* /P—Pause when screen full.
/X—Sort by extension.
/S—Sort by size.
/D—Sort by date/time.
/N—Do not sort, original order.

Default = *.* sorted by name.ext with screen erase.
*—Option may be combined with other options.

MEMBRAIN, (#198,#273)

MEMBRAIN.EXE creates a file named 'MEMBRAIN.SYS', a DOS device driver for an emulated disk drive configured to your specifications. DOS will assign to the drive the next available drive letter. For example, if your system has two diskette drives (A & B), then the emulated drive will be drive C. The emulated drive will function identically to a hardware drive with a few exceptions. First, this drive need not and cannot be formatted. Second, when you turn the system off, the drive ceases to exist. Be sure to copy any files that must be saved to a hardware drive before turning power off. Third, it's fast!!!

SYSTEM REQUIREMENTS: An IBM PC or XT with at least 128K of memory and DOS 2.x operating system.

MEMBRAIN allows you to specify disk size, sector size, cluster size, and number of directory entries.

GCOPY, (#140,#204,#273)

GCOPY is used to copy files from one drive to another. The user may enter an ambiguous file request and drive specifier. The program then goes through the matching files it finds in the directory and asks the user if he wants to copy the file again. The program keeps track of the desired files, then copies them after all have been specified.

Format: GCOPY <source filespec> <destination filespec>

GDEL, (#140,#204,#273)

GDEL is similar to VCOPY and may used to delete files from the current drive. The user may enter an ambiguous file name. The program then goes through the matching files it finds in the directory and displays them for the user. The user marks the files that are to be deleted. When all are marked, the user hits the ESC key, and the files will be deleted.

Format: GDEL <filespec>

L4, (#198)

To display the contents of an ASCII file, line by line, with operator positioning commands. A super file lister.

Format: LIST [d:][path]filename[.ext]

Type: H or ? for a list of commands

NDOSEDIT, (#205,#273)

NDOSEDIT makes it easy to edit commands on the DOS command line. You may conviently create your next DOS command from one of the previous commands you entered. It is a VM style editor for DOS commands. It can be used with DOS 1.1 and 2.0.

The DOS editing keys are different than the standard DOS keys and are more natural for the average user. The function keys on the left side of the keyboard are not used.

The information below summarizes the functions of the new editing keys.

Right arrow:	Advances the cursor one character position.
Left arrow:	Backs up the cursor one character position.
Ctrl-Right:	Advances the cursor to the next word.
Ctrl-Left:	Backs up the cursor to the previous word.
LeftShift-tab:	Backs up the cursor to the previous tab position.

RightShift-tab:	Advances the cursor to the next tab position.
Home:	Moves the cursor to the beginning of the line.
End:	Moves the cursor to the end of the line.
Del:	Erases the character at the cursor position.
Back Space:	Erases the character to left of the cursor.
Esc:	Erases the entire line.
Ctrl-Home:	Erases from the beginning of the line to the cursor.
Ctrl-end:	Erases from the cursor to the end of the line.
Up arrow:	Recalls the previous instruction from the stack.
Down arrow:	Recalls the following instruction from the stack.
Ctrl-PgUp:	Clears the current stack of all entries.
Ctrl-PgDn:	Erases the currently displayed stack entry.
Ins:	Toggles the insert mode. If active, cursor size changes.
Ctrl-A:	Displays alias list when under DOS control.
Ctrl-Z:	End of file marker (1AH). Replaces the F6 key.
F1 thru F10:	Not used.

BROWSE, (#205,#273)

BROWSE allows full screen viewing of any file. It is very similar to the VM/CMS browse command. The arrow keys are used to scroll up, down, left and right. Home takes you to the top left corner of the file, End goes to the bottom left. Press Esc to exit browse.

Note: Browse is not an editor. It can only be used to VIEW a file, not change it.

FILEDUMP, (#109,#273)

FILEDUMP is a fast and easy command that dumps out a hexidecimal display of a file's contents. Displayed next to the hex are the ASCII characters so that the file may be read directly.

To use the command enter:

```
FILEDUMP filename
```

Where "filename" is the full name of the file you want dumped.

CWEEP13 v1.30, (#283)

CWEEP13 is a program to make it easier to copy and delete files It was inspired by the CP/M utility SWEEP. CWEEP provides the same capabilities to a Z-DOS/MS-DOS system user which SWEEP13 provides to the CP/M user. See the documentation file with program for a complete list of features.

BASIC programming aids

BASIC Necessities v1.12, (#162) u-s $25

SB.EXE is a preprocessor program for Microsoft BASIC on the IBM PC. It takes a program containing special Structured BASIC statements and translates it into a program containing BASIC statements. Using SB.EXE helps you write more concise, better structured BASIC programs, because the preprocessor lets you take advantage of these features:

- You now have the ability to write free-form, indented statements without line numbers.
- You can now include statements from many separate files into a single BASIC program. This lets you write and maintain your programs in small modules.
- You can organize your subroutines into procedures, each with its own alphanumeric name.
- You can use structured programming statements similar to those found in programming languages like Pascal and C.

PROGRAM REQUIREMENTS: To successfully use these utility programs, you need an IBM PC, XT, or jr with:—at least 64KB of memory,—at least one single-sided diskette drive,—a color or monochrome adapter, and a monitor capable of displaying 80-character lines,—PC DOS version 1.1 or 2.0, and—the files BASICA.COM or BASIC.COM.

BASREF 3.1, (#60) u-s $20

The BASREF program is a utility program designed to help in developing programs in MICROSOFT BASIC on the IBM PC. The program requires 64K of memory to run, and a printer for hardcopy. The program uses a form length of 66 lines, 80 characters per line. BASREF produces a cross- reference list for every variable and line number referenced by a GOTO, GOSUB, THEN, ON... that appear in a BASIC program.

The program will read any type of file, ASCII or TOKENIZED. You just specify the name of the file when requested, and the program does the rest. The listing can be sent to the screen, printer or disk file. An interactive menu guides the user through the program, with help menus available. A formatted listing of the program can also be generated if the original file was in ASCII, i.e. saved with the ",A" option.

It is not possible (in this release) to obtain a listing of a tokenized program through BASREF.

EXPLIST, (#7) u-s $15

Computerenergy's Expanding Lister was created to make programming and maintenance jobs easier. We feel that a computer should help as much as possible in its own development efforts. The Expanding Lister is a tool that performs a number of formatting functions as a program is listed. It provides powerful aids to visualize what is happening (and where) within a program.

Expanding Lister will do several things to help you improve the readability of your program listings. Most of its functions are designed to display the structure of a program without the burden of any additional effort from the programmer. However, as you become more familiar with Expanding Lister's capabilities, you may wish to slightly adjust the way you enter code in order to take greater advantage of some of the features.

CROSSREF, (#8) u-s $15

Computerenergy's Cross Reference was created to make programming and maintenance jobs easier. We feel that a computer should help as much as possible in its own development efforts. CROSSREF is a tool that produces a cross-reference for each reference to a variable or a line number within a program.

BPRINT, (#236) u-s $25

A BASIC printer formatter.

SYSTEM REQUIREMENTS: • 128K memory • any monitor • 1 disk drive • printer

Gerry J. Danen
106 Abbotsfield Road
Edmonton, AB T5W 4S9
CANADA
403/474-0732

NUMZAP, (#284)

NUMZAP is a utility for removing line numbers from BASIC programs. Just removing the line number from the beginning of each line is rather easy, and somewhat pointless. NUMZAP is slightly more selective, however. NUMZAP removes only those line numbers which are not referenced from other parts of the program.

UNPROT, (#2, #67, #28)

Program for "unprotecting" or allowing you to list and modify a BASIC program which has been saved using the P option.

File Encryption

COMPUTER CRYPTOGRAPHY v1.53, (#112) u-s $25

The PC-CODE package is an Ultra High Security Cryptographic series of seven programs intended to provide a superior level of security in excess of the National Bureau of Standards DES algorithm and to approach the level of security that might be provided United States Government for its internal use. However, no endorsement or certification is implied for use in sensitive National Security applications.

The seven programs that make up this package include:

- PC-MENU — A simple Menu program to execute the various different programs in a user friendly manner.
- PC-CODE1 — A file oriented encryption/decryption program.
- PC-CODE2 — A text and printable ASCII oriented version of the above.
- PC-HELP — A simple program to display sources of help and documentation.
- PC-ZERO — A program to securely Erase and delete files.
- PC-TAMP1 — A program to do simple tests to verify if the most important files have been altered or tampered with.
- PC-TAMP2 — A program to test if PC-TAMP1 was altered.

To get information on PC-CODE1 in DOS type:

```
COPY PC-CODE1.DOC LPT1:
```

To get information on PC-CODE2 in DOS type:

```
COPY PC-CODE2.DOC LPT1:
```

The process used in PC-CODE1 & PC-CODE2 is super-encipherment. This involves two forms of encoding or decoding. First, each letter or character is exclusively OR'ed (EOR) bit by bit for the eight bits in each byte (character). Next, each character is transposed or scrambled, thus changing its position and order in the message. PC-CODE1 allows not only transposition of characters but also scrambling of bits if desired. This creates extremely powerful codes but is very very CPU compute-bound intensive (in other words it's slow).

If you don't have to worry about the Soviet KGB reading your mail the NBS DES algorithm is faster but certainly not more secure. The source code is provided and is intended for IBM BASIC Compiler (and not BASICA). If you can compile it with an 8087 oriented compiler or come up with a pseudo random number generator that's faster or doesn't use floating point, the cryptographic process could be speeded up to 10-30 times faster.

Recommended Memory: 128K PC-DOS V1.10 or V2.0+ Recommended IBM Compatibale Monitor; Color or Monochrome

The CONFIDANT, (#230) u-s $10

The Confidant encodes sensitive data using either one of two encryption procedures. The national Data Encryption Standard (DES) provides very high security. A faster "privacy" procedure that is somewhat less secure provides encryption for normal use—where speed is important and the material to be encrypted is not highly sensitive.

You can also use The Confidant to enter data into the computer, to copy files and to print files. Input to the program may come from either a disk file or the keyboard of the console. Output may be directed to a file, the screen of the console or a printer.

The program requires an IBM Personal Computer or a BIOS-compatible computer with 64K bytes of RAM; one 5.25 inch double-sided double-density disk drive; an IBM-compatible color or monochrome display capable of showing 80 columns, and PC-DOS 1.1 or higher. It can also use a printer and additional disk drives.

The disk includes a Description and Startup Guide, a casebook-style Tutorial, a detailed Reference manual and a Quick Reference Card.

It's easy to use the Confidant. Just place the disk in the logged drive and type: CONFIDE. A menu will appear.

Next fill in the SOURCE, DESTINATION, and PASSWORD boxes. The DESTINATION tells The Confidant where to send the text it processes; it can be a file or the console. The SOURCE tells The Confidant where to take its text FROM for processing; it can be a file or the console. The Confidant combines the PASSWORD with the text in the SOURCE to create encrypted or decrypted text. The PASSWORD may consist of any characters you can generate from the keyboard, except for the special editing keys.

After you've entered this information, you simply press a function key. These are the tasks The Confidant will perform:

<F1> DES Encipher: encrypts the text in the SOURCE using the Data Encryption Standard (DES) algorithm.

<F2> DES Decipher: decrypts the text in the SOURCE using the Data Encryption Standard (DES) algorithm.

<F3> Privacy: encrypts or decrypts the text in the SOURCE using a special algorithm that is faster than the Data Encryption Standard (DES).

<F4> Copies the text from the SOURCE to the DESTINATION.

<F5> Exchanges the names in the SOURCE and DESTINATION fields.

<F6> Toggles between hiding and revealing the information in the PASSWORD, SOURCE and DESTINATION fields.

<F7> Displays a directory listing of all files that match the file specification in the SOURCE field.

<F8> Erases the file or files specified in the SOURCE field.

<F9> Help: explains The Confidant's functions.

<F10> End: stops The Confidant at any time and returns you to the place at which you gave the last command.

<SHIFT> <Prtsc> prints a copy of the screen on the printer.

Printer utilities

SP 3.4, (#186,#275) u-s $15

SP is a software printer buffer that holds data intended for the printer. It works like a buffer that can be installed in the printer but the data is stored in RAM storage instead of in the printer. The buffer is unloaded to the printer at the printer's speed while DOS proceeds at its speed. The size of the buffer is specified as a parameter when SP is invoked. For example,

```
SP 14
```

will produce a buffer of 14K (1K = 1024 bytes). If the parameter is omitted, a default buffer of 16K is used.

The program will work for all data sent to the printer whether it is from the DOS TYPE command, a PrtSc command, a BASIC LLIST or LPRINT command, or a print command from EasyWriter 1.1, etc. If you start a printout and decide you don't want it, turn the printer off and then back on. This will re-set the buffer.

If you want the printing to pause, hold down the ON LINE button until the printer stops (which it will do at the end of a line). Pressing the ON LINE button again will allow printing to resume with no loss of data.

You can change the size of the buffer by re-invoking SP with the new parameter. In this case, SP determines that there is already a copy present in the machine and alters the size of the buffer of the older copy only. (This feature not available for DOS 2.0.) You can remove SP from the machine by specifying a buffer of zero. That is:

```
SP 0
```

will return DOS to its original state (except with DOS 2.0).

MULTIPLE COPIES

You can produce multiple copies of a document as long as the document is smaller than the buffer specified. To produce more than one copy, say 3 copies, invoke SP as follows:

```
SP 16 3
```

where 16 is the buffer size and 3 is the number of copies. Note that if you specify the number of copies you must specify the buffer size. If your document is larger than the buffer, SP will default to one copy. You can respecify the number of copies at any time even if there is another program resident beyond SP. In this case, the buffer size is not changed.

SP has been tested in the following environments: • PrtSc command • WordStar • DOS TYPE to printer • EasyWriter 1.1 • BASIC LLIST • VisiCalc • BASIC LPRINT • With Communications • BASIC PRINT# • The Personal Editor • Lotus 1-2-3 • Multiplan • PC-FILE • PC-TALK • DOS 2.0 PRINT; and with the following printers: IBM Printer and Printer-2, TI-800, C. Itoh PROWRITER, Okidata, Epson MX-80 or MX-80 F/T, NEC 7730

Alan Jones
3717 Wildwood Drive
Endwell, NY 13760

FASTPRT 2.0, (#59) — u-s $10

Speeds up the Print Screen function by not printing blank after end of line. FASTPRT is a speed-up utility for the PrtSc function on the IBM Personal Computer and IBM Personal Computer XT.

For all printers, it allows you to terminate an active PrtSc operation early (if you've seen enough or changed your mind, for instance).

For printers which don't have the foresight to ignore trailing blanks and empty lines, FASTPRT provides this capability. This look-ahead feature allows a screen with trailing blanks and blank lines to print in a fraction of the time it takes if all extraneous blanks have to be "printed".

It has been tested under DOS 1.00 through 2.0.

PC-FONT 2.04, (#225) u-s $20

PC-Font allows an Epson MX (with Graftrax), RX, or FX printer to print 243 of the 256 ASCII characters. The remaining 13 are used by the program to control printer font options. In contrast, only 94 characters (in the ASCII range 32-126) can currently be transferred from the screen to the Epson printer.

PC-PRINT CONTROL, (#250) u-s $15

PC-PRINT CONTROL is a printer utility for the EPSON printer. Both the compiler and interpretive BASIC versions are included on the program diskette. PC-PRINT CONTROL is run before your favorite software to preset font type, line spacing, page length, and paper width for your programs which do not have an internal printer control. It is an ideal tool to be used to prolong use of a worn out printer ribbon.

- PC-PRINT CONTROL is menu driven and extremely easy to use. No documentation is required other than the instructions given from the main title screen.
- Use the BASIC version with you BASIC programs. Use the compiled version with your EXE or COM files.
- PC-PRINT CONTROL uses the standard EPSON printer control codes to set the printers internal memory for font types, etc.
- PC-PRINT CONTROL includes bold, double strike, compress, italics, subscript, superscript, and all legal combinations of the font types.
- PC-PRINT CONTROL sets non-standard form lengths and widths.
- PC-PRINT CONTROL controls the paper out sensor in the ESPON printer.

PC-PRINT CONTROL requires 64k, one disk drive, DOS 1.1 or later, and EPSON printer. Start the compiled version by typing PRINTCTL at the A> prompt. Start the BASIC version by typing BASICA PRINTCTL.

BASICA.COM must be installed on your system diskette. Later versions, when available, will be obtainable by sending $15 to:

Charles Little
807 Lipton Drive
Newport News, VA

PRINTGR, (#61) u-s $9

The two programs, PRINTGR1 and PRINTGR2, will produce printed copies of screen displays in either medium (320x200) or high (640x200) resolution mode. PRINTGR1 prints a small (5.3'W x 2.5'H) upright image. PRINTGR2 prints an expanded (6.6'W x 8.9") image that is rotated clockwise by 90 degrees.

PRINTER UTILITIES, (#220-#222) u-s $45

Printer utilities for the Prowriter, NEC 8023A, and Transtar printers.

PRINT_SCREEN—This program will make it possible for you to make a print of any graphics screen that is visible on your display.

PRINT_CHARACTERS—With this program loaded to memory, you will not only be able to print italics characters, but also print characters from the Extended ASCII Set (those are the characters above ASCII 126 that IBM so kindly provided for your use).

PRINTER_SET—With this program running, you can set the most often used (and some not so often used) printer parameters, and it can be done with very few keystrokes: sometimes only one (1) is needed.

PRINT_SCREEN is designed for one purpose, to transfer any graphics screen displayed to the printer. (Computer types refer to that as a screen dump). As you may know, PC DOS has a built-in program to print text screens, until DOS 2.0 came on the scene, IBM did not supply a method for dumping graphics. For some reason (an oversight I'm sure) the one they now supply doesn't work with all printers.

It is really very easy. You don't have to learn anything new to use PRINT_SCREEN. Just press "Shift-PrtSc" and it goes into action. Look familiar? That's right, the very same keystrokes that IBM designated for the printing of a text screen. So, all you have to do is get the display just how you want it, either by programming the display yourself or by using another program that handles the generation of screen graphics, then press "Shift-PrtSc". There is even a way to access PRINT_SCREEN directly from within a BASIC program.

When you have PRINT_SCREEN in memory, just press Shift-PrtSc to print any screen. It doesn't matter whether it's a text or graphics screen. The software will handle it from there.

Contact the authors for a list of other printers supported. Registered users may pay an additional $50 for the source code to the programs.

VOLKSWRITER/TOSHIBA, (#236) u-s $15-25

These printer tables are used with VOLKSWRITER DELUXE to allow that word processing program to use the TOSHIBA P1340-1 and P1350-1 printers. With the tables it is possible to take advantage of most of the advanced features of the Toshiba printers when using VOLKSWRITER DELUXE. More is offered than is possible using the Toshiba printer table supplied with VOLKSWRITER. Use of the VOLKSWRITER Configure program cannot achieve these results.

Features:

- Seven printer tables for maximum choice and flexibility.
- Ability to use downloaded fonts on the P1351 printer.
- Choice of any of the five Toshiba supported fonts plus condensed print.
- Double width printing in any font.
- Choice of character width (5, 6, 8, 10, 12, 15, 17, 20 CPI).
- Complete documentation on the disk—with examples of use.
- Batch files for installation and copying on the disk.

To start, print the file README on your printer using the type command. It gives complete instructions for proceeding and getting the documentation printed. The documentation printed on your Toshiba with VOLKSWRITER uses many of the features of the printer. It also gives an explaination why things are done this way.

Graphics

DESIGNER, (#69) u-s $20

The Designer is a programming tool for BASIC users working with animated graphics on an IBM-PC. It can be of significant value to people writing graphic games and to people interested in experimenting with animation.

The Designer is written in IBM advanced BASIC (BASICA). The source code is included for those who wish to study and/or modify it. Included with The Designer is a demonstration program which illustrates one way to program animation. "Demo" is also provided in source code form so you can study and/or modify it as you wish.

The objective of The Designer is to create data files of two types, "screens" and "sprites". A "screen file" contains the image of a fixed background (the scenery behind your game). A "sprite file" contains the image of a character which your BASIC program can move about. The completed screen and sprite files are input data for your animation programs.

With The Designer, your PC can be used like an artist's canvas. You can draw on the screen in color, store your work in either "screen" or "sprite" form, and recall it later to make changes. All calculations required to create the files are performed automatically and you need concern yourself only with the artwork and the graphic appearance of your images.

Your programs can directly read both screen and sprite files created by The Designer, limiting your programming effort to the game logic and its presentation to the user.

The Designer features full use of the PC's function keys to control program function. It has online-help capabilities and is able to print a handy reference card on your printer. Documentation is included on the disk.

The Designer requires an IBM-PC with at least 64K of memory, PC-DOS with BASICA, a color/graphics adapter, an 80-character display, and at least one disk drive (two recommended).

SLIDE (#244) u-s $25

The purpose of this program is the production of medium quality slides and overhead transparencies (both referred to as sLides). A sLide is created, edited, saved, displayed, and printed using this program. Overhead transparencies are produced by copying the printed output onto transparent material. Photographic slides are produced by photographing the printed output. Both the IBM Graphics printer and Epson MX- and FX-printers are supported.

Type -readme- (dash readme dash) for instructions to print the manual or to begin to use the program.

The Author requests a user-supported donation of $7.

John R. Lehmann
11403 Rolling House Road
Rockville, MD 20852

Computer education

PC-Professor, (#105) u-s $30-50

PC-Professor is a tutorial program that teaches the BASIC programming language. It is designed to gradually increase in complexity and difficulty. The program encourages experimentation and allows you to make your own mistakes and learn from them. This is a fun program with a cute introduction that should help almost anyone get started in the BASIC programming language.

There is no separate documentation with this program and none is needed. Once the program is started by entering the introduction, directions and menus lead the way.

PC-DOS Help, (#254) u-s $15

This software package provides full on-screen help for all PC-DOS version 2.00 and 2.10 commands. It may be run on any IBM PC, XT, PCjr or compatible with one or more disk drives and an 80 column display. The package contains two levels of help for all DOS commands, an abbreviated version and a detailed explanation including examples. In addition, many topics not normally discussed are explained at length, including solutions to common computer problems and clarifications of some DOS concepts.

The package is easily configured for use with any combination of fixed or floppy disk drives. Unique help descriptions are presented for DOS versions 2.00 and 2.10 using the PC/XT, and PCjr using DOS 2.10; ensuring that the correct keys and manual pages are referenced in the help presented.

The actual help text may be altered, allowing customized descriptions to be displayed that best match the vocabulary level of the end user. HELP topics may be added as well, making the package ideal for a "notebook" type of function used to keep track of programs written and what they do. In short, this package should prove useful for all PC-DOS users from novice to expert.

Start by viewing the package description and installation instructions in the file "HELP.DOC".

Educational programs

The programs listed here are intended to assist in the educational process. The program, NAEPIRS, listed in the "Databases" section provides information on how well education is being carried out in the US.

HISTORY, (#76) u-s $5

A well presented educational game, which teaches American History while having fun. There are 7 periods of history covered and 4 periods left open for you to use on each disk, each period having 25 questions. You travel back in time, then have an adventure trying to return to the present. Winning and losing gold, getting trapped in time warps, etc.

Questions can be changed or new questions added at anytime, without going into the program code. This is achieved by a second program which generates a Data file. Instructions for this program are contained on the disk. There is no end to the possible uses of this program.

PC-TOUCH, (#249)

PC-TOUCH is a simple program with a simple purpose: to help you practice touch-typing.

PC-TOUCH will display on the screen lines of text for you to type. You can't correct mistakes as you go along, because that won't help you learn how not to make them in the first place. Just do the best you can, and as you continue you will find yourself making fewer and fewer errors.

As you are typing, PC-TOUCH will update statistics along the bottom two rows of the screen. On the left you will see the total number of keystrokes and the total number of erroneous keystrokes. On the right you will see your typing accuracy as the percentage of keystrokes which have been correct, and your typing speed in words per minute. The statistics on the left are updated whenever you press any key, while those on the right are updated whenever you get to the end of a line. Remember that when you are just learning to type, accuracy is more important than speed.

To use PC-TOUCH, just key in:

pc-touch

PC-TOUCH starts by giving you instructions on how to use the program. Aside from the keys you will use to type the lines of text displayed, there are only three special keys recognized:

ENTER	Press this key when you get to the end of each line.
ESC	Press this key when you are done with the program.
F1	Press this key when you want to stop typing for a while (for example, to answer the phone) and don't want to lose credit for the elapsed time during which nothing will be typed. (When you are ready to restart, just press F1 a second time.)

PC-TOUCH doesn't recognize any other special keys because the idea was to practice touch-typing in a way that would be valid for ANY keyboard, including ancient office typewriters you may be stranded with once in a while. (If enough people ask for more sensitivity to the special keys on the IBM/PC [like INS, DEL and the cursor control keys], the author be glad to include this in a future release.) PC-TOUCH should work with any display device that supports 80-column output.

EQUATOR, (#249) u-s $20

The EQUATOR is an equation learning aid. The purpose of this product is to help you, the student, learn the function, use, and application of various general purpose formulas used in the fields of Math, Finance, and Science.

This product consists of 35 equations divided equally among the three subjects. Each equation appears on its own screen or worksheet. The EQUATOR is designed to allow you to experiment with each equation as much as you like. The more you work with an equation, the easier it will be for you to understand it, remember it and use it at home or at school. As the actual equation is shown on your screen, you can type in your numbers and let the EQUATOR compute the right answer. Entering the numbers is easy and telling the EQUATOR to compute the answer is even easier. Everything you need to know about using the EQUATOR is on the screen at all times.

The Equator is menu-driven. This means the screen you are working with will always contain information on what actions you can take next. These actions will include ending the program, computing the next answer, or going to another screen. So there is no need for you, the user, to memorize a series of long and confusing commands.

The following equations are in the Math Menu of the EQUATOR:

1. Area of a square of rectangle.
2. Area of a circle.
3. Area of a triangle.
4. Hypotenuse of a right triangle.
5. Circumference of a circle.
6. Volume of a cylinder.
7. Surface area of a cylinder.
8. Volume of a cone.
9. Surface area of a cone.
10. Surface area of a sphere.
11. Volume of a sphere.
12. Distance between two points.

The following equations are in the Finance Menu of the EQUATOR:

1. Simple interest.
2. Compound interest.
3. Years to double investment.
4. Return needed to keep up with inflation.
5. Equivalent taxable return of a non-taxed investment.
6. Monthly mortgage payments.
7. Annual simple interest rate on loans.
8. Payoff balance on a loan.
9. Gross profit margin.
10. Net profit margin.
11. Earnings per share.
12. Price / Earnings ratio.

The following equations are in the Science Menu of the EQUATOR:

1. Celsius to Farhrenheit.
2. Farhrenheit to Celsius.
3. Density Ratio.
4. Average velocity.
5. Metric to English.
6. English to Metric.
7. Acceleration.
8. Force.
9. Work.
10. Power.
11. Pressure.

REQUIREMENTS: • IBM PC with at least 64K of memory • DOS 2.0 operating system • 1 disk drive • A printer.

To start the EQUATOR, do the following:

1) Boot up Your IBM PC with DOS 2.0
2) Insert your diskette containing the EQUATOR files into your default disk drive. This will usually be your "A:" disk drive.
3) Type EQ after the "A>" prompt and press the RETURN key. This will start the EQUATOR program.

   or

4) Type PRT after the "A>" prompt and press the RETURN key. This will list the EQUATOR's user manual to the printer.

Games

A good percentage of time spent on computers is done playing games. Even on secret national defense computers the games sneak in. There are many fine games in the PC-SIG library. Games that run on monochrome monitors, games that run on color monitors, arcade games, word games, adventure games, educational games, games for the young, and games for the not so young.

In the category of color arcade games there are PANGO and 3-DEMON on disk #293, for adventure fans CASTLE on disks #198, #210 and #274. Disk #274, "Best Games" has some great games. For those with monochrome displays try BUGS (#274) or PITFALL (#293). SPACEWAR on disk #292 has one version just for the Hercules Graphics Card.

Part of the fun of games is comming upon unexpected treasures. Perhaps this is true because no two people will like exactly the same games with the same enthusiasm. So explore the library and pick the games you like. Fire photon torpedoes (or old fashioned ones as on a sub), slay those dragons, shiver those timbers, and may the force be with you, live long and prosper.

FUNNELS & BUCKETS, (#229) u-s $10

Funnels & Buckets is a learning game. Playing it improves your skill in adding, subtracting, multiplying, and dividing. The object of the game is to earn points by solving them within a short span of time.

The screen shows a room called The Cleaning Closet. On its floor are several buckets. A funnel glides across its ceiling. Arithmetic problems fall from the funnel into the buckets below. You must type in the correct answer to each problem before it reaches the buckets. That will POP it, and the more problems you POP, the higher your score. At fast speeds, POPping will challenge even an adult.

The dastardly villain Burglar runs the funnel. He wants to fill all the buckets in The Cleaning Closet with equations. Burglar gets his name because he tries to steal the points you earn from typing in an answer. Even worse, if you type the wrong answer when he's around, he steals TWICE the points.

Meggie, the cleaning woman, is the game's heroine. This is her cleaning closet, and the buckets belong to her. She's busy cleaning, but she drops by often to reward you with bonus points for stopping Burglar. If you type in the correct answer when she's around, you get TRIPLE the points.

When you don't know an answer, Meggie will help you. (Her cleaning job is just a money-making sideline. In real life she is a math teacher). Press the <space bar> when an equation is falling and she'll show you how to get the right answer. You can remember it for the next time Burglar drops that problem.

Funnels & Buckets allows you to set up the game the way you want it. You control the type of problems (addition, subtraction, multiplication, division, or mixed). Difficult problems are worth more points than easy ones. You can also control whether you want sound effects, and you control how fast the game will go; there are six different speeds. The computer will automatically speed things up as you get better and your score gets higher.

You may change the speed, the sound, and the type of problems anytime. This will not cause you to lose points. Press the <esc> key to interrupt play. Make the changes you want. Then press the <space bar> to continue play.

The computer will compare your score with that of previous players. If you beat all previous scores, it will ask you to enter your name as the new record holder. Then you may decide if you want to play again.

The value of Funnels & Buckets is that it makes learning fun. Some people like the excitement of outpacing the burglar. They lose track of time as they POP equations. Others prefer the gentle explanations Meggie gives when they press the <space bar>. A player learns best by playing the game in his or her own way. That keeps it fun without becoming threatening or boring.

Many children between the ages of four and seven prefer to watch Meggie's explanation instead of playing for points. Older children usually prefer both explanations and play.

The game is designed so you only have to use the numeric keypad, the <space bar>, the <backspace> key and the <esc> key. The <esc> key, which is used for exiting, is separated from the playing keys to prevent accidental use. For children this makes play easier and more enjoyable.

Funnels and Buckets is written for the IBM PC under PC-DOS. It requires 96K of RAM, one diskette drive, and a color or monochrome monitor which can display 80 columns.

Data Sage
Yale Station 2902
New Haven, CT 06520

Norland HANGMAN 4.1, (#153) u-s $15

Hangman presents four adaptations of the traditional Hangman game designed to challenge accomplished players. In Basic Hangman the computer chooses a secret word which the player must guess by selecting letters of the alphabet. Educational Hangman uses much more esoteric words, but provides brief definitions of each word as a clue for the player. Literate Hangman is stocked with famous sayings and quotations from throughout the ages—the author of each phrase is provided as a clue.

Finally, Personalized Hangman allows two or more players to enter their own words or phrases. To satisfy the most discriminating players, Hangman includes over 1000 words and phrases and four levels of difficulty. This game is definitely not for children!

Requires 80-column display, one disk drive, 64K of memory under DOS 1.1, 96K of memory under DOS 2.0, 128K of memory for the PCjr.

Eric N. Miller
Norland Software
1014A West Badger Road
Madison, WI 53713

LIFE2, (#79)

The original game of life was invented by mathematician John Conway. The idea is to initialize the screen with a pattern of bacteria in 'EDIT' mode. The 'RUN' mode then brings life to the colony. The population increases and decreases according to fixed rules which affect the birth and death of individual bacterium. A rectangular grid (2-dimensional matrix) will be shown on the screen. Each cell in the grid can contain a bacterium or be empty. Each cell has 8 neighbors except that cells on the boundary have less than 8 neighbors. The existance of cells from one generation to the next is determined by the following rules:

1. A bacteria with 2 or 3 neighbors survives from one generation to the next. A bacterium with fewer neighbors dies of isolation. One with more neighbors dies of overcrowding.
2. An empty cell spawns a bacteria if it has exactly three neighboring cells which contain bacteria.

   To start type: LIFE2

SPACEVAD, (#176,#274)

This is a modified version of SPACE INVADERS. It has excellent graphics. The object is to shoot the invaders before they invade earth. Be careful or you may get SPACEDOUT!

XWING, (#174,#274)

Relive "Star Wars". This is an outstanding game. As a XWING fighter pilot you will have to locate the DEATHSTAR and destroy it. (Graphics required)

PACKMAN, (#24, #274)

PACKMAN is an excellent graphics version of the arcade game, PacMan. It's a fun game of gobbling power pellets and eating monsters.

BREAKOUT, (#177,#274)

This is a hard PONG game. It is a very fun, fast, and skillful game, where in the player attempts to break out of a brick wall.

WIZARD, (#71,#274)

IPCO WIZARDS CASTLE is a fun game similar to DUNGEONS & DRAGONS. Complete with a castle , treasures, monsters, and all sorts of weird creatures. (no graphics)

Spacewar, (#292) u-s $20

Spacewar is a commercial quality, high resolution graphics, game that combines the best features of Asteroids and Startrek with a few tricks of its own. This is perhaps the best game that this author has seen in a very long time. Can be played by either one or two people and has some very interesting options. Versions for the standard PC color graphics card and the Hercules graphics card.

3-DEMON, (#293) u-s $10

3-DEMON is an excellent color graphics game that is similar to a 3 dimensional pack-man. Run around the maze looking down hallways and trying not to be eaten by the ghosts. Lots of fun with good sound. Make sure to listen to the music in this one, it has some old favorite tunes.

BRICKS, (#293)

The bouncing ball knocks out bricks. Pretty colors, good sound, lots of action, and 3 levels of play.

KONG, (#293)

Run up ladders and ramps to rescue the girl. Jump barrels and balls of fire. Once at the top it starts again. Second screen has a twist—but to see that you have to get the disk.

PANGO, (#293)

A very colorful game with excellent sound. Lots of action and 9 levels of play. A maze made of movable blocks. Watch out for the KILLER BEES. Move the blocks with a good swift kick—squish both bees and then you're done—only to start again, and have more fun.

PC-GOLF, (#293)

This is a good game for a golfer on a rainy day. It is written for the amateur golfer, is easy to use and understand, and it is a very friendly program.

PYRAMID, (#293)

Climb the blocks that change color as you go. Watch out for the ball, and the bug, and all. This game is quick so you have to be fast, but when you tire—hop the elevator at last.

CASTLE, (#198, #210, #274) u-s $10

Castle is an adventure game, but much more than the normal word game. Castle runs on the monochrome screen and displays the rooms and objects you are after. The cursor control keys on the numeric pad are used to direct your character around the castle. If you have a vague interest in adventure games, this one will hook you for sure.

LANDER, (#55, #274)

Land a spaceship, after negotiating mountains, on a little pad, and with a limited amount of fuel. Challenging game with good graphics.

BUGS, (#177, #274)

Similar to the popular game, CENTIPEDE. BUGS is a simple, easy to play game. This is a good version, which will keep you occupied.

EAMON, (#296, #297)

EAMON is a computerized version of what are called "fantasy role-playing games." When you enter the universe of one of these games, you are no longer

Jon (or Jane) Smith, mild-mannered computer hobbyist. Instead, you become a character in a land of adventure, doing almost anything you want to.

In the land of Eamon, you will be a member of the select free adventurers guild, which is made up of hardy individuals like yourself who want to live by your wits, defeating horrible monsters and finding glorious treasures.

Unlike most games, there is no single set goal for you to achieve, no way to "win" the game. Instead, in Eamon, you have a lasting goal to both better yourself and also get rich. If you set for yourself another goal (do good to all princes and princesses, kill all evil wizards, that sort of thing), you may also work towards it in you quests.

EAMON was created by Donald Brown and converted to the PC Dy Jon Walker

Music

PC-MUSICIAN, (#127) u-s $20

PC MUSICIAN is an onscreen music composition and editing system for the IBM PC family which allows amateur musicians, music students, and anyone else to quickly and easily create, play, modify, and save single-voice tunes on their PC. Its features include:

- Easy onscreen music entry using cursor and function keys.
- Online help always available while creating or editing.
- Note by note or "cut and paste" editing supported.
- Note preview: hear note before selecting it.
- Plays part or all of your tune at any time during creation.
- Plays saved songs like a jukebox.
- Requires only 64K PC or PC Jr.
- Versions for both monochrome and graphics display adapters.
- Works with any version of DOS.
- Extensive documentation file on disk for easy printout.

PC MUSICIAN is being used throughout this country and abroad by schools and individuals interested in using their PC's to explore the world of music.

PC MUSICIAN is distributed in single-sided, single-density format.

Please start by typing at the DOS prompt:

type **read.me** [hit enter key]

PIANO MAN, (#279) u-s $25

PIANO MAN is an excellent well developed program that allows you to write and edit music on your PC with remarkable ease. The program will record your music as you play it and lets you go back and edit later. Along with the program are several fine tunes.

PIANO MAN lets you play your PC's keyboard like a piano. You don't really need any instructions to start playing right away.

Type: PIANOMAN to start the program.

PIANO MAN REQUIREMENTS: • IBM PC or equivalent with 128K or more. 128K gives enough memory to record about 3,700 notes. • monochrome or color display in 80 columns.

Unfortunately, PIANO MAN does not work very well on the PC jr.

Other applications

PC-FLY "FLITEPLN" 2.1, (#261) u-s $20

PC-Fly "FLITEPLN" is written to be practical & useful for the busy pilot and only requires essential information all pilots use when planning a flight. The program consists of 3 modules:

AIRCRAFT FLIGHT DATA—permits saving pertinent information on 15 various airplanes! Information readily available for flight. Hard copy printed also.

FLIGHT LOG—User enters: 1) estimated groundspeed 2) fuel/hour 3) departure airport, checkpoints, and leg distances are ONLY entered INITIALLY, then saved for future use.

"FLITEPLN" then calculates:

DISTANCE, total & to-go,
TIME: leg, cumulative & total in hr. & min.,
FUEL, per leg, cumulative, & total for flight.

It also prints hard copy as needed.

PC-FLY "FLITEPLN" saves flight routes in files for future use AND can be re-used with different groundspeed and fuel rates added as needed. (OR with different airplanes without change).

FAA FLIGHT PLAN—dept., route, time, dest. fuel, name, address, etc. are printed without re-entering. Permanent data is stored for future use.

SYSTEM REQUIREMENTS: Program was written on an IBM-PC, PC-DOS 2.1 interpreted Basic and can run with 1 disc drive with 64 K RAM. It is written to run in color when available or on a standard monitor.

STARTUP: Begin BASIC then type "RUN FLITEPLN.2V1" (or FLITEPLN.2-1 if one has that version.)

REGISTERED USERS: (contributors) will be sent copy of program that permits adding and changing aircraft data. Space is available for 15 airplanes and data. Registered users will also be able to change FAA Flight Plan data.

Others will only be able to use the Flight Log portion of the program. A $20 Contribution gives user enhanced, completed version & notification of future updates & programs.

D.A. Gullickson
19 Custer Street
Lander, Wyoming 82520

FT-Etc 1.25, (#240) u-s $35

'Family-Tree, Etc' is a general purpose genealogy system designed for charting and maintaining information pertaining to family trees and relationships between individuals. The system is menu driven with single keystroke commands, scrolling, mini-windows and screen/printer/ diskette report output capability.

The MAINTENANCE option of the system allows the user to:

1) Enter the known facts about an individual and then establish parent/spouse relationships. The selection of the individuals for the relationships is accomplished by 'pointing' to persons in the data base, thereby ensuring the integrity of the data base and eliminating duplicate data.
2) Correct the spelling of a data element once and related entries (parents/spouse/children) are corrected automatically.

Data gathering utilizes a 'mini-window' concept with formatted fields for the required data entry. The system maintains up to 999 names with the following information fields:

Name and Sex of Individual	Dates of Birth/Death/Marriage(s)
Mother/Father/Spouse(s) Names	Place of Birth/Death/Marriage(s)

The CHARTS portion of the system uses the data base created by MAINTENANCE to generate the typical genealogy reports for pedigree, ancestors, family groups, descendants, and relationships. The output may be viewed on the screen, directed to a (optional) printer, or routed to a diskette file for later printing.

REQUIREMENTS: IBM-PC, PCjr, Compaq, etc., 128K 1 double-sided, double- density diskette DOS 1.1+ (BASIC not required, FT-ETC is compiled).

START-UP: Distribution diskette contains a twenty page User Reference Manual in file 'FT-ETC.TXT'.

Pine Cone Software
P.O. Box 1163
Columbus, Indiana 47202

GENEALOGY ON DISPLAY, 3.0 (#90) u-s $35

Genealogy ON DISPLAY, Version 3.0, is an integrated, menu-driven group of twenty unprotected BASIC programs for IBM PCs (including the PCjr), which assist users in organizing, entering, and reporting their own Genealogical Data.

When shipped, Genealogy ON DISPLAY, Version 3.0, provides for 500 persons and 200 marriages within its data base, with no specific generation limit. The number of persons and the number of marriages may be changed by a user.

Information may be displayed on the screen, and it may be printed on a printer. Output available for printing or for displaying on the screen includes:

1. Pedigree (Family Tree) Charts.
2. Family Group Charts.
3. Descendents Charts (new in Version 3.0).
4. Detailed Personal Information.
5. Detailed Marriage Information.

Additional output available for printing includes:

1. Lists of Persons (by number or alphabetized).
2. Lists of Marriages (by number or alphabetized).
3. A list of Parent/Child Relationships.

Documentation, including a Program Directory and an eighty-eight page User's Manual, is provided on the diskette with the programs. The User's Manual provides details about how to begin, and how to enter and update

Genealogical information. It describes how to obtain output on the printer, and how to view information on the display screen.

Genealogy ON DISPLAY, Version 3.0, requires PC-DOS (any level from 2.0 upward), BASIC (on Diskette or Cartridge), an 80 column display (either Color or Monochrome), one double-sided diskette drive, and at least 96K of (RAM) memory. An IBM Graphics Printer (or equivalent) may be used for printing the charts, lists, etc., and the documentation. A wider printer may be used with Standard (LDS) preprinted charts.

Changes required to print the documentation on other printers is included on the diskette. Changes required to use other printers for output from the programs is included in an appendix within the User's Manual.

Start by running the BASIC Program "runfirst".

MAPMAKER, (#219) u-s $75

MapMaker can be used by scientists, planners, business persons, or others who need to show numerical values for specified geographical areas. The program combines LOCATIONAL and STATISTICAL data sets to produce two types of maps, Choropleth (area coloring) and Proportional Circle.

The Choropleth routine colors map areas according to the range into which the associated values fall. The Circle routine draws circles in each map area, the size being determined by the associated values.

Locational data sets contain many areal units, such as counties in a state, census tracts in a city, or sales districts in a total sales area. There may be no more than 65 units within any locational data set, and each must have a closed boundary.

Statistical data sets contain a range of values, with only one value for each locational unit. All values must be positive numbers.

Sample locational and statistical data sets are provided on the program diskette in order to demonstrate the program.

** IMPORTANT ** MapMaker requires a 2-monitor configuration, one of which must be a color graphics monitor. 192K of RAM is also required.

A step-by-step guide through MapMaker's routines is provided in a text file named "MANUAL", although directions are provided on the screen throughout the program. The manual also contains descriptions of the sample data sets, instructions for creating customized data sets, and general information for producing meaningful map displays.

Those not familiar with mapping principles are urged to read the manual carefully in order to understand fully the production of each map type.

A hardcopy version of maps can be made by printing the contents of the screen on a matrix printer.

Begin the program by typing MAPMAKER, with the program diskette in the appropriate drive. The sample data sets described in the manual can be used to demonstrate the program and can later be replaced by user-generated data sets.

SAGE TAG, (#243) u-s $25

Sage Tag is designed to produce tags for sacks or bags. This is not another label program. Label programs are designed to print a single copy of many different labels. This program is designed to print multiple copies of a single label. Because bag tags often have the same format, titles and headings, this program lets you enter a format and template for repeated use. The format options give you full control over the printed form of the tag. The template can save you time, because you only need to enter the common elements of your tags once.

Sage Tag includes a number of convenient features:

- It is designed to operate quickly. You won't need to wait for it to do its tasks.
- Where possible, choices can be made by pointing with the arrow keys.
- Help screens are available at all times by pressing the [F1] function key.
- All major features are available from a single menu.

The program requires an IBM PC, PC XT, PCjr or IBM PC compatible computer with one disk drive and at least 64K of user memory. The more memory you have, the more data that you can store. The IBM Monochrome or color graphics screens are supported. A parallel printer is required.

Start by copying the 18 page manual in file, "TAG.PRN" to your printer.

PERSONAL DATEBOOK, (#261) u-s $12.95

PERSONAL DATEBOOK is a program that maintains a daily calendar of appointments, birthdays, memos, events and whatever else you choose to record. It also generates a monthly calendar and allows you to create and maintain a personal address list.

The program will work with any IBM Personal Computer: (XT, PC, PC Portable or PC Jr.) with either a color or monochrome display. It may also be used with most IBM "compatible" computers running IBM PC DOS. You must have at least one disk drive (floppy or hard) and your display must be 80 columns wide.

If you have a printer connected to your computer, you will be able to print a day's memos along with the current month's calendar.

SAGE CALENDAR, (#243) u-s $25

Sage Calendar is designed for anyone who has ever forgotten an appointment, meeting, or anniversary. Sage Calendar is an electronic desk calendar. Use it as you would any other calendar. Review memos at the beginning of the day. Add memos as required. Locate a particular memo quickly and easily. Review the calendar for this month, next month or any month in the twentieth century.

Sage Calendar includes a number of convenient features:

- It is designed to operate quickly. You won't need to wait for it to do its tasks.
- Where possible, choices can be made by pointing with the arrow keys.
- Help screens are available at all times by pressing the [F1] function key.
- All major features are available from a single menu.

The program requires an IBM PC, PC XT, PCjr or IBM PC compatible computer with one disk drive and at least 64K of user memory. The more memory you have, the more data that you can store. The IBM Monochrome or color graphics screens are supported. A parallel printer is suggested.

Start by copying the 19 page manual in file, "CAL.PRN" to your printer.

iRecipe83, (#281) u-s $20

Isn't it time the cook benefitted from computer indexing?

iRecipe83(tm) is a database index to 1800 recipes that appeared in Family Circle magazine, and Woman's Day magazine in 1983. If these magazines are saved in your home, this database will provide the advantages of computer indexing. Note: it is necessary that you have saved the magazines, or have them readily available from a library. iRecipe83 is an INDEX not a repeat of the recipes. iRecipe83 is available on disk for three database programs that run on the IBM-PC/XT, IBM compatible micros, and the IBM PC Jr. It is available for LOTUS 1-2-3, dBASEII, and PC-FILE III.

PC-GOLF 1.4, (#262) u-s $35

Player performance is the primary subject of PC-GOLF. It keeps track of your scores and putts for each hole on your home course. It shows you how you are doing on each hole. PC-GOLF helps you concentrate on the main event so you can see where improvement is most desirable and most likely to be achieved. It will even mark the holes you should not make presses on.

PC-GOLF will help you improve your golf game. The program is easy to use and understand. It is a very friendly program. PC-GOLF is written especially for the amateur golfer, the IBM Personal Computer and compatibles. Use it with confidence that it will help lower your scores and raise your enjoyment on the course. PC-GOLF can help you and your foursome to lower scores. PC-GOLF works for you in six areas.

1. Introduction.
2. Tally the scores for a round.
3. Get the golfer's score sheet.
4. Get the golf course list.

5. Get the golfer's roster.
6. Quit. Going to the 19th hole.

1. Introduction. This tells you what the six parts of PC-GOLF do. The way PC-GOLF prompts you and the way you give directions to PC-GOLF are explained.

2. Tally the scores for a round. This is where you record your putts and scores for a round. You also tell PC-GOLF whether a round is for handicapping, performance or just for practice. You see the gross and the adjusted gross scores here too.

3. Get the golfer's score sheet. This is where you see each golfers performance in nine tables and graphs. You see putt and stroke averages for each hole. The double diamond flag marks the holes where you should not press your opponents. See your Personal Best scores here.

4. Get the golf course list. This is where you add, change and delete courses and provide the information about par, course rating and hole handicaps. You also review the golf course information here. The course list holds nine golf courses.

5. Get the golfer's roster. This is where you add, change and delete players, assign the player's home course and initial handicap. You review the golfer's roster here. The roster holds sixteen golfers.

6. Quit. Going to the 19th hole. This provides a smooth exit from PC-GOLF, safeguards your scores and returns to IBM DOS.

To get started: Boot up DOS; Load Basic; put the PC-GOLF diskette in the "A" drive; type RUN"A:USER.DOC" and press the ENTER KEY.

Magazines on Disk

PC FIRING LINE/PC UNDERGROUND, (#159-#161)

PC Firing Line/PC Underground is a collection of programs, tips, reviews and other information that might be interesting to a PC user. See the directory section for the type of material on each disk.

PC Firing Line/PC Underground is available for $12 per issue or $72 per year (6 issues). Contact:

ABC Computing
P0 Box 5503 Dept S
North Hollywood, CA 91616
(818) 509-9002

IBM User Group NEWSLETTER, (#156-#158)

See what IBM has been sending to computer clubs across the country. Many useful tips, comments and programs.

4.0 DISK CONTENTS

The files on each of the disks in the PC-SIG library are described in this section.

The "v" following the disk name in the disk header indicates the PC-SIG version number of the disk. A "DS" or "DS2" following the version number indicates a double-sided (320K) or double-sided DOS 2.0 format disk respectively. Those using a version of DOS before 2.0 will not be able to read "DS2" disks.

A "+" after the file extension indicates that a color graphics adapter is required. Those with PCjrs or Compaqs don't need to worry, graphics is built in.

Disk No 1 **GAMES #1** **v1**

This disk is one of the original game disks for the IBM PC. Many of these games are primitive compared to ones on latter disks, but they may all be addressed from a single menu. Run program "MENU" to start.

PATTERNS	BAS+	Generates random patterns on color monitor
BLACKJCK	BAS	Blackjack game on the monochrome display
YAHTZEE	BAS	Yahtzee game on the monochrome display
MENU	BAS	Menu for selecting programs on this disk
DOTS	BAS	Displays dot patterns for display characters
HATDANCE	BAS	Plays the Mexican Hat Dance song
KALEID	BAS+	Generates random patterns on the color display
MAXIT	BAS+	Number game
STRINGS	BAS+	Generates random patterns on the color display
WOMBAT	BAS	Generates word problems
CIRCLES	BAS+	Draws random patterns on the color display
PONGPONG	BAS	Pong type game
COPYOVER	BAT	Copies games from DOS 1.0 or 1.1 disk
COPYOVER	DOC	Description of how to use COPYOVER.BAT

Disk No 2		Spoolers	v1.1
MSPOOL	COM	Print spooler for monochrome/printer adapter	
CSPOOL	COM	Print spooler for printer adapter	
DISKMOD	BAS	Utility to examine and modify disk sectors	
SDIR	COM	Displays the directory on one screen (DOS 1.1 only)	
CLEAN	COM	Exercises disk when using a cleaning diskette	
GRAF2	COM	Graphic screen dump using the PrtSc key	
MONITOR		Toggles between monochrome and color display	
CR	BAS	Cleans up downloaded BASIC files	
KYBD	BAS	Outputs keyboard input to the printer like a typewriter	
SYSTAT	COM	Displays system status	
PROGRAM	DOC	Details for running the programs on this disk	
STARTREK	BAS	The game of	
CLS	COM	Clears the screen from DOS	
ADDCR	BAS	Adds a carriage return to each line in a text file	
LISTER	BAS	Generates a formatted listing of BASIC programs	
NEWKEY	BAS	Reassigns the ten function keys	
CROSSREF	BAS	Generates a cross-reference listing for BASIC programs	
UNPROT	TXT	Procedure for unprotecting BASIC programs	
HEXCONV	BAS	Converts binary files to ASCII for transmission	
HGRI	EXE	Graphics screen dump using PrtSc key	

Disk No 3		RATBAS	v1

RATBAS stands for RATionalized BASic. RATBAS allows BASIC programs to be written in a more structured way without line numbers. Programs written in Rationalized BASIC are converted by the RATBAS translator into standard BASIC.

RT	EXE	The RatBAS translator
RT	UM	User's Manual for RT.EXE
RATBAS	UM	User's Manual for the RatBAS language
RATBAS	TXT	Paper on RatBAS by the authors. The RatBAS article in PC Magazine Volume 1 No. 6, Oct 1982 is a slightly edited version of this paper.
TEST	RAT	A sample program written in RatBAS
SORT	INC	An 'include' routine which will be used by TEST.RAT
TEST	BAS	TEST.RAT after being processed by RT.EXE. This is an ASCII file which may be read by the BASIC interpreter or The BASIC compiler. It is also quite readable by humans.

Disk No 4		DBMS/MODEM7	v1
DBMENU	BAS	Menu program for Data Base Management System (DBMS)	
CREATE	BAS	Part of DBMS	
INSERT	BAS	Part of DBMS	
LOOKUP	BAS	Part of DBMS	
SCREEN	BAS	Part of DBMS	
DUMP	BAS	Part of DBMS	
BACKUP	BAS	Part of DBMS	
CHESS	EXE	Chess program (See Disk No 120 for a better version)	
SURVIVAL	BAS	Adventure type game—survive a crash landing on the moon	
SATURN	BAS +	Graphics demo—the ringed planet with orbiting moon	
CATCH88	BAS	Catch falling goodies—improve typing skills	
METEOR	BAS	Arcade type game—eat goodies while dodging meteors	
HANGMAN	BAS	Popular word guessing game	
ELIZA	BAS	Talk your problems out with ELIZA the psychotherapist	
MODEM7	COM	Communications & file transfer program adapted from CP/M	
MODEM7	DOC	Documentation file for MODEM7.COM	

Disk No 5 **PC-FILE III** **v4 DS**

This is Jim Buttons' very popular database filing program. Users comment on its ease of use and excellent documentation. It is a must for anyone desiring an inexpensive, useful filing system.

DOC	BAT	File for printing PC-FILE.DQC. Type "DOC" to print documentation.
PC-DEF	EXE	PC-FILE utility
PC-EXPOR	EXE	PC-FILE utility
PC-FILE	EXE	PC-FILE main program
PC-FILE	PRO	PC-FILE utility
PC-FILE	DOC	Documentation (108K)
PC-FIX	EXE	PC-FILE utility
PC-IMPOR	EXE	PC-FILE utility
PC-LABEL	EXE	PC-FILE label utility
PC-OVL	EXE	PC-FILE utility
PC-PRINT	EXE	PC-FILE utility
PC-SETUP	EXE	PC-FILE printer setup parameter file
PC-SORT	EXE	PC-FILE utility
PC-UTIL	EXE	PC-FILE utility
SAMPLE	BAS	Sample program for assessing PC-FILE data bases

Disk No 6		RAM disk v1
CHARS	BAS	Full character set display. Requires Monochrome card
CHARS	EXE	Compiled, stand alone version of CHARS.BAS
GDUMP	BAS +	Med. resolution graphics to C.Itoh 8510/NEC 8023 printers
GDUMP	EXE +	Compiled, stand alone version of GDUMP.BAS
FREE1	EXE	ELECTRONIC DISK-Generates 160KB RAM drive (256KB rqd)
FREE1	BIN	Part of ELECTRONIC DISK
FREE1	DOC	Documentation for FREE1
FREE3	COM	NEW RESET—Softer resets save RAM drive data
FREE3	DOC	Documentation for FREE3
COLOR40	COM +	DOS switch to colorgraphics 40 col text mode
COLOR80	COM +	DOS switch to colorgraphics 80 col text mode
COLORG	COM +	DOS switch to colorgraphics med. resolution graphics mode
MONO	COM	DOS switch to monochrome 80 col text mode
PROFILE	BAS	Generates PROFILE.MEM. See PC MAGAZINE, October, 1982
PROFILER	BAS	Demos use of PROFILE.MEM
STARLANE	BAS	2-4 players invest in interstellar trading & shipping
DCBA	HOW	Patch to DISKCOPY for production copying
KB_FLAG	BAS	Software control of keyboard modes [TUTORIAL]
GUIDE1	REF	Reference Guides—DOS, BASIC & Volkswriter function keys
GUIDE2	REF	Reference Guide—C.Itoh/NEC command codes [A>TYPE fname CtrlPrtSc Enter]-require C.Itoh/NEC printer
NUM-WORD	BAS	Routine converts numeric value to literal expression
PRTSET	BAS	Printer setup program for C.ITOH/NEC printers
GRAFHAT	BAS +	Draws "industry standard" graphic pattern in high resolution mode
GRAFHAT	EXE +	Somewhat faster compiled version of above
ZELLER	BAS	Determines day of week using Zeller's congruence
CNTRLBK	BAS	Demos CtrlBreak disable & imbedded protect/unprotect
CHECKOUT	BAS	Checkout various ports, devices—strong on modems
STICK	BAS	Displays joystick/paddle gameport values
ACRS	BAS	Accelerated Cost Recovery System, Creative Computing 2/83

Disk No 7 — EXPLIST — v1

User-supported program to expand the listing of BASIC programs to make them more readable.

EXPLIST	EXE	Expanding lister for BASIC programs
EXPLISTR	EXE	Expanding lister requiring compiler runtime library
EXPLIST	DOC	Documentation file for Expanding Lister
EXPOPT		Options file—EXPLIST.EXE
EXPMAIL	EXE	Generates a reply/contribution letter to author
PRINT	BAS	Prints ASCII files with title banner and page #'s
PRINTNEC	BAS	Same as "print" for NEC 8023/C.Itoh 8510 printers
BIHEX	BAS	Converts binary files to ASCII hex and back again
LF	COM	Directory list sorted alphabetically by extent & name

Disk No 8 — CROSSREF — v1

User-supported program to produce a cross-reference listing of variables referenced in a BASIC Program.

CROSSREF	EXE	Extensive cross-reference generator for BASIC programs
CROSSREF	DOC	Documentation file
CRMAIL	EXE	Generates a reply/contribution letter to the author
CROSSOPT		Options file
CROSSWDS	DAT	Data file
MONITOR	BAS	BASIC subroutines for formatted screen displays
MONITOR	DOC	Documentation file

Disk No 9 — SQUISH — v1

ACATALOG	BAS	A catalog of the programs on this disk (Items 1-31)
ASCICHAR	BAS	Display or Prints primary and alternate character sets
ASCII	BAS	A chart of ASCII Characters (Decimal)
AUTOINST	BAS	Prints Autostart Program Instructions (AUTOST.BAS)
AUTOPEEK	BAS	Displays 10 locations of memory in dec or hex
AUTOST	BAS	Sets date and time, displays files and runs program
CHECKOUT	BAS	Checks Serial and Parallel equipment & handshake
COLORSET	BAS	Displays color options on a color monitor
KEYSBAS	BAS	Programs Function keys for BASIC and prints OVERLAY
KEYSMP	BAS	Prints a Function Key OVERLAY for Multiplan programs
LONGZONE	BAS	Computes GMT (UCT) and local time for any longitude
MENU	BAS	Runs AUTOST.BAS program
MINIPROG	BAS	A Skeleton BASIC program used to start a new program
MODULO	BAS	Demonstrates Modulo Arithmetic
MONOSET	BAS	Displays screen options for the monochrome monitor
NUMVERT	BAS	Displays numbers in ASCII, dec, oct, hex and binary

OPKEYS	BAS	Programs the Function Keys for BASIC programming
PAYMENT	BAS	Computes payment for a fully amortized loan
PEEK	BAS	Peeks at a location in memory
Q	BAS	Returns to DOS with a clear screen and keys reset
REAL$	BAS	Displays and prints a table of Real Estate Appreciation
SYS	BAS	Returns to DOS with a clear screen and keys reset
TIME	BAS	Displays system date and time on the screen
!	BAT	Boots up BASICA and AUTOST from DOS
AUTOEXEC	BAT	Boots up BASICA and AUTOST from power ON Startup
STARTUP	BAT	Transfers DOS and BASICA from DOS Disk in B to Disk in A
2COLOR	COM	Transfers to Color Graphics Adapter and Monitor from DOS
2MONO	COM	Transfers to Monochrome Adaptor and Monitor from DOS
DISKID	REV	Contains Disk ID Label and Year for AUTOST program
2COLOR	SYS +	Transfers to Color Graphics Adapt and Monitor from BASICA
2MONO	SYS	Transfers to Monochrome Adaptor and Monitor from BASICA
INDEX	DOC	This contains details on files on this disk
MDM7I	COM	This is a MODEM and TERMINAL file transfer program
MDMIBM	ASM	Part of MDM7I above
MDM7	DOC	This describes how the modem program is to be used
CRCK4	COM	This a file checksum program
CRCK4	CPM	Part of CRCK4.COM
LOOK	COM	This is a memory byte search program
FIND	COM	This is a disk file string search program
WASH	COM	This is a disk maintenance program
WASH	DOC	This documents WASH.COM
SQUISH	BAS	This program removes spaces, REM's and condenses lines
SQUISH	DOC	Documentation for SQUISH program

Disk No 10 — CHASM Version 2.01 — v2.1 DS

CHASM stands for CHeap ASseMbler. It is a user-supported assembler useful for those wishing to learn about assembly language. Programs are converted directly into .COM files.

CHASM	BAS	CHeap ASseMbler (Version 2.01)
CHASM	DOC	Documentation file (128K)
CHASM	BAT	Starts CHASM (BASIC or BASICA must be on the same disk)
CHASM	CFG	Part of CHASM
CHASM	DAT	Mnemonic data file
COM2DATA	BAS	Part of CHASM
COM2DATA	DOC	Documentation for COM2DATA.BAS
EXAMPLE	ASM	Sample assembly language program
PRIMER	DOC	Primer (48K)

Disk No 11 — SPEEDUP — v1

Some of the programs on this Disk and on Disk No 12 were used as part of the original IBM PC dealer demo.

SPEEDUP	COM	Speeds up disk operations—do not use with VISICALC
SPEEDUP	BAS	Source to create SPEEDUP.COM on system disk in Drive A
AUTOEXEC	BAT	Sample autoexec file to load speedup and request date
TWOSIDE	COM	Allows 2 double-sided disk drives addressed a,b,c,d
TWOSIDE	BAS	Source for TWOSIDE.COM; contains setup instructions
HEAPSORT	BAS	HEAPSORT demo
QSORT	BAS	Quick internal sort for array—string or numeric
PRINT	BAS	Prints or displays any ASCII text file
BASICPRT	BAS	Prints BASIC programs with highlighted rems & print ctrl
MENU	BAS	Program from dealer demo a-disk
IBMDIY	BAS	Program from dealer demo a-disk
IBMMC	BAS	Program from dealer demo a-disk
IBMCS	BAS	Program from dealer demo a-disk
B	BAS+	Switches display to monochrome
C	BAS+	Switches display to color
LUNAR	BAS	Game—apollo lunar landing
PRDEMO	BAS	Prints all 12 MX80 printer fonts
CHRSET	BAS	Prints all 244 printable chars—244 out of 255
TRANDUMP	BAS	Hex file display program
CANNON	BAS	Cannon firing game—elev control and sound effects
NIM	BAS	Game of NIM
START	BAS+	Color display demo consisting of 17 programs and one data file
GTEST	BAS+	" (Requires color display and BASICA)
PSTYLES	BAS+	"
DISPLAY	BAS+	"
SATURN	BAS+	Picture of Saturn
TESTSCRN	BAS+	"
PLOTTER	BAS+	"
GRAPH1	BAS+	Draw on screen with 8 cursor keys or light pen
WAITIN	BAS+	"
HAPPYB	BAS+	"
LOGOC	BAS+	IBM logo
SCREENS	+ D	0 questions (May need empty PEOPLEF file)
SNOW1	BAS+	Random patterns
SNOW2	BAS+	"
SNOW3	BAS+	"
PATTERNS	BAS+	More random patterns
DEFEND	BAS+	Animated war game—uses joy stick controllers

Disk No 12		DEMO3	v1
FENCE	BAS	Game—hit shifty prey with ball using / paddles	
DEMO3	BAS+	Use with menu on Disk No 11	
LOGO40	BAS+	IBM logo on 40 char screen	
GRAPHICS	BAS+	"	
MOUNTX	PIC+	Pictures used by DEMO3	
WORM	PIC+	"	
COMPLEX1	PIC+	"	
WORM2	PIC+	"	
QUILT	PIC+	"	
EGGS	PIC+	"	
FLOWERS	PIC+	"	
BULLSEYE	BAS+	Program using circle statements	
MEDBULL	BAS+	Program using circle statements	
PAINT	BAS+	Program with circle and paint statements	
ARKTRAV	BAS	Music—a short melody	
SIREN	BAS	Wailing siren that doesn't stop until "ctrl break"	
LIFE	BAS	Input pattern is char string(s)—last one is "done"	

Disk No 13		PDRAW	v1
STARTREK	BAS	Starship Enterprise—space war with sound effects	
STARTREK	HOW	Screens of instructions—invoked by BASIC program	
STARTREK	DUM	Data file used by program	
PDRAW	DOC	Comprehensive documentation of PDRAW package (15K)	
PDRAW	BAS+	Drawing program	
COLOR	BAS+	Color sub-program	
MONO	BAS+	Monochrome sub-program	
COLOR	BAT+	Batch files used by PDRAW	
RUNCOLOR	BAT+	"	
SETCOLOR	BAT+	"	
MONO	BAT+	"	
DEMO	PIC+	Pictures used by PDRAW	
HELP1	PIC+	"	
HELP2	PIC+	"	
USASTATE	PIC+	"	
USATEMP	PIC+	"	
USA	PIC+	"	
IBMSONG	BAS	IBM rally song—lyrics & bouncing ball—80 screen	

Disk No 14		BARGRAPH	v1
BASMENU	BAS	Automatic menu for BASIC programs	
METEOR	BAS	Fast-moving game using cursor movement keys	
YAHTZEE	BAS	Yahtzee game rolls the dice & keeps score	
COREFIX	BAS	BASIC program to inspect & patch storage	
BIRDS	BAS	Sound effects	
BLKLETER	BAS	Generate block letters on the printer	
SPSHIPS	BAS	Sound effects	
TICKTOCK	BAS	Sound effects	
FINANCE	BAS	Large package of financial programs	
SHELLSRT	BAS	Shell-metzger sort written in BASIC	
SORT	BAS	Another sort written in BASIC	
PDSOFTWR	DOC	Package of public domain software	
ASYN-PGM	BAS	Asynchronous communication program	
BKSPACE	BAS	Patch for DOS-disk COMM.BAS to handle backspaces	
DWNLOAD	BAS	Patch for DOS-disk COMM.BAS to download files	
PRINTER	BAS	Patch for DOS-disk COMM.BAS to toggle printer	
BRKEVEN	VC	VISICALC program—break-even points	
COSINES	VC	VISICALC program—calculate table of cosines	
FEDTAX	VC	VISICALC program—federal income tax	
GRAPHS	VC	VISICALC program—plotting points	
HOMEBDGT	VC	VISICALC program—home budget program	
PRTSETUP	VC	VISICALC printer setup hints	
		BARGRAPH	
BARGRAPH	BAS	Program to produce bargraphs on the mono display—well liked	
BACKLOG	BAR	Sample BARGRAPH input	
FCST	BAR	Part of BARGRAPH	
PLANACT	BAR	Part of BARGRAPH	
QTR2G	BAR	Part of BARGRAPH	
S	BAR	Part of BARGRAPH	
SS	BAR	Part of BARGRAPH	
SSS	BAR	Part of BARGRAPH	
SSSSS	BAR	Part of BARGRAPH	
SSSSSS	BAR	Part of BARGRAPH	
YR17	BAR	Part of BARGRAPH	
YR20	BAR	Part of BARGRAPH	

Disk No 15		COLORDEMO	v1
PCMAN	BAS +	Color game using joysticks (Untested)	
PATHMAN	BAS +	Color game using keypad—no joysticks needed	
DRAW	EXE +	Block-read a file directly to color/graphics buffer	
DRAW	ASM +	Assembler source for DRAW.EXE	
SCREEN	EXE +	Set color/mono/40/80/low/med/high resolution	
SCREEN	ASM +	Assembler source for SCREEN.EXE	
MONSW	BAS +	Another color/mono program (Good as a subroutine)	
PRTGRAF	BAS +	Draw a polygon, optionally print with graftrax	
MONO	EXE +	Set display to monochrome	
COLOR	EXE +	Set display to color	
		COLORDEMO	
COLORDEM	BAT +	Part of COLORDEMO—run color demo (impressive demo)	
START	BAS +	Part of COLORDEMO	
NEXTSHOW	BAS +	Part of COLORDEMO	
FAMILYDA	Y +	Part of COLORDEMO	
BLASTOFF	BAS +	Part of COLORDEMO—rocket blasts off	
ESSXFADE	BAS +	Part of COLORDEMO	
FLYBY	BAS +	Part of COLORDEMO—objects in space	
LANDSEQ	BAS +	Part of COLORDEMO—landing	
WELCOME	BAS +	Part of COLORDEMO	
ELEPHANT	BAS +	Part of COLORDEMO—dancing elephant	
BUTTRFLY	BAS +	Part of COLORDEMO—butterflies flying	
OTHDEMO	BAS +	Part of COLORDEMO—game demonstration	
BLIMP	BAS +	Part of COLORDEMO—blimp flying	
FINISH	BAS +	Part of COLORDEMO—end of demo	
ADVLAND	PIC +	Part of COLORDEMO	
ELEPH	EXE +	Part of COLORDEMO	
ELEPH	DAT +	Part of COLORDEMO	
MCODE	%%% +	Part of COLORDEMO	

Disk No 16		GAMES	v1
BREAKOUT	BAS	Game—uses cursor keys to move paddle	
CHESS1	BAS	Game—multi-level skills (Slow)	
CRAPS	BAS	Game—casino type, single player	
MASTMIND	BAS	Game—guess numbers instead of colored pegs	
SUPRTREK	BAS	Game—another version for the "Trekies"	

STARTREK	BAS	GAME—original on Disk No 13 minor updates
STARTREK	HOW	Documentation used by STARTREK.BAS
STARTREK	DUM	Data used by STARTREK.BAS
PC-TALK	BAS	Original version of popular communications program
PC-TALK	DOC	Extensive documentation for PC-TALK 2
LPCTALK	BAS	Used with PC-TALK.OR SCREEN
REMOVE	BAS	Used with communications (PC-TALK)

Disk No 17		**GAMES #2**	**v1**
MENU	BAS	Menu to execute programs on this diskette	
PCMAN	BAS	Game—Pac-Man look alike for 80 column display	
SURVIVAL	BAS	Game—can you survive a trip to the moon?	
MOON	BAS	Game—enhanced version of SURVIVAL	
STARTREK	BAS	Game—another STARTREK version with minor changes	
STARTRK2	BAS	Documentation for STARTREK game	
STARTREK	DUM	Overlay module for STARTREK	
JBREAK	BAS	Game—bounce the ball off of the wall (BREAKOUT)	
BREAKOUT	BAS	Game—a more sophisticated version of BREAKOUT	
METEOR	BAS	Game—enhanced version of game on Disk No 14	
FENCE	BAS	Game—enhanced version of game on Disk No 12	
PCINIT	BAS	Initialize a high score file for PCMAN	

Disk No 18		**IQBUILD**	**v1**
MENU	BAS	Menu to select programs for execution	
READING	BAS	Game—improve your reading speed	
MASTER	BAS	Game—mastermind. Guess the code	
MATH	BAS	Game—drill of simple math problems	
FRANK	BAS	Game—HANGMAN by another name	
WORDS	BAS	Data for FRANK	
NIM	BAS	Game—ancient game of skill and strategy	
BACKGAM	BAS	Game—BACKGAMMON	
BLACK	BAS	Game—BLACKJACK. For 1 or 2 players	
TRUCKER	BAS	Game—make your fortune in the trucking business	
		IQBUILD	
IQBUILD	BAS	Game—sub-menu to run the IQ-Builder Series	
NUMBERS	BAS	Data 1 for numbers section of IQ-Builder Series	
NUM2	BAS	Data 2 for "	
NUM3	BAS	Data 3 for "	
ANALOG	BAS	Data 1 for analogy section of IQ-Builder Series	
ANALOG2	BAS	Data 2 for "	
ANALOG3	BAS	Data 3 for "	
ANALOG4	BAS	Data 4 for "	
ANALOG5	BAS	Data 5 for "	

ANALOG6	BAS	Data 6 for "
SYNONYM	BAS	Data 1 for synonym section of IQ-Builder Series
SYNONYM2	BAS	Data 2 for "
ANTONYM	BAS	Data 1 for antonym section of IQ-Builder Series
ANTONYM2	BAS	Data 2 for "

Disk No 19		**ARCHIE**	**v1**
MENU	BAS	Menu program for Disk No 19	
ARCHIE	BAS	Archie la cucharacha—game, BASIC tutorial & fun program	
ARCHIE	DOC	Documentation for ARCHIE	
PCS	DOC	Program control system description	
CONTROL	BAS	Runs the prime program on a BASIC diskette	
CONTROL	PCS	Returns control to Drive "A"	
AUTOEXEC	BAT	Requests date & time and gives control to SYSTEM.BAT	
SYSTEM	BAT	Loads BASICA, runs TRANSFER.BAS, runs b:CONTROL.BAT	
RUN	BAT	Runs the program passed as a parameter	
TRANSFER	BAS	Displays disk swap message, waits for keystroke	
MENU	PCS	Sample menu file for BASIC programs	
COVER	PCS	Mergeable cover page and exit hierarchy	
EXIT	PCS	Mergeable exit hierarchy	
CONTROLB	PCS	Copy to CONTROL.BAT on BASIC program diskettes	
CONTROLD	PCS	Copy to CONTROL.BAT on data diskettes	
CONTROLM	PCS	Copy to CONTROL.BAT on machine language program diskettes	
RV-EDIT	BAS	Full screen editor (Limited usefulness)	
RV-EDIT	DOC	Full screen editor documentation	

Disk No 20		**DRAW**	**v1.1**
CHSONG	BAS	Music—Christmas songs ('Tis the Season!)	
WORM1	BAS	Game—watch him tunnel through the ground	
SCOPE	BAS+	Game—display symmetric random patterns	
DRAW	BAS+	Game—program to draw pictures on color screen	
HANGMAN	BAS+	Game—color version of HANGMAN	
BLACKJCK	BAS	Game—upgraded to use color monitor if on	
YAHTZEE	BAS	Game—upgraded to use color monitor if on	
B-SIMPLE	BAS	Utility—aid to create & structure BASIC programs	
CROSSREF	EXE	Utility—cross-reference program for BASIC programs	
CROSSREF	SCR	Documentation for CROSSREF (SCRIPT source)	
EDIT	BAT	Utility—invoke RV-EDIT from DOS (See Disk No 19)	
BASMENU	BAS	AUTOMATIC MENU FOR BASIC PROGRAMS (See Disk No 14)	
CONTROL	BAS	Lets this diskette run under PCS	

Disk No 21		PC-MAN	v1
PCMAN	EXE	Game—text mode, any monitor, keeps high 10 scores	
JOYSTICK	EXE	Lets you use a joystick for PCMAN	
JOYSTICK	DOC	Explains joystick setup for PCMAN	
PACGIRLA	EXE	Game—Text mode, any monitor, variation on PAC* theme	
PCHEERS	BAS	Song—Bonnie's Version of 12 Days of Christmas	

Disk No 22		CHECKDIR	v1.1
PC-MAP	BAS	A utility to help you use PC-FILE (Disk No 5)	
BMENU	BAS	Program to create menus for BASIC programs (Needs BASICA)	
BMENU	DOC	Documentation for BMENU.BAS	
BMENUD	BAS	Same as BMENU except uses Disk BASIC	
CHECKDIR	EXE	Check a disk against catalog to see if duplicates	
CHECKDIR	DOC	Documentation for CHECKDIR.EXE	
LDIR	BAS	List Directory / FAT	
LDIRC	BAS	Input for BASIC COMPILER version of above	

Disk No 23		BOWLING	v1
DRAW2	BAS+	Update to PDRAW (graphics)	
MOUNTAIN	BAS	Game	
STARWARS	BAS	PC adaptation of popular space game	
TAXRETRN	VC	VISICALC template to use for your income taxes	
		BOWLING	
BOWLING	BAT	Batch file to start League Secretary Bowling Programs	
BOWLING	DOC	Documentation for League Secretary Bowling Programs	
BOWLFILE	FD	Part of League Secretary Bowling application	
BOWLPRT1	EWF	EASYWRITER format documentation for Bowling program—Part 1	
BOWLPRT2	EWF	EASYWRITER format documentation for Bowling program—Part 1	
MENU	BAS	League Secretary Bowling application—run this program first	
*	BAS	League Secretary Bowling application program files (11 files)	

Disk No 24		GAMES #3	v1.1
WUMPUS	BAS	Game—Hunt the Wumpus in its cave	
JAMMER	BAS	Game—"Head On" Variation	
RACJAM	SCO	DATA for JAMMER game, scoring categories	
GOBBLE	BAS	Game—PAC MAN variation	
TICTACTO	BAS	Game—Tic-Tac-Toe	
MOON	BAS	Game—Survival on the MOON	
NEWTREK	BAS	Game—Another version of StarTrek	
NEWTREK	HOW	Documentation for NEWTREK.BAS	

OPERATOR	BAS	Game—Simulates S/370 VM Operator Console
PACKMAN	EXE+	Game—Excellent graphics version of PacMan
PACKMAN	DOC	Documentation for PACKMAN.EXE
		SONGS
SONGS	BAS	Song—Choose from several on "menu"
YESTER	BAS	Song—Yesterday
EVRONWRD	BAS	Song—Ever Onward
RANGERD	BAS	Song—The William Tell Overture (Lone Ranger Theme)
PUFF	BAS	Song—Puff the Magic Dragon
LITUPLIF	BAS	Song—You Light Up My Life

Disk No 25 FINANCE v1.1

FINANCE	BAS	20 Miscellaneous financial programs
FINANCE1	BAS	5 more financial programs
GROWTH	BAS	Growth rate and projections
GROWTH1	BAS	Calculates compound growth
REPORTS	BAS	Budget management report
PRLIST	BAS	Miscellaneous printer routines
KALCOL	BAS	Kaleidescope—mono/color (Subroutine form)

Disk No 26 BOOK INDEX v1

INFO	BAT	Informational file for Book Indexing programs
START	BAT	Start-up program. Creates empty data file
ENTER	BAT	Begin index entries
COMBINE	BAT	Sort/merge new entries with any previous entries
INDEX	BAT	Format an index from the data
INPUT	EXE	Compiled programs for Book Indexing
SORT	EXE	Compiled programs for Book Indexing
MERGE	EXE	Compiled programs for Book Indexing
BUILD	EXE	Compiled programs for Book Indexing
INPUT	PAS	Pascal source code for Book Indexing Program
SORT	PAS	Pascal source code for Book Indexing Program
MERGE	PAS	Pascal source code for Book Indexing Program
BUILD	PAS	Pascal source code for Book Indexing Program

Disk No 27 ZOOSORT v1

NOISE	BAS	Demo—Produces different cycle sounds
LANDER	BAS	Game—Fuel consumption
CRASHER	BAS	Game—Planet landing
TREK	BAS+	Game—Yet another Startrek game (color)
FOILS	BAS	Utility—Produces foils from script-type file
DATETIME	BAS	Utility—Easier way to set DOS date & time

DISKMOD	BAS	Utility—Examine & modify disk sectors
MSPOOL	DOC	Documentation for use with print spooler programs
MSPOOL	COM	Printer spooler for use with the monochrome/print adaptor
CSPOOL	COM	Printer spooler for use with a separate printer adaptor
SETCOLOR	COM+	Utility. Sets background and border color to blue
SETCOLOR	ASM	Assembler source code for SETCOLOR
		ZOOSORT
STARTUP	BAS+	Initial program to run for ZOOSORT
ZOOSORT	BAS+	Graphical demonstration of bubble sort—sort animals by weight
ZOOTIME	BAS+	Part of ZOOSORT program
FLAG	BAS+	"
MONTOCOL	BAS+	"
COLTOMON	BAS+	"
AUTHOR	BAS+	"
AUTHOR2	BAS+	"
FLIP	MEM+	"
FLIPD	MEM+	"
GRAPHICS	COM+	"
??	BAS+	Binary files used in ZOOSORT program

Disk No 28		**DISKMODF**	**v1.1**
BIGTYPE	BAS	Displays character set in large block font	
DDATE	COM	Allows quick updating of date and time on bootup	
DISKMODF	BAS	Improved version of disk sector modifier program	
JUMBLE	BAS	Permutes jumbled words	
PALLETTE	BAS+	Displays colors available in low resolution (160x200) graphics	
SPEED411	COM	Sets disk step rate to 4 ms—test with format and copy	
TIMING	BAS	Accurately times the execution of short BASIC programs	
HALS	DOC	Doc on BIGTYPE, DDATE, DISKMODF, JUMBLE, PALLETTE, SPEED411, TIMING	
LF	COM	Directory lister sorted by extension & filename	
VDEL	COM	Provides for OK's when doing wildcard deletes	
CD	COM	Sets default drive and .NAM file information and sorted directory	
WAIT	COM	Batch file PAUSE for three seconds	
GUMUP1	DOC	Doc on LF, VDEL, CD, WAIT	
SYSTAT	COM	Status report on all drives including information from .NAM files	
SYSTAT	DOC	Documentation on SYSTAT.COM	
FK	COM	Function key handler (with reset) for DOS 1.0 & 1.1	
FK	DOC	Documentation on FK.COM	
SD	COM	Directory lister, 4 up	
SDIR	EXE	Directory lister, 2 up—slight upgrade of SDIR.COM on Disk No 2	
UNPROT2	TXT	Ultra simple technique for unprotecting BASIC programs	
ARTILL	BAS+	Artillary for 2, random terrain & winds—Quite good	
GRAFGE	BAS+	Uses graphic screen to develop your own ASCII 128-255 set	
GRAFGE	DOC	Documentation for GRAFGE.BAS	

MEMPEEK	BAS	Similiar to disk modify programs except for RAM memory
SQUISH	SRC	Upgrade of SQUISH on Disk No 9, modified for compiler
SQUISH	EXE	Compresses BASIC programs, removes REM's, etc
SQUISH	DOC	Documentation on SQUISH
GSDUMP	BAS+	Graphics Sideways memory DUMP to C.Itoh 8510 (or NEC8023)
COLOUR	DOC	Tutorial + small routines re: Artifacting, high resolution color, 16-color
CPCPRO	DOC	Tutorials—BASIC PrtSc, Printer bit graphics, Keyloc
RESCMD	BAS	Generates resident COMMAND.COM
RESCMDCK	BAS	Resident COMMAND.COM with BEEP, PAGE, CLS (Requires clock)
RESCMD	DOC	Documentation on resident COMMAND.COM

Disk No 29 FINANCE v1

BALANCE	BAS	Calculate remaining balance of loan
BESTLINE	BAS	Calculate best fit to points—technique 1
BOND	BAS	Calculate accrued bond interest
BUDGET	BAS	Recursive personal budget model
COMPOUND	BAS	Calculate compound interest
CRITICAL	BAS	Critical path method for activities (Not CP/M!)
FUTURE	BAS	Calculate future value of an investment
INCOME	BAS	Calculate income averages for taxes
LEASE	BAS	Calculate lease versus buying values
MEAN	BAS	Calculate mean, variance and stnd dev
NETPREST	BAS	Calculate net present value of investment
NUMERIC	BAS	Convert number to new base
PERT	BAS	Program evaluation and review technique
PVTAX	BAS	Calculate the value of an interest tax deduct
REGRESS	BAS	Calculate best fit to points—technique 2
TREASURY	BAS	Calculate value of treasury bill

Disk No 30 PASCAL I/O v1

The Pascal programs on this disk show how to do disk I/O from Pascal. They require the IBM Pascal compiler.

IOSTUFF	DOC	Describes files below
DISKREAD	EXE	Displays disk contents by sector
DISKREAD	OBJ	Object for DISKREAD.EXE
DISKREAD	PAS	Source for DISKREAD.OBJ
INTRPT	OBJ	Object to be linked to your PASCAL program object

INTRPT	ASM	Source for INTRPT.OBJ
IOSTUFF	OBJ	Object to be linked to your PASCAL program object
IOSTUFF	PAS	Source for IOSTUFF object
IOSTUFF	INC	Source to be INCLUDED with your PASCAL program source
PRIME	PAS	Source for DEMO
SAMPLE	PAS	Source for DEMO

Disk No 31 — MVP-FORTH — v1.1

This disk contains the Mountain View Press Public Domain FORTH language. For documentation refer to the book "Starting Forth" by Leo Brodie.

COMMAND	COM	Boots FORTH on initial startup
MVPFORTH	ASM	Assembly language source for MVPFORTH
MVPFORTH	EXE	Executable FORTH—type MVPFORTH to start from DOS
MVPFORTH	DOC	Where to look for documentation—"Starting Forth"

Disk No 32 — MVP-FORTH 2 — v1

Screens for MVPFORTH (Disk No 31). Directory is on screen 11. This disk is not a DOS disk and has no DOS files, directory, or file allocation table. DOS 2.0 will indicate error when copying this disk.

Disk No 33 — DIR — v1.1

BATMAN	BAS	Sample menu/batch manager program; requires SHELL.BAT
BATMAN	DOC	Documentation file
BSR	BAS	Simple program to drive ABM/BSR controller
BSR	DAT	Data file for BSR.BAS
BUZOFF	COM	Turn off paper out buzzer on Epson (Can execute from WORDSTAR)
COMPRS	COM	Enables compressed print on Epson (Can execute from WORDSTAR)
CVTHEX	EXE	Binary/hex conversion for files larger than 32K
DCPATCH	DOC	Patch for DISKCOPY.COM 2.0
DIAL	COM	Dials Hayes Smartmodem
DIR	BAS+	Disk cataloging program—very colorful
DIR	DAT	Sample data file
DIR	DOC	Documentation file
FK203	ASM	Source code for FK203.EXE
FK203	EXE	Function key reassignment program for DOS 2.0
GRAFTRAX	ASM	Screen dump using PrtSc key for Epson/Nec/C.Itoh
GRAFTRAX	BAS	Sample BASIC program to call GRAFTRAX.COM as a subroutine
GRAFTRAX	COM	Executable program file
GRAFTRAX	DOC	Documentation file

HANG	COM	Hangs up Hayes Smartmodem
HOST	BAS	Communication program for remote access
HOST	DOC	Documentation file for HOST.BAS
PEPATCH	DOC	Patch to IBM's Personal Editor
POSTER	BAS	Prints large character posters
PRTFIX	COM	Corrects "DEVICE TIMEOUT" errors with printer
PRTFIX	DOC	Documentation file
QD	COM	Quadram RAMDRIVE program—FOR QUADRAM BOARD ONLY
QD	DOC	Documentation file
SCROLL	ASM	Scrolls specified area of display screen
SCROLL	BLD	Program file to "BLOAD" from BASIC
SCROLL	DOC	Documentation file
SCROLL1	BAS	Sample program
SCROLL2	BAS	Sample program
SHELL	BAT	Bat file used with BATMAN.BAS
SOUNDS	BAS	Generates different sounds—contains documentation

Disk No 34 — SDIR22 — v1.1

PC3SC	MRG	Adds split screen capability to PC-Talk III
PC3SC	DOC	Documentation file
SDIR22	ASM	Sorted directory program for DOS 2.0
SDIR22	COM	Executable program file
VDISK	ASM	Sample RAM disk program from DOS 2.0 manual
VDISK	COM	Executable program file
VDISK2	ASM	Same as VDISK.COM modified for double-sided disk
VDISK2	COM	Executable program file
VOLSER	COM	Program to write 2.0 volume labels on diskettes
VOLSER	DOC	Documentation file
XOFF	MRG	Adds XMODEM protocol to PC-Talk 2.0
XOFF	DOC	Documentation file
DEFKEY	COM	Keyboard reassignment program; DOS 1.1 and 2.0
ORIGINAL	KEY	Original keyboard configuration file
BSLASH	KEY	Backslash keyboard configuration file
DEFMAIL	EXE	Mail/donation assistance
DEFCOPY	BAT	Copies distribution disk
DEFKEY	DOC	Documentation file

Disk No 35 — GAMES #4 — v1

23MATCH	BAS	The match game
ADDRESS	BAS	Addresses and phone numbers
BANKER	BAS	Checking account maintenance, expense categories
BARGRAPH	BAS	Creates bargraphs
BULLSEYE	BAS	Simulated dart game

CAPTURE	BAS	Logic game, try to capture the enemy space ship
CHESS	BAS	Play chess with the computer (Basis for CHESS.EXE on Disk No 4)
CHIEF	BAS	Math game
DECIDE	BAS	Helps decide between alternatives
DESERT	BAS	Try to cross the desert without getting killed
GOLF	BAS	Play golf, pick your club and stroke
ICICLE	BAS	A race to the top of the screen
KENO	BAS	Nevada style bingo
KINGDOM	BAS	Can you survive your term as king?
LANDER	BAS	Another moon lander program
LEM	BAS	A moon lander program
LOAN	BAS	Loan amortization program
MISSLE	BAS	Earth under attack from another planet
SECRETNO	BAS	You try to guess the number
STARS	BAS	Challenging permutation puzzle to solve
STORY	BAS	Creates four stories from user-supplied words
STRIKE9	BAS	Dice roll numbers game
TRAP	BAS	Number guessing game
ZAP-EM	BAS	Space shoot'em on the monochrome

Disk No 36 — PASCAL — v1

CONTENTS	TXT	Description of files on this disk
TABSET1	PAS	Sets tabs on Epson MX-100 printer
TABSET2	PAS	Simular to TABSET1 but treats printer as binary file
TIMM	PAS	Illustrates concept of Pascal unit (Main program)
TIMI	PAS	Illustrates concept of Pascal unit (Interface)
TIMU	PAS	Illustrates concept of Pascal unit (Unit)
SCREEN	PAS	Short program to assess specific memory addresses
PRINTER	PAS	Utility to print multiple files
PARSE	P	Part of PRINTER
INDEX	P	Part of PRINTER
DSNAME	P	Part of PRINTER
XREF	PAS	Cross-reference utility
COPYFILE	PAS	Program to show how files are defined, read and copied
DUMPFILE	PAS	Produces hexadecimal and ASCII dump of a disk file
UNSQ	PAS	Unsqueezes files compressed by Huffman encoding
PRETTY	PAS	Utility for listing Pascal programs in pretty format
PARTA	PAS	Part of PRETTY
PARTB	PAS	Part of PRETTY
PARTC	PAS	Part of PRETTY
GETDIR	PAS	Program to read disk directory
GETDIR	OBJ	Object module of GETDIR
GETSEC	ASM	Assembly language utility used by GETDIR
GETSEC	OBJ	Object module of GETSEC
GETDIR	EXE	Executable program to read disk directory

VIDEO	ASM	Pascal callable routine to perform BIOS video interrupts
PASCLG	BAT	Batch file to compile, link and go
PASCL	BAT	Batch file to compile and link
PASC	BAT	Batch file to compile only
FLUSH	BAT	Batch file to clean up Pascal compilation and test residue

Disk No 37	GAMES #5	v1

ATTACK	BAS +	Game—Destroy the Apple computer manufacturing plant
BLACKBOX	BAS	Game—A game of strategy
CHR	BAS	Displays complete character set on screen
CIAGAME	BAS	Game—An adventure to recover the stolen ruby
EQNSOLVE	BAS	Solves n linear equations in n unknowns, n < = 10
GALLERY	BAS	Game—Arcade game
INVEN	BAS	48K inventory program
MATH	BAS	Game—Addition, subtraction, multiplication & division problems
PERMUTE	BAS	Displays all possible permutations of a set of characters
ROMCHAR	BAS	Displays dot matrix characters from ROM patterns
SCRAMBLE	BAS	Game—Guess scrambled words in shortest time
SERPENT	BAS	Game—Guide a serpent through obstacles
SLOTMACH	BAS	Game
SPINOUT	BAS +	Game—High resolution version of breakout
SURROUND	BAS	Game—Guide expanding character through a maze
WILLTELL	BAS	Music—An amazing musical selection
WILLTELL	DAT	Data for WILLTELL.BAS
ZAP'EM	BAS	Game—Arcade game
MENU	BAS	Menu program—run it to assess other programs

Disk No 38	DRAW	v1

COLOR	EXE	Sets display to color from DOS
MONO	EXE	Sets display to monochrome from DOS
SCROLLK	BAS	Allows scrollock key to enable/disable scrolling
SCROLLK	COM	Compiled version of SCROLLK.BAS
WS-DOS	BAS	Converts WORDSTAR files to DOS files
SPOOLBAS	BAS	Allows scrolling to continue from BASIC to DOS
SPOOLER1	COM	Printer spooler for monochrome display card
SPOOLER2	COM	Printer spooler for color display card
SPOOLER	DOC	Documentation file for spooler programs
DISKRTN	EXE	Examine and modify disk directory
DISKRTN	DOC	Documentation for DISKRTN
FILTER	BAS	Removes control characters from downloaded files
FILTER	DOC	Documentation for FILTER program
DM	BAS	Sets up Dot Matrix printer under WORDSTAR
DMLQ	DOC	Documentation for DM and LQ

LQ	BAS	Sets up Letter Quality printer for use under WORDSTAR
LIST	EXE	Lists files to screen, one page at a time
		DRAW Programs
DRAW	DOC	Documentation file for MDRAW and HDRAW
DRAW	CMT	Comment lines for HDRAW and MDRAW programs
MODROW	TXT	Additional information on graphics programs
MDRAW	BAS	Medium resolution DRAW program
HDRAW	BAS	High resolution DRAW program
HELP1	PIK	Help picture for DRAW programs
HELP1	PIC	Help picture for DRAW programs

Disk No 39 — Flight Simulator — v1

Not up to the commercial versions.

JETSET	BAS	Combines AJETOFF.BAS & AJETCRUZ.BAS in one
JETSET	DOC	Documentation for flight simulator program
AJETOFF	BAS	Half-source of program (For mono display)
AJETCRUZ	BAS	Half-source of program (For mono display)
JETSET	EXE	Faster, compiled version of above (Also mono)
OJETCRUZ	EXE	Faster, compiled version of above (Also mono)

Disk No 40 — Stock Market Analyser — v1

Stock Market Analysis Program for creating, analyzing and plotting security data files.

MAKSTKFL	BAS	Main program to create stock data file
MAKSTKFL	DOC	Documentation for MAKSTKFL.BAS
PLTSTKFL	BAS	Main program to print stock data
PLTSTKFL	DOC	Documentation for PLTSTKFL.BAS
SCHWABCM	BAS	Part of stock market program
TRANSFER	BAT	Backup batch file
AELPW	NYS	Stock data file
GANNETT	NYS	"
PUTNAMHL	MUT	"
DUPONT	NYS	"
INDUST	DJA	"
AMPINC	NYS	"
ESKOD	NYS	"
COMSHARE	OTC	"
FLIGTSF	NYS	"
GENEL	NYS	"
GMOT	NYS	"
KELLYSER	OTC	"
AUTODT	NYS	"
BOEING	NYS	"

AT&T	NYS	"
GEMAR70	OPT	"
MONEYMKT	INT	"
DISNEY	NYS	"
CORNG	NYS	"
DELTAA	NYS	"
UPDSTKFL	ALL	Lists all securities files
PLTSEQFL	ALL	Lists all plot files
UPDSTKFL	DAT	Lists all active files

Disk No 41		**Kermit Communication System Version 2.26A**	**v2.1 DS**
MSCMD	ASM	Kermit assembly language source code	
MSCOMM	ASM	"	
MSFILE	ASM	"	
MSKERM	ASM	"	
MSRECV	ASM	"	
MSSEND	ASM	"	
MSSERV	ASM	"	
MSSET	ASM	"	
MSTERM	ASM	"	
MSXDMB	ASM	"	
MSXIBM	ASM	"	
MSYIBM	ASM	"	
MSDEFS	H	"	
MSKERMIT	INI	"	
MSXDMB	HLP	Help file	
MSBUILD	HLP	"	

Disk No 42		**Kermit Communication System Version 2.26A**	**v2 DS**
MSKERMIT	HLP	Part of Kermit system—help file	
MSKERMIT	DOC	Part of Kermit system—documentation (104K)	
MSXGEN	ASM	Part of Kermit system—assembly source code	
MSXSYS	DOC	Part of Kermit system—documentation (13K)	
MSXHP150	ASM	Part of Kermit system—assembly source code	
MSXRB	ASM	Part of Kermit system—assembly source code	
MSXWNG	ASM	Part of Kermit system—assembly source code	
MSKERMIT	EXE	Part of Kermit system	
COMMER	DOC	Part of Kermit system	

Disk No 43		Exidy Word Processor Demo	v2
EDIX	EXE	Program to run	
TEXT		Sample text	
STUDENT	BAT	Used to turn on tutorial mode	
GRADUATE	BAT	Used to turn off tutorial mode	
EXELOAD	EXE	Part of Exidy system	
KEYCODES	EDX	Exidy text file	
LSN	EDX	"	
LSNCFG	EDX	"	
HELP	EDX	"	
CONFIG	EDX	"	

Disk No 44		GAMES #6	v1
1500	BAS	Game	
21	BAS	Game	
BALL	BAS	Game—shoot ball at target	
BANNER	BAS	Produces large letters on printer	
BIORYTHM	BAS	Print your biorythms	
BLKFRI3	BAS	Game—Black Friday on the stockmarket	
CHASE	BAS	Game	
DECISION	BAS	Executive decision maker	
ENTEP	BAS	Produces Starship Enterprise on printer	
HANOI	BAS	Game—Towers of Hanoi	
HANOI	DOC	Documentation for HANOI.BAS	
HOBBIT	BAS	Game—adventure type	
HORSE	BAS	Game—horserace	
KING	BAS	Game—manage your kingdom	
LINES	BAS+	Draws pattern of lines on screen	
MSQUARE	BAS	Builds magic squares	
ROCKET	BAS	Rocket launch	
ROULETTE	BAS	Game	
SLOT	BAS	Game—slotmachine	
STARTREK	BAS	45K version of popular game	
TREKINFO	DOC	Documentation for STARTREK.BAS above	
USALIST	BAS+	Draws map of USA on color display	

Disk No 45		GAMES #7	v1
ANTONYMS	BAS	Game—educational	
AWARI	BAS	Game—classic African sticks and stones	
BACCRRT	BAS	Game—card game	
BASEBALL	BAS	Game	
BIO	BAS	Biorythms for printer	

BIRTHDAY	BAS	Find the day of the week you were born
BOMB	BAS	Game—find the bomb
CIVILWAR	BAS	Game
CLIMATES	BAS	Game—educational
CLOUD-9	BAS	Game—educational
DOTS	BAS	Game—connect the dots
DRAGRACE	BAS	Game
FOOTBALL	BAS	Game
GALAXY	BAS	Behold the stars
GALAXY2	BAS	Behold the stars and be inspired
GREEKRTS	BAS	Game—educational—match Greek words with their meaning
HIDESEEK	BAS	Game
IQUEEN	BAS	Game
MEMBRAIN	BAS	Game—educational—keep cells alive
MINIMATH	BAS	Game—educational
REVERSE	BAS	Game—arrange the numbers correctly
SHOP	BAS	Game—educational—go shopping
SNOOPY	BAS	Print Snoopy on printer
SQUARE	BAS	Game—competative square building
SWARMS	BAS	Game—you are attacked by bees
SYNONYMS	BAS	Game—educational—learn synonyms
TAXMAN	BAS	Game—beat the taxman
TRADE	BAS	Game—intergalactic training game
WEATHER	BAS	Predict the weather

Disk No 46 — UTILITIES #1 — v1.2

CAT	COM	Directory sort
CLOCK	COM	Puts clock in upper right corner of display
CONFIG	SYS	Setup for alternate keyboard programs (DOS 2.0)
DVORAK		Alternate keyboard program (DOS 2.0 only)
DVORAK	DOC	Documentation for above
DVORAK	BAT	Batch file for above
QWERTY		Alternate keyboard program (DOS 2.0 only)
QWERTY	BAT	Batch file for above
MA	BAT	Batch file for above
FULLEDIT	BAS	Stopgap full screen editor
PRINTFIX	COM	Run once to be rid of early DOS 1.1 printer bug (or autoexec load...takes 368 bytes off memory)
WS-ASCII	BAS	WORDSTAR-to-ASCII conversion
EFS	BAS	Electronic (database) file system
ASDADEL	BAS	Part of screen format program
ASDA	BAS	"
ASDARUN	BAS	"
HELPCOM	BAS	"
EDIT	BAS	"

FORMDISP	BAS	"
RESTATTR	BAS	"
HIDEFILE	BAS	Remove/modify hidden files
CHECKCON	BAS	Simple checkbook balancing program
CPRINT	BAS	Setup parameters of C-Itoh 8510 (NEC 8023) printer
GPRINT	BAS	Setup parameters of IBM/Epson printer
MEMDUMP	BAS	Memory dump program
DVORAK	COM	Command file for DVORAK
CONTROL	COM	Part of alternate keyboard system
QWERTY	COM	Command file for QWERTY
KEYMOVE	BAS	Part of alternate keyboard system

Disk No 47 CASTLE v1

CASTLE	BAS	Wizards castle game from July/Aug, Recreational Computing
CASTLE	DOC	Documentation for CASTLE game
CHRONSET	BAS	Sets Hayes stack chronograph
COMCHRON	BAS	Program to read Hayes stack chronograph
DISRTN	EXE	Disk file utility—undeletes and recovers lost first sectors
ELECTRIC	BAS	Computes electric usage
FINPAK	BAS	Package of 20 financial programs
GDUMP1	BAS	Graphics dump program
GDUMP2	BAS	Graphics dump program
KILLNULL	BAS	Removes nulls from sequential files
MAILLIST	BAS	Mailing list program
PLOT	BAS +	Creates plots on color display
SORT-BLK	BAS	Sorts fixed length record files
XMAS	BAS	Plays Christmas song

Disk No 48 RUNOFF v1

DATAFIX	BAS	Utility to add or delete line numbers from sequential files
EDIPAGE	BAS	Produces formatted listing of BASIC programs
FF	BAT	Sends formfeed to printer
FF	DOC	Description of FF.BAT
FF	TXT	Used by FF.BAT
FORTH	BAS	Implimentation of FORTH language in BASIC (From Dr Dobbs)
GROWTH2	BAS	Analysis trends and projects future growth rates
LOAN2	BAS	Calculates the missing loan amortization factor
PCFORM	BAS	Form generater example
QUADRIVE	DOC	Documentation for QUADRAM board
RUNOFF	BAS	Simple text formatter
RUNOFF	RNO	Sample text for RUNOFF text formatter
SERIAL	BAS	Allows printscreen command to work with serial printer

Disk No 49		FINISH	v1
ADDRFLCD	BAS	Prints 3x5 cards	
BIGTYPE1	BAS	Displays dot matrix characters in ROM pattern	
CALEPSON	BAS	Modification to CALENDAR.BAS (1.0 & 1.1) for Epson printer	
CALEPSON	DOC	Documentation for CALEPSON	
CHARDISP	BAS	Displays screen character set	
CLOCK	BAS	On screen digital clock	
CUBE	BAS	Rubic cube simulation	
DAYLOG	BAS	Calender program	
EMBEDDED	BAS	Demonstrates embedded printer commands	
FINISH	BAS	Text formatter written in BASIC	
FINISHTX	BAS	Documentation for FINISH.BAS (Use FINISH.BAS to list)	
GREATCIR	BAS	Calculate great circle crossings	
GREATRHM	BAS	Great circle calculations	
HEARING	BAS	Hearing test	
JOYSTEST	BAS	Test joystick	
JOYSTICK	BAS	Display joystick values	
LOAN3	BAS	Loan amortization	
NCCLSPRE	BAS	Statistics program—precision based on collected data	
PCHALLEN	BAS	Game—hit the bouncing ball	
PRINTER2	BAS	Sets up printer and lists files	
PRINTSET		Sets up Epson printer to 1/8 inch line spacing	
PRINTSET	DOC	Description of how to use PRINTSET	
RHMLINE	BAS	World navigation	
SEC&BYTE	BAS	Prints a table listing number of bytes as a function of sectors	
SPINOUT	BAS+	Game using color graphics	
XREFMOD	BAS	Produces cross-reference of variables used in a BASIC program	

Disk No 50		ROFF	v1
REBOOT	ASM	Source code for REBOOT program	
REBOOT	EXE	Program to reboot operating system	
SDIR	ASM	Source code for SDIR.COM	
SDIR	COM	Routine to list sorted directory	
MUSICBOX	BAS+	Music editor	
DEPREC	BAS	Calculate depreciation based on Economic Recovery Act of 1981	
TABLET	BAS+	Color graphics editor	
TICCLOCK	BAS	Digital screen clock	
ADDCRS	BAS	Adds carriage returns to downloaded files	
ASCFILTR	BAS	Removes control characters from downloaded files	
COLOR	COM	Go to color display	
MONO	COM	Go to monochrome display	
		ROFF	
ROFF	EXE	Executable RUNOFF program	

ROFF	DOC	Documentation for RUNOFF program
ROFF	H	Suggestions for compiling and linking ROFF
ROFF	HE	Suggestions for compiling and linking ROFF
ROFF1	C	Source code for RUNOFF program
ROFF2	C	Source code for RUNOFF program
ROFF3	C	Source code for RUNOFF program
FILEIO	C	Source code for RUNOFF program

Disk No 51		**HYPERDRIVE**	**v1**
FOUR	EXE	Game—get four in a row	
FUTRDATE	BAS	Determines date—x days, months, years from now	
FUTRDATE	DOC	Documentation for FUTRDATE.BAS	
GOMOKU	DOC	Documentation for GOMOKU.EXE	
GOMOKU	EXE	Game—simular to tic-tac-toe but played on 20x20 board	
GOMOKU	PAS	Source code for game of GOMOKU	
HDD512	EXE	RAM disk program for 512K of memory	
HDS320	EXE	RAM disk program for 320K of memory	
HYPERDRV	DOC	Documentation for RAM disk program	
INTERUPT	MAC	Macro assembly language interrupt routine	
PCGLOBE	BAS	Draws globe	
RAMDISK	ASM	Source code for RAM disk program	
TMDAY	BAS	Digital clock	

Disk No 52		**FREE4**	**v1**
BEEP	COM	Generates beep sound—useful for match files	
CRETURN	BAS	Adds carriage returns to downloaded files	
DISRTN	EXE	File directory utility	
DSKPGM2	BAS	Creates batch file for copying files	
FILTER	BAS	Removes control and non-ASCII characters from disk files	
FIXDEL	EXE	Disk file utility	
FIXIT	BAS	Creates PRINTFIX.COM	
FREE4	COM	160K electronic disk drive—update to FREE1	
FREE4	DOC	Documentation for FREE4.COM	
FREE5	COM	New reset program—update to FREE3	
FREE5	DOC	Documentation for FREE5.COM	
HEX	BAS	Convert binary files to and from hex format for downloading	
HIDEFILE	BAS	Modifies a file's directory status	
PARTCOPY	EXE	Copies files from double-sided disk to 2 single-sided disks	
PATCH256	ASC	Patches various printers into PR256	

POKEPEEK	DOC	Memory locations in ROM BIOS accessable from BASIC
PR256	ASM	Printer patch
SHIFTBS	COM	Converts backslash key into left shift key
SHIFTIBM	COM	Converts backslash key back to IBM standard configuration
TUNE	COM	Plays tune
UTSCAN	BAS	Scans text files for specified string and prints

Disk No 53		SOUNDS	v1
ATTRIB	ABS	Abstract for ATTRIB.BAS	
ATTRIB	BAS	Sets up video display attributes	
BASECONV	BAS	Numeric base conversion	
CHARMAP	BAS	Displays character set on screen	
CLOCK	BAS	Displays clock on screen	
DISKPGM1	ABS	Abstract for DISKPGM1.BAS	
DISKPGM1	BAS	Produces alphabetical list of programs on disk	
FILESORT	BAS	File sort routine	
KYBDSET	SUB	Keyboard subroutine	
QUICKSRT	BAS	Quicksort demo	
SCROLL	SUB	Scroll subroutine (In BASIC)	
SEESWTCH	BAS	Displays computers switch settings	
SHELLSRT	BAS	Shellsort demo	
UNWS	ASM	Source for UNWS.COM	
UNWS	COM	Converts WORDSTAR files to DOS files	
WSFIX2	TXT	WORDSTAR fixes	
WSMOD	DOC	Instructions for modifying WORDSTAR 3.2 screen/printer controls	
WSPATCH2	TXT	Installs various printers for WORDSTAR	
		SOUNDS	
SOUND1	BAS	Makes sound	
CHIRP	BAS	Makes sound	
PHASER	BAS	Makes sound	
BOMB	BAS	Makes sound	
UPBEAT	BAS	Makes sound	
SORRY	BAS	Makes sound	
TADAA	BAS	Makes sound	
TADADADA	BAS	Makes sound	
SIREN	BAS	Makes sound	
ENGINE	BAS	Makes sound	
SRS	BAS	Makes sound	
LRS	BAS	Makes sound	
PHASERB	BAS	Makes sound	
TORPEDOB	BAS	Makes sound	
SHIELDS	BAS	Makes sound	
COMPUTER	BAS	Makes sound	

Disk No 54		**XMODEM**	**v1.1 DS**
TUTORIAL		Tutorial for IBM ASYNC COM PROGRAM	
PROGRAMN	OTE	Programming notes for IBM ASYNC COM PROGRAM modifications	
DESCRIPT	ION	Program description for IBM ASYNC COM PROGRAM modifications	
SHORTERM	BAS	64K version—see PROGRAMN.OTE	
LONGTERM	BAS	96K version—see PROGRAMN.OTE	
PROFEEL		Sony Profeel monitor modifications (Text file)	
		XMODEM	
XMODEM	ASM	Source code (52K)	
XMODEM	DOC	Documentation for XMODEM.COM	
XMODEM	COM	Modem communication program (DOS 1.1)	

Disk No 55		**GAMES #8**	**v1**
BIO	BAS	Biorythms—from today's date	
CRAZY8	BAS	Game—uses character graphics for cards	
DESERT	BAS	Game	
HRSERACE	BAS	Game—horse race	
IPCOGOLF	BAS	Game—golf	
IPPOKER	BAS +	Game—Buck Mann's poker for one—uses graphics	
IPPOKER	DOC	Documentation for IPPOKER.BAS	
JETPILOT	BAS	Fly from pilots control panel	
JETPILOT	DOC	Documentation for JETPILOT.BAS	
LANDER	BAS +	Game—land space vehicle—graphics and sound	
LANDER	BIN	Used by LANDER.BAS	
LANDER	SCR	Used by LANDER.BAS	
NADIA	BAS	Song	
PHOENIX	BAS	Song	
ROULETTE	BAS	Game—roulette.	
SESAME	BAS	Song	
STARWARS	BAS	Song	

Disk No 56		**Keyboard Utilities**	**v2**
BASIC-KB	ASM	Assembly language source for BASIC-KB.EXE	
BASIC-KB	EXE	Executable program file	
BASIC-KB	DOC	Documentation for BASIC-KB.BAS	
DISTAR	BAS	IPCO Computes stellar parameters	
DECIDE	BAS	IPCO Decision maker	
XMASCARD	BAS +	IPCO Animated Christmas card	
KEYBOARD	ASM	Assembly language source for KEYBOARD.EXE	
KEYBOARD	EXE	Executable program file	

KEYBOARD	DOC	Documentation for KEYBOARD.BAS
MINI-WP	BAS	Mini word processor
SPEECH	BAS	IPCO Produces test of speech
ADDR-PH	BAS	IPCO Filing system for names, addresses and telephone numbers
PROVERB1	BAS	IPCO Prints proverbs

Disk No 57 — Text Processing Tools—Volume 1 — v1

Tools to manipulate text files. See Disks No 130-132 for more complete and better documented versions of the utilities on this disk and Disk No 58.

TRANSLIT	EXE	Transliteration utility
SORT	EXE	Sorts text files
FIND	EXE	Finds text strings in files
CHANGE	EXE	Changes text strings in file
COMPARE	EXE	Compares two files

Disk No 58 — Text Processing Tools—Volume 2 — v1

FORMAT	EXE	Text formatter
DEFINE	EXE	String replacement macroprocessor
MACRO	EXE	Expands macros with arguments
EDIT	EXE	Text editor

Disk No 59 — PEPSON, FASTPRT, QUICKREF — v1

There are 3 user-supported programs on this disk.

		PEPSON Epson printer utility
PRINT	DOC	Documentation for PRINT.BAS
PEPCON	DOC	Documentation for PEPCON.BAS
PEPSON	BAS	Printer formatter to work with Epson printer
PEPSON	EXE	Compiled version of PEPSON.BAS
PSCREEN	BAS	Printer formatter to show results to screen
PSCREEN	EXE	Compiled version of PSCREEN.BAS
		FASTPRT, a faster PrtSc function
ADD	BAT	Part of FASTPRT
AUTO	BAT	Part of FASTPRT
AUTOADD	BAT	Part of FASTPRT
AUTOEXEC	BAT	Part of FASTPRT
FASTPRT	COM	Main program—Speedup utility for the PrtSc function on PC or XT
FASTPRT	DOC	Documentation for FASTPRT.BAS
INSTALL	BAT	To install FASTPRT
TWO	BAT	Part of FASTPRT

		QUICKREF to create quick reference templates for your keyboard
AUTOEXEC	BAK	Part of QUICKREF
GUIDE	BAT	Prints QUICKREF.DOC file
QUICKREF	BAS	Main program to create keyboard reference templates
QUICKREF	DOC	Documentation for QUICKREF.BAS (May not print on all printers)
BASIC	KEY	Part of QUICKREF—template file for BASIC
EW	KEY	Part of QUICKREF—template file for Easywriter
TEMPLE	KEY	Part of QUICKREF—template file for Temple of Apshai
QR	KEY	Part of QUICKREF—blank template file
VOLKSWTR	KEY	Part of QUICKREF—template file for Volkswriter

Disk No 60 — UTIL 1.2/MAKE/BASREF — v1.2

Three user-supported programs. UTIL is a flexible text file manipulator. MAKE converts Easywriter 1.1 files to DOS files. BASREF produces a listing of variables in a BASIC program.

		UTIL 1.2 for text file manipulation
UTIL	EXE	Main program
UTIL	HLP	Documentation for UTIL program (15K)
DEMO1	BAT	UTIL demo
DEMO2	BAT	UTIL demo
DEMO3	BAT	UTIL demo
DEMO4	BAT	UTIL demo
DEMO5	BAT	UTIL demo
DEMO6	BAT	UTIL demo
DEMO7	BAT	UTIL demo
DEMO8	BAT	UTIL demo
TF1		UTIL dummy text file
TF2		UTIL dummy text file
		BASREF, a BASIC cross-reference lister
BASREF	DOC	Documentation for BASREF
BASREF	EXE	Produces cross-reference list of variables in BASIC program
		MAKE, Easywriter to DOS file conversion
MAKE	COM	Main program to convert EASYWRITER (1.1) files to DOS files
MAKEDOC1	DOC	Documentation for MAKE—Part 1
MAKEDOC2	DOC	Documentation for MAKE—Part 2
MAKE-REF	DOC	Documentation for MAKE—Reference
MAKECONV	DOC	Documentation for MAKE

Disk No 61		PRINTGR, IPCO Programs	v1

PRINTGR is a user-supported program to print graphics on a printer in either a small (5.3''x2.5'') upright mode or a (6.6''x8.9'') sideways mode.

SLOTMACH	BAS	IPCO Roulette type game
YAHTZEE	BAS	IPCO game
BANNER	BAS	IPCO Creates large letters on printer
STATCAPS	BAS +	IPCO Names, states and capitals—needs BASICA, good graphics
NFL-PK	BAS	IPCO Picks point spreads between the 29 teams of the NFL
ITALICS	BAS	IPCO Prints ASCII text files in italics on Epson MX-80 printer
MEMSIZE	BAS	IPCO Resets top of memory—may be used to avoid startup delay
EPSONUTL	BAS	IPCO Epson printer utility
		PRINTGR, prints screen graphics on Epson printer
PRINTGR	ASM	Common assembly language source for PRINTGR1&2.EXE
PRTSC_1	ASM	Assembly language source for PRINTGR1.EXE
PRTSC_2	ASM	Assembly language source for PRINTGR2.EXE
PRINTGR1	EXE	Prints medium and high resolution graphics—5.3''x2.5'' upright
PRINTGR2	EXE	Prints medium and high resolution graphics—6.6''x8.9'' sideways
PRINTGR	DOC	Documentation for PRINTGR1&2.BAS

Disk No 62		Applications	v1

HEBREW	ASM	Assembly language source for HEBREW character set
HEBREW	COM	Loads HEBREW character set
CHARS2	BAS	Displays ASCII character set with octal, hex or decimal value
LINREGRS	BAS	Calculates multiple linear regression coefficients
WB-UPTLE	BAS	Modification for PC-TALK 2.0 to allow file transmission while using host computers editor
		Applications
MAILIST2	BAS	Mailing list program—with search and alphabetic sort
INVENTRY	BAS	Helps to keep list of possessions on computer
INVENTRY	DAT	Data file for INVENTRY.BAS
INVENTRY	DOC	Few notes for INVENTRY.BAS—very short
CASHACC	BAS	Simple cash accounting system
REMCACC	BAS	Remark lines which may be merged with CASHACC.BAS
TESTDATA	ACC	Part of CASHACC.BAS

Disk No 63 withdrawn

Disk No 64 DESKTOP—Volume 1 v1 DS

DESKTOP is a LOTUS 1-2-3 worksheet which implements some of the functions of a managers desktop. LOTUS 1-2-3 is required to use this disk.

SAMPLE	WKS	DESKTOP sample worksheet
DESKTOP	WKS	DESKTOP main worksheet
COPYIT	BAT	Batch file to copy DESKTOP
DTCOPY	BAT	Batch file

Disk No 65 DESKTOP—Volume 2 v1

DESK	DOC	Documentation for DESKTOP
INSTRUCT	WKS	DESKTOP instruction worksheet

Disk No 66 GINACO Programs v2 DS

This is a very popular and well-liked disk full of useful utilities and games. All programs may be accessed by running the main menu program BLUEMENU.BAS.

ALPHAHEX	BAS	Alpha to hex reference display
BLUEBERY	BAS	Label creator, filer, record system—simular to LABELPRO.BAS
BLUEBERY	DOC	Documentation for BLUEBERY.BAS
BLUEBRY2	DOC	Documentation for BLUEBRY2.BAS
BLUEMENU	BAS	Menu for running programs on this disk
BOXINBOX	BAS	Displays border boxes on CRT—can be used as subroutine
BOXINPUT	BAS	Disables all input keys except those needed by your program
BUSCHECK	BAS	Checking or cash account reconciliation aid
CALULATE	BAS	Simple calculator
CHEKFORM	BAS	Check ledger & statement reconciliation form sheet
CHR$PRNT	BAS	Prints you printers character set
CIRCLE	GRA+	Hypnotic circle
COLORSEE	CLR+	Displays full-color range
COMPOUND	BAS	Annual compounded value of a sum at end of each year
D&CFORM	BAS	Debit/credit worksheet
EASYRITE	BAS	Word processor
EASYWORD	BAS	Simple text editor with no file storage
EPSONSET	BAS	Epson printer control and tester
ESCKEY	BAS	Converts ESC key to Continue key
FILEDATE	BAS	Date and time stamp on PC files
GASFORM	BAS	Mileage and trip log form
HEADCLN	BAS	Diskette drive head cleaning utility
HEXPRINT	BAS	Hex/decimal display printout
HEXSAY	BAS	Converts hex to decimal
IBMLABEL	BAS	Label print routine
KEYSET	BAS	BASIC function key settings

LABLFILE	BAS	Label creator, notebook, record keeper, file system
LISTSKIP	10P	10 pitch program listing
LISTSKIP	17P	17.5 pitch program listing
LPT12SET	BAS	Toggles between LPT1 and LPT2 if you have 2 printers
MENUPRNT	BAS+	Graphics print routine
NECLABEL	BAS	NEC 8023A label printer
NICELIST	BAS	Print an ASCII file with page skip and header
PC-COLOR	BAS+	Color monitor test
PCADD	GRA+	Graphics print routine
PEEKPRNT	BAS	Alpha to hex reference display
PRNTCALL	BAS	Subroutine for printer control
PROGHEAD	BAS	BASIC program heading
QUICKBOX	CLR	Part of showbox
RANDSEED	BAS	Random number generator
SAMPLE	TWD	Data for TESTWRIT.BAS
SAVINGS	BAS	Display & print savings or checking account information
SHOWBOX	BAS	BASIC subroutine—border
SIXBOXES	BAS	Program example—6 nested boxes
STARTUP	BAS	Example of menu display
STARTUP	CLR	Example of menu display
TASKLIST	BAS	Daily phone call and to-do list
TESTWRIT	DOC	Documentation for TESTWRIT.BAS
TIMESHOW	BAS	Display, retains elapsed time
WEIGHTFM	BAS	Daily health record form
WORKFILE	BAS	General ledger—daily journal entry form
WORKFILE	DAT	Part of WORKFILE
YESORNO	BAS	Yes/no response subroutine
YOURMENU	BAS	Menu subroutine
ZIPCLEAR	BAS	Clears designated screen area

Disk No 67 **NONLIN** **v1**

GROWTH	BAS	Growth rate projections
PRINTER	BAS	Epson printer routine
UN	P	File used to unprotect a BASIC program
UNPROT	DOC	Description of how to unprotect a BASIC program
REGRESS	BAS	IPCO game—linear regression
NONLIN	BAS	Performs non-linear least squares fit
FUNC2	BAS	Part of NONLIN—Gausian function
FUNC1	BAS	Part of NONLIN—Lorentzian function
DATA		Part of NONLIN—set of test data
BIGCHAR	BAS	Displays big characters on screen
LABELS	BAS	Quick label printer
APPLECOM	BAS	Simple communication program
CLKMOD	BAS	Prints day of week
TM-BREAK	BAS	PC-TALK 2.0 modifications to add true break with ALT-B

TM-DIAL2	BAS	PC-TALK 2.0 modifications to add automatic redial function
TM-LDIR1	BAS	PC-TALK 2.0 modifications to expand directory to 4 pages
TM-TIME1	BAS	PC-TALK 2.0 modifications to leave correct system on program exit
LABELEPS	BAS	Label maker
SCISUBV1	BAS	Simple plotting program
MATHFUNC	BAS	IPCO 20 complex math functions

Disk No 68 — WORDFLEX Word Processor Version 1.60 — v2.1 DS

There are two versions of this word processing program. Version 1.60 is on this disk. If you make a $35 contribution NEMCO will send you a version with more features.

AUTOEXEC	BAT	Automatic start file
COLOR		File containing WORDFLEX default parameters
CONFIG	WWW	Part of Wordflex
DEFAULTS	EXE	Program for modifing WORDFLEX default parameters
HELP	TXT	Online help file containing summary of WORDFLEX commands
IBM		File containing WORDFLEX default parameters
INSTALL	EXE	WORDFLEX installation program—run this program first
INSTALL	TXT	Instructions for installing WORDFLEX
MANUAL1	TXT	Part 1 of WORDFLEX manual (18K)
MANUAL2	TXT	Part 2 of WORDFLEX manual (19K)
MANUAL3	TXT	Part 3 of WORDFLEX manual (19K)
MONOCHR		File containing WORDFLEX default parameters
NEW_IN_2	54	What's in version 2.54
READ_ME		Read this file first
START	BAT	File for creation of your first working WORDFLEX diskette
TRANSFER	BAT	File for creation of additional working WORDFLEX diskettes
TUTOR1	TXT	WORDFLEX tutorial—Part 1
TUTOR2	TXT	WORDFLEX tutorial—Part 2
TUTOR3	TXT	WORDFLEX tutorial—Part 3
TUTOR4	TXT	WORDFLEX tutorial—Part 4
TUTOR5	TXT	WORDFLEX tutorial—Part 5
VERS_1	60	Whats in this version
WX	EXE	WORDFLEX main program
WXO	EXE	Another version of program

Disk No 69 — DESIGNER — v1.1

DESIGNER is a user-supported graphics editing program. A color graphics card is required to run this program.

DESIGNER	BAS	DESIGNER main program (Requires BASICA)
DESIGNER	DOC	Documentation for DESIGNER.BAS (45K)
DEMO	BAS	Animation demo

MAZE	BAS	Part of DEMO
MAZE	RES	Part of DEMO
MOUSE	SPR	Part of DEMO
TEXTCHAR		Text character images
VERBIAGE		Used by DESIGNER.BAS—messages, menus, etc.

Disk No 70 DISKCAT v1

DISKCAT is a disk cataloging system for keeping track of your disk files. It works with DOS 1.1 format disks only (not DOS 2.0).

PAGE	BAT	Sends formfeed to printer (lpt1:)
PAGES	KIP	Formfeed character—used by PAGE.BAT
PAGESKIP	DOC	Documentation for PAGESKIP.BAS
SMALLPR	INT	Commands to put Epson in condensed double-strike mode
SMALLPRT	BAT	Batch file to put Epson in condensed double-strike mode
SMALLPRT	DOC	Notes for using SMALLPRT.BAT
UNSMALLP	BAT	Batch file to reset Epson in normal print mode
UNSMALLP	DOC	Notes for using UNSMALLP.BAT
UNSMALLP	RNT	Commands to reset Epson printer in normal mode
DISKCAT	BAS	Disk cataloging program
DISKCAT	EXE	Compiled version of DISKCAT.BAS
DISKCAT	DOC	Documentation for DISKCAT.BAS
DC-SORT	BAS	Disk cataloging sort program—Part of DISKCAT
DC-SORT	EXE	Compiled version of DC-SORT.BAS
VPRINT	COM	Redirects printer output to file
VPRINT	ASM	Assembly language source for VPRINT.COM
VPRINT	DOC	Documentation for VPRINT.COM
DIRMANIP	EXE	Directory manipulation program

Disk No 71 GAMES #9 v1

ZAP'EM	BAS	IPCO game—shoot'em type game
STARTREK	BAS	Another Startrek
STARTREK	DOC	Documentation for STARTREK.BAS
CYCLE	BAS	IPCO motorcycle race, Q&A type game
DROIDS	BAS	IPCO Hunt for minerals—board game
LOSTGOLD	BAS	IPCO Adventure type game
WIZARD	BAS	IPCO The Wizards Castle
MEMORY	BAS	IPCO—Game to test your memory
SPELLER	BAS	IPCO—Spelling word drill—input your own words

Disk No 72		GAMES #10	v1
TICTACTO	BAS	IPCO Tic-tac-to	
DOCTOR	BAS	IPCO Talk your problems out with the doctor	
ROADRALY	BAS	IPCO Roadrally—Q&A type game	
BLCKJACK	BAS	IPCO Blackjack—no color	
BLACKBOX	BAS	IPCO Discover position of atoms by projecting rays	
FIFTEEN	BAS	IPCO Puzzle game	
ELIZA	BAS	The psychoanalyst	

Disk No 73		3D	v1
TEMPCONV	BAS	IPCO Temperature conversion	
MPG-CAL	BAS	IPCO Miles per gallon calculator	
%-DIFF	BAS	IPCO Calculates percentages—educational value	
MOLY-PAY	BAS	IPCO Catalog books in your library	
SERIALNO	BAS	IPCO serial number generator	
GROWTH	BAS	IPCO Growth rates and projections	
WINDCHIL	BAS	IPCO Calculates windchill factors	
SHIP		Data file for 3-D-ROT.BAS	
JET		Data file for 3-D-ROT.BAS	
CUBE		Data file for 3-D-ROT.BAS	
PYRAMID		Data file for 3-D-ROT.BAS	
3-D-ROT	BAS+	IPCO Rotate and display objects	
3D	GRF	BASIC source for 3D.EXE	
3D	DOC	Documentation for 3D	
3D	EXE+	Creates 3D images on graphics board	
3DTEST1	PLT	Part of 3D—image file	
3DTEST2	PLT	Part of 3D—image file	
PCFILECH	BAS	Recreates PC-FILE data base in different format	
CLERK	BAS	IPCO Record keeping program	
SHIFTS	BAS	Subroutines to set/test shift keys	

Disk No 74		Pascal Utilities Demo from Software Labs	v1.1 DS
README		Description of files on disk	
DEMO	EXE	Demostrates music, animation, bar, pie, and screen	
DEMO	PAS	Source code for the main program for demo.exe	
DEMOG	PAS	Source code for graphics and music demo	
DEMOG	INC	Interface file for the demos	
DEMOS	PAS	Source code for displaying a table of color text	
DEMOS	INC	Interface file for the demos	
SLIB	INC	Screen/keyboard control module declarations	

PLIB	INC	Peripheral control and sound/music module declarations
GLIB	INC	Graphics (line drawing) module declarations
ALIB	INC	Animation (pattern fill, get/put picture) declarations
GUNIT	INC	Graphics using world coordinated (Window and viewport)
MANUAL	TXT	Manual for the Pascal Utilities
MINI	OBJ	Library object module for the Pascal Utilities
MINI	INC	Function declarations to be include by the Pascal program
DEMOMINI	EXE	Demo random number, sound, screen control, and drawing
DEMOMINI	PAS	Source codes
DEMOMINI	OBJ	Object codes

Disk No 75 **Forms Manager Demo** **v1 DS**

Type "demo" from default drive for a demonstration of this forms management system.

Disk No 76 **History Education** **v1**

AUTOEXEC	BAT	Batch file to automatically invoke program
CATALOG	ASC	Additional programs from Mypro
HISTORY	BAS	Educational history program
QUEST	BAS	Program to create new lessons
*	DAT	Lesson data files for use HISTORY.BAS

Disk No 77 **1RD** **v1**

1RD	COM	Modem communications from the author of PC-FILE—see Disk No 129 (PC-DIAL) for the new version of this program
1RD	DOC	Documentation for 1RD (49K)
1RD	PRO	File of setup commands
DOC	BAT	Batch file for printing documentation

Disk No 78 **PC-WRITE Version 2.4** **v2.4 DS**

GO	BAT	Types READ.ME
READ	ME	A short introductory note
QUICKS	ME	A quick start for the knowledgable operators
PRINTMAN	COM	Part of PC-WRITE
TYPEMAN	COM	Part of PC-WRITE
FILEMAN	COM	Part of PC-WRITE
MANUAL1	CRN	Part 1 of manual for PC-WRITE (118 pages in all)
MANUAL2	CRN	Part 2 "
MANUAL3	CRN	Part 3 "
MANUAL4	CRN	Part 4 "
SPECIAL	DOC	Manual page with special characters

REGFORM	DOC	Registration form for PC-WRITE
TUTORIAL	DOC	Tutorial for PC-WRITE
ADDEND24	DOC	Brief notes
ED	EXE	PC-WRITE editor main program
PR	EXE	PC-WRITE paginate and print program
MANYCOPY	BAT	Batch file to print over and over
RULER	DEF	Initial ruler file, standard version
HELPE	DEF	Used by PC-WRITE for help screens
COLOR	DEF	Initial ruler file, for color editing
SHIFT	DEF	Initial ruler file, special version
M_PCWRIT	COM	Part of PC-WRITE
PRINT	TST	Part of PC-WRITE
PRINTER	DOC	Information about printer ruler files
		Ruler files used by printer
ANJAC830	PRT	" "
ANJAC832	PRT	" "
BROTHER1	PRT	" "
CENTR351	PRT	" "
CENTR739	PRT	" "
DAIS2000	PRT	" "
DAISTRS2	PRT	" "
DATAS180	PRT	" "
DATAS220	PRT	" "
DIABLO16	PRT	" "
DIABLO63	PRT	" "
EPLQ1500	PRT	" "
FOREPSON	PRT	" "
HPTHINKJ	PRT	" "
IBMCOLOR	PRT	" "
IBMEPSON	PRT	" "
IBMW5216	PRT	" "
IDSPR132	PRT	" "
IDSPR460	PRT	" "
OKI8283A	PRT	" "
OKI84A92	PRT	" "
OKIBMSON	PRT	" "
OKIP2350	PRT	" "
OKIP2410	PRT	" "
OKIWRITE	PRT	" "
OLDEPSON	PRT	" "
OLY2CRX1	PRT	" "
PINWRITE	PRT	" "
PKXP1091	PRT	" "
PROWRITE	PRT	" "
PRTEK912	PRT	" "
QUMESP20	PRT	" "

SIMPLE	PRT	" "
SMITD100	PRT	" "
SPIN3510	PRT	" "
SPIN3550	PRT	" "
SPIN5530	PRT	" "
SREED550	PRT	" "
STAR1015	PRT	" "
STARWRIT	PRT	" "
TALLY160	PRT	" "
TINST855	PRT	" "
TOSH1350	PRT	" "
TRANS315	PRT	" "
TTXC1014	PRT	" "

Disk No 79 RAMdrive v1.1

AD	COM	Quadram's Alphabetic Directory (Name & Extent in 5 columns.)
ADD-LF	BAS	Adds linefeeds to files that contain only carriage returns
BALL	BAS	Shoot pea into cup—simple text mode game
CONV	BAS	Converts COM/EXE to transmittable BASIC which will rewrite file
DESIGN	BAS +	Nice graphics demo program
DISPLAY	BAS	Program portion of IBM Bulletin UU-12
DISPLAY	TXT	IBM Bulletin UU-12. Faster screen writes
DRIVETST	BAS	Disk Drive Test program
DSKTST	BAS	Disk Drive Test program
KEYLOC	ASM	Source code for KEYLOC.EXE
KEYLOC	DOC	Documentation for KEYLOC.EXE
KEYLOC	EXE	Converts momentary keys (Alt,Ctrl,Shift) to toggle keys
LIFE	ASM	Source code for LIFE.EXE—bugs
LIFE	EXE	Rabbit paced version of John Conway's famous Game of Life
LUNAR	BAS +	Pick a flat spot and try to land, not too hard!
MAIL1	BAS	Mail list program. Keeps sort indexes on four fields
MAIL1	DOC	Documentation for MAIL1.BAS
MEMORY	COM	Sets memory size independent of system board switches
MEMORY	DOC	Documentation for MEMORY.COM
PEEKPOKE	TXT	Information on memory locations and their contents
QD	EXE	QUADRAM 8 sector drive 0 to 320KB
QDXT	EXE	QUADRAM 9 sector drive 0 to 360KB
QM	EXE	QUADRAM 8 sector multidrive 0 to 320KB
QMXT	EXE	QUADRAM 9 sector multidrive 0 to 360KB
QSPOOL	COM	QUADRAM print spooler
QSWAP	COM	QUADRAM printer swap, LPT1:/LPT2:

QUADRAM	DOC	Documentation for QUADRAM programs
ROD	BAS +	Draws every varying mosaic pattern
SETPRTR	C	Source for SETPRTR.EXE
SETPRTR	EXE	Setup MX-80 printer from Menu Screen
LIFE2	BAS	Another version of Life, runs on color monitors
LIFE2	EXE	Compiled super fast version of LIFE2

Disk No 80 — UTILITIES #2 — v1

ALTER	COM	Utility to change file attributes (DOS 2.0)
ALTER	DOC	Documentation file for ALTER.COM
ASK	COM	Allows interactive input to a batch file (DOS 2.0)
ASK	DOC	Documentation file for ASK.COM
BIGANSI	SYS	Enlarged ANSI.SYS (DOS 2.0)—allows for redefinition of 40 keys
CISEXE	COM	Communications program that supports CompuServe protocol
CISEXE	DOC	Documentation file for CISEXE.COM
CL	ASM	Source for CL.COM
CL	COM +	Sets blue bkgnd, yellow frgnd. and block cursor on C/G monitor
CL	DOC	Documentation file for CL.COM
COLOR	COM +	Machine language equivalent of BASIC's COLOR statement
COLOR	DOC	Documentation file for COLOR.COM
EDITNO	BAS	Formats numeric output in ways that PRINT USING cannot
EDITNO	DOC	Documentation file for EDITNO.BAS
ET4	BAS	BASIC text file line editor—an alternative to EDLIN
ET4	EXE	Compiled BASIC version
FCBCRT	BAS	Creates BLOADable program for reading directories from BASIC
FCBEXM	BAS	Demonstrates use of BLOADable file
FCBREAD	BSV	BLOADable file created by FCBCRT.BAS
FKREST	ASM	Source for FKREST.COM
FKREST	COM	Companion to FKSET.COM—resets keys to original functions
FKSET	ASM	Source for FKSET.COM
FKSET	COM	Upgrade of function key definition routine for DOS 2.0
FLIGHT	NEW	How to modify the Flight Simulator for color on a RGB monitor
HIQUE	BAS +	Board game that supports light pen input
KEYLK	DOC	Documentation for KEYLK and KEYLK3
KEYLK3	ASM	Source code for KeyLock program for latest BIOS ROM
KEYLK3	EXE	KeyLock program for latest BIOS ROM. Updated from Disk No 79
MEM640	DOC	Documentation file for MEM640.ZAP
MEM640	ZAP	Modifies BIOS to handle memory greater than 544KB
MOVE	COM	Utility to move files across directories without copying
MOVE	DOC	Documentation file for MOVE.COM
OKIMOD	DOC	Documentation on how to modify MODE.COM for different printers

SD20	COM	Sorted directory for DOS 2.0. Includes several run options
SD20	DOC	Documentation file for SD20.COM
SOLFE	BAS	Plays "Solfeggietto" by Carl Phillip Emanual Bach
WMTELL	BAS	Plays William Tell Overture
XDIR	COM	Extended directory—shows file attributes
XDIR	DOC	Documentation file for XDIR.COM

Disk No 81 — Communications — v1

HOST2	BAS	Upgrade of HOST.BAS on Disk No 33
HOST2	DOC	Documentation for HOST2.BAS
MAGDALEN	BAS	Music from Bach
MODEM	ASM	Source for MODEM.COM
MODEM	COM	IBM PC version of Ward Christensen's MODEM.ASM (Version 3.0)
SCNMAP	BAS	Generates screen layout form on Epson with script
SCNMAP	DOC	Documentation for SCNMAP.BAS
SORTS	BAS	Sort routines, various types, times different cases
SORTS	DOC	Documentation for SORTS.BAS (References)
UNWS	ASM	Source for UNWS.EXE
UNWS	EXE	Strips high order bits from WORDSTAR files

Disk No 82 — Batch File Utilities — v1

This disk enhances the Batch file capabilities of DOS.

RUNME	BAT	The first batch file in the tutorial "chain"
__QUERY	BAT	The rest of the tutorial "chain"
__RUNME2	BAT	"
__RUNME3	BAT	"
__FUNKY	BAT	"
__WHAT	BAT	"
__FIND	BAT	"
FILELIST		Summary list of files on this disk in wildcard format
CATALOG		Full list of files
__SLASH	REM	Text files displayed during the tutorial
__ELEM	REM	"
__WHAT	REM	"
__QUERY	REM	"
__FUNKY	REM	"
EXTCODES	REM	"
__PERFORM	REM	"
__FIND	REM	"
__EPILOG	REM	"
QUERY	COM	The six batch file utilities
WHAT	COM	"
SLASH	COM	"

FUNKY	COM	"
FINDFILE	COM	"
SETDISK	COM	"
FUNKY	ASM	Source code for the six utilities
WHAT	ASM	"
QUERY	ASM	"
SLASH	ASM	"
FINDFILE	ASM	"
SETDISK	ASM	"
PARSER	INC	Source code "include" files for the utilities
Q_CMDS	INC	"
QDISPLAY	INC	"
QGETKEY	INC	"
TESTQ	BAT	Batch files used to test utilities
TESTF	BAT	"
TESTERR	BAT	"
TESTFIND	BAT	"
TESTSET	BAT	"
SIDIR	BAT	Generates a directory file sorted by file size
EXDIR	BAT	Generates a directory file sorted by extension
ALDIR	BAT	Generates a directory file sorted by filename

Disk No 83 FRED v1

15PUZZLE	BAS+	Well known puzzle, arrange 15 numbered pieces in order
COM2ASM	BAS	Adds labels to DEBUG's UNASSEMBLE, aids modification of ASM code
COM2ASM	DOC	Documentation for COM2ASM
DISKMDF2	BAS	DISKMDF upgraded for DOS 2.0's nine sector tracks
GRPH64K	BAS	Sample register settings as used with GRPH64K board modification
GRPH64K	DOC	How to convert IBM color board for higher resolution
HANOI	BAS	Towers of Hanoi—Standard programming exercise, nicely done
KEYFLAGS	ASM	Source for KEYFLAGS.COM
KEYFLAGS	COM	Display @ and #in corner of screen to show CapsLock & NumLock
LANDER	BAS+	Simple, but not easy "land on the pad" game
MENU2	BAS	Menu program to load and run .BAS programs (DOS 2.0 version)
NWCLOCK	BAS	Displays time in very large HH:MM:SS format
PCGLOBE	BAS+	Globe of PC World's premier issue, page 220
STARMAP	BAS	Starmap for any date/time
TARGET	BAS+	Arcade aim and shoot game
TARGET	DOC	Documentation for TARGET.BAS
TARGET	PIC	Data file for TARGET.BAS
WORMCITY	BAS+	Help the worm eat an apple, escape maze

		FRED, a simple, fast text editor
FRED	EXE	FRee EDitor with many similarities to IBM's Personal Editor
FRED	DOC	Documentation for FRED.EXE
FRED	SUM	Summary of FRED's features
FREDDIE	EXE	Compiled version of FRED to use with BASRUN.EXE

Disk No 84 — UTILITIES #3 — v1

CHMOD	C	Source for CHMOD.EXE, written in C86
CHMOD	EXE	Changes file attribute byte
DOWDIF	BAT	Batch file to print DOWDIF.DOC file
DOWDIF	COM	Converts Dow Jones date to DIF format for VISICALC & 123
DOWDIF	DOC	Documentation file for DOWDIF.COM
DOWTRY	TXT	Sample data for DOWDIF.COM
DRAWIT	BAS+	Graphics draw utility—relatively simple, but very good
FILECMD	BAS	Loads, runs, renames or deletes .BAS files (DOS 1.1 version)
FILECMD2	BAS	Loads, runs, renames or deletes .BAS files (DOS 2.0 version)
FPR	C	File print routine written in C86. Personalize and compile
KILL	BAS+	Deletes multiple files selected from a menu (Color required)
QPRINT	ASM	Source for QPRINT.BIN from Byte, July 83, page 408
QPRINT	BAS	Demo of QPRINT vs PRINT
QPRINT	BIN	BLOADable BASIC CALL for fast screen writes, color or mono
TXTPRO	DOC	Documentation for TXTPRO.EXE
TXTPRO	EXE	Filter utility for ASCII files (Requires BASRUN.LIB)
UPVC	DOC	How to unprotect VISICALC

Disk No 85 — VISICALC Templates — v1 DS

BPR	VC	VISICALC templates
F1040	VC	"
F104064K	VC	"
F1040A	VC	"
F1040B	VC	"
F1040D	VC	"
F1040DOC	VC	"
F1040INS	VC	"
F1040SIM	VC	"
OPT123	VC	"
OPTCASH	VC	"
OPTMAR	DOC	"
OPTMAR	GIN	"
OPTTEST	VC	"
PR	VC	"

VBARCHRT	VC	"
VBREAKEV	VC	"
VCHKBK1	VC	"
VSPREAD	VC	"
VSPREAD1	VC	"
SORTDIF	BAS	DIF file sort program

Disk No 86 — SCREEN Text Editor — v1.1 DS

A user-supported text editor.

SCREEN	EXE	Main program
SCREEN	TXT	Documentation file (125K)
AUTOEXEC	BAT	Batch file to autoboot SCREEN
HELPME	BAT	Instructions on how to begin
INSTALL	BAT	Batch file to install program
MMOUSE	BAT	Batch file to copy Microsoft Mouse software onto disk
PRTCOM1	BAT	Batch file to copy documentation to com1:
PRTCOM2	BAT	Batch file to copy documentation to com2:
PRTLPT1	BAT	Batch file to copy documentation to lpt1:
PRTLPT2	BAT	Batch file to copy documentation to lpt2:
SAMPLE	TXT	Sample text—list of features

Disk No 87 — Programmer's Calculator — v1.2

PC	EXE	Programmer's calculator—main program
GC	EXE	Number base conversion program for use with PC.EXE
MANUAL	DOC	Documentation file (41K)
MANUAL	BAT	Batch file to print documentation
DUP	BAT	Batch file to copy program files to another disk

Disk No 88 — EPISTAT Statistics Package Version 3.0 — v2.1

ANOVA	BAS	One and two way analysis of variance
AUTOEXEC	BAT	Batch file to auto boot program
BAYES	BAS	Uses Bayes theorem to calculate rates of false positive and negative tests
BINOMIAL	BAS	Binomial distribution
CHISQR	BAS	Chi-square test
CORRELAT	BAS	Calculates Pearson's correlation coefficient
DATA-ONE	BAS	Main data entry program
EPIMRG	BAS	Used by every EPISTAT program
EPISETUP	BAK	Backup for EPISETUP.DAT
EPISETUP	DAT	Used by every EPISTAT program
EPISTAT	BAS	Lists available programs and guides user to proper program to use

FILETRAN	BAS	Transfers data from one data file to another
FISHERS	BAS	Fisher's exact test to evaluate 2 by 2 tables of discrete values
FORTRANS	BAS	Transfers FORTRAN to EPISTAT files
HISTOGRM	BAS	Graphs data sample on high resolution graphics screen
LNREGRES	BAS	Linear regression
MCNEMAR	BAS	McNemar's test or paired Chi-square test
MHCHIMLT	BAS	Mantel-Haenszel Chi-square test for multiple controls
MHCHISQR	BAS	Mantel-Haenszel Chi-square test
NORMAL	BAS	Calculates normal distribution
POISSON	BAS	Calculates Poisson distribution
PRINTDOC		Documentation file (25K)
RANDOMIZ	BAS	Random sample generator
RANKTEST	BAS	Three tests—signed rank, rank correlation and rank sum
RATEADJ	BAS	Rate adjustment program
SAMPLSIZ	BAS	Calculates sample sizes for statistical significance
SCATRGRM	BAS	Graph scatergrams
SELECT	BAS	Select from other programs
T-TEST	BAS	T-test compares mean of 2 samples
XTAB	BAS	Print crosstab reports
EXAMPLE		Sample data set

Disk No 89 — Tools — v1

COLBLNK1	COM	Blanks color display after 5 minutes
MINICALC	DOC	Documentation for MINICALC.EXE
MINICALC	EXE	Single screen spreadsheet calculator—11 columns, 22 rows
MONBLNK1	COM	Blanks monochrome display after 5 minutes
MONBLNK1	DOC	Documentation for MONBLNK1.COM and COLBLNK.COM
MSPOOL	COM	Flexible spooler program
MSPOOL	DOC	Documentation for SPOOL.COM
PC-LIB	BAS	Disk file library program
PC-LIB	DOC	Documentation for PC-LIB
VOLSER	COM	Create/alter volume labels
VOLSER	DOC	Documentation for use of VOLSER.COM
		Text Tools programs
XUP	BAS	Prints textfiles in columnar tables
PRNT2	BAS	Wild card print program—prints all files *.* or other file specifications
MAIL	BAS	Mailmerge program
MAIL	TXT	Sample input file for MAIL.BAS with instructions for use
PR1	LET	Sample letter for MAIL.BAS

Disk No 90		Genealogy On Display Version 3.0	v3 DS
RUNFIRST	BAS	Copy of cover letter—how to start	
MENU	BAS	Program to run first	
DISPLAY	BAS	Displays file information	
CREATMAR	BAS	Creates marriage file	
INDEXMAR	BAS	Creates marriage index	
CREATORD	BAS	Creates ordinances file	
CREATPER	BAS	Creates persons file	
INDEXPC	BAS	Creates persons index	
UPDATMAR	BAS	Updates marriage file	
UPDATORD	BAS	Updates ordinance file	
UPDATPER	BAS	Updates persons file	
LISTMAR	BAS	Lists marriages	
LISTPCI	BAS	Lists parent/child index	
LISTPER	BAS	Lists persons file	
ALPHAMAR	BAS	Prints alphanumeric marriage list	
ALPHAPER	BAS	Prints alphanumeric persons list	
DESCEND	BAS	Prints descendents	
FAMILY	BAS	Prints family group sheets	
PRINTMAR	BAS	Prints marriage file	
PEDIGREE	BAS	Prints pedigree charts	
PRINTPER	BAS	Prints persons and ordinance file	
DIRECTOR	BAS	Prints program directory	
TESTFILE		Test file to verify BASIC /S:256	
		Programs to run to print documentation	
TABLEOFC	BAS	Program to print table of contents (1)	
INTRODUC	BAS	Program to print manual introduction (2)	
GENERAL	BAS	Program to print general information (3)	
USINGTHE	BAS	Program to print "Using the programs" (4)	
REFERENC	BAS	Program to print reference material (5)	
APPENDIX	BAS	Program to print Appendices (6)	
PRINTERS	BAS	Program to print documentation on other printers	

Disk No 91		Adventure	v1.1
ADVENT	DOC	Documentation for Adventure game compiler	
BASCOM	PAT	Patches for IBM BASIC compiler	
BOGGLE	BAS	Game—find as many words as you can	
CHESS	BAS	New version of the old game	
COMPIL	BAS	Adventure system database compiler	
DKSPAT	TXT	DISKCOPY and DISKCOMP patches for large memory (+320K) machines	

DRIVER	BAS	Driver for Adventure system
GLOBE	BAS +	Creates rotating globe on graphics screen
GLOBE	DAT	Data file for GLOBE.BAS
GOLF2	BAS	Golf game
HIQUE2	BAS	Puzzle game—uses lightpen if you have one
MUGGER	DAT	Sample adventure definition

Disk No 92		**MUSIC**	**v1**
PATTERNS	BAS +	Creates patterns on graphics display	
SOUNDEMO	BAS	Generates several sounds selected from menu	
TWINKLE	BAS	Generates twinkling stars on screen (Use BASICA)	
MUSIC	BAS	Music scoring system	
MUSIC	DAT	Data file for MUSIC.BAS	
NAMCNV	TXT	Naming convention suggestions for public domain software	
QDCOPY	DOC	Diskcopy modification—eliminates prompts	
RACE	BAS	Game	
SCHROE	DER	Image of Schroeder in characters—may be printed	
SQUARE	BAS	Rubic cube type game	
SQUARE	DOC	Documentation for SQUARE.BAS	
SQUARE	SUM	Part of SQUARE.BAS	
STLOUIS	BBS	Information on using St. Louis bulletin board and others	
SW-PEG	BAS +	Game—move the pegs to the other side of the board	
UPVC	DOC	Instructions on how to make backups of VISICALC disks	
VCCOM	DOC	How to make VISICALC load as a .COM file	
GLOBE	REF +	Draws picture of earth on graphics adapter	

Disk No 93		**ASMGEN**	**v1**
ASMGEN	COM	Generates IBM Macro Assembler source code from executable file	
ASMGEN	DOC	Documentation for ASMGEN	
DETAB	DOC	Documentation file for DETAB.EXE	
DETAB	EXE	Expands tabs in text file to correct number of spaces	
FLASHCRD		Data file for FLASHCRD.BAS	
FLASHCRD	BAS	IPCO—Allows the creation and drill of flashcards	
FLASHCRD	LST	Sample flashcard data file	
FLIPPER	BAS	IPCO puzzle game—flip the tokens	
LOANANAL	BAS	Loan analysis	
MORSECOD	BAS	Morse code program	
TANK	BAS	IPCO Game—tank fighting for 2 players	
VW128FIX	BAT	Modifies Volkswriter to bypass title page	
VW128FIX	INS	Instruction for using VW128FIX.BAT	
WORLDMAP	BAS +	IPCO world map drawing game	

Disk No 94 — Ladybug Version 1.0C — v1.2 DS

Ladybug in a user-supported version of LOGO, a popular graphics oriented language useful for teaching computer concepts to kids.

LADYBUG	EXE	Ladybug main program
README		Notes about using Ladybug
LADYBUG	LST	Documentation (150K)
STATUS	LST	Version 2.0c adenda
LADYBUG	GET	Summary of Ladybug features and where to get it from
HELP*	BUG	Help files
PROBLEM		Form for reporting problems on
		Ladybug proceedures
BCAKE	BUG	"
BUG	BUG	"
C	BUG	"
CCIRCLE	BUG	"
CIRCLES	BUG	"
DRAGON	BUG	"
DUOPOLY	BUG	"
DYNA	BUG	"
HILBERT	BUG	"
INSPI	BUG	"
LUDWIG	BUG	"
MISC	BUG	"
MOVEBUG	BUG	"
POLY	BUG	"
POLYSPI	BUG	"
PROFILE	BUG	"
RAIL	BUG	"
SLINKY	BUG	"
SNOWFLAK	BUG	"
SOUNDS	BUG	"
SPINSQ	BUG	"
SPIRO	BUG	"
SQUARE	BUG	"
TOOLS	BUG	"
TREES	BUG	"

Disk No 95		Math Tutor	v1
ANSI	SYS	Enhanced version of program offered with DOS 2.0 (larger key buffer)	
TUTOR	BAS	Math tutor program	
INSTR	BAS	Part of Math Tutor package	
SETUP	BAS	"	
MATH	BAS	"	
GRD1		Data files for different grade levels	
GRD2		"	
GRD3		"	
GRD4		"	
GRD5		"	
GRD6		"	
SAV1		"	
SAV2		"	
SAV3		"	
SAV4		"	
SAV5		"	
SAV6		"	
TDATA		"	
MIS		"	
READ	ME	Instructions for using Math Tutor	

Disk No 96		THE SOURCE Introduction—Volume 1	v1
S-CHAT		Instructions for CHAT function on THE SOURCE	
S-INFO	SIG	Information about SIGs on THE SOURCE	
S-INTRO	ED	Introduction to THE SOURCE and ED, its editor	
S-LBRARY		Library of functions on THE SOURCE	
S-MAIL		Electronic mail function on THE SOURCE	
S-MGRAM		How to send a MailGram on THE SOURCE	
S-POST		Information about the public bulletin board on THE SOURCE	
S-PUBLSH		How to publish on THE SOURCE at a profit	
S-USERS	IBM	List of IBM users on THE SOURCE	

Disk No 97		**THE SOURCE—Volume 2 Free BSS Functions**	**v1**
S-AIRLIN		Information about Airline Guides on THE SOURCE	
S-BARTER		Information about bartering service on THE SOURCE	
S-DADATE		Information about "dating" service on THE SOURCE	
S-INFOX		Information about "4th generation" language on THE SOURCE	
S-LAWYER		Information about getting PUBLIC legal forms on THE SOURCE	
S-MOBIL		Information about Mobil restaurant & travel guides on THE SOURCE	
S-MODEL1		Business modeling language on THE SOURCE	
S-MUSES		Information about art and humor PUBLIC functions on THE SOURCE	
S-PUBLIC	CAT	Catalog of PUBLIC functions on THE SOURCE	
S-STOCK		Information about quick stock quotes on THE SOURCE	
S-STORE		Information about purchasing at a discount store on THE SOURCE	
S-TRAVEL		Information about a travel service on THE SOURCE	
S-WINE		Information about getting wine guidance on THE SOURCE	
S-XWORDS		Information about crossword puzzles on THE SOURCE	
STL-BBS1		Sample from a St. Louis area BBS	
STL-BBS1	INS	Instructions on a St. Louis BBS service	
STL-BBS1	NOS	National & local BBS access numbers (11/83)	
STL-BBS2		Sample from another St. Louis area BBS	

Disk No 98		**SOURCE & CompuServe Access Numbers 11/83**	**v1**
S-PHONE	NOS	Telenet, Uninet, Tymnet & SOURCEnet SOURCE access numbers	
CS-PHONE	NOS	Telenet, Tymnet & CompuServeNet CompuServe access numbers	

Disk No 99		**Public BBS & CompuServe IBM SIG—as of 11/83**	**v1**
CS-IBM	SIG	Instructions & information about CompuServe's IBM SIG	
CS-USERS	IBM	List of CompuServe IBM SIG members & their interests	
S-BBS		List of public BBS from THE SOURCE	
TBBS-NOS		List of public BBS from a St. Louis local BBS	

Disk No 100		**Games#11**	**v1**
MENU	PGM	Menu program for running programs on this disk	
BAGPIPES	BAS	Plays the bagpipes	
JUKEBOX	BAS	Jukebox music player	
JUKEDOWN	MUS	Music for JUKEBOX.BAS	
JUKEGARO	MUS	"	
JUKESATI	MUS	"	
JUKESOUN	MUS	"	

JUKECARA	MUS	"
JUKEIMPO	MUS	"
JUKESUNR	MUS	"
JUKESECO	MUS	"
JUKETHIR	MUS	"
JUKETAKE	MUS	"
ALIEN	BAS	Adventure type game
ALIEN	SPC	Files for ALIEN.BAS
ALIEN	DOC	"
A2	SPC	"
A5	SPC	"
3DTT	BAS+	Play 3-D tic-tac-toe on a 4x4x4 board
ANIMATE	BAS+	Animation demo
EGGS	BAS+	Draws patterns of eggs on graphics screen
EGGS	DOC	Brief description of EGGS.BAS
MANOR	BAS	Adventure type game
TRADER	BAS	Interstellar trading game
CIA	BAS	Adventure type game

Disk No 101 — The Portworth Package — v1

The PORTWORTH package is a user-supported set of applications programs that you can use for monitoring and evaluating your stock portfolios. Portfolios of up to 25 stocks can be processed.

README	TXT	Description of files on disk
PORTPACK	BAT	Prints PORTPACK.DOC: insert disk in Drive A, type portpack
PORTPACK	DOC	32-page user guide
DRIVE	DTA	System configuration parameter file
HOLDLIST	DTA	Sample input file
DLTAFILE	DTA	Sample input file
SETDRIVE	BAS	System configuration program
PORTCOST	BAS	Portfolio cost valuation program
PORTMRKT	BAS	Portfolio current valuation program
DLTAPRNT	BAS	Portfolio valuation change bar chart program
DLTAPLOT	BAS+	Portfolio valuation change line graph program

Disk No 102 dBASE II Ad Agency Accounting Package v1

ACCTG	PRG	To run, key "DO ACCTG" at the dBASE II prompt
*	PRG	dBASE II program file (36)
*	DBF	Database files (11)
*	FRM	Format files (3)
*	NDX	Index files (6)
CONSTANT	MEM	Memory constants
TEST	SUB	Part of Ad Agency accounting package

Disk No 103 CompuServe & BBS Sampler v1

CS-BUS		CompuServe—Business Services Sampler
CS-INSTR		CompuServe—General Instructions
CS-POST		CompuServe—Public Bulletin Board Instructions
CS-PRO		CompuServe—Professional Services Sampler
CS-TRAVL		CompuServe—Travel Services Sampler
ALCATRAZ	BBS	Sample from a St. Louis public BBS
EMC80	BBS	Sample from a TRS80 St. Louis public BBS
MIDWEST	BBS	Instructions for sex-oriented St. Louis public BBS

Disk No 104 CompuServe Sampler v1

CS-EDUCA		CompuServe—Educational Services Sampler
CS-HOME		CompuServe—Home Services Sampler
CS-INDEX		CompuServe—Index to All Services, as of 12/83

Disk No 105 PC Professor BASIC Tutorial v1

PC-Professor is a well liked tutorial for teaching the BASIC programming language. Start by running the BASIC program "intro".

INTRO	BAS	Part of PC-Professor—program to run first
AUTOEXEC	BAT	Batch file to start PC-Professor
*	*	Other PC-Professor files called from INTRO.BAS

Disk No 106 DISKCAT 4.3f v2.1 DS

A user-supported program for cataloging your diskettes.

DC4-CAT	EXE	Program to add descriptions to DISKCAT data files
DC4	DOC	Documentation file for DISKCAT (41K)
DC4-CNVT	BAS	Converts pre-DC3 format to current
DC4-DOC	EXE	Prints DISKCAT documentation
DC4-FIND	EXE	Finds a file in DISKCAT catalog

DC4-PGM	DTA	DISKCAT program data file
DC4-READ	EXE	Program to read & catalog disk files
DC4-SAMP	DT2	Sample data file for DISKCAT
DC4-SAMP	DTA	Sample data file for DISKCAT
DC4-SORT	EXE	Program to sort & print DISKCAT catalog
CNVRTDC	COM	Conversion program
INVOICE	DC4	Invoice for your records or to bill your company

Disk No 107 **Home Finance** **v1**

SCRNSAVE	COM	Program to turn off screen if no keys depressed after 3 minutes
SCRNSAVE	DOC	Short description for SCRNSAVE.COM
MUSIC	BAS	Plays notes
SETUP	BAT	Initialization routine for this diskette
FOS	BAS	Home financial management system
FOS2	BAS	Second part of FOS
FOS-DESC		FOS documentation—Key "TYPE FOS-DESC" to look at it Strike Ctrl and PrtSc first if you want it printed
FINANCE	BAS	A collection of financial analysis routines
TAX1982	VC	A VISICALC template for 1982 Federal Income Taxes
HAL-PC	TXT	Description of how one PC users group formed

Disk No 108 **APL** **v1**

BASTODOS	BAS	Subroutines for BASIC to access DOS 1.1 and 2.0 functions
BATMENU	COM	Flexible menu prompting for batch files
BATMENU	DOC	Documentation for above
DEPRE___	APL	Depreciation functions in APL
DISKTYPE	EXE	Tells you a diskette's format (Sides, sectors/track)
DISKTYPE	DOC	Documentation for above
FORECAST	APL	Forecasting model in APL
MATH___	APL	Determinant, integrate by Simpson's rule, in APL
MUSIC	BAS	Color graphics music editor/player
MUSIC	DOC	Documentation for above
NOECHO	DOC	Tells how to make DOS 2.0 batch default to no echo
PEPATCHS	DOC	Add color to Personal Editor and other improvements
PMODE	COM	Command to set EPSON printer modes and fonts
PMODE	ASM	Source and documentation for above
PRTSCFX	COM	Allows PrtSc to print the FULL monochrome character set
PRTSCFX	DOC	Documentation for above
PRTSCFX	ASM	Source for above
UNDOC	DOC	Lots of undocumented DOS 2.0 bugs and gotchas
UTILITY__	APL	String, time/date, and other utility functions in APL
		APL programs on this disk require the IBM APL compiler

Disk No 109		BBS Utilities #1	v1.1 DS
BREAKPT	COM	Makes ctrl-esc do a breakpoint to trace any program	
BREAKPT	DOC	Documentation for above	
BREAKPT	ASM	Source for above	
DATE	PRG	dBASE II program to validate dates	
FEDTAX83	WKS	123 worksheet for 1040 form, schedules A, B, C, W	
FILEDUMP	COM	Hex dump a file to screen	
MACTEST	ASM	Illustrates structured assembler macros in STRUCT.MAC	
PV_____	APL	Present value functions in APL	
REGDISP	ASM	Source for program to display 8088 regs in real time	
STRUCT	MAC	Assembler macros for structured programming	
UTIL	EXE	Fantastic set of screen/file/directory, etc. functions	
UTIL	DOC	Documentation for UTIL.DOC	
UTILREAD	ME	Introductory note about these utilities	
DATABASE		Sample database	
READ	ME	List of files on this diskette	

Disk No 110		BBS Utilities #2	v1
AUTOFILE	BAS	Free format filer/indexer with keyed lookup	
AUTOFILE	BAT	Batch file for invoking AUTOFILE	
AUTOFILE	DOC	Documentation for AUTOFILE	
DEFINE	BAS	Create pictures your BASIC programs can GET/PUT	
DEFINE	DOC	Documentation for DEFINE	
DOSCOLOR	BAS	Program to set colors used by DOS 2.0	
DOSCOLOR	BAT	Batch/documentation file for DOSCOLOR	
HC	COM	Fast, assembly coded hex-binary file converter	
HC	DOC	Documentation for the above	
PRINTER	COM	Menu-driven printer mode setup program	
PRINTER	DAT	File to customize the above for your printer	
PRINTER	DOC	Documentation for PRINTER program	
PRINTER	ASM	Source for PRINTER program	
RAMDISK	SYS	DOS 2.0 RAM disk sized by parameter in CONFIG.SYS	
RAMDISK	DOC	Documentation for RAM disk program	
ROMBIOS	ASM	Source include file for ROM BIOS data areas	
SCRN	ASM	BASIC-callable routines for display windowing	
SCRN	DOC	Documentation for the above	
SIZER	COM	Checks the size of a file and sets ERRORLEVEL	
SIZER	DOC	Documentation for SIZER program	
SIZER	ASM	Source for SIZER program	
STEEPDES	APL	Steepest descent equation solution in APL	
TABLET	BAS	Interactive graphics editor	

UPPER	COM	Filter program to convert file to upper case
UPPER	DOC	Documentation for UPPER program
UPPER	ASM	Source for UPPER program
WHEREIS	COM	Names all the subdirectories containing a given file
WHEREIS	DOC	Documentation for WHEREIS
XT370	DOC	Insider information on the new PC XT/370

Disk No 111	BBS Utilities #3	v1

BIGCALC	BAS	100 digit precision calculator!
BIGCALC	DOC	Documentation for above
CAL	COM	Prints calendar for any month/year after 1900
CAL	DOC	Documentation for above
COVER	COM	Prints file directory on Epson
DETAB	C	Convert tabs in file to blanks (Source program)
DETAB	EXE	Executable file for above
DIRECTRY	BAS	Creates machine program to read disk directory
ENTAB	C	Convert blanks in file to tabs (Source program)
ENTAB	EXE	Executable file for above
FIXTEXT	BAS	DOS-to-WORDSTAR converter, better than UNWS
GETMEM	ASM	Program to reserve memory areas (Source program)
GETMEM	COM	Executable file for above
LABELPRT	BAS	Print diskette directory as a diskette label
LAR	DOC	Program to manage file libraries (Documentation)
LAR	EXE	Executable file for above
MEMDRV	ASM	DOS 2.0 device driver to allow 640K RAM (Source program)
MEMDRV	SYS	Executable file for above
PI-COMP	COM	Replacement for DOS COMP command—better!
PI-COMP	DOC	Documentation for above
PRINT	C	Print text files on printer (Source program)
PRINT	EXE	Executable file for above
SHELL	COM	Fix for DOS SHELL command bug
SHELL	DOC	Documentation for above
ST	COM	Type files to full screen with PgUp/PgDn
ST	DOC	Documentation for above

Disk No 112	Computer Security Package Version 1.53	v1.3 DS

Computer security package is a set of user-supported for encrypting data files to prevent unauthorized access or for transmission across phone lines.

COPYRIGH	T	Copyright notes—disk not for export
READ	ME	Notes from the author
AUTOEXEC	BAT	Auto execute file
PC-CODE1	EXE	Encodes/decodes files
PC-CODE2	EXE	Encodes/decodes text files

PC-HELP	EXE	Type "PC-HELP" for help
PC-MENU	EXE	Execute other programs from this one
PC-TAMP1	EXE	Checks to see if files have been tampered with
PC-TAMP2	EXE	"
PC-ZERO	EXE	Writes "zeros" to file before deleting it
*	153	Program versions to use with BASRUN.EXE
DIALOG??	DOC	Sample dialogues for using programs
FILES	DOC	Documentation
I-8087	DOC	Source of 8087 BASIC compiler versions
PC-CODE1	DOC	Documentation for PC-CODE1
PC-CODE2	DOC	Documentation for PC-CODE2
PC-TAMP1	DOC	Documentation for PC-TAMPx
PC-ZERO	DOC	Documentation for PC-ZERO
NEW1	KEY	Key files
NEW2	KEY	"
SAMPLE	KEY	"
PC-STAT2	LOG	Sample files
SAMPLE1	COD	"
SAMPLE2	COD	"
SAMPLE3	COD	"
SAMPLE	MSG	Sample message

Disk No 113 — 3 User-Supported programs — v1.1

The 3 user-supported programs on this disk are: 1) the Datamorphics Screen package for greater display control, 2) PC-COMPARE for comparing data files, and; 3) DEFKEY, a keyboard reassignment program simular to Prokey.

		Datamorphics Screen programs
READ	ME	Brief description of Datamorphics Screen programs
INVOICE		Form for generating invoice for screen package
PC-BW	DOC	Documentation for PC-BW (3 pages)
PC-PAGE	DOC	Documentation for PC-PAGE (3 pages)
PC-TTY	DOC	Documentation for PC-TTY (4 pages)
PC-TTY	COM	Program modifies TTY emulation of BIOS
WRAP	COM	Sets line wrapping on or off
PC-BW	COM	Program to make monochrome screen calls work on color board
PAGE	COM	Modifies page length setting of PC-PAGE
PC-PAGE	COM	Prevents text from scrolling off screen
PC-BW	D11	DOS 1.1 optimized versions of screen programs
PC-PAGE	D11	"
PC-TTY	D11	" (Last file in Datamorphics Screen package)
		PC-COMPARE 1.30
RUN	BAT	Invokes the PC-COMPARE 4-part screen tutorial and program
COMPARE1	DOC	Part of PC-COMPARE documentation
COMPARE2	DOC	Part of PC-COMPARE documentation

COMPARE3	DOC	Part of PC-COMPARE documentation
COMPARE4	DOC	Part of PC-COMPARE documentation
COMPARE5	DOC	Part of PC-COMPARE documentation
COMPARE6	DOC	Part of PC-COMPARE documentation
COMPLETE	DOC	Documentation for COMPARE.COM to be printed out (3 pages)
PRINTDOC	BAT	Used to send COMPLETE.DOC to the printer
SAMP1	TXT	Sample file to be used with RUN.BAT
SAMP2	TXT	Sample file to be used with RUN.BAT
COPYCOMP	BAT	Makes a backup PC-COMPARE files from Drive A to Drive B
COMPARE	COM	The COMPARE program itself
CLS	COM	Utility to clear the screen, for those running under DOS 1.10
BEEP	COM	Used by PC-COMPARE
FILES	LST	Listing of the PC-COMPARE files
		DEFKEY
PROGRAM	DOC	Instructions for running DEFKEY program
DEFKEY	BAS	Program to reassign keyboard keys (Requires DOS 2.0)
DEFKEY	BAT	Batch file to automatically run DEFKEY program
DEFKEY	DOC	Instructions for running DEFKEY program (3 pages)
KEYS	BAS	Program to redefine BASIC program keys
BASICAK	BAT	Loads BASIC and runs KEYS.BAS from DOS
MOD100IN	BAS	Program to load files from Radio Shack Model 100
MOD100IN	DOC	Documentation for MOD100IN.BAS (5 pages)

Disk No 114 — Assembly Language Tutorial and More — v1

ASMTUT	DOC	Tutorial on Assembly Language programming
BASCOM	DOC	Four patches for the BASIC Compiler
FPLOT	BAS	Plots math functions in polar and Cartesian coordinates
FPLOT	DOC	Documentation file for FPLOT.BAS
KBDFIX	BAS	Fix for keyboard buffer program in September Softalk
NEWCLOCK	SYS	Fix for DOS 2.0 clock update function
NEWCLOCK	DOC	Documentation file for NEWCLOCK.SYS
PCT3VT	BAS	Adds Vidtex, VT52, VT100 & ANSI cursor control to PC-Talk III
PROFEEL	DOC	Review of Sony KX 1211 HG monitor/TV
CABLE	DOC	Procedure for making a cable for the Sony Profeel
TERM	BAS	Adds auto-dial and auto log-on to IBM ASYSC. Comm. 2.0
TERM	DOC	Documentation file for TERM.BAS
TREND123	MAC	LOTUS 123 macro for straight line/exponential curves
TREND123	DOC	Documentation file for TREND123.MAC
UASMLS	EXE	Formats DEBUG unassemble output file
UASMLS	DOC	Documentation file for UASMLS.EXE

Disk No 115		UTILITIES #4	v1
FREE	DOC	Catalog of user-supported software	
SURF87	EXE	Produces wave forms on graphics printer (Requires 8087)	
SURFPR	BAS	Printer installation program for SURF87.EXE	
SURF87	DOC	Documentation file for SURF87.EXE	
SQUEEZE	EXE	File compression program	
USQUEEZ	EXE	Uncompress program	
SQUSQ	DOC	Documentation file for SQUEEZ.EXE and UNSQUZ.EXE	
DSKHND	BAS	Disk handler program from October Softalk	
DHDEMO	BAS	Demo program for DSKHND.BAS	
123KEY	PRO	PROKEY file to enable numeric keypad with LOTUS 123	
123KEY	BAT	Batch file to run LOTUS 123 with PROKEY	
123KEY	DOC	Documentation file for 123KEY.PRO	
NOCOLOR	ASM	Suppress color signal when using mono monitor on C/G adapter	
NOCOLOR	COM	Executable program file	
NOCOLOR	DOC	Documentation file for NOCOLOR.COM	
SCROLL	BAS	Scroll window program from PC Magazine, October, 1983, page 650	
PINUP1	PIC	Pinup picture; COPY to LPT1:	
PINUP2	PIC	Pinup picture; COPY to LPT1:	
PINUP3	PIC	Pinup picture; COPY to LPT1:	
PINUP4	PIC	Pinup picture; COPY to LPT1:	

Disk No 116 **microGOURMET—Volume 1** **v1**

MicroGOURMET is a set of dBASE II data files containing information about foods.

READ	ME	Notes about microGOURMET programs and listing documentation
GOURMET	HI	Version of microGOURMET for 360K and HDU disk drives (rename .PRG)
GOURMET	LOW	Version of microGOURMET for single-sided disk drives (rename .PRG)
ITEM	DBF	microGOURMET dBASE II database file
SHOP	DBF	microGOURMET dBASE II database file
TYPE	NDX	microGOURMET dBASE II index file
NUMBER	NDX	microGOURMET dBASE II index file
ITEM	NDX	microGOURMET dBASE II index file
MANUAL	DOC	microGOURMET manual in listable DOS file format

Disk No 117 — microGOURMET—Volume 2 — v1

GOURMET	DBF	microGOURMET dBASE II database file
MANUAL	TXT	microGOURMET manual (WORDSTAR format)
UNWS	BAS	Program for converting WORDSTAR files to DOS files

Disk No 118 — QSYS DOS Menu & Security Package Version 3.0 — v2 DS

QSYS is an operating environment, menu system, an appointment calendar and message system. Features include password access for up to 24 users and an extensive menu system. Documentation for QSYS is on disk No 278.

QSYS	EXE	Main QSYS program
AUTOEXEC	BAT	Installation startup procedure batch file
QINST	EXE	Part of QSYS
QMSG	EXE	Message handler
QCNFG	EXE	Part of QSYS
QINT	EXE	Part of QSYS
QLDR	COM	Part of QSYS
CONFIG	SYS	Initial bootup file
MEMBRAIN	EXE	RAMdisk
MEMBRAIN	SYS	RAMdisk initial bootup file

Disk No 119 — ABC Database — v1.1 DS

ABCFILE	EXE	ABC database main program
ABCFILE	HLP	Help data
ABCFILE	DOC	Documentation
ABCONVRT	BAS	Convert files to ABC format
AUTOEXEC	BAT	Boot start up file
DBII-ABC	EXE	Translate dBASE II files to ABC
NUMSAM	CFG	Sample configuration
NUMSAM	DAT	Sample program data
NUMSAM	NUM	Part of sample program
NUMSAM1	NDX	Sample program
README	1ST	Initial documentation
SAMPLE	CFG	Sample configuration
SAMPLE	DAT	Sample program data
SAMPLE	NUM	Part of sample program
SAMPLE1	NDX	Sample program

Disk No 120		PC-CHESS	v1
SETUP	BAT	For 2-drive systems this BAT file will create a useable program and documentation diskette (double-sided drive required) or separate documentation and program diskettes.	
PCCHESS	PRT	Compressed PCCHESS.PRT (Documentation in printer output format)	
PCCHESS	EXE	Initialization/setup program	
PCCH1	EQE	Compressed PCCH1.EXE (Player vs computer program)	
PCCH2	EQE	Compressed PCCH2.EXE (2 player program)	
UNSQ	EXE	Program to expand the compressed files	

Disk No 121 — Letus A-B-C #1 — v1 DS

Letus A-B-C is a database (in PC-FILE III format) containing references to articles in most of the major PC magazines. It is designed to work with PC-FILE III. (Disk No 5).

SOFT82	DTA	Softalk 1982 magazine reference files
SOFT82	INX	"
SOFT82	HDR	"
SOFT82	KEY	"
PCMAG82	DTA	PC Magazine 1982 magazine reference files
PCMAG82	INX	"
PCMAG82	HDR	"
PCMAG82	KEY	"
PCAGE82	DTA	PC Age 1982 magazine reference files
PCAGE82	INX	"
PCAGE82	HDR	"
PCAGE82	KEY	"
BYTE82	DTA	Byte 1982 magazine reference files
BYTE82	INX	"
BYTE82	HDR	"
BYTE82	KEY	"
LETUS	BAT	Batch file for starting Letus
LOGO82	COM	Generates Letus logo
PLOGO82	COM	"
LETUS	DOC	Documentation for using Letus (11 pages)

Disk No 122		Letus A-B-C #2	v1 DS
SOFT83	DTA	Softalk 1983 magazine reference files	
SOFT83	INX	"	
SOFT83	HDR	"	
SOFT83	KEY	"	
PCMAG83A	DTA	PC Magazine first 6 months 1983 magazine reference files	

PCMAG83A	INX	"
PCMAG83A	HDR	"
PCMAG83A	KEY	"
PCAGE83	DTA	PC Age 1983 magazine reference files
PCAGE83	INX	"
PCAGE83	HDR	"
PCAGE83	KEY	"
LETUS	BAT	Batch file for starting Letus
LOGO83A	COM	Generates Letus logo
PLOGO83	COM	"

Disk No 123 Letus A-B-C #3 v1 DS

PCW83	DTA	PC World 1983 magazine reference files
PCW83	INX	"
PCW83	HDR	"
PCW83	KEY	"
PCMAG83B	DTA	PC Magazine second 6 months 1983 magazine reference files
PCMAG83B	INX	"
PCMAG83B	HDR	"
PCMAG83B	KEY	"
PCTEC83	DTA	PC Tech Journal 1983 magazine reference files
PCTEC83	INX	"
PCTEC83	HDR	"
PCTEC83	KEY	"
BYTE83	DTA	Byte 1983 magazine reference files
BYTE83	INX	"
BYTE83	HDR	"
BYTE83	KEY	"
LETUS	BAT	Batch file for starting Letus
LOGO83B	COM	Generates Letus logo
PLOGO83	COM	"

Disk No 124 — Extended Batch Language Version 2.0 by Seaware — v1

The extended batch language is a program which adds additional features to the batch processing supported by DOS. With the extended batch language, you can write batch file programs that prompt for responses and keep track of values of variables.

BACKUP	BAT	Utility to backup BAT
BAT	COM	Extended Batch Language
BATDEMO	BAT	Demonstrations—number guessing, menu, directory, etc.
BATDOC	BAT	Documentation start
EDIT	BAT	General purpose "editor & file to be edited" caller
ERRATA		Items corrected from previous BAT versions
TELE	BAT	Telephone list sample program
VCOPY	BAT	Demo of READSCRN command to copy file with 80 column display

Disk No 125 — HOST-III Public Bulletin Board Package — v1 DS

This disk allows your PC to act as a Bulletin Board and have others call you, upload and download files and leave messages. See Disk No 152 and 212 for simular systems.

HOST-III	DOC	Documentation for HOST-III
HOSTCALL	DOC	Documentation for HOSTCALL
HOST-III	EXE	Program that receives telephone calls
HOSTCALX	EXE	Program that initiates telephone calls—Part 1
HOSTCL2X	EXE	Program that initiates telephone calls—Part 2
HOSTCALL	BAT	Batch file that starts up HOSTCALX
README		Information about HOST-III use & other programs available
CS-NEW		New CompuServe (1/84) services, ie, Electronic Gourmet
RACKET	BBS	Tennis-oriented BBS example

Disk No 126 — dBASE II Items — v1

BACKUP	PRG	dBASE II backup routine
SUPERBAK	PRG	dBASE II backup routine
STATEX	NDX	dBASE II state & zipcode checker
STATEZIP	DBF	Part of dBASE II state & zipcode checker
STATEZIP	PRG	Part of dBASE II state & zipcode checker
DOC	TXT	Documentation
		dBASE II form letter generator
MAIL	PRG	dBASE II form letter generator
MAIL	DBF	Part of dBASE II form letter generator
MAILENTR	PRG	Part of dBASE II form letter generator
MAILFMT	FMT	Part of dBASE II form letter generator
MAILINFO	PRG	Part of dBASE II form letter generator
MAILLAB	PRG	Part of dBASE II form letter generator
MAILLTTR	PRG	Part of dBASE II form letter generator

MIS	DBF	Part of dBASE II form letter generator
PRINT	TXT	Part of dBASE II form letter generator
		dBASE II mailing label manager
ML2	PRG	dBASE II mailing label manager
ML2	DOC	Documentation for dBASE II mailing label manager
ML2	DBF	Part of dBASE II mailing label manager
ML2*	PRG	Mailing label manager program files (16)
MLABEL5	PRG	Part of dBASE II mailing label manager
		dBASE II library routines
ADDSUB	PRG	dBASE II library routine
BLANK	PRG	"
ENTER	PRG	"
GUIDE	PRG	"
NAMEBRK	PRG	"
REFDEX	NDX	"
REFERALS	DBF	"
REFS	PRG	"
SEARCH	PRG	"
SHOWFIL	PRG	"
SOME	DBF	"
SORTED	DBF	"
STRINGS	DBF	"
SUBDEX	NDX	"
SUBJECTS	DBF	"
SUBS	PRG	"

Disk No 127 PC-MUSICIAN Version 1.9 v1.2

With PC-MUSICIAN you can create and play songs on your PC. PC-MUSICIAN is a user-supported program.

READ	ME	How to list documentation
AUTOEXEC	BAT	Batch file for automatic execution
PRINTDOC	BAT	Batch file to print documentation
MAKECOPY	BAT	Batch file to files to disk b:
MUSICIAN	EXE	PC-MUSICIAN main program
TXTMUSIC	EXE	PC-MUSICIAN main program to use with monochrome display
EXNOTES	FNT	Part of PC-MUSICIAN
MUSICIAN	DOC	Documentation for PC-MUSICIAN (13 pages)
MAXWELLS	SNG	Song files
DONA	SNG	"
BUTCHER	SNG	"
SHEEPMAY	SNG	"
OLDWOMAN	SNG	"
SHEWALKS	SNG	"
MICHELLE	SNG	"

YESTRDAY	SNG	"
I_WILL	SNG	"
YNKEDODL	SNG	"
JNGLEBLS	SNG	"
MAKEMONO	BAT	Setup routine for monochrome display & > = 128K memory
MAKEG64	BAT	Setup routine for graphics display & 64K memory
MAKEM64	BAT	Setup routine for monochrome display & 64K memory
GMUS64	EXE	Main program—see MAKEG64.BAT
TMUS64	EXE	Main program—see MAKEM64.BAT

Disk No 128 dBASE II Utilities v1

ANIMAL	BAS	Guess the animal game
ANIMAL	GME	Sample data file of animals for ANIMAL.BAS
BANNER	BAS	Make large banners on the screen
LBANNER	BAS	Make large banners on the printer
BARIC	BAS	Two person Tron like game
HAMURABI	BAS	Game—be king for a ten year term
PICTURE	BAS+	3-D graphic demo (Requires color/graphics)
PINWHEEL	BAS	Animated program listing
KBD_FIX	BAS	Creates KBD_FIX.COM
KBD_FIX	COM	Increase keyboard buffer to 159 characters
DAY	PRG	dBASE II program to find day of week
DATE	PRG	dBASE II program to set date from system date
TIME	PRG	dBASE II program to get system time
COMSTRIP	PRG	dBASE II program to strip comments from other dBASE II programs
GEMINI	ABS	Fix to use DOS 2.0 graphic dump on Gemini printer
CATALOG	TXT	List of files on this disk
DBS	PRT	Documentation for DBS.EXE program (9 pages)
README		How to list DBS documentation
DBS	EXE	Program to generate dBASE II screens

Disk No 129 PC-DIAL v2 DS

PC-DIAL is a modem communications program from Jim Button, the author of PC-FILE III. It has the ability to create autologon scripts but lacks some of the functions of PC-TALK III. With this version the author provides a special program just for PCjr owners to communicate with.

PC-DIAL	COM	PC-DIAL main program (For modem communications)
PC-DIAL	PRO	Initial setup file for PC-DIAL
ENCRYPT	EXE	File encryption main program
ENCRYPT	DOC	Documentation for file encryption program
BACKSCRL	DOC	Documentation for BACKSCROLL program
BACKSCRL	COM	BACKSCROLL main program
DOC	BAT	Program to print PC-DIAL documentation
PC-DIAL	DOC	PC-DIAL documentation file
JR-DIAL	COM	PC-DIAL for the PC jr
READ	ME	Introduction letter for JR-DIAL

Disk No 130 Pascal Tools—Volume 1 v1 DS

The Pascal Tools are routines adapted from the book "Software Tools in Pascal" which are useful for processing and extracting information from text files.

README1		Notes about using Pascal Tools
ARCHIVE	EXE	File archiving program
CHANGE	EXE	Changes patterns in text
CHARCNT	EXE	Count characters in input
ECHOARG	EXE	Echo arguments to output
FINDP	EXE	Find patterns in text
FMT	EXE	Produce formatted output
KWIC	EXE	Produce lines for KWIC index
CITOH	FNT	Printer setup files
FMT	FNT	"
MX80	FNT	"
MAN	IM	"
ARCHIVE	MAN	Portions of manual
CHANGE	MAN	"
CHARCNT	MAN	"
ECHOARG	MAN	"
FINDP	MAN	"
FMT	MAN	"
KWIC	MAN	"
LINECNT	MAN	"

MACRO	MAN	"
PRINTF	MAN	"
SORTF	MAN	"
TED	MAN	"
TOOLS	MAN	File used to print documentation—see readme file
TRANSLIT	MAN	Portions of manual
UNIQUE	MAN	"
UNROTATE	MAN	"
WORDCNT	MAN	"

Disk No 131 — Pascal Tools—Volume 2 — v1 DS

README2		Notes about using Pascal tools
LINECNT	EXE	Counts number of lines in a text file
MACRO	EXE	Expands string definitions
PRINTF	EXE	Print files with headings
SORTF	EXE	Sort lines in text file
TED	EXE	Line editor for text files
TRANSLIT	EXE	Transliterate characters
UNIQUE	EXE	Deletes adjacent duplicate lines
UNROTATE	EXE	Formats lines for a KWIC index
WORDCNT	EXE	Counts words in standard inputs

Disk No 132 — Pascal Tools—Volume 3 — v1 DS

README3		Notes about using Pascal tools
ARCHIVE	AR	Source code for Pascal tools
CHARCNT	AR	"
ECHOARG	AR	"
FINDP	AR	"—needed for Change
FMT	AR	"
KWIC	AR	"
LINECNT	AR	"
MACRO	AR	"
PRIMS	AR	"—general primitives
PRINTF	AR	"
SORTF	AR	"—needed for sortf and KWIC
TED	AR	"
TRANSLIT	AR	"
UNIQUE	AR	"
UNROTATE	AR	"
UTILITY	AR	"—general utilities
WORDCNT	AR	"
GETFCB	ASM	Pascal callable routine to fill File Control Block (FCB)
GLOBCONS	INC	Include files

GLOBTYPS	INC	"
GLOBVARS	INC	"
CMDFILE	BAT	Batch files used to create utilities
LKTOOL	BAT	"
MK*	BAT	"
*	DCL	Procedure definition files
*	OBJ	Object files

Disk No 133 — Ultra-Utilities 4.0 — v2 DS

The Ultra-Utilities are a collection of useful tools everyone with a PC should have. With these utilites you can recover a file that you may have accidently erased (with U-FILE), modify and look into any file on a disk or create a database program written in BASIC (with U-MIND). Unsqueezed copies of files from this disk are on Disk No 245.

README	NOW	Instructions for files on disk
U-ZAP	EXE	Program to look at disk sectors
U-FILE	EXE	Modify/recover disk files
U-OPT	EQE	Squeezed U-OPT (Optomize) program
U-OPT	DQC	Squeezed documentation for U-OPT
U-FORMAT	EXE	Disk format utility
U-MIND	BQS	Squeezed U-MIND BASIC program
U-MIND	DQC	Squeezed documentation for U-MIND
SKELETON	BQS	Squeezed BASIC program for U-MIND
TEST	ATR	Part of U-MIND
TEST	HDR	Part of U-MIND
USQ	COM	Unsqueeze program
DOC41	TQT	Squeezed documentation for Ultra-Utilities—Part 1
DOC42	TQT	Squeezed documentation for Ultra-Utilities—Part 1

Disk No 134 — LISP — v1

8087	ASM	Assembler macros for 8087 instructions
AUTODEX	EXE	Fantastic fullscreen directory/file manipulator
CC	C	c source program checker, catches mismatched parens
DOSINTS	TXT	Tells all about secret DOS interrupt functions!
DOS_ERR	TXT	Information on DOS I/O redirection bugs
FIND	PAT	Patch to DOS FIND command, makes it a better filter
LOAD	COM	Load COM files bigger than 64K: LOAD <FILENAME>
LOAD	ASM	Source for above
MENUMAKR	BAS	Interactively create menus callable from BASIC

PIL	LSP	Micro-Prolog interpreter written in XLISP
PTURTLE	LSP	Programmable logo turtle written in XLISP
STEEPDES	APL	Steepest descent equation solution in APL
TURTLE	LSP	Interactive logo turtle programmed in XLISP
XLISP	DOC	Documentation for XLISP Interpreter
XLISP	EXE	A Lisp interpreter with object-oriented extensions

Disk No 135 — BBS Utilities #5 — v1

APLCHIP	DOC	Where to get an APL character generator chip for IBM APL
BASCOM	PAT	Fixes for BASCOM.COM (See BASCOM.TXT)
BASCOM	TXT	Instructions for program to fix all BASIC Compiler bugs!
BASLIB	PAT	Fixes for BASCOM.LIB
BASRUN	PAT	Fixes for BASRUN.LIB (See BASCOM.TXT)
DOSFTE	PAS	Part of DOSFUN.PAS
DOSFUN	INC	Part of DOSFUN.PAS
DOSFUN	PAS	Procedures for extended DOS file access from Pascal
DRIVER	ASM	Interrupt driven comm I/O driver for Lattice c
DRIVER	OBJ	Linkable module for above
FILKQQ	INC	Part of DOSFUN.PAS
FILUQQ	INC	Part of DOSFUN.PAS
IBMPCTIP	DOC	Tips on using PCDOS
LAR	DOC	Documentation for file library program
LAR	EXE	Program to combine files into libraries to save space
PAD	WKS	123 desktop-type worksheet, lots of useful functions
PATCHER	BAS	Program to apply patches to IBM BASIC (See BASCOM.TXT)
PRTSCRN	ASM	Replacement print screen driver, filters ctrl chars
PRTSCRN	COM	Executable version of above
SCAV2XX	ASM	Program to make diskette with bad sectors useable
SCAV2XX	COM	Executable version of above
SYSCOM	INC	Assembly language includes for DOS functions

Disk No 136 — PC-Picture Graphics by E. Ying — v1 DS

PC-Picture allows you to create graphics images on your color graphics card. An extensive library of readymade images is included with this user-supported program.

PCPG	EXE	Great graphics drawing package (Requires graphics board)
PCPG	FT?	Part of PC-Picture
PCPG	HLP	PC-Picture help file
PCPG	PIC	Part of PC-Picture
PCPG	SYM	Part of PC-Picture
DEMO*	GFL	Demo files for PC-Picture containing graphic immages

Disk No 137 — c Screen Editor — v1

This disk contains a complete screen editor written in the c language.

EDIT	EXE	Compiled program
READ	ME	Implementation notes (3 pages)
ED	DOC	Documentation of commands
ED*	C	Source files
ED11	A	Assembler source code for screen input and output
ED0	C	Include files
ED1	CCC	"
LINK	BAT	Batch file for linking program
LIST	BAT	Batch file list source files

Disk No 138 — BBS Utilities #6 — v1

BLYPROGS	DOC	General description of BLY programs
RE-VIEW	COM	BLY's color card support for 100-line virtual screen in DOS!
RE-VIEW	DOC	Documentation for above
ANSIPCH	EXE	Part of RE-VIEW
CLA	COM	Part of RE-VIEW
UP	COM	Part of RE-VIEW
BRICKS	EXE	BLY's version of BREAKOUT
SETPRN	COM	BLY's printer setup program
SETPRN	ASM	Source for above
SETPRN	DOC	Documentation for above
CASE	COM	BLY's resident utility for auto case switching during program entry
CASE	ASM	Source for above
VTYPE	EXE	BLY's replacement for DOS type command, many extensions
VTYPE	C	Source for above
VTYPE	DOC	Documentation for above
C	ASM	DOS 2.0 version of entry point routine for Lattice c
_MAIN	C	DOS 2.0 version of main routine for Lattice c
IOS1_20	ASM	DOS 2.0 version of level 1 I/O routines for Lattice c
ENVIRON	DOC	How to access DOS environment variables from batch files
LIBRIAN	MRG	Merge file to upgrade IBM diskette librarian to DOS 2.0
LIBRIAN	DOC	Documentation for above
NORTPAT2	DOC	Patch to Norton utilities 2.0 to support teac 42 track drives
RMSPC	COM	Interrupt handler for diagnosing parity errors
RMSPC	ASM	Source for above
VECTS	EXE	Program to display interrupt vectors

Disk No 139 — BBS Utilities #7 — v1 DS

BAT200D	COM	Version 2.00d of SEAWARE BAT program
ANSI	BAT	Demonstrations of buggy interactions between BAT and ANSI.SYS
DIAL	BAT	Front end dialer for PC-TALK III (Uses BAT)
EDIT	BAT	Generalized editor or word processor invoker (Uses BAT)
FORMAT	BAT	Generates a formatted listing to screen or printer (Uses BAT)
FSKEL	BAT	Skeleton for function-key driven user menu (Uses BAT)
MENU	BAT	Another menu system for BAT (Uses BAT and UTILITY.BAT)
TELE	BAT	Online telephone directory (Uses BAT)
UTILITY	BAT	Required by MENU.BAT
VCOPY	BAT	Copies multiple files with yes/no prompt for each (Uses BAT)
DOSPATH	C	Lattice c functions for DOS 2.0 command line args and pathnames
CHAROP	ASM	Used by DOSPATH.C. Reads/sets switch char and device avail
DIR201	BAS	Diskette cataloging program. Very friendly user interface
DIR201	EXE	Compiled version of above
LORES	BAS	Does 160x100 16-color graphics (The PC's secret graphics mode!)
LORES	DOC	Documentation for 160x100 graphics support package
LORES	ASM	Assembly language subroutines for 160x100 16-color graphics
LORES	OBJ	Assembled version of LORES.ASM
LODEMO	BAS	Demo of 160x100 16-color graphics on IBM PC
LORES	EXE	Another 160x100 demo program
LORES	USR	BASIC-callable 160x100 graphics functions
NUSQ	COM	Assembly-coded version of unsqueeze program—super fast!
PRINTXT1	CMD	dbase II command to print multiple text lines on screen
PRINTXT1	DOC	Documentation for above
PRINTXT1	INC	Include routines for PRINTXT1.CMD.

Disk No 140 — BBS Utilities #8 — v1

EJLUTIL	LBR	A library of useful utilities. Unpack with LU.EXE
EJLUTIL	DOC	Documentation for the utility library
FLCHART	WKS	123 worksheet macros for drawing flowcharts
FREE	COM	Reports free space on hard or floppy disk
GCOPY	EXE	Choose multiple files to copy from full-screen menu
GCOPY	DOC	Documentation for GCOPY.EXE
GDEL	EXE	Choose multiple files to delete from full-screen menu
GDEL	DOC	Documentation for GDEL.EXE
INTOOLS	PAS	A set of interactive keyboard I/O procedures and functions
LU	EXE	The latest and best library maintainer
LU	DOC	Documentation for LU.EXE
M8087	MAC	Macros for issuing 8087 instructions
PAS87	ASM	Assembler subroutines for using 8087 from Pascal
P87_INT		Pascal interface to PAS87.ASM routines

SQPC161	EXE	The latest file squeeze utility
USQLC10	COM	The latest file unsqueeze utility
SQ-USQ	DOC	Documentation for SQPC161.EXE and USQLC10.COM
X2COLOR	COM	Copies the monochrome screen to the color display

Disk No 141 — BBS Utilities #9 — v1

123PREP	EXE	Converts a simple text file to a form loadable by 123
123PREP	DOC	Documentation for 123PREP.EXE
AID	BAS	A BASIC programming development aid
AID	EXE	Compiled version of AID.BAS
AID	BAT	Batch file for invoking AID
AID	DOC	Documentation for the AID system
SCREENIN	BAS	Full-screen formatted input subroutine for BASIC
SCREENIN	DOC	Documentation for SCREENIN.BAS
W20	COM	Directory "wash" program—list/copy/view/delete multiple files

Disk No 142 — BBS Utilities #10 — v1

AFT8087	MAC	Assembly macros and interface for Fortran access to 8087
BASSUB	BAS	Call DOS 2.0 functions from BASIC
BASSUB	OBJ	Part of BASSUB.BAS
BIOS	MAC	Assembly macros for accessing all BIOS functions
CLINK	COM	Program to load text fonts for graphics display
CLINK	ASM	Source for CLINK.COM
DOS	MAC	Assembly macros for accessing all DOS 2.0 functions
GRDRAW LF		Logo program for interactive graphics drawing
HP	C	HP-style RPN calculator in c (Requires TRAN.C—see below)
KVUTIL	COM	Display control functions (Auto screen blank, scroll lock...)
KVSET	COM	Part of KVUTIL.COM
KVUTIL	DOC	Documentation for KVUTIL.COM
LDIR	EXE	List the table of contents of library files made by LAR and LU
LDIR	DOC	Documentation for LDIR.EXE
LDIR	C	Source for LDIR.EXE
LTYPE	EXE	Type a library file without extracting it—very useful
LTYPE	C	Source for LTYPE.EXE
LISP	PAS	A simple LISP interpreter in Pascal
PCUTIL	COM	Several screen and keyboard utility functions
PCUTIL	DOC	Documentation for PCUTIL.DOC
TRAN	C	Transcendental functions in c
UTILITES	MAC	A set of utility macros and subroutines for IBM Assembler
VUE	EXE	View file in hex and ASCII
XENIX	ASM	Xenix-like subroutines for accessing DOS 2.0 functions in c

Disk No 143		BBS Utilities #11	v1 DS
CMP	COM	Intelligent file compare—works on binary files of different size	
CMP	DOC	Documentation for CMP.COM	
COPYFLD	PRG	dBASE II program to copy fields from one file to another	
COPYFLD	DOC	Documentation for COPYFLD.PRG	
D	EXE	Display selected diskette sides/sectors/tracks	
D	DOC	Documentation for D.EXE	
PC-ZAP	EXE	Apply patches to disk(ette)—supports auto-patch files	
PC-ZAP	DOC	Documentation for PC-ZAP.EXE	
PROJECTS	BAS	Home projects database manager	
PROJECTS	DAT	Sample database for PROJECTS.BAS	
RUSQ	EXE	Another (different) file unsqueezer—try this if others fail!	
SCRIPT	DOC	A Crosstalk script for menu-driven operation	

Disk No 144		Fabula 1	v1
DNXSD	DOC	Documentation for .BAT files	
DN	BAT	Sorts Directory by fileName	
DX	BAT	Sorts Directory by eXtension	
DS	BAT	Sorts Directory by Size	
DD	BAT	Sorts Directory by Date	
DXSAVE	BAT	Sorts Directory by eXtension and saves sorted directory in file DXS on default-drive disk	
TALK450	MRG	Adds 450 baud capacity to PC-TALK III	
TALK450	DOC	Documentation for TALK450.MRG	
SCROLLK	COM	Enables SCROLLLOCK key	
SCROLLK	DOC	Documentation for SCROLLK	
SCRNSAVE	COM	Prevents screen "burn-in"	
SQIBM	COM	Squeezes files	
SQIBM	DOC	Documentation for SQIBM	
USQIBM	COM	Unsqueezes files	
USQIBM	DOC	Documentation for USQIBM	

Disk No 145		Fabula 2	v1
ASMGEN	COM	Converts EXE and COM to ASM files	
ASMGEN	DOC	Documentation for ASMGEN.COM	
BASICAID	BAS	Squeezes and unsqueezes files	
BASICAID	DOC	Documentation for BASICAID.BAS	
BINSIX	DOC	Documentation for BINSIX.DOC	
BINSIX	EXE	New squeeze program, 20% less then hex	
COMP	BAS	Compares two tokenized BASIC files	
CROSSOPT		Data file for CROSSREF.EXE	
DIP-MEM	COM	Bypasses power-up memory test	

DIP-MEM	DOC	Documentation for DIP-MEM.COM
MAKEDATA	BAS	Checksumed data files for COM/EXE
RSVD	COM	Changes the size of VDISK
SQIBM	COM	Squeezes files for faster transfer
SQIBM	DOC	Documentation for SQIBM.DOC
TABS	BAS	Puts tab codes in or removes them
UPNUM	COM	Shows if NumLock or CapsLock in use
UPNUM	DOC	Documentation for UPNUM.DOC
USQIBM	COM	Unsqueezes files squeezed by SQIBM
USQIBM	DOC	Documentation for USQIBM.COM
VDISK	COM	160k RAM disk program (see RSVD.COM)
WRITECOM	BAS	Converts data from MAKEDATA.BAS to EXE/COM
WRT	DOC	DOC for WRTE.COM and WRTP.COM
WRTE	COM	Erases read-only attribute from a file
WRTP	COM	Sets read-only attribute of a file

Disk No 146 — EasyRite/LabelFile from GINACO — v2 DS

		EasyRite
ER	EXE	Word processor program (compiled)
DEMOFILE		Sample Word Processor file
EASYRITE	BAS	Word processor source code
FACTS		EasyRite instructions
TEXT	ONE	Sample text file—information about EasyRite/LabelFile
TEXT	TWO	Sample text file—information about Blueberry from GINACO
		LabelFile
LF	EXE	Label/File program (compiled)
LABLFILE	BAS	Source for Label/File program
README		Notes about using programs (short!)

Disk No 147 — SDB—A Simple Database System — v1 DS

SDB is a partly relational database system written in c

README		Note about programs on this disk
SDBGEN	ARF	Batch files for generating system
SDBGEN	BAT	"
SDBGREP	BAT	"
SDBLUMP	BAT	"
SDBXC	BAT	"

SDB	EXE	Database program
SDB	HLP	Help screen
SDB	MEM	Document file (30 pages)
*	C	c Source files
*	OBJ	Object files
SDBIO	H	Source files

Disk No 148 XLISP Version 1.4 v2 DS

This is a version of the LISP language. LISP is the preferred language for artificial intelligence. This is version 1.4 from the author.

XLISP	MEM	XLISP documentation (34 pages)
README	TXT	Description of files
XLISP	EXE	XLISP for MS-DOS (CI-C86 small model)
		Sample programs
ART	LSP	Code from the Byte article on XLISP
TRACE	LSP	Simple trace facility
FACT	LSP	Factorial function
PT	LSP	Programmable turtle program
INIT	LSP	Sample initialization file
PROLOG	LSP	Tiny prolog interpreter
		XLISP Source code
XLINIT	C	Initialization code
XLREAD	C	Reader (Including the load function)
XLIO	C	I/O support routines
XLOBJ	C	Object-oriented programming support
XLSTR	C	String functions
XLSTUB	C	Stubs for XLOBJ.C (To remove object support)
XLJUMP	C	Non-local jump routines
XLBIND	C	Symbol binding routines
XLSYS	C	System functions
XLSYM	C	Symbol table routines
XLISP	C	The main entry point
XLSUBR	C	Built-in SUBR/FSUBR support routines
XLSETF	C	SETF function
XLDBUG	C	Debugging and error handling routines
XLPRIN	C	Printer
XLMATH	C	Arithmetic functions
XLCONT	C	Control functions
XLLIST	C	List functions
XLBFUN	C	BASIC functions

XLFIO	C	File I/O functions
XLDMEM	C	Dynamic memory routines (Garbage collector)
XLFTAB	C	Function initialization table
XLGLOB	C	Global variable declarations
XLEVAL	C	Evaluator
XLISP	H	XLISP include file

Disk No 149 — c Utilities — v1

LUMP	DOC	Documentation for LUMP
LUMP	C	Source code for LUMP
UNLUMP	C	Source code for UNLUMP
LUMP	EXE	Program to lump files together
UNLUMP	EXE	Program to split files apart
GREP	DOC	Documentation for GREP
GREP	EXE	Unix like grep command to find strings in files
GREP	C	Source code for LUMP
XC	DOC	Documentation for XC
XC	C	Source code for LUMP
XC	EXE	Xreference utility for c programs
CC	DOC	Documentation for CC
CC	EXE	c program checker
CC	OBJ	Object file for CC
CC	C	Source code for CC
README		Notes about the files on this disk

Disk No 150 — IBM BBS by Gene Plantz — v1 DS

BBSCOMP	BAT	BAT startup file
BBSLOGO	BAS	Logo displayed upon BBS startup
CALLERS		List of each logon, excepting SYSOP
COUNTERS		Workfile containing next message #, next caller, etc.
FLASH		File displayed after WELCOME file
HARDWARE		Information file on hardware prices
HELP	BBS	Help file
IBBS	BAS	Compiler BASIC source code
IBBS	DOC	Limited documentation
IBBS	EXE	Compiler object code for IBBS
MESSAGES		Main messages file
NEWCOM		Message file for first-time callers
RBBSUTIL	BAS	Source code for file cleanup utility
RBBSUTIL	EXE	Compiled object code for file cleanup utility

SOFTWARE		Information file on software prices
SUMMARY		Messages summary file
USERS		List of logon IDs
WELCOME		First file displayed after logon
XFER	HLP	Help file for file transfer function
XFERLIST		List of files that can be transferred

Disk No 151 — Finance Manager from Genesis Software 3.1 — v2.1 DS

README		Description of files listed below
FM	DOC	Documentation file (55K)
FM	EXE	Main program.
FMUTIL	EXE	Configuration program.
FM	DEF	FM system file.
FM	CNF	System active configuration data file.
IBM	CNF	Configuration file for IBM/Epson printer (copy to fm.cnf)
JUKI	CNF	Configuration file for Juki 6100 printer (copy to fm.cnf)
AUTOEXEC	BAT	Autoboot batch file.
INSTALL	BAT	Batch procedure to install/configure program for first use
WORK	NAM	Sample: Small business...name.
WORK	CRT	Sample: Small business...chart of accounts.
WORK	TRN	Sample: Small business...transaction file.
HOME	NAM	Sample: Personal use.....name.
HOME	CRT	Sample: Personal use.....chart of accounts.
HOME	TRN	Sample: Personal use.....transaction file.

Disk No 152 — RBBS for the IBM PC — v1 DS

This is a really nifty package from the Capital PC Users Group that allows you to set your own PC up as a BBS.

-README-	DOC	Initial suggestions for starting out
BULLET1		Sample bulletin
BULLETIN		Menu for bulletins
CAPITAL	PC	Capital IBM PC Users Group information
CONFIG	BAS	Sets up RBBS configuration
DIR		Description of file directories
DIR99		Description of most recent file uploads
FIXFILES	BAS	Cleans up caller file
HELP01		User help file—commands
HELP02		User help file—functions supported
HELP03		User help file—message protection
HELP04		User help file—editing messages
HELP05		User help file—file menu
HELP06		User help file—file subsystem extra help
HELP07		User help file—message read help file

MENU1		Menu—SYSOP utilities
MENU1G		Menu—SYSOP utilities—with border
MENU2		Menu—main RBBS menu
MENU2G		Menu—main RBBS menu—with border
MENU3		Menu—RBBS files
MENU3G		Menu—RBBS files—with border
NEWUSER		Welcome message
RBBS-PC	BAS	BASIC version
RBBS-PC	DOC	Documentation
RBBS-PC	EXE	Compiled version
RBBS-PC	REM	Remarks used by RBBS-PC.xxx programs
STARTUP	BAT	Installs RBBS onto two diskettes
USRINIT1	BAS	Clears user download/upload counts
USRINIT2	BAS	Reads callers file & updates
UTSPACE	OBJ	Part of RBBS-PC.xxx programs

Disk No 153 **Norland Software Hangman Version 4.1** **v1.1**

HANGMAN	EXE	Nifty Hangman game—larger vocabulary than most versions
AUTOEXEC	BAT	Automatic start-up file if set up on bootable disk
README		Start-up instructions
DOCUMENT		Documentation file
HANGADV1	WRD	Part of HANGMAN.EXE—Quotations
HANGBAS1	WRD	Part of HANGMAN.EXE—Riddles
HANGCMT	REF	Part of HANGMAN.EXE
HANGED1	WRD	Part of HANGMAN.EXE—Vocabulary words
HANGMAN	REF	Part of HANGMAN.EXE
HANGMUSE	MSC	Part of HANGMAN.EXE—Music

Disk No 154 **Printer Art** **v1**

CINDY	NUD	Nude female
CLOWN	ART	Clown
DARTH	BAS	Darth Vader
DRU	NUD	Nude female
ELLEN	NUD	Nude female
ENTEP	BAS	Enterprise (From Startrek)
GIRL	NUD	Nude female
HONEY	NUD	Nude female
JANE	NUD	Nude female
PANTHR	PIC	Pink Panther
PHANT	PIC	McDonnell Douglas F-4E Phantom II
PINUP1	NUD	Nude female
ROXANN	NUD	Nude female
SANTA	BAS	Santa and his raindeer

SCHROE	DER	Schroeder (From Peanuts)
SHUTTL	PIC	Challenger space shuttle
SNOOPY	BAS	Snoopy
SNOOPY3	BAS	Snoopy
SUSAN	NUD	Nude female

Disk No 155 Budget-Taskplan-Loan v1.2

		BUDGETRK 3.3
BUDGETRK	BAS	Budget tracking program
BUDGETRK	DOC	Documentation for BUDGETRK.BAS (2 pages)
BUDGETRK	MOD	Part of BUDGETRK
		TASKPLAN
TASKPLAN	BAS	Task planning program
DESCRIPT	DOC	Task plan documentation
SAMPLE	TPN	Sample task plan
		LOAN
LEAS-BY1	BAS	Lease—buy analysis for auto purchase or lease
LOAN-MTG	BAS	Loan mortagage schedules, after tax impact
LOANSVGS	BAS	Loan payment solutions

Disk No 156 IBM Users Group Newsletter #1 v1 DS

This is an electronic newsletter published by IBM Boca Raton. It will run on either a color or mono display. To read it, type NEWS. You will be presented with a menu of topics and stories, including new product announcements, tips, techniques and other stuff. The newsletter includes some programs also.

Disk No 157 IBM Users Group Newsletter #2 v1 DS

Second issue of IBM's Users Group Newsletter. To read it, type NEWS.

Disk No 158 IBM Users Group Newsletter #3 v1 DS

Third issue of IBM's Users Group Newsletter. To read it, type NEWS.

Disk No 159 PC Firing Line/PC Underground #1 v1 DS

This is the first issue of the PC Firing Line Newsletter on disk. To read it, type PCFL.

0	BAT	Use with LIST1 files below
1-2-3	TXT	LOTUS article by J. Benedict
8087	REV	Book review by G. Hearne
ADA1	TXT	ADA G. Noel

ADA1CMP	REV	ADA compiler review by G. Noel
ASM1	TXT	Introduction to Assembler by B. Salkin
BIGDEAL	ASM	Sample ASM program
C1	TXT	UNIX article by D. Roady
COLORFUL	EXE	Changes colors for foreground/background/border
CPYRIGHT	TXT	Copyright notice
DEBUG	PAT	Sample
DOS1	TXT	Article by D. Buresh
DOS2	TXT	Article by R. Levaro (DOS 2.0 bug)
DOS3	TXT	DOS interrupts
FORT1	TXT	Fortran Ellipses
GRABBAG	ASM	Source for GRABBAG.EXE
GRABBAG	EXE	Change colors for foreground/background
INTRO	TXT	Introduction to PC Firing Line
LISP1	TXT	LISP article by G. Rader
LIST1	ADA	ADA routines
LIST1	ASM	ASM routines
LIST1	C	c routines
LIST1	PAS	Pascal routines
MEMORY	TXT	Article about expanding memory by K. Holcombe
METABAS	TXT	MetaBAS review
ODDS	TXT	Microcomputer terms definitions
PAS1	TXT	PASCAL article by R.Levaro
PATCH2	BAT	COMMAND.COM patch
PCFL	EXE	Start up of PC Firing Line magazine
PCUGINTR	TXT	PC UnderGround magazine text
PE	TXT	Personal Editor review
PRETTY1	COM	Printer interface routine
SPONSORS	TXT	About the publications' sponsors
THINKING	TXT	B. Sweeney & B. Salkin article
TXT	ADS	Advertisements
WRITERS	GDE	Writers Guide
WRITEUS	TXT	Plea for feedback from readers

Disk No 160 — PC Firing Line Issue 2 Volume 1 — v1 DS

ADA1	TXT	ADA tutorial
ADABOOK	REV	Review of 6 ADA books
ASM1	TXT	Tutorial on DOS & BIOS routines
ASM2	TXT	Sequential file reading under DOS 1.1, 2.0
BASIC1	TXT	SIMPMAZE documentation
C1	TXT	c tutorial
CHANGES	TXT	Improvements in PCFL/PCUG
CPYRIGHT	TXT	Copyright notice
DOS1	TXT	DOS article
DOS2	TXT	Compatibility article

EDITOR	TXT	Editorial
FORT1	TXT	Roots of 3rd & 4th order polynomials (Fortran)
FORTH1	TXT	Forth article
FORTH2	TXT	Forth documentation
FORTH3	TXT	Forth compiler documentation
GRABBAG	C	Source for GRABBAG.EXE
ITOP	LSP	LIST module
KEDIT	TXT	Review of Kedit
LISP1	TXT	LISP—convert infix to prefix notation
LIST1	ADA	Two source ADA routines
LIST1	ASM	Five assembler routines
LIST1	BAS	SIMPMAZE BASIC program
LIST1	C	Two c modules
LIST1	FOR	Fortran source for 3rd, 4th order polynomials
MASTHEAD	TXT	Newsletter masthead
PAS1	TXT	Pascal article
PCFL	EXE	Main newsletter program
PCUGINTR	TXT	Description of Volume 2 of newsletter
PRETTY1	COM	Printer interface routine
READISCO	PE	Readiscope article
SPLITA	BAT	Splits this volume into two 160KB diskettes
SPONSORS	TXT	Sponsors (Advertisements)
TOC	TXT	Table of contents
WRITERS	GDE	Writers guide

Disk No 161 — PC Firing Line Issue 2—Part 2 — v1 DS

FORTH	BAT	Start up batch file to read FORTH.MSG and start DEBUG
FORTH	MSG	Documentation for FORTH.OBJ
FORTH	OBJ	FORTH compiler
GC	EXE	General calculator—Part of PC Calculator
GRABBAG	EXE	Unsqueezes files, removes carriage returns, etc.
MANUAL	BAT	Prints MANUAL.DOC—Part of PC Calculator
MANUAL	DOC	Documentation—Part of PC Calculator
PC	EXE	Programmers Calculator main program
POLYMAZE	EXE	Interesting maze challenge (Requires color graphics)
SPLITB	BAT	Splits this diskette into two 160KB diskettes
SQ	C	Source for SQ.EXE
SQ	EXE	File shrinker
T86	BAT	Batch file to start Trace 86
T86D	EXE	Trace 86 main program—programming aid
T86TXT1	TXT	Documentation file for Trace 86
T86TXT2	TXT	Documentation file for Trace 86
XXXXXXXX	XX?	Part of Trace 86

Disk No 162 — BASIC NECESSITIES Version 1.12 — v1.1 DS

BASIC NECESSITIES is a user-supported preprocessor program for Microsoft BASIC on the IBM PC. It takes a program containing special statements and translates it into a program containing BASIC statements. Using this helps you write more concise, better structured BASIC programs, because the preprocessor lets you write free-form, indented statements without line numbers, include statements from many separate files and organize your subroutines into procedures, each with its own alphanumeric name.

ED	EXE	Program editor
SB	EXE	Structured BASIC preprocessor
LLIST	EXE	Lister
XREF	EXE	Cross-reference
ARCH	EXE	Source code archiver
ENTAB	EXE	Utility to put tabs in files
DETAB	EXE	Utility to remove tabs from files
ATTRIB	SB	Sample program
CHARS	SB	Sample program
LC	SB	Sample program
DEBUG	INC	Debug functions
SCREEN	INC	Screen functions
INPUT	INC	Input functions
CLS	INC	Fast screen clear functions
SB	DOC	Preprocessor manual (30k)
ED	DOC	Editor manual (26k)
UTIL	DOC	Utilities manual (17k)
READ	ME	File to read first

Disk No 163 — Dscreen and Text Filters — v1

CRYPT	C	Source code for CRYPT.EXE
CRYPT	DOC	CRYPT.EXE documentation
CRYPT	EXE	Encryption/decryption filter—uses a key to encode files
DBS	PRT	Documentation for DBS.EXE
DBS	EXE	Screen generator for dBASEII
DETAB	C	Source code for DETAB.EXE
DETAB	DOC	Documentation for DETAB.EXE
DETAB	EXE	Replaces tabs with appropriate number of spaces
ERR	C	Source for subroutines used here
ERRS	C	"
ESCT	C	"
FILP	C	"
FILPS	C	"
INDE	C	"
INDEX	C	"
LOCAL	H	"

SETS	C	"
SPSCN	C	Source code for SPSCN.EXE
SPSCN	DOC	Documentation for SPSCN.EXE
SPSCN	EXE	Removes spaces at the ends of lines in a text file
TRANSLIT	C	Source code for TRANSLIT.EXE
TRANSLIT	DOC	Documentation for TRANSLIT.EXE
TRANSLIT	EXE	Translates a character string into a different string
VERSION	C	Source for subroutine used here
WC	C	Source code for WC.EXE
WC	DOC	Documentation for WC.EXE
WC	EXE	Counts characters, words and lines in a text file

Disk No 164 — TeleWare Personal Finance Manager Version 4.5 v2.1 DS

FINANCE4	EXE	Main program
FINANCE4	DOC	Documentation (56K)
?????	DAT	Data files

Disk No 165 — Personal General Ledger — v1 DS

RECTJRNL	WKS	Cash receipt journal
DISBJRNL	WKS	Cash disbursements journal
SLRYJRNL	WKS	Salary journal
GENLJRNL	WKS	General journal—everything else
AUTO123	WKS	Sets up automatic menu when first accessing 1-2-3
GENLEDGR	WKS	Full general ledger
LEDGER	DOC	Documentation for Person General Ledger
CHART	DOC	Full chart of accounts

This disk requires LOTUS 1-2-3

Disk No 166 — IBM Macro Assembler Items — v1

ASMTUTR1	DOC	Assembler tutorial—Part 1
ASMTUTR2	DOC	Assembler tutorial—Part 2
ASMTUTR3	DOC	Assembler tutorial—Part 3
ASMTUTR4	DOC	Assembler tutorial—Part 4
ASMTIPS	DOC	Assembler tutorial—Part 5
ASMGEN	COM	Generates assembler code from executable files—Version 2.01
ASMGEN	DOC	Documentation for ASMGEN.BAS
COM2ASM	BAS	Converts COM file to assembler
COM2ASM	DOC	Documentation

Disk No 167		BASIC Aids	v1
ADVANCED	BAS	Checks to see if a program requires BASICA or not	
ADVANCED	DOC	Documentation	
ANIMATE	BAS	Demonstrates how to use several BASICA graphics commands	
BASKEYS	BAS	Sets up BASIC programming function keys	
BASTODOS	BAS	Several callable assembler routines for BASIC programs	
BASTOFOR	BAS	Converts BASIC to Fortran	
BASTOFOR	DOC	Documentation	
CHARDISP	BAS	Displays ASCII character set	
PSQUISH	BAS	BASIC program squisher	
REMREM	BAS	Removes REMarks from BASIC programs	
STOPGAP	BAS	Screen text editor for BASIC programming	
TRANDUMP	BAS	Dump utility	
TRS2PC	BAS	Converts TRS80 BASIC partways to IBM PC BASIC	

Disk No 168		Music and Educational Items	v1
ALGEBRA	BAS	Displays several algebra functions in 3-d (Color required)	
BABYMATH	EXE	Select a number, displays same number of dots (Color required)	
BACH	BAS	J. S. Bach Prelude 1 in C Major	
BACH2	BAS	Compose your own music (Bach to BASIC Version 1.2)	
BIBLE	BAS	The Bible Song	
CHEMQUES	BAS	Chemistry test aid	
CHEMTEST	BAS	Chemistry test aid	
CLASROLL	BAS	Update, print class roll, attendance, labels	
CLASROLL	DOC	Documentation	
COFFEE	BAS	Percolating coffee (Color required)	
GODFATHR	BAS	Theme from "The Godfather"	
JESUSLOV	BAS	Jesus Loves Me	
MINUET	BAS	Bach Minuet in D Minor	
MINUET2	BAS	Bach Minuet	
PIANO1	BAS	Play the piano from your keyboard (Color required)	
PIANO2	BAS	Same as above, except it guides you through sample songs	
SPELL	BAS	Spelling bee	
SPELL1	DAT	Part of SPELLBEE.BAS	
SPELL2	DAT	"	
SPELL3	DAT	"	
SPELL4	DAT	"	
SPELLBEE	BAS	Another spelling bee program	
SPELLDAT	BAS	Part of SPELLBEE.BAS	
STORY	BAS	Supply the words to complete the story	
TELLTIME	BAS	Good way to teach youngster to tell time (Color required)	

Disk No 169		Mailing List Programs	v1
EASYMAIL	ASC	Documentation for EASYMAIL.BAS	
EASYMAIL	BAS	Mailing label system	
ADDMAIL	BAS	Part of EASYMAIL.BAS	
BROWMAIL	BAS	"	
BUILDML	BAS	"	
CHGMAIL	BAS	"	
DELMAIL	BAS	"	
DISPMAIL	BAS	"	
LABMAIL	BAS	"	
LABPRINT	BAS	"	
LABSELEC	BAS	"	
LISTMAIL	BAS	"	
LOCMAIL	BAS	"	
MAILMENU	BAS	"	
REORMAIL	BAS	"	
STATMAIL	BAS	"	
MEMBER	ASC	Documentation for MEMBERS.BAS	
MEMBERS	BAS	Membership system based on EASYMAIL.BAS	
ADDMEMB	BAS	Part of MEMBERS.BAS	
BUILMEMB	BAS	"	
DISPMEMB	BAS	"	
MAILMEMB	BAS	"	
RENUMEMB	BAS	"	
REVUMEMB	BAS	"	
STATMEMB	BAS	"	
UPDMEMB	BAS	"	
MAILIST1	BAS	Another mailing list system	
MAILIST1	DOC	Documentation for MAILIST1.BAS	
MAILLIST	BAS	Another mailing list system	
MAILSORT	BAS	Sort for MAILIST1.BAS	

Disk No 170		Spreadsheets	v1.2 DS2
		FreeCalc	
FC	EXE	FreeCalc Version 1.01—main FREECALC spreadsheet program	
FC	HLP	FreeCalc Version 1.01—help files used by FC.EXE	
FC	DOC	FreeCalc Version 1.01—documentation for FC.EXE	
READ	ME	FreeCalc Version 1.01—how to print FC.DOC	
DEMO1	FC	FreeCalc Version 1.01—sample spreadsheet—home budget	
DEMO2	FC	FreeCalc Version 1.01—sample spreadsheet—home budget	
DEMO3	FC	FreeCalc Version 1.01—sample spreadsheet—home budget	
		PC-PAD	
AUTOEXEC	BAT	Part of PC-PAD—boot start up file	

PC-PAD	ABS	Part of PC-PAD—abstract of PC-PAD
PC-PAD	BAS	PC-PAD Version 1.3 text oriented spreadsheet main program
PC-PAD	BAT	Part of PC-PAD—start PC-PAD spreadsheet
PC-PAD	DOC	Part of PC-PAD—documentation
PC-PAD	LST	Part of PC-PAD—commented source & 20 add-on functions
ROWCOL	BAS	Part of PC-PAD—instruction for row/column totaling
TEMPLE	KEY	Part of PC-PAD
VOLKSWTR	KEY	Part of PC-PAD
BASIC	KEY	Part of PC-PAD
COPYPAD	BAT	Part of PC-PAD
DEMOPAD		Part of PC-PAD
EW	KEY	Part of PC-PAD
		MINICALC
MINICALC	DOC	Documentation for MINICALC.EXE
MINICALC	EXE	Small compiled spreadsheet (DOS 2.0 or later required)

Disk No 171		**Misc Financial Items**	**v1**
B1	BAS	Future value of an investment	
B2	BAS	Future value of regular deposits	
B3	BAS	Regular deposits	
B4	BAS	Regular withdrawals from an investment	
B5	BAS	Initial investment	
B6	BAS	Minimum investment for withdrawals	
B7	BAS	Nominal interest rate	
B8	BAS	Effective interest rate on investment	
B9	BAS	Earned interest table	
B10	BAS	Depreciation table	
B11	BAS	Depreciation amount	
B12	BAS	Salvage value	
B13	BAS	Discount commercial paper	
B14	BAS	Principal on a loan	
B15	BAS	Regular payment on a loan	
B16	BAS	Last payment on a loan	
B17	BAS	Remaining balance on a loan	
B18	BAS	Term of a loan	
B19	BAS	Annual interest rate on loan	
B20	BAS	Mortgage amortization table	
BUSIN	BAS	Menu for above B??.BAS programs	
FINANCE	BAS	Amortization, present values, future values, interest rate	
INTEREST	BAS	Prints compound interest factors	
		POS Inventory	
CASHREG	BAS	POS Inventory—Cash register transaction processing	

INVENPRC	BAS	POS Inventory—Inventory transaction processing
INVENRPT	BAS	POS Inventory—Inventory reporting
INVENTRY	DOC	POS Inventory—Documentation
PICKER	BAS	POS Inventory—Picking list generation
PICKTRAN	BAS	POS Inventory—Picking list transaction processing
START	BAS	POS Inventory—Main menu

Disk No 172 Steve's disk v1 DS

BEEP	ASM	Source code for BEEP.EXE
BEEP	COM	Program to produce "tone" on speaker
BEEP	DOC	Documentation for BEEP program
BEEP	EXE	Program to produce "tone" on speaker
CLS	ASM	Source code for routine to clear screen
CLS	DOC	Documentation for CLS.ASM
DSKTEST	BAS	Examines the status byte from the floppy disk controller
DSKTEST	DOC	Documentation for DSKTEST.BAS
EDIT-MOD	PAS	Source code for part of editor
EDITOR	DOC	Documentation for editor written in Pascal
EDT-MAIN	PAS	Source code for main editor module
INPORT	ASM	Routine to interrogate requested port
INPORT	DOC	Documentation for INPORT.ASM
LOCATE	ASM	Routine to locate curser position
LOCATE	DOC	Documentation for LOCATE.ASM
MSBEDIT	EXE	Compiled version of editor written in Pascal
PAS-BEEP	DOC	How to create a beep in Pascal
PORTS	DOC	Documentation for PORTS.EXE
PORTS	EXE	Program to examine I/O ports
PORTS	PAS	Source code for PORTS.EXE
PRNSTATS	BAS	Program to examine status of lineprinter port
PRNSTATS	DOC	Documentation for PRNSTATS.BAS
RAMDISK	COM	Virtual disk driver from DOS 2.0 manual
RAMDISK	DOC	Documentation for RAMDISK.COM
SETKEY	BAS	Keyboard reassignment program (Requires DOS 2.0 up)
SETKEY	DOC	Documentation for SETKEY.BAS

Disk No 173 PCMAN & ESP v1

CPOKEMAN	EXE	Good monochrome Pacman-type game
ESP	DOC	Documentation
ESP	EXE	Extra Sensory Perception testing
PCMAN	BAS	Fair monochrome Pacman-type game
PACMANGL	EXE	Slow Pacman-type game—good color (Requires color graphics)
SELLERS		Part of ESP

Disk No 174		Game Mixture	v1 DS
CIA	BAS	CIA adventure simulation	
CIVILWAR	BAS	Civil war simulation	
COMBOT	BAS	Program two robots to fight each other with lasers	
COMBOT	DOC	Documentation	
FOOTBAL	BAS	Big-8 football simulation—K.U. versus your choice	
FOOTBALL	BAS	Another football simulation	
FROG	EXE	Good Frogger-type game (Graphics required)	
GRINCH	BAS	El Grinch game—cute, neat game	
MARS-ESC	BAS	Escape from Mars adventure	
RACECAR	BAS	Good race car game	
SEAWOLF	BAS	Excellent game—sink subs, PT's, tankers	
SOLITARE	BAS	Solitare card game—you can't cheat with this one	
XWING	BAS	Re-live Star Wars—outstanding game (Graphics required)	

Disk No 175		Simulation & Board Games	v1
ACEY-DUE	BAS	Acey-duecy card game	
ALIEN	BAS	Adventure version	
BASEBALL	BAS	Baseball simulation	
BLACKBOX	BAS	Find the balls in an 8x8 grid using rays	
BLKFRDY	BAS	Stock market simulation	
BLOCK	EXE	Pong—requires graphics and BASRUN.EXE	
CHECKERS	BAS	Checkers—slow but okay	
HUSTLE	BAS	Like Hoser—good game	
HUSTLE	DAT	Part of HUSTLE.BAS	
HUSTLE	DOC	Documentation	
KNOCK	ASC	Documentation	
KNOCK	BAS	Knock-knock joke teller	
MUSICFIL	BAS	Music class management program	
JHORCH	MUS	Sample data created by MUSICFIL.BAS	
JHBAND	MUS	Sample data created by MUSICFIL.BAS	
SHORCH	MUS	Sample data created by MUSICFIL.BAS	
MEDLEY	BAS	Name that tune—plays favorite songs (Requires DOS 2.0)	

Disk No 176		Space Invaders and Graphics Demos	v1
CIRCLE	BAS	Circle patterns	
CIRCLOOP	ASC	Documentation	
CIRCLOOP	BAS	Circle patterns	
CURVE	BAS	Sine wave	
CURVE2	BAS	Draws curve to your selection of coordinates and color	
CURVE3	BAS	Draws circle, ellipse to your selection of coordinates and color	
DOWN	BAS	Pattern by Robbie Khedouri	

JAIME	BAS	Moving line pattern
NEWYEAR	DOC	Documentation
NEWYEAR	EXE	Main program—welcome in the New Year with your PC
NEWYEAR	PAS	Pascal source code
NUDE	BAS	Excellent female nude on color monitor by G. Wesley & Dave Moon
NYTEST	BAT	Part of NEWYEAR.EXE—test execution
NYTEST1	BAT	Part of NEWYEAR.EXE—test execution
ROUNDER	BAS	Curve plot to your selection of coordinates
ROUNDER1	BAS	Curve plot to your selection of coordinates
ROUNDER2	BAS	Curve plot to your selection of coordinates
ROUNDER3	BAS	Curve plot to your selection of coordinates
ROUNDER4	BAS	Curve plot to your selection of coordinates
SPACEVAD	EXE	Space Invaders game—excellent public domain version
SQUARE	BAS	Square pattern
SWIRL	BAS	Pattern by Robbie Khedouri
TRIANGLE	BAS	Draws triangle to your selection of coordinates
WALLS	BAS	Pattern by Robbie Khedouri

Disk No 177 — Arcade Games — v1

BOMB	BAS	Find the bomb in 1 of 1,000,000 rooms before BLAM!
BREAKOUT	BAS	Hard Pong game (Requires color graphics)
BUGS	EXE	Centipede-like game—good version
BUGS!	SCR	Part of BUGS.EXE
CUBE	BAS	Cube game (Color required)
DRIVER	BAS	Drive racecar around track—tough on eyes!
HS	DAT	High scores for JUMPJOE.EXE
JUMPJOE	EXE	Version of Miner 2049'er or Donkey Kong (Color required)
JUMPJOE	SOL	Part of JUMPJOE.EXE
PENCIL	BAS	Sketch on color monitor with joystick

Disk No 178 — Startrek, Chess and Misc Games — v1

AWARI	BAS	Old African game played with 7 sticks & 36 stones
CHESS	EXE	Color Graphics—plays well at first, not tough later
CHESS88	EXE	Same as above game, either later or earlier version
COLLIDE	BAS	Simple minded but not easy—shoot falling bombs
HAMURABI	BAS	Play King and find out its not such a good life
STAR3D	DOC	Documentation for STAR3D.EXE
STAR3D	EXE	Sensation of traveling through space on color monitor
STARTREK	BAS	Super version of Startrek
STARTREK	EXE	Outstanding version of Startrek

Disk No 179		Pizza & Check Register Systems	v1
PIZZA	EXE	Pizza recipes—main program	
MA	BAS	Micro Accounting check register system	
MA	DOC	Documentation for MA.BAS	
MACOPY	BAT	Batch file to copy MA files	
MADOC	BAT	Batch file to print MA.DOC	
SCR*	DOC	Data for PIZZA.EXE	

Disk No 180		Math and Statistics Routines	v1
TRADENET		TRADENET network sampler	
DATANET		DATANET network sampler	
M1	BAS	Greatest common demoninator	
M2	BAS	Prime factors of integers	
M3	BAS	Area of polygon	
M4	BAS	Analysis of two vectors	
M5	BAS	Parts of a triangle	
M6	BAS	Operations on two vectors	
M7	BAS	Coordinate conversion	
M8	BAS	Coordinate plot	
M9	BAS	Angle conversion	
M10	BAS	Plot of polar equation	
M11	BAS	Plot of function	
M12	BAS	Linear interpolation	
M13	BAS	Curvilinear interpolation	
M14	BAS	Integration: Simpson's rule	
M15	BAS	Integration: Gaussian quadrature	
M16	BAS	Integration: Trapeqoidal rule	
M17	BAS	Derivative	
M18	BAS	Roots of quadratic equation	
M19	BAS	Real roots of polynomials: Newton	
M20	BAS	Roots of polynomials: half interval sear	
M21	BAS	Trig polynomial	
M22	BAS	Simultaneous equations	
M23	BAS	Linear programming	
M24	BAS	Matrix add, subtract & scalar multiplication	
M25	BAS	Matrix multiplication	
M26	BAS	Matrix inversion	
MATH	BAS	Menu for above math programs	
MATRIX	BAS	Solves simultaneous equations	
NCCLSPRE	BAS	Calculates a sample's precision	
NORMAL-Z	BAS	Normal distribution routines	
REGRESS	BAS	Regression analysis	
S1	BAS	Permutations & combinations	

S2	BAS	Mann-Whitney U test
S3	BAS	Geometric mean and deviation
S4	BAS	Binomial distribution
S5	BAS	Poisson distribution
S6	BAS	Normal distribution
S7	BAS	Chi-square distribution
S8	BAS	Chi-square test
S9	BAS	Student's T distribution
S10	BAS	Student's T test
S11	BAS	F-distribution
S12	BAS	Linear correlation coefficient
S13	BAS	Multiple linear regression
S14	BAS	Linear regression
S15	BAS	Nth order regression
S16	BAS	Geometric regression
S17	BAS	Exponential regression
S18	BAS	Mean, variance, standard deviation
STAT	BAS	Menu for above S??.BAS statistics programs

Disk No 181 — Keyboard Utilities — v1

DOSKEY1	DOC	Documentation
DOSKEYS	BAS	Redefines function keys (C. Haapala)
DOSKEYS	DOC	Documentation continued
KBBUFF	BAS	Keyboard buffer—extends buffer by 160 characters
KBBUFF	DOC	Documentation (3K)
		NEWKEY
NEWKEY	EXE	NEWKEY Version 1.1—key customization package by Frank Bell
NEWKEY1	EXE	NEWKEY—additional functions
PRINTDOC	EXE	Prints NEWKEY documentation
NEWKEY	DOC	Documentation (42K)
TEST	KEY	Part of NEWKEY.EXE—Demos of features
WS	KEY	Part of NEWKEY.EXE—WORDSTAR
LOADNEW	BAT	Part of NEWKEY.EXE—loads NEWKEY and WORDSTAR key definitions
ASM	KEY	Part of NEWKEY.EXE—Sample for assembler
DVORAK	KEY	Part of NEWKEY.EXE—Dvorak keyboard

Disk No 182 — EasyFile, AutoFile and Time, Date Utilities — v1

		AUTOFILE
AUTOFILE	BAS	AUTOFILE small indexed file system
AUTOFILE	BAT	AUTOFILE batch start up file
AUTOFILE	DOC	AUTOFILE documentation
AUTOFILE	FIX	Part of AUTOFILE

		EASYFILE
EASYFILE	BAS	EASYFILE main program—small simple file manager
ADDFILE	BAS	Part of EASYFILE—add to a file
BUILFILE	BAS	Part of EASYFILE—builds initial file
COLRFILE	BAS	Part of EASYFILE—switches to color monitor
COPFILE	BAS	Part of EASYFILE—copies file
DCATFILE	BAS	Part of EASYFILE—displays file categories
DISPFILE	BAS	Part of EASYFILE—displays files
DTEXFILE	BAS	Part of EASYFILE—displays text
EZFDOCM	BAS	Part of EASYFILE—documentation—use BASICA LIST to view
FILEFILE	BAS	Part of EASYFILE—file selection
FILEMENU	BAS	Part of EASYFILE—EASYFILE menu
LISTFILE	BAS	Part of EASYFILE—list file
MONOFILE	BAS	Part of EASYFILE—switch to monochrome
STATFILE	BAS	Part of EASYFILE—status report

AREACODE	BAS	Displays major cities within an area code
CALENDAR	BAS	Displays calendar for any month & year (Irvan Krantzler)
DDATE	COM	Last date used routine
MONOCLKF	COM	Monochrome clock time display
MONOCLKF	DOC	Documentation
SPEC-OCC	BAS	Keeps track of special occasions by month (Phil Michitsch)
SPEC-OCC	DOC	Documentation
TCLOCK	BAS	Displays large date & time, has alarm feature (William Vath)
TIME	BAS	Displays time

Disk No 183 — Sundry DOS Utilities — v1

BOARD	TST	Check for famous QUADRAM parity error design defect
CHECKOUT	BAS	Diagnostics on all ports
CMD99	COM	Command processor
COMPROM	EXE	Compares two ROM programs from diskettes
COMSPEC4	ASM	Assembler source
COMSPEC4	COM	DOS patch to activate COMMAND.COM in subdirectories
COMSPEC4	DOC	Documentation
CONFIG	EXE	Displays your PC's configuration
COPYROM	EXE	Copies ROM programs onto diskette for later use
CRL	BAS	Change cursor shape & size (John Herzfeld)
CRL	COM	Compiled version
CRS	BAS	Change cursor shape & size (John Herzfeld)
CRS	COM	Compiled version
INFO1	BAT	Documentation for COPYROM.EXE & COMPROM.EXE
MEM640	DOC	Documentation
MEM640	ZAP	DOS patch to permit older BIOS PC's to use 544KB-640KB memory
MY-DATE	BAT	Part of COPYROM.EXE utility

OLD-NEW	BAT	Part of COMPROM.EXE utility
RESCMD	BAS	DOS 1.1 patch to make COMMAND.COM memory resident (John Chapman)
RESCMD	DOC	Documentation
ROMREAD	BAS	Reads & displays ROM BIOS dates, type IBM PC (Tom Allen)
ROMREAD	DOC	Documentation
VTYPE	DOC	Documentation
VTYPE	EXE	Improved TYPE command (Vincent Bly)
MOVE	COM	Utility—COPY command which prompts at each file
MOVE	DOC	Documentation for MOVE.COM

Disk No 184 — Diskette Utilities — v1.1

COVER

COVER	COM	Generates a listing of a directory to put into diskette envelope
(READ	ME)	Part of COVER.COM
COVER	DOC	Part of COVER.COM (13K)
COVER	ASM	Part of COVER.COM
COVERPRO	COM	C.Itoh Prowriter version of COVER.COM.
COVERPRO	ASM	Source for COVERPRO.COM.
CO*	ASM	Assembly language source code for COVER.COM modules
CO*	OBJ	Object modules for COVER.COM

ALTER	COM	Alter file attributes
ALTER	DOC	Documentation
CHMOD	BAS	Change file attributes
CHMOD	DOC	Documentation
CLEAN2	COM	Update to disk drive cleaning utility
CLEAN2	DOC	Documentation
COPY40	COM	Copy utility that breaks some protected items
COPY40	DOC	Documentation
COPYALL	COM	Copy utility that breaks some protected items
CV	COM	Changes diskette labels (DOS 1.1, 2.0, 2.1)
CV	DOC	Documentation
DCOPY	COM	Copies some protected items
DFORMAT	COM	Format utility (Buggy)
DOSBUG	DOC	Fix DOS 1.1 bugs
MINIPRT	DOC	Prints directory in small shape for diskette envelopes
PURGE	COM	Deletes selected files
PURGE	DOC	Documentation
RAMDSK16	COM	160KB RAM disk
RAMDSK18	COM	180KB RAM disk
RAMDSK32	COM	320KB RAM disk
RAMDSK36	COM	360KB RAM disk
RM18	ASM	Assembler source for RAM disks
SPEEDUP2	DOC	DOS 2.0 diskette drive speed up utility

123STAR	UNP	How to unprotect LOTUS 123
BASIC	UNP	How to unprotect BASIC compiler
EASYWR11	UNP	How to unprotect EASYWRITER
FLTSIM	UNP	How to unprotect FLIGHT SIMULATOR
LOTUS1A	UNP	How to unprotect LOTUS 123 1A
MEMSHIFT	UNP	How to unprotect MEMORY SHIFT
MS2	UNP	How to unprotect MEMORY SHIFT
NEW123	UNP	How to unprotect LOTUS 123
PFSFILE	UNP	How to unprotect PFS File
VISICALC	UNP	How to unprotect VISICALC
WORD	UNP	How to unprotect WORD
WORDNEW	UNP	How to unprotect WORD
ZORK3	UNP	How to unprotect ZORK

Disk No 185 — Diskette Utilities — v1

CATALOG	COM	Sorted directory
DD	BAT	Directory sorted by date (Part of DNXSD.BAT)
DIR2	BAS	Diskette sorted directory by Wes Meier, Version 2.0
DN	BAT	Directory sorted by filename (Part of DNXSD.BAT)
DNXSD	DOC	Series of batch sorted directory utilities
DS	BAT	Directory sorted by file size (Part of DNXSD.BAT)
DX	BAT	Directory sorted by file extension (Part of DNXSD.BAT)
DXSAVE	BAT	Sample change in BAT to save sorted directory on a diskette file
SDIR	COM	Sorted directory by Ted Reuss
SDIR	DOC	Documentation
SDIR24C	ASM	Assembler source
SDIR24C	COM	Sorted directory Version 2.4 by John Ratti
SDIR24C	DOC	Documentation
SEC&BYTE	BAS	Prints table of diskette sectors & bytes
SQIBM	COM	Squishes a file
SQIBM	DOC	Documentation
USQIBM	COM	Unsquishes a squished file
USQIBM	DOC	Documentation
ZSQ	EXE	Squishes a file
ZSQ-ZUSQ	DOC	Documentation
ZUSQ	EXE	Unsquishes a squished file

Disk No 186		CRT and Epson Printer Utilities v1
NOCOLOR	COM	Switch color graphics card to B/W mode
NOCOLOR	DOC	Documentation
SCRLKY	ASM	Assembler source
SCRLKY	COM	Better screen scrolling control
SCROLLK	COM	Another screen scrolling control utility
SCROLLK	DOC	Documentation
COMPRSOF	COM	Set compressed print off
COMPRSON	COM	Set compressed print on
CREATOR	BAS	Displays characters in dot matrix pattern
DBLHITOF	COM	Set enlarged print off
DBLHITON	COM	Set enlarged print on
DBLWDEOF	COM	Set wide print off
DBLWDEON	COM	Set wide print on
EMPHASOF	COM	Set emphasized print off
EMPHASON	COM	Set emphasized print on
EPSONCHR	ASM	Assembler source
EPSONCHR	DOC	Documentation
EPSONCHR	EXE	Permits printing all characters
ITALICOF	COM	Set italics off
ITALICON	COM	Set italics on
KYBD	BAS	Send printing directly to monochrome parallel port
PRINT20	DOC	Patch to skip LPT1: prompt from PRINT.COM
PRINTSET		Sets Epson to compressed print
PRINTSET	DOC	Documentation
PRTSCFX	COM	Graphics printing for Epson FX & RX
PRTSCFX	DOC	Documentation
RESET	COM	Reset printer to power-on settings
SET-PRTR	C	Source
SET-PRTR	EXE	MX-80 printer settings
SET51LNS	COM	Set 51 lines per page
SETCW132	COM	Set 132 columns per page
SETPRF19	COM	Perforation setting
SKP6PERF	COM	Perforation setting—6 lines/inch
SKP8PERF	COM	Perforation setting—8 lines/inch
SP	DOC	Documentation
SP	EXE	Print spooler by Alan Jones
SPC	EXE	Print spooler for use with data communications
TOPOFORM	COM	Skip to top of form
UNDERLOF	COM	Set underline off
UNDERLON	COM	Set underline on

Disk No 187		Data Communications Items	v1
AUTODIAL	BAS	Auto telephone dialer	
BASECONV	BAS	Converts to/from hex, binary, decimal (Robert West)	
CONVERT	BAS	Converts EXE & COM files to BASIC for transmission (Version 1.1)	
EZSIG3	HLP	CompuServe IBM SIG instructions (1/84)	
HAYSMODM	BAS	Hayes SmartModem demo—nifty!	
KILLNULL	BAS	Converts nulls in a file to spaces	
PC-SPEAK	BAS	Data communications program by Larry Jordan	
TALK450	DOC	Documentation on how to speed up Hayes to 450 baud	
TALK450	MRG	BASIC code to program 8250 to run at 450 baud	

Disk No 188		MINITEL Communications System Version 1.0	v1
IBMMINI	EXE	IBM PC version of MINITEL	
MINITEL	ABS	Abstract	
MINITEL	DOC	Documentation	
MINITEL	DQC	Compressed documentation	
MINITEL	LBR	File transfer program	

Disk No 189		TECH PRINT Version 2.01	v1
FLIER		Start documentation—read with WORDSTAR	
TECH	CLR	Color switch	
TECH	EXE	Improved WORDSTAR printing on FX Epson	
TECH	KEY	Prokey key definitions	
TECH	MNL	Documentation manual	

Disk No 190		Text Editors and Misc	v1
CUSTOM	BAS	Custom characters by Gary Antrim	
FIX-TEST	BAS	Inserts carriage returns & line feeds	
MEMO	BAS	Quick memo writer (John Harrington)	
PC-FORM	EXE	PC-FILE form generator Version 1.1 (William Bailey)	
RV-EDIT	BAS	Full screen editor Version 1.2 (Bob Vollmer)	
RV-EDIT	DOC	Documentation	
TXTSCAN	BAS	Searches ASCII file for character string	
VUE	BAS	Nifty look into text files Version 1.0 (Buzz Hamilton)	
		FULLSCRN	
FULLSCRN	BAS	Full screen data entry	
PGMCVRT	BAS	Part of FULLSCRN.BAS	

XXXX	DAT	Part of FULLSCRN.BAS
FULLSCRN	BSC	Part of FULLSCRN.BAS
FRM001	DAT	Part of FULLSCRN.BAS
FUL001	DAT	Part of FULLSCRN.BAS
FULLSCRN	BSN	Part of FULLSCRN.BAS
INFO	DOC	Part of FULLSCRN.BAS—Documentation

Disk No 191		**DVED Screen Editor, Easel & Easygraf**	**v1 DS**
COLOR	BAS	Part of PIECHART.BAS	
CURVEFIT	BAS	Curve fitting program by T S Cox	
CURVEFIT	DOC	Documentation for CURVEFIT.BAS	
DIGIDRAW	BAS	Nifty drawing program (Requires graphics & BASICA)	
DIGIDRAW	DOC	Documentation for DIGIDRAW.BAS	
DVED	COM	Good screen-oriented text editor (Version 6.02)—Can use with mouse	
READ	ME	Part of DVED.COM	
GRAPH	BAS	Graphs data (x, y coordinates and function)	
GRAPH2	BAS	Graphs data (x, y coordinates and function)	
HISTGRAM	BAS	Displays and prints simple histogram	
INFO	BIN	Binary file for DIGIDRAW.BAS	
LOGO	BIN	Binary file for DIGIDRAW.BAS	
PIECHART	BAS	Draws pie charts—Version 1.0	
PLOT	BAS	Creates plots from your coordinates	
SKETCH	BAS	Etch-a-sketch with cursor keys	
		EASEL	
EASEL	BAS	Easel drawing package (Requires light pen, color graphics)	
EASEL	ASC	Part of EASEL.BAS—documentation	
PENCIRC	BAS	Part of EASEL.BAS—draw circles	
PENCLEAR	BAS	Part of EASEL.BAS—clear screen	
PENDRAW	BAS	Part of EASEL.BAS—draw dots	
PENLINE	BAS	Part of EASEL.BAS—draw lines	
PENPAINT	BAS	Part of EASEL.BAS—demo—color train with light pen	
PENSAVE	BAS	Part of EASEL.BAS—save drawing	
		EASYGRAF	
EASYGRAF	BAS	EasyGraf drawing package (Requires color graphics)	
BUILGRAF	BAS	Part of EASYGRAF.BAS—build graph file	
COLRGRAF	BAS	Part of EASYGRAF.BAS	
DISPGRAF	BAS	Part of EASYGRAF.BAS—display graph	
DISPGRDR	BAS	Part of EASYGRAF.BAS—display graph directory	
DRAWGRAF	BAS	Part of EASYGRAF.BAS—draw a graph	
EASYGRAF	ASC	Part of EASYGRAF.BAS—documentation	
EZGDOCM	BAS	Part of EASYGRAF.BAS—use BASIC LIST to view	
GRAPHIT	BAS	Part of EASYGRAF.BAS—draws with cursor & function keys	
MONOGRAF	BAS	Part of EASYGRAF.BAS—monochrome graph	
PRINGRAF	BAS	Part of EASYGRAF.BAS	

PRN2GRAF	BAS	Part of EASYGRAF.BAS
PRNTGRAF	BAS	Part of EASYGRAF.BAS
PRNTSAVE	BAS	Part of EASYGRAF.BAS
SAMPDRAW	BAS	Part of EASYGRAF.BAS—sample drawing—part of house
SAVEGRAF	BAS	Part of EASYGRAF.BAS
TEMPGRAF	BAS	Part of EASYGRAF.BAS—temporary graph storage
TESTPRNT	BAS	Part of EASYGRAF.BAS

Disk No 192 Health/Risk v1 DS

A IBM PC conversion of the Center For Disease Control health/risk appraisal program.

HRAINP1	EXE	Interactive input module
HRA1	EXE	Main health/risk program
HRAPRINT	EXE	Program to set up printer
SYSTAB		Data tables
DIATAB		" "
M1		" "
OWTAB		" "
AGETAB		" "
TITLES		" "
RRSKFCT		" "
EDT		" "
RM2		" "
RWTTAB		" "
RTOP12		" "
RDTH		" "
RPRTHED		" "
RSMOHED		" "
HDATA		Active pt. data
HRADATA		Archival file
PRINTSTY		Printer parameters
HRADOC	TXT	Documentation

Disk No 193 FREEWILL v1

This disk contains text used to prepare a California will.

FREEWILL	DOC	Introduction
PRINTING	DOC	Information on printing FREEWILL GROUP
C2	BAT	Execute "C2" in default drive for explanation
BANNER	ASC	FREEWILL LOGO
PAGEII	ASC	Explanation text
PAGEIII	ASC	Explanation text
PAGEIV	ASC	Explanation text
PAGEV	ASC	Explanation text
PAGEVI	ASC	Explanation text

PAGEVII	ASC	Explanation text
PAGEVIII	ASC	Explanation text
PAGEIX	ASC	Explanation text
FREEWILL	ASC	California Civil Code
WILL		First of two FORMS for your "Do-It-Yourself" will
TRUST		Second choice of FORMS

Disk No 194		**ROFF and PC-READ**	**v1.1**
INTEGRAL	C	Source in c for integration routine	
INTEGRAL	PAS	Source in Pascal for integration routine	
INTEGRAL	DCL	Declaration of integral for calling Pascal program	
TSTINTEG	C	Source in c for example of use of integral	
TSTINTEG	PAS	Source in Pascal for example for use of integral	
RKF45	C	Source in c for RKF45 integrator	
RKF45	PAS	Source in Pascal for RKF45 integrator	
RKF45	DCL	Declaration of RKF45 for calling Pascal program	
TSTRKF45	C	Source in c for example of use of RKF45	
TSTRKF45	PAS	Source in Pascal for example of use of RKF45	
		ROFF	
ROFF	H0	Header common to all ROFF source	
ROFF	H1	Header specific to ROFF1	
ROFF	H2	Header specific to ROFF2	
ROFF1	C	Part 1 of ROFF source (Modified from PC-SIG Disk No 50).	
ROFF2	C	Part 2 of ROFF source	
ROFF3	C	Part 3 of ROFF source	
ROFF	DOC	Documentation of ROFF	
ROFF	EXE	Version of ROFF produced from source code on this disk	
		PC-READ by Joey Robichaux	
PC-READ	COM	Program to determine the clarity of text	
PC-READ	DOC	Documentation for PC-READ.COM	

Disk No 195		**GRAFH2 & SKETCH**	**v1 DS**
AUTOEXEC	BAT	System reset bootstrap batch file	
BAS	BAT	Batch file that loads BASIC & sets function keys	
BUFEXTEN	BAS	BASIC program to generate BUFEXTEND.COM	
BUFEXTEN	COM	Extends keyboard buffer to 149 characters	
COLOR	BAS	Sets default color for text in DOS	
COLOR	BAT	Simple batch file to call COLOR.BAS	
COLOR	SCR	File containing commands to set text color	
DIRLIST	DOC	Directory of files on this disk	
DISPLAY	BAS	BASIC program to load screen image from file	
DISPLAY	BAT	Batch file to call DISPLAY.BAS	
GRAPH2	BAS	Program to plot line figures x-y plots	
GRAPH2	DOC	Documentation file for GRAPH2.BAS	

MONOGRPH	BAS	Monochrome version of GRAPH2—Hercules
HAT	BAS	BASIC program to generate graphics test screen
HAT	DMP	Screen dump of result of HAT.BAS
KEYDEF	BAS	Program to define function keys for DOS
MONOKEYD	BAS	Monochrome version of KEYDEF.BAS
MEMO	BAS	Program to keep and display daily memos
MEMO	FIL	File of memos used by MEMO.BAS
MONOMEMO	BAS	Monochrome version of MEMO.BAS
MENU	BAS	Program to give menu display of BASIC files
MONOMENU	BAS	Monochrome version of MENU.BAS
PLOT	BAT	Batch file to run GRAPH2
QUERY	ASM	Program that allows interactive batch files
QUERY	BAS	BASIC program to generate QUERY.COM
QUERY	COM	Program that allows interactive batch files
SCRNSAVE	BAS	BASIC program that generates SCRNSAVE.COM
SCRNSAVE	COM	Blanks screen after 3 minutes of no use
SETUP	BAS	Defines 10 function keys in BASIC
SKETCH	BAS	Joystick drawing program
SKETCH	DOC	Documentation file for SKETCH.BAS
SUBGRAPH	BAS	Subroutine that does plotting in GRAPH2
TEMP	SPC	Sample file of specifications for GRAPH2
TESTDATA	DTA	Sample file of data for GRAPH2
PRINTQUE	DOC	Documentation for PRINTQUE.BAS (12K)
PRINTQUE	BAS	Program to establish a que for printing multiple file copies

Disk No 196		**BBS Utilities #12**	**v1**
DIRCOMP	COM	Compares two directories and lists files found in both	
EQUIP102	COM	Displays system equipment configuration	
EQUIP102	DOC	Documentation for above	
MV	EXE	Sophisticated file move/rename utility	
MV	DOC	Documentation for above	
SLIDE	COM	Prepare slides on graphics display	
SLIDE	ASM	Source for above	
SHOW	EXE	Show prepared slides on graphics display	
SHOW	ASM	Source for above	
UTIL102	COM	Copy/delete multiple files	
UTIL102	DOC	Documentation for above	

Disk No 197		**BBS Utilities #13**	**v1**
TREKRUN	EXE	Fantastic STARTREK game, works on graphics or mono screen	
TREKPIK	EXE	Part of STARTREK game	
DATA	DAT	Part of STARTREK game	
IBMMINI	EXE	Communications program with several file transfer protocols	

Disk No 198		BBS Utilities #14	v1
CASTLE	EXE	Great adventure game—combines text, pictures, animation	
CASTLE	RAN	Data file for CASTLE.EXE	
L4	EXE	Full-screen list program with 4-way scroll and search!	
L4	DOC	Documentation for above	
L4	ASM	Source for above	
MEMBRAIN	EXE	Best RAM disk yet—supports many config parameters	
MEMBRAIN	DOC	Documentation for above	

Disk No 199		PC-CALC	v2 DS
PC-CALC	EXE	Spreadsheet program from author of PC-FILE	
PCCALC	DOC	Documentation for PC-CALC (86K)	
DOC	BAT	Batch file to print documentation	
PCCALC	EXE	Part of PC-CALC	
PCCALC2	EXE	Part of PC-CALC	
PCCALC3	EXE	Part of PC-CALC	
PCCALC	MSG	Part of PC-CALC	
PCOVL	EXE	Part of PC-CALC	
EXAMPLE		Part of PC-CALC	
RESPONSE		Part of PC-CALC	

Disk No 200	IBM Users Group Newsletter #4	v1 DS

June 1984 issue of the electronic newsletter published by IBM Boca Raton. To read it, type NEWS. You will be presented with a menu of topics and stories, including new product announcements, tips, techniques and other material.

Articles include:

BASIC and machine code interfacing
Running DOS commands from BASIC
Using numbers in random files
Installing half-height drives
Comparing microprocessors
Using macros
Recovering data from bad directories
Speeding up memory check
POKing around on the fixed disk

Disk No 201		WORDSTAR and Financial Items	v1
78INT	BAS	Rule of 78's interest/principle calculating utility	
DISBURSE	BAS	Disbursements register, single entry, with annual summaries	
DISBURSE	TXT	Documentation	
FIXWS	COM	Converts WORDSTAR files to ASCII	
FIXWS	DOC	Documentation	
FORMGEN	BAS	Simple word processor	
FORMGEN	TXT	Documentation	
OUTPUTS	PRF	Part of DISBURSE.BAS	
POW	DOC	Documentation	
POW	COM	Simple word processor by Michael Maioli (Version 3.0)	
UNDOWS	DOC	Documentation	
UNDOWS	EXE	Version 1.0 by Gary Elfring—converts WORDSTAR to standard ASCII	
WS-DOS	BAS	Converts WORDSTAR files to ASCII, and ASCII to WORDSTAR	

Disk No 202 — MIT/ISI COMM GROUP — v2

This is a serial I/O package originally developed by John Romkey and Jerry Saltzer of MIT. Modifications have been made by Dick Gillmann and Craig Rogers. It is fully interrupt driven on transmit, receive and error detection. It will run at 9600 baud, and even faster if you don't plan on doing anything else.

		MIT/ISI COMM GROUP
COMMREAD	ME	Release letter for MIT/ISI communications package
COMMMSGS	DOC	Details about IBM ASYNC port & BIOS and MIT/ISI communication package
LPT_PKG	ASM	An interrupt driver and interface package for the line printer. It uses the same circular buffer scheme as the COM package. It is primarily intended for special applications, such as printing graphics.
INT_PKG	ASM	These routines save and restore interrupt vectors. "Chained" vectors are not directly supported. Vectors may be saved/restored in one of three ways: DOS 1, DOS 2 or no DOS.
EXMEM	ASM	These routines provide additional physical memory access. Memory is accessed with 20-bit addresses. All of physical memory may be accessed, regardless of the programming "model".
EXIO	ASM	These routines provide additional machine I/O functions beyond the Lattice-supplied inp() and outp(). The new functions solve certain interrupt-and DMA-related problems in devices which require multi-I/O control sequences. These routines are not used by the rest of the distribution at present, but may be used in the future.
COM_PKG	ASM	The interrupt-driven COM package

COM__PKG1	ASM	Provides a library of serial port routines
BMACTST	ASM	This program tests the BMAC macros
TSTLPT	C	A test program for LPT__PKG
TSTINT	C	A test program for INT__PKG
TSTEXMEM	C	This program tests the routines in EXMEM. For complete confidence, the test should be run under the control of a debugger to verify the results.
TSTCOM	C	A test program for the COM package. Allows the IBM PC to act like a glass TTY connected to a host via COM1:. This program is more useful when you are running the ANSI terminal driver. There is no protection against DOS character traps (control-C, etc.).
TSTCOM2	C	A second test program for the COM package. It allows the IBM PC to approximate an (expensive) null modem between COM1: and COM2:.
TITLE	MAC	These macros provide functional replacements for the standard TITLE and SUBTTL macros. A table of contents appears in the symbol table at the end of an assembly listing.
DOS	MAC	This file comes from the Lattice c distribution. It defines which programming "model" is being used, for the benefit of assembly routines. It defines the PSECTs used for code and data. Edit this file to select your programming "model". This version of DOS.MAC fixes a bug in the standard Lattice c version.
BMAC	MAC	Assembly language macros which encapsulate the sub-routine call interface. The macros define names for subroutine arguments and temporary variables on the stack. This version interfaces with Lattice c (AKA Microsoft c). Both large small programming "models" are supported. A separate version of BMAC could be created to interface to IBM Pascal, if desired.
TRUTH	H	Contains type definitions for the bool (boolean) data type
EXMEM	H	This file defines the P__ADDR (Physical address) data type, and defines the return values of some of the EXMEM functions.
BEAUTY	H	A set of macros and type definitions which enhance c program portability and reliability. The macros define an enhanced set of character and integer data types. Edit this file to select your programming "model" (long pointers vs. short pointers).
GLASSTTY	PAS	Simple dumb terminal for IBM PC. (Microsoft Pascal)

Disk No 203 — Games & Music — v1

ADVEN1	BAS	Adventure by Scott Adams
ASTEROID	BAS	Asteroid Pilot by Dorn Stickle & R A Bower (Color graphics)
BLESS	BAS	God Bless America (With flag display)
FLY	BAS	Simple fly swatting game (Color graphics)
HINT1	DOC	Part of ADVENT1.BAS
HINT2	DOC	Part of ADVENT1.BAS
HINT3	DOC	Part of ADVENT1.BAS

MOON	BAS	Lunar lander (Color graphics) (Allan & Andrew Lee)
NEWCHESS	BAS	Chess game by M. C. Rakaska (Modified by S. W. Huggins)
SLOTCOLR	BAS	Good color graphics slotmachine (Modified by Arnold Thomson)
SOLITAIR	BAS	Klondyke solitaire (Jeff Littlefield, modified by Ken Handzik)
SURVIVAL	BAS	Space adventure-like game (Allan and Andrew Lee)
TRAILER	BAS	Trailer for rent
TRUMPET	BAS	Trumpeters Lullaby (Leroy Anderson)
WELLTEMP	BAS	Praeludium I from The Well-Tempered Clavier by J S Bach
WHEEL	BAS	Wheel of Fortune (David Lien)
WORDPLAY	BAS	Generates sentences from lists of nouns, adjectives and verbs

Disk No 204 — Copy & Delete Utilities — v1

FCOPY	EXE	Copies & formats SS diskette in 30 sec (Peter Norton)
FCOPY	PAS	Pascal source code
FCOPY	OBJ	Object code
FCOPY	LNK	Part of FCOPY
READ	ME	FCOPY documentation
FCMAGIC	ASM	Assembler routines for FCOPY.EXE
FCMAGIC	OBJ	Object code
FILECOPY	BAS	Paginates & prints text files
FILEOUT	BAS	Epson printing utility (Don Withrow)
GCOPY	DOC	Documentation
GCOPY	EXE	Enhanced DOS copy utility (Gordon Waite)
GDEL	DOC	Documentation
GDEL	EXE	Enhanced DOS delete utility (Gordon Waite)
MSPOOL2	COM	Up to 4 simultaneous printer spoolers (Rich Winkel)
MSPOOL2	DOC	Documentation
VDL	COM	File delete utility for DOS 2.0 (Tom Roberts)
VDL	DOC	Documentation
VISIPROT	DOC	Unprotect VISICALC
WRT	DOC	Documentation—WRTE.COM & WRTP.COM (Kent Quirk)
WRTE	COM	Make a read-only file copyable
WRTP	COM	Make a file read-only

Disk No 205 — Batch and Misc DOS Utilities — v1

BAT	COM	Version 2.0 Extended Batch Language
BAT2DEMO	BAT	BAT.COM demonstration
BAT2DOC	BAT	BAT.COM documentation and demonstrations
BROWSE	COM	View file contents—similar to CMS BROWSE command
BROWSE	DOC	Documentation
CAT	COM	Directory utility: scrolling, sorted display, etc.
CAT	DOC	Documentation
CGCLOCK2	COM	Color display clock, beeps every 15 minutes

CGCLOCK2	DOC	Documentation
CMD185	COM	Creates resident COMMAND.COM with good internal commands
CMD185	DOC	Documentation
CURSOR	COM	Changes cursor shape—enter "cursor8" for block shape
CV2	COM	Changes diskette labels under DOS 2.0
EDLIN	BAS	Better documentation for EDLIN (Mel Rothman)
FILELIST	BAS	Displays text files with pause for each full screen
KEY	BAS	Something like simple Prokey for DOS 2.0
NDOSEDIT	COM	VM style editor for DOS commands, with command stack
NDOSEDIT	DOC	Documentation

Disk No 206 — BASIC Aids & Math — v1

CMP	COM	File compare utility Version 1.0 (Jack Gersbach)
CMP	DOC	Documentation
FACTOR	BAS	Calculates factorials
KEYPUNCH	BAS	Programmable keypunching
MULTREG	EXE	Outstanding multiple regression analysis program
PERT	DAT	Part of PERTCHT.BAS
PERTCHT	BAS	PERT schedule Version 1.1
PROFILE	MEM	Helps optimize BASIC programs—load co-resident with BASIC
PUNYCALC	BAS	Four function simple calculator (S. Mones)
PUNYCALC	DOC	Documentation
SORT	BLD	Machine language subroutine for BASIC programs
SORT	DOC	Documentation
SORTEST	BAS	Demo of SORT.BLD
VISICOM	DOC	Convert VISICALC to standard COM file (Corrected by J Wright)

Disk No 207 — LOTUS 123 Templates and Tools — v1 DS

123KEY	BAT	Batch start up file
123KEY	DOC	Documentation
123KEY	PRO	Prokey template—permits using numeric key pad with LOTUS
AUTO	WKS	Calculates your gas usage and mileage (Vince Heiker)
FEDTAX83	WKS	1983 Tax Schedules 1040, 1040A, B, C, W (Les Wheeler)
JOGLOG	WKS	Simple jogging log (Vince Heiker)
PAD	WKS	Version 1.2 (Frank Girard)—Desktop-like template
TREND123	DOC	Documentation
TREND123	MAC	Version 1.0 (John Dannenfeldt)—Curve fitting macro for LOTUS

Disk No 208 — Graphics, Printer Art, Game, Music — v1

DESIGN	EXE	Neat graphics demo
FLASHDAN	BAS	Flashdance (Music—Judith Penner)
JSB	BAS	J.S. Bach Violin Sonata No 6, in E Major, 1st Movement

MASTER2	BAS	Mastermind (Les Penner)
NUDE	BAS	Graphics nude (G. Wesley)
NUDE84	TXT	Text nude with 84 calendar
PRF	PRF	Part of MASTER2.BAS
SMURF	BAS	Smurf printer art (James Card, Phil Gill)

Disk No 209 — Arcade Games (Color Graphics Required) — v1

JUMPJOE2	DOC	Documentation & hints (Tim McClarren)
JUMPJOE2	EXE	Improved version of Miner 2049'er-like game (Kevin Bales)
DATNOIDS	BAS	Similar to robot arcade game (Casey Roche)
NUKE-NY	BAS	Simulation of nuclear attack on NYC area (J. R. Dukat)

Disk No 210 — Castle Game — v1

CASTLE	DOC	Documentation
CASTLE	EXE	Like Temple of Apshai (Kevin Bales)
CASTLE	RAN	Part of CASTLE.EXE

Disk No 211 — JUSTIFY and Speed Reader Demo — v1

ART	TXT	Part of Speed Reading demo
EYE	TXT	Part of Speed Reading demo
JUSTIFY	ASM	Assembler source code
JUSTIFY	EXE	Right/left micro-justifies text (COMFAX)
LINEBUG	BAS	Part of JUSTIFY.EXE
SR	BAS	Speed Reading demo (BBP)
TIMED	TXT	Part of Speed Reading demo
TUTOR2		Part of JUSTIFY.EXE
TUTORIAL		Part of JUSTIFY.EXE

Disk No 212 — RBBS Version 12.2 — v1 DS2

CALLERS		Part of RBBS-PC.EXE
CONFIG	BQS	Sets up RBBS configuration (Squeezed)
DIR		Description of file directories
DIR99		Description of most recent file uploads
FIXFILES	BAS	Cleans up caller file
FILESEC		Part of RBBS-PC.EXE
FIX-2A-1	DOC	Documentation for FIX-2A-1.MRG
FIX-2A-1	MRG	Fixes for bugs in Version 12.1
FIXUSERS	BAS	Converts RBBS Version 12.1 to Version 12.2
HELP01		User help file—commands
HELP02		User help file—functions supported

HELP03		User help file—message protection
HELP04		User help file—editing messages
HELP05		User help file—file menu
HELP06		User help file—file subsystem extra help
HELP07		User help file—message read help file
HELP08		User help file—commands
MENU1		Menu—sysop utilities
MENU1G		Graphics Menu—sysop utilities
MENU2		Menu—main RBBS menu
MENU2G		Graphics Menu—main RBBS menu
MENU3		Menu—RBBS files
MENU3G		Graphics Menu—RBBS files
MENU4		Menu—additional utilities
MENU4G		Graphics Menu—additional utilities
MENU5		Menu—Windows function
MENU5G		Graphics Menu—windows function
MESSAGES		Part of RBBS-PC.EXE
NEWUSER		Welcome message
PASSWRDS		Part of RBBS-PC.EXE
RBBS-PC	BQS	BASIC version (Squeezed)
RBBS-PC	DEF	Part of RBBS-PC.EXE
RBBS-PC	DQC	Documentation (Squeezed)
RBBS-PC	EXE	Compiled version
RBBS-PC	REM	Remarks used by RBBS-PC.xxx programs
RINGBACK	MRG	Ringback function source code
UNSQ	EXE	Unsqueezes *.?Q? files
USRINIT1	BAS	Clears user download/upload counts
USRINIT2	BAS	Reads callers file & updates
UTSPACE	OBJ	Part of RBBS-PC.xxx programs
WELCOME		Welcome message
WELCOMEG		Graphics welcome message

Disk No 213 — Adventure Game Compiler — v1

ADVCOMP	DOC	Documentation for ADVCOMP.EXE
ADVCOMP	EXE	Adventure game compiler—create your own adventure games
ADVRUN	EXE	Part of ADVCOMP.EXE—interpreter for running compiled games
MUGGER	ADV	Source for sample MUGGER game for ADVCOMP.EXE
MUGGER	DAT	Memory resident file for sample MUGGER game
MUGGER	HDR	Header message file for MUGGER sample
MLGGER	REF	Reference file addressed by ADVRUN.EXE for MUGGER adventure

Disk No 214	Data Base of Steel—Volume 1 Version 3.1	v2 DS

This is the first volume of Potomac Engineering's database, spreadsheet and expert system offerings. The purposes of each file is more fully explained in the manual on Disk No 215. The other volumes in this set are Disks Nos 215, 267 and 268.

		Database of Steel—Source Code
MAIN	BAS	Main database program
SCAN	BAS	Database extract and select program
CHANGE	BAS	Global database change and replacement
FORM	BAS	Report format program
TRANSFER	BAS	Transfer data from one file to another
SORT	BAS	Sorts database
CFILE	BAS	Creates (defines) database file
CINPUT	BAS	Sets up new data entry for the file
CTRANSFE	BAS	Customizes transfers between files
CFORM	BAS	Creates print forms
CLIMITS	BAS	Sets range limts for numeric fields
CREAL	BAS	Realtime transfers between files
CSCREEN	BAS	Sets up screen display for record
ASCII	BAS	Convert from random access format to ASCII
TESTASCI	BAS	Reads file created from above and display it
READ	ME	Descriptions of files on disk

Disk No 215	Data Base of Steel—Volume 2 Version 3.1	v2 DS

		Database of Steel—Sample Programs and Files, Documentation
READ	ME	Descriptions of files on disk
MASTER	TXT	Manual (WORDSTAR format—153K)
PRINTMAN	BAS	Procedure to print the manual
REMARKS1	BAS	Program remarks
REMARKS2	BAS	Program remarks
REMARKS3	BAS	Program remarks
REMARKS4	BAS	Program remarks
ACCTSUM		Sample program
ARSUMARY		"
ASCIDATA		"
BILL		"
CHECKS		"
CLS	OBJ	"
CTEMP	BAS	"
CUSTOMER		"
EXTRA		"
FFILE		"
FORMLIST		"

IDEX		"
INVOICE		"
IPUTD		"
IPUTD1		"
IPUTD10		"
IPUTD11		"
IPUTD12		"
IPUTD13		"
IPUTD14		"
IPUTD15		"
IPUTD2		"
IPUTD3		"
IPUTD4		"
IPUTD5		"
IPUTD6		"
IPUTD7		"
IPUTD8		"
IPUTD9		"
JOBCOSTS		"
JOURNAL		"
KEYLISTS		"
KYLIST		"
LCATE	OBJ	"
MAXMIN1		"
MAXMIN8		"
PAYCHECK		"
PAYCHKS		"
PAYSUM		"
PRTEXTRA	BAS	"
REAL1		"
REAL3		"
REALTIME		"
RECIEABL		"
SCREEN1		"
SCREEN14		"
SCREEN4		"
SCREEN6		"
SCREEN8		"
SCTEST		"
SECOND		"
STOCK		"
TAXSCH		"

TEMP	BAS	"
TEST		"
TESTIPUT		"
TESTTWO		"
TFER		"
W2		"

Disk No 216	"c" utilities	v1
README	DOC	Notes about programs on this disk
WEEKDAY	C	Function to determine the day of the week a given Gregorian date
READS	C	Reads string from stdin
SCONTROL	H	Header file used by screen and keyboard control library
CHOSIT	C	Function to display menu, prompt for a response and validate
ELINE	C	Function to erase line of screen
JTOG	C	Function to convert Julian date to Gregorian date
DOSDATE	ASM	Returns DOS month, day, year as integers
JTOJ	C	Returns Julian day from date in form (yddd)
SCRINIT	C	Initializes screen and keyboard arrays
SCRATT	C	Toggles screen attributes (ie BOLD, blink, reverse video)
FRAME	C	Function to draw box given two corners
CURSOR	C	Function to move cursor to a specific r,c position
CURDOWN	C	Function to move curser down y relative lines
GETLINE	C	Read record from file to string
CVTDATE	C	Unpacks Gregorian date (1/1/84) to (01/01/84)
GTOJ	C	Converts Gregorian date to Julian date
CURFOR	C	Move cursor forward x columns
CURBACK	C	Move cursor back x columns
PAUSE	C	Pauses a program for period of time
CURUP	C	Mover cursor up y lines
ESCREEN	C	Function to erase line from screen
DOSTIME	ASM	Return DOS time in hours, minutes, seconds and 1/100 seconds
GETTIME	C	Gets time in form HH:MM:SS (24 hour clock)
GETDATE	C	Gets date in string form MM/DD/YY
BIOSIO	ASM	Assembly routines which interface directly with BIOS
READC	C	Function to read string from stdin
WRITES	C	Function to write string to stdout
WRITEC	C	Function to write character to screen using DOS function
MENCON	C	Function to open menu file and display it on screen
COMM	MNU	Menu for communications program
IBMTTY	C	Terminal emulation program with file upload and download capabilities
VI	BAT	Batch files to emulate UNIX commands
LS	BAT	"
RM	BAT	"
CL	BAT	"

CAT	BAT	"
MV	BAT	"
LD	BAT	"
L	BAT	"
CC	BAT	"

Disk No 217		**ELIST and disk ALIGNment**	**v2 DS**
RESWORDS	TXT	Key word list used by NELIST	
SUPERDIR	BAS	"Super directory" program (Compute Magazine April, l984)	
SUPERDIR	DOC	Documentation for SUPERDIR.BAS	
DUMPSCRN	BAS	BLOADable high resolution screen dump (Softalk, July, 1983)	
DUMPSCRN	MRG	Model BASIC program for using DUMPSCRN.BAS	
DUMPSCRN	DOC	Documentation for DUMPSCRN	
ALIGN	EXE	Disk alignment program	
ALIGN	DOC	Documentation for disk alignment program	
NELIST	DOC	Documentation for NELIST	
NELIST	COM	Turbo Pascal source lister—underlines key words etc.	
NEPRN	DAT	Printer control data for NELIST	
NEINST	COM	Installation program to create NEPRN.DAT	
NELIST	PAS	Source code for NELIST	
NEINST	PAS	Source code for NEINST	
WA-TOR	COM	Predator-prey simulation (Scientific American, Dec., 1984)	
WA-TOR	000	Overlays used by WA-TOR.COM	
WA-TOR	PAS	Turbo Pascal source code for WA-TOR	
WA-TOR	DOC	Documentation for WA-TOR	

Disk No 218		**Address Manager**	**v1**
ADDRESS	EXE	Executable program file—Address Manager	
ADDRESS	MEN	Program menu file	
ADDRESS	DAT	Data base file	
ADDRESS	DOC	Documentation (Approximately 5 pages)	
PAPER	OUT	Disables paper out detector on printer	
SCREEN	ASM	Source for SCREEN.COM	
SCREEN	COM	Screen utility to change fgd/bkgd colors	
COLOR	BAT	.BAT version of screen (Uses prompt cmd)	
SCREEN	EXE	Link command output [will not run...only .COM]	
READ-ME	DOC	How to use screen & color programs	

Disk No 219		**MapMaker**	**v1 DS**
MANUAL		Documentation (Approximately 20 pages)	
MAPMAKER	EXE	Main program	
FLAPAN		Data set—NW Florida	

GNV		Data set—Gainsville, Florida
OFFICES		Data set—sample floorplan
USA		Data set—contigous USA
FLA-POP		Statistical data—number of residents by county (FLAPAN)
FLA-INC		Statistical data—per capita income (FLAPAN)
OFF-YRS		Statistical data—number of years of occupancy by present occupan
tGNV-65		Statistical data—percent of residents 65 years and older in 197
0GNV-POP		Statistical data—number of residents in 1970
USA-SUN		Statistical data—percent sunny days during an average year
USA-FUND		Statistical data—Federal funding of universities in 1979
FLA-CENT		Centroid data set (FLAPAN)
USA-CENT		Centroid data set (USA)
SCREEN1	BAS	Screen image files—Choropleth—Office Residency
SCREEN2	BAS	Screen image files—Circle—Gainesville Population
SCREEN3	BAS	Screen image files—Circle—N.W. Florida Population
SCREEN4	BAS	Screen image files—Choropleth—Gainesville Elderly
SCREEN5	BAS	Screen image files—Choropleth—U.S. Sunny Days

Disk No 220 — Prowriter Utilities (S&F) — v1 DS

Disks No 220 through 222 are Soft & Friendly's user-supported printer utilities.

PRNT-SCN	COM	Print screen utility
PRNT-CHR	COM	Allows italics and extended ASCII characters to be printed
PRNT-SET	COM	Program to allow printer to be setup easily
SCN-DEMO	BAS	Demonstration program for PRNT-SCN
CHR-DEMO	BAS	Demonstration program for PRNT-CHR
USMAP	PIC	Graphic test image of USA for use with SCN-DEMO
PRN-MAN	BAT	Batch file to print manual
MANUAL	DOC	Formatted manual (Use Prowriter I or II only—takes 50 minutes—125K)
PRN-APX	BAT	Batch file to print appendix
APPENDIX	DOC	Appendix (Use Prowriter I or II only—takes 20 minutes—65K)
NOTICE		Message to those who print manual and/or appendix
README		Instruction for printing documentation

Disk No 221 — NEC 8023A Utilities (S&F) — v1 DS

PRNT-SCN	COM	Print screen utility
PRNT-CHR	COM	Allows italics and extended ASCII characters to be printed
PRNT-SET	COM	Program to allow printer to be setup easily
SCN-DEMO	BAS	Demonstration program for PRNT-SCN
CHR-DEMO	BAS	Demonstration program for PRNT-CHR
USMAP	PIC	Graphic test image of USA for use with SCN-DEMO
PRN-MAN	BAT	Batch file to print manual

MANUAL	DOC	Formatted manual (Use NEC 8023A only—takes 50 minutes—124K)
PRN-APX	BAT	Batch file to print appendix
APPENDIX	DOC	Appendix (Use NEC 8023A only—takes 20 minutes—61K)
NOTICE		Message to those who print manual and/or appendix
README		Instruction for printing documentation

Disk No 222 — Transtar Utilities (S&F) — v1

PRNT-SCN	COM	Print screen utility
PRNT-CHR	COM	Allows italics and extended ASCII characters to be printed
SCN-DEMO	BAS	Demonstration program for PRNT-SCN
CHR-DEMO	BAS	Demonstration program for PRNT-CHR
USMAP	PIC	Graphic test image of USA for use with SCN-DEMO
PRN-MAN	BAT	Batch file to print manual
MANUAL	DOC	Formatted manual (Use Transtar 315 only—takes 50 minutes—48K)
PRN-APX	BAT	Batch file to print appendix
APPENDIX	DOC	Appendix (Use Transtar 315—takes 30 minutes—36K)
NOTICE		Message to those who print manual and/or appendix
README		Instruction for printing documentation

Disk No 223 — Assembly/Pascal Utilities — v1 DS

BEEP	ASM	Program to make "beep" on speaker
BEEP	DOC	Documentation for BEEP
CANCEL	ASM	Source for CANCEL
CANCEL	EXE	Program to cancel the setting that SETP causes
CLS	ASM	Program to clear screen
CLS	DOC	Documentation for CLS
CLS	OBJ	Object file
CONTENTS	DOC	Description of file on this disk
CONTRACT	ASM	Procedure to restore the cursor to its system size
CONTRACT	DOC	Documentation for CONTRACT
CONTRACT	OBJ	Object file
EXPAND	ASM	Procedure to expand curser to solid blinking rectangle
EXPAND	DOC	Documentation for EXPAND
EXPAND	OBJ	Object file
FILE	PAS	Pascal Program to manage a small data base type program
INFO	BAT	Batch file to list file information on screen
LOCATE	ASM	Procedure to set curser position from Pascal
LOCATE	DOC	Documentation for LOCATE
LOCATE	OBJ	Object file
MODULE	OBJ	Object file
MODULE	PAS	Module to be linked with FILE.PAS

MORE	COM	Filter to one screen at a time
MSBFILE	EXE	Executable image of file
PREVIEW	EXE	A Pascal utility to preview a text file prior to printing
PREVIEW	PAS	Pascal source code for PREVIEW
READCHAR	ASM	Procedure to read a specified number of characters
READCHAR	DOC	Documentation for READCHAR
READCHAR	OBJ	Object file
REPLY	ASM	Source code for REPLY
REPLY	COM	Produces beep
REPLY	EXE	Produces beep
RESPOND	ASM	Produces beep
RESPOND	DOC	Documentation for RESPOND
RESPOND	OBJ	Object file
SETANSI	ASM	Source code for SETANSI
SETANSI	COM	A procedure to communicate with ANSI.SYS to reset keys
SETANSI	EXE	Executable file version of SETANSI
SETP	ASM	Source code for SETP
SETP	EXE	Program to setup Epson printer to skip perforations
SETP	OBJ	Object file

Disk No 224 — Gray Gordon's PC-CALC — v1 DS

This disk contains PC-Calc, as small spreadsheet written by John Vandegrift and Guy Gordon. PC-Calc is distributed free, and should not be confused with a later program of the same name by Jim Button (of PC-File fame).

README		List of files
PC-CALC	DOC	Documentation for PC-Calc (65K)
PC-CALC	BAS	Source code for PC-Calc
PC-CALC	EXE	Compiled version
SCRNSAVE	COM	Advanced Screen Save
SCRNSAVE	DOC	Allows user to set time out
SCRNSAVE	ASM	Source code for new version
KBUFF	COM	Advanced keyboard buffer expander
KBUFF	DOC	Documentation and Source for above
SDIR1	COM	Enhanced SDIR for DOS 1.xx
SDIR1	DOC	Documentation explains enhancements

Disk No 225 — PC-FONT — v1

PC-FONT2	EXE	Program to print 243 of PC's 256 characters
PC-FONT2	TST	Test file
DESCRIPT	TXT	Brief program description
PC-FONT2	PRN	Manual (70K bytes)
README		How to print manual

Disk No 226 — FREECOPY Version 1.10 — v1.1 DS2

FREECOPY	COM	A user-supported version of DISKCOPY
FREECOPY	ASM	Source code for FREECOPY.COM
FREECOPY	DOC	Users manual (28K)
FREECOPY	LST	Assembly listing for those without an Assembler
FREECOPY	REF	Assembler reference listing
FREECOPY	MAP	Assembler map listing

Disk No 227 — FINANCE — v1.1

A user-supported finance program to determine present and compound values.

FINANCE	EXE	Main program
FINANCE	DOC	Documentation (20K)

Disk No 228 — GAMES — v1

CRIBBAGE	BAS	Game—same rules as board game one player vs PC
CRIBBAGE	BLD	Subroutines for CRIBBAGE.BAS
PAC-GAL	EXE	Game—eatem up dots
COLSLOT	BAS	One arm bandit in color—its a winner (Requires color)
FIREFIRE	BAS	Game—reflexes on keyboard
MAZE	BAS	Produces mazes of any size for screen or printer
T-ROAD	BAS	A neat and interesting adventure game
SLOT	BAS	Same as you have, but graphics are much better and in color
VAMPIRE	BAS	Adventure game
NEWFONT	BAS	The program in PC—bugs?
NUKE-SF	BAS	A well done nuclear war demo

Disk No 229 — Funnels & Buckets — v1 DS

FUNNELS	EXE	A user-supported Funnels & Buckets game
FUNNELS	DOC	Funnels documentation (15K)
FUNNELS	INV	Invoice for author contribution
ATC	EXE	Air Traffic Control game (US)
ATC1	BLD	Part of ACT
ATC2	BLD	Part of ACT
AUTOEXEC	BAT	Part of ACT
ATC	DAT	Part of ACT
EUCHRE	BAS	"Squished" version of EUCHRE
EUCHRE	DOC	Rules for the card game EUCHRE
EUCHRE	SRC	Source code for EUCHRE including comments
EUCHRE	INS	Instructions for computer EUCHRE

Disk No 230 The Confidant Version 2.0 v1 DS

The Confidant is a user-supported program which encodes sensitive data in order to keep it confidential. The Confidant protects information transmitted by communications lines from alteration as well as from unauthorized use by anyone intercepting it or trying to change it. The Confidant gives a choice of two encryption procedures. The national Data Encryption Standard (DES) provides very high security. A faster "privacy" procedure that is somewhat less secure provides encryption for normal use, where speed is important.

CONFIDE	EXE	Main program
CONFIDE	HLP	Help file
CONFIDE	CRY	Part of CONFIDE
CONFIDE	INV	Part of CONFIDE
REFCARD	DOC	A brief summary of the main commands
TUTORIAL	DOC	A step-by-step tutorial (69K)
DESCRIPT	DOC	An overall description of the program (24K)
REFER	DOC	A technical reference manual (60K)
TYPE	ME	How to list documentation

Disk No 231 REFLIST 2.0 v1.1

User-supported program to maintain list of references.

FILEREFS	EXE	Program to file your reprints
REFLIST	EXE	Program to formats references
REFLIST	DOC	Instruction manual (32K)
MASTFILE		Reprint master file
PROTOTYP	???	Prototype formats
EXAMPLE	MSS	Text to practice on
FILECATA	LOG	List of files on disk

Disk No 232 SPPC System Demo v1.1 DS

This is a demo of SPPC, a fully interactive statistical package that enables you to enter, manage and analyze simple and complex sets of data. In order to use the SPPC, you must enter your data and store it on a diskette or hard disk file. You can then conduct any statistical analysis that is available.

READ	ME	Instructions for installing the SPPC system
AUTOEXEC	BAT	Autostart file
README	BAT	Type the readme message on screen
LETTER	TXT	Introductory letter describing features of package
SUMSTAT	HLP	Part of SPPC system—help file
MULREG	HLP	Part of SPPC system—help file
LEARN	HLP	Part of SPPC system—help file
SP	SHR	Part of SPPC system

SPPC	HLP	Part of SPPC system—help file
CORR	HLP	Part of SPPC system—help file
RPNC	HLP	Part of SPPC system
PROB	HLP	Part of SPPC system
SUMSTAT	EXE	Part of SPPC system—program file
MULREG	EXE	Part of SPPC system—program file
SPPC	EXE	Part of SPPC system—main program
CORR	EXE	Part of SPPC system—program file
PROB	EXE	Part of SPPC system
LONGLEYS	DAT	Part of SPPC system—data file
LONGLEYR	DAT	Part of SPPC system—data file

Disk No 233 newBASE v1.1 DS

User-supported data base program. Type or list READ_ME.DOC for directions on how to make a working disk and run the program.

READ_ME	DOC	How to make a working disk

Disk No 234 TPNCALC v1

User-supported program for Pharmacists to calculate intravenous electrolyte additives needed to compound a Hyperalimentation order according to the medical doctors specifications.

TPNCALC	EXE	Main program
TPNDOC		Documentation (14K)

Disk No 235 Parts Inventory Control v1.1 DS

This diskette contains the documentation and program for Parts Inventory Control, Version 1.0. There are eleven datasets:

INVENT	COM	Program driver, enter INVENT from DOS to load and run program
DISKETTE	COM	Loaded by INVENT.COM—formats and copies diskettes
FILE	COM	Loaded by INVENT.COM—create inventory records
RECORD	COM	Loaded by INVENT.COM—update inventory records
PRINT	COM	Loaded by INVENT.COM—prints current and history reports
HISTORY	COM	Loaded by INVENT.COM—transfer data to history diskettes
UTILITY	COM	Loaded by INVENT.COM—transfer data to DOS formatted diskettes
INVENT	DOC	Tutorial and User's Guide, print using DOS support (161K)
README	DOC	Notes about files on disk and printing documentation
NOTICE	DOC	Press release
AUTOEXEC	BAT	Loads INVENT.COM at power on or with Alt, Ctrl, and Del

Disk No 236	Printer	v1.1

This disk contains two user-supported programs for printers. The first one is BPRINT (for BASIC program lister). The second contains tables for using the Toshiba printer with Volkswriter Deluxe.

		BPRINT (BASIC program lister) Version 1.05
BPRINT	EXE	List BASIC programs
FPRINT	EXE	List ASCII files
FPRINT	DOC	Documentation for FPRINT.EXE
FPRINT	HLP	Help file for FPRINT.EXE
FPRINT	TRY	Sample file for FPRINT.EXE
		Toshiba/Volkswriter printer tables
README		How to use the Toshiba printer/Volkswriter tables
INSTVXPT	RCE	Part of Toshiba printer/Volkswriter tables
IN12	FMT	Part of Toshiba printer/Volkswriter tables
IN12HS	FMT	Part of Toshiba printer/Volkswriter tables
IN12INDT	FMT	Part of Toshiba printer/Volkswriter tables
IN12TITL	FMT	Part of Toshiba printer/Volkswriter tables
INCOND	FMT	Part of Toshiba printer/Volkswriter tables
COPYPRTR	BAT	Part of Toshiba printer/Volkswriter tables
COPYINST	BAT	Part of Toshiba printer/Volkswriter tables
COPYALL	BAT	Part of Toshiba printer/Volkswriter tables—copies all files
VXPRINT*	TBL	Part of Toshiba printer/Volkswriter tables

Disk No 237	PC-General Ledger Version 1.3a	v1.1 DS

PC-General Ledger, a user-supported program from Charter Software, was written by a financial executive with over 25 years of experience in all areas of accounting, finance, taxes and general management. The The program has all of the controls necessary to make sure that everything is kept in balance and that a complete audit trail always exists. The manual and the programs assume that you have a working knowledge of bookkeeping, know the difference between debits and credits and know how to prepare and post entries.

GLCHECKS	EXE	Part of PC-General Ledger
GLSTATE	EXE	Part of PC-General Ledger
GLTRIAL	EXE	Part of PC-General Ledger
GLMENU	EXE	Part of PC-General Ledger
GLCHART	EXE	Part of PC-General Ledger
GLENTRY	EXE	Part of PC-General Ledger
GLCTRL	FIL	Part of PC-General Ledger
MANUAL		PC-General Ledger Manual (38K)
MANUAL	BAT	Batch file to print manual
AUTOEXEC	BAT	Part of PC-General Ledger—autostart file

Disk No 238 SPRITE v1 DS

There are several unrelated programs on this disk. SPRITE is a user-supported program which lets you conveniently create Sprite charaters. A Sprite character is a graphics figure made from a set of colored pixels. Instead of displaying this figure pixel by pixel, BASIC lets you display the figure in one step with the graphics form of the PUT statement. This is similar to the Sprite graphics available on other microcomputers.

SPRITE	COM	This is the SPRITE Program
SPRITE	SAV	This is a sample SPRITE save file.
SPRITE	BAS	A sample BASIC program created with the SPRITE program
SPRITE	DOC	Documentation message—SPRITE is self documenting
BASTOD	BAS	BASIC program shows how to call DOS functions (50K)
SEIV	DOC	Benchmark test for several computers including c test program
CVTBIN	BAS	Converts CIS (Intel hex format) .BIN files to true Binary files
TIMER		Explains how to get around PRINT/SIDEKICK incompatibility
QUIET	DOC	How to quiet Tandon drives (DOS 2.0 +)
HARDBO	DOC	How to reboot off hard disk
NKYPKY	TXT	Comparison of NEWKEY and PROKEY
TKSOLVER	UNP	How to unprotect TKSOLVER
PROKEY	UNP	How to unprotect PROKEY
LAYOUT	UNP	How to unprotect LAYOUT
RBASE	UNP	How to unprotect RBASE
SK	UNP	How to unprotect Sidekick
PC-PRINT	EXE	German, Spanish, Banner, EPSON printer utilities
PC-PRINT	DOC	Documentation file (11k)

Disk No 239 IPCO Graph and Higher Math Mix v1 DS

This disk has an interesting mix of programs with the majority dealing with higher math functions and graph capabilities. CURVE.BAS requires color graphics and the rest run well on momochrome. 4028-A.BAS is a musical program that allows an interlude in a hard day of pounding simultaneous equations.

1004-B	BAS	Mini word processor/mail merge
1005-A	BAS	Prints 3x5 recipe cards for address listing
1009-A	BAS	Form generation, daily log sheet
3002-A	BAS	A neat non-graphics mini graph plot
3003-A	BAS	Plots probability curve
3006-A	BAS	Matrix inversion & simultaneous equations
3012-A	BAS	Multiple linear regression coefficients
3014-A	BAS	Multiple regression analysis package
CURVE	BAS	Linear exponential logorithmic & power equation
CURVE	ABS	Introduction for CURVE.BAS
CURVE	NFO	Documentation for CURVE.BAS (12K)
4028-A	BAS	Musical change of pace

5006-A	BAS	Spelling bee exercisor
7013-A	BAS	Prints in italics on Epson printer
LOGMENU	LOG	A BASIC program that records entry and exit times
LOGON	LOG	Used by LOGMENU.LOG to log on
LOGREV	LOG	Used by LOGMENU.LOG to keep times
LOGOFF	LOG	Used by LOGMENU.LOG to leave system
7037-A	BAS	Changes printer mode
7042-A	BAS	Mini data menu: directories, printer mode etc.

Disk No 240 — FT-Etc Genealogy 1.25 — v1.1 DS

Genealogy program from Pine Cone Software. Lets you keep track of the old family tree. This program has a good menu system.

FT-ETC	EXE	This is the main geneology program
FT-ETC-C	EXE	One of the branches
FT-ETC-M	EXE	Another branch
FT-ETC-R	EXE	Still another branch
FT-ETC	PCS	Documentation
FT-ETC	TXT	Documentation and directions

Disk No 241 — PCjr Educational Games — v1 DS

This is an excellent collection of games for kids of ages 6 through 60. There are things to tease and tantilize the intellect and some that are just plain fun.

MENU	BAS	Menu that allows selection and calls up the games
AUTOEXEC	BAT	A batch file that helps create a working disk
11	BAS	Word matching game, similar to concentration
12	BAS	Black and white version of word matching game
0	BAS	End program and goodbye screen
2	BAS	Alphabetize a word list
3	BAS	Fun arcade type bowling game
4	BAS	A graphics display program
5	BAS	Maxit, a strategy numbers game
6	BAS	Othello, an old standby
7	BAS	Word problems game
8	BAS	Find-a-word puzzle (Requires printer)
10	BAS	Finds your age in days
15	BAS	Word scramble (1)
9	BAS	Creates a unique maze each time (Requires printer)
13	BAS	Hangman, an old favorite
BRIEFLY	BAS	Part of titles used by TITLE.BAS
ACS	PIC	Picture file—used by ?

1	BAS	Spelling bee
GRADE-2	LST	Wordlist for grade 2—used by spelling programs
GRADE-3	LST	Wordlist for grade 3
17	BAS	Mazes number 2
GRADE-1	LST	Wordlist for grade 1
GRADE-4	LST	Wordlist for grade 4
14	BAS	Word scramble number 1
16	BAS	Screen machine, a draw program (Requires color graphics)
README	DOC	Documentation by authors
TITLE	BAS	Title page and pointer to other documentation
TITLE2	BAS	Additional titles
GRADE-5	LST	Wordlist for grade 5
20	BAS	Program descriptions—called from menu

Disk No 242 Sage Trader v1 DS

Sage Trader was written to provide the commodity trader with an analysis and graphics program that would run on the IBM monochrome display. Requires DOS 2.0. It is a user-supported program.

ST	EXE	Main program
ST	HLP	On line help for ST.EXE
ST	SPC	Points to data files
ST	ARF	Same as above
LCFEB84	CCC	Example data files
LCAPR84	CCC	"
CNMAR84	CCC	"
CNMAY84	CCC	"
INSTALL	BAT	Makes a working copy of original disk
TRADER	PRN	Documentation for Sage Trader

Disk No 243 Sage Calendar/Tag v1 DS

Sage Calendar is an electronic desk calendar. It allows you to create memos, store addresses or record events. The program will display active memos and create calendars for any date you select. Tag was written for a seed company to produce tags. It may be useful to others who need to produce multiple copies of several different tags. Both programs are user-supported and include documentation on disk.

		Sage Calendar
CAL	COM	Sage Calendar main program
SCRN	OVL	On line help for Sage Calendar
CAL	PRN	Documentaion for Sage Calendar
CALINST	BAT	Batch program to make working copy

		Sage Tag
TAG	COM	Sage Tag main program
TAG	HLP	On line help for Sage Tag
TAG	PRN	Documentation for Sage Tag
TAGINST	BAT	Batch program to make working copy

Disk No 244 — Slide Generation — v1 DS

The purpose of this program is the production of medium quality slides and overhead transparancies. Images may be created, edited, saved, displayed and printed using this program. Overhead transparancies are produced by copying the printed output onto transparent material. Photographic slides are produced by photographing the printed output. This is a user-supported program.

SLIDE	EXE	Slide master program
SLIDE	SDE	Character definition file
SLIDE	CTR	Printer control code file
-README-	BAT	Initiates the display of instructions
INSTRUCT	ION	Instructions for printing the slide manual and running the slide program
SLIDEDOC	EXE	Expand and print slide manual
SLIDE	MAN	Squeezed manual

Disk No 245 — Ultra-Utilities Files—Unsqueezed — v1 DS

U-MIND	DOC	Documentation for U-MIND (51K)
U-OPT	DOC	Documentation for O-OPT (2K)
DOC41	TXT	Ultra-Utility documentation—Part 1 (52K)
DOC42	TXT	Ultra-Utility documentation—Part 2 (23K)
U-OPT	EXE	Ultra-Optimize program
SKELETON	BAS	Used with Ultra-Mind
U-MIND	BAS	Ultra-Mind program (Intelligent database)

Disk No 246 — Stock Charting System — v1 DS

The purpose of this system is to draw and/or print volume-high-low-close charts for any stock. Bonds, commodities, or other securities that have high-low-close prices can also be charted. Short and longterm moving average lines can optionally be included on each chart. This is a user-supported program. Color graphics is needed to display the graphs.

REL1_5		Release number
AUTOEXEC	BAT	Starts program on system reboot if COMMAND.COM is on disk
AUTOSTRT	BAT	Starts program at initial start if COMMAND.COM is on disk
SPECCOPY	BAT	Batch program to copy to a working disk
SMCONFG1	BAS	Main configuration program that calls others
SMADDEL1	BAS	Maintains indes file directory

SMENTRY1	BAS	Sets up data entry to data files
SMGRAPH1	BAS+	Uses entered information to create bargraphs
SMCONFG1	HS1	Help screen that displays on line documentation
SMADDEL1	HS1	" "
SMENTRY1	HS1	" "
SMENTRY1	HS2	" "
SMGRAPH1	HS1	" "
SMGRAPH1	HS2	" "
SMGRAPH1	HS3	" "
SMCOVER	DOC	Cover documentation and summary of program (3K)
SMUSERG	DOC	10 page user guide
INDEXFIL	SMX	Index to data files
WAHP	SMP	Sample data file
WDOW	SMP	" "
WIBM	SMP	" "
WMD	SMP	" "
WDJ20B	SMP	" "
WTE	SMP	" "

Disk No 247 — BOBCAT—Business Database — v1.1 DS2

BOBCAT is a database of small business computer information. Reviews, tutorials, general articles, buying guides, even ads on special products that apply to small businesses are listed. The database may be searched by any combination of category, subject, form, product or company name. BOBCAT is distributed as user-supported software in Jim Button's PC-File III format. Needs PC-File or other similar program to sort and print information and indexes in a usable format.

BOBCAT01	DTA	Data base
BOBCAT01	INX	Index
BOBCAT01	HDR	Header information
BOBCAT	TXT	Help program
ORDERFRM	TXT	Order form and information to communicate with author
MAG	HDR	Header information
MAG	INX	Index
MAG	DTA	Data base
MAG	RPT	Formats a report for data from BOBCAT01.DTA
CATEGORY	RPT	Part of BOBCAT

Disk No 248 — Math Library — v1.1 DS

User-supported complex function library—version 1.2

COMPLEX	LIB	Function library
COMPLEX	DOC	Documentation (32K)
COMPLEXP	PAS	Pascal sample program
COMPLEXF	FOR	Fortran sample program

		Pascal programs
LISTING	COM	Lists Turbo Pascal files with xreference, begin/end blocks...
LISTING	DOC	Instructions for above
LISTING	PAS	Source code for above
PRINTER	COM	Sets Epson printer for condensed, double, wide, normal print
PRINTER	PAS	Source code for above
FUNCTION	PAS	Additional functions for Turbo Pascal (time, date, min, max...)
FUNCTION	DOC	Documentation for above

Disk No 249 — Equator/PC-TOUCH Educational Programs — v1.1 DS

There are some excellent educational programs on this disk. Equator is a user-supported educational system for teaching math, science, and finance. It uses a novel non-drill exploratory approach. PC-TOUCH is a typing tutor which lets you go at your own pace and keeps track of how well you are doing. UTMP is a math drill program.

		EQUATOR 1.1 (u-s)
EQ	EXE	Main program—start by typing "EQ"
SCIENCE	EXE	Science lessons
MATH	EXE	Math lessons
PRT	BAT	To print documentation type: "PRT"
EQUATOR	TXT	Documentation (20K)
FINANCE	EXE	Finance lessons
		PC-TOUCH Touch typing tutor (u-s)
PC-TOUCH	BAS	Source code for PC-TOUCH.EXE
PC-TOUCH	FIL	Part of PC-TOUCH
PC-TOUCH	EXE	Compiled version—type "PC-TOUCH" to start
PC-TOUCH	DOC	Documentation (4K)
UTMP	BAS	Math drill program

Disk No 250 — SYSMENU/FINDFILE — v1.1 DS

There are two user-supported programs on this disk. SYSMENU is a menu driven directory program primarily for hard disk users. FINDFILE searches out specific files on disk.

		Sysmenu
SYSMENU	COM	Main SYSMENU program, allows file selection from menu
SYSMENU	DOC	Documentation for SYSMENU (7K)
		Findfile programs
START	BAT	Prints documentation for FINDFILE program
START	TXT	Cover information for FINDFILE
BUG		Bug report form to be sent to author if you have problems
COVER		Installation instructions
DOC		Findfile documentation (41K)
ORDER		Order and license form to be sent to author

LISTER	EXE	Lists your found file on the printer
DSKLABEL		Creates a disk label for FINDFILE
MOVEFF	BAT	Move FINDFILE to a different disk or directory
FINDFILE	BAT	Runs FINDFILE and MAPTREE
SORTTREE	BAT	Runs $$TRESRT.BAT
$$TRESRT	BAT	Sorts directories and subdirectories
MAPTREE	BAS	Maps the tree structure
SAMENAME	BAS	Looks for duplicate filenames
FFILE	EXE	FINDFILE main program
FFILE	LIB	Library used by FFILE
		PC-CHECK Manager and PC-PRINT control have moved to disk No. 275

Disk No 251 Time and Money 1.1B v1.1 DS

Time and Money is a simple financial record keeping system that also keeps a budget, calculates interest, compares rent/buy options, etc.. All of the programs on this disk are designed to be called from the menus that are displayed. In order to run the program or see documentation type in "TAMSTART" and hit the enter key. This is a user-supported program.

Disk No 252 ListMate/Load-US by SWFTE v1.1 DS

This disk contains two user-supported programs from SWFTE. ListMate is a menu driven label producer with all documentation and help displayed from the program. After DOS is active type "LISTMATE" and you're into the program. Load-US (tm) allows you to run Lotus 123 and Symphony directly from a hard disk without the system disk in Drive A. This saves you the aggravation of locating your System disk each time you need to run 123 or Symphony.

LISTMATE	EXE	This is the main ListMate program
LISTMATE	SYS	ListMate system files
LISTMATE	TXT	ListMate text files
LISTMATE	HLP	ListMate help files
LISTMATE	DOC	ListMate documentation (not listable)
LISTMATE	ABS	ListMate abstract
LOAD-US	COM	Main program
LOAD-US	DOC	Documentation (listable)
LOAD-US	ABS	Abstract

Disk No 253	3x5 Card	v1 DS

This program is an information handling system that allows your computer to act like a very efficient 3x5 card system, thus its name. This program would be great for keeping track of small pieces of information such as a patient listing or small library card catalog.

3BY5	EXE	Main program—type "3BY5" to start.
SAMPLE1	3X5	Sample data file
SAMPLE2	3X5	" "
SAMPLE3	WP	" "
SAMPLE4	WS	" "
SAMPLE1	MAP	Map for sample data file
SAMPLE2	MAP	" "
SAMPLE3	MAP	" "
SAMPLE4	MAP	" "
CHAP1&2	BAK	Backup documentation for chapters 1&2
CHAP3	DOC	Documentation for chapter 3
CHAP4&5	DOC	" " 4&5
CHAP6	DOC	" " 6
PRINTALL	BAT	Batch file to print all of the documentation (144K)
README		One page, explains how to print all the documentation
CHAP1&2	DOC	Documentaion for Chapters 1 & 2

Disk No 254	PC-DOS HELP	v1.1 DS2

This program gives you an on-line help capability for DOS commands. Just type HELP if you don't remember the command for the function. This is a user-supported program.

HELP	EXE	The HELP Function program
HCONFIG	EXE	HELP Function configuration program
HELP	DOC	Documentation for HELP.EXE (10K)
HELPREG	DOC	Registration form for HELP
MAKEBKUP	BAT	Makes a backup of this disk
CNV2_00	BAT	Convert HELP for DOS 2.0
CNVPCJR	BAT	Convert HELP for the PC jr
CLEANUP	BAT	After HELP is configured for your system, this file cleans out the stuff that's no longer needed.
* <DIR>		Directories containing help files

Disk No 255		Utilities #5	v1 DS
NEWBELL	COM	Run once to shorten DOS (not BASIC) bell tone	
NEWBELL	ASM	Source for NEWBELL.COM	
HERMREAD	ME	Notes on BATQUES, SCRNCOLR, Compaq video, and FORMAT	
BATQUES	COM	Prompts for character returned as error level	
BATQUES	DOC	Documents BATQUES.COM (2K)	
BATQUES	ASM	Source for BATQUES.COM	
SCRNCOLR	COM	Intercepts screen writes to change colors	
SCRNCOLR	DOC	Documents SCRNCOLR.COM (2K)	
SCRNCOLR	ASM	Source for SCRNCOLR.COM	
DOS-SIZE	DOC	Reference table, size of various DOS versions	
WHEREIS	COM	Searches subdirectories for filename	
WHEREIS	ASM	Source for WHEREIS.COM	
OLDER	COM	Returns information on relative age of two files	
OLDER	ASM	Source for OLDER.COM	
LABEL	EXE	Change/Create Volume Labels—command line input	
LABEL	C	Source for LABEL.EXE	
LABEL	DOC	Documentation for LABEL.EXE	
SCREEN	BAS	Utility for data input and verification	
SCREEN	DOC	Documentation for SCREEN.BAS (3.6K)	
TIMER	EXE	Provides continuous time of day clock on screen	
MORSE	BAS	Morse code practice program	
PURGEDUP	COM	Compares DIRs & erases = fnams with < = date/time	
PURGEDUP	DOC	Documentation for PURGEDUP.COM	
DOSEDIT	COM	Provides re-executable history file of DOS commands	
DOSEDIT	DOC	Documentation for DOSEDIT.COM (3.2K)	
DOCUFILE	BAS	Generates BASIC program Help screens from text file	
DOCUFILE	DOC	Documentation for DOCUFILE.BAS (3.6K)	
DOCUFDOC	BAS	Sample made using DOCUFILE.BAS and DOCUFILE.DOC	
BYE	BAS	Protects screen, provides date & time on idle system	
SDIR	COM	Sorted Directory with numerous options—best to date	
SDIR	DOC	Documentation for SDIR.COM	
LIST	COM	ASCII file lister, viable alternative to TYPE/MORE	
LIST	DOC	Documentation for LIST.COM (2.1K)	
CRYPTO	BAS	Aids in solving cryptograms	
PX	COM	Procedure Cross Referencer for ASM and MASM	
PX	DOC	Documentation for PX.COM (14K)	
SPEED	COM	Modifies disk parameter table	
SPEED	ASM	Source for SPEED.COM, easily modified to your taste	
CHN	PAS	Provides command line execution of Turbo .CHN files	
L4	COM	Displays file w/ up/down paging, horz scroll, find	
L4	DOC	Documentation for L4.COM (4K)	
L4	ASM	Source for L4.COM	
KBFIX	COM	CAPS, NUM & SCROLL flags plus a 127 byte kybd buffer	
KBFIX	ASM	Source for KBFIX.COM	

KBFIX	DOC	Documentation for KBFIX.COM
KBD_FIX	COM	Expands DOS typeahead buffer to 160 characters
KBD_FIX	ASM	Source for KEY_FIX.COM (See Softalk PC, November 83 & January 84)
BAT-CD	COM	Changes working directory based on standard input
BAT-CD	DOC	Documents BATCD.COM
BAT-CD	ASM	Source for BATCD.COM

Disk No 256 — Utilities #6 — v1 DS

SAVE	COM	Copy current screen to alternate monitor
DISPRE	COM	Displays the 8088 registers after being loaded
DISPRE	EXE	by different programs, ie: DEBUG vs COMMAND.COM
DISPRE	ASM	Source for DISPRE.COM/EXE
DISPRE	DOC	Documentation for DISPRE.COM/EXE
MONOCLOK	COM	Time in UR corner of mono display, graphics unaffected
LABEL	EXE	Diskette label program (Softalk March 84)
LABEL	ASM	Source for LABEL.EXE
FREE	COM	Reports free space on one or all drives
FREE	ASM	Source for FREE.COM
FREE	DOC	Documentation for FREE.COM
WHEREIS	COM	File searcher, upgraded with 23 line pause feature
WHEREIS	ASM	Source for WHEREIS.COM
DEFRAG	BAS	Defragments diskette space
DEFRAG	DOC	Documentation for DEFRAG.BAS
NUSQ	COM	New UnSQueeze program, small, fast, improved
NUSQ	DOC	Documentation on NUSQ.COM
DUMP	EXE	Displays a file in hex and ASCII (From May Softalk)
DUMP	ASM	Source for DUMP.EXE
PARCHK	COM	Replaces std parity routine, errors don't stop machine
PARCHK	ASM	Source for PARCHK.COM
PARCHK	DOC	Documentation for PARCHK.COM
REFCD	DOC	INT 21 reference card, DOS 2.1 version
TABS	EXE	Converts spaces to tabs (Shrinks files)
TABS	ASM	Source for TABS.EXE
TABS	DOC	Documentation for TABS.EXE
LOOK	COM	Memory display program
LOOK	ASM	Source for LOOK.COM
LOOK	DOC	Documentation for LOOK.COM
ZAPDEB	BAS	Patch DEBUG.COM to fix timer interrupt bug
ZAPDEB	DOC	Documentation for ZAPDEB.BAS
ZAPTRE	BAS	Patches TREE.COM to support a filename operand WHATWHATWHAT
ZAPTRE	DOC	Documentation for ZAPTRE.BAS
QS	RIO	Quick Startup patch for BIOS
QS	TXT	Documentation for QS.RIO

CLOCK	SYS	Device driver for AST and TECMAR boards with clock
CLOCK	ASM	Source for CLOCK.ASM
CAPSDEF	COM	Defeats the CapsLock key
CAPSDEF	DOC	Documentation for CAPSDEF.COM
CAPSDEF	ASM	Source for CAPSDEF.COM
BIGCAL	BAS	High precision calculator; default is 100 digits
BIGCAL	DOC	Documentation for BIGCAL.DOC
EXPAND	BAS	Replaces tabs with appropiate number of spaces
EXPAND	DOC	Documentation for EXPAND.BAS
DIRECT	BAS	Creates BLOADable file to directly read disk directory
DIRDEM	BAS	Demonstrates DIRECTORY function created by DIRECT.BAS
WHEREIS	COM	Searches all directories for specified file
WHEREIS	BAS	Generates WHEREIS.COM
DSKTYP	EXE	Reports the format of the selected diskette
DSKTYP	ASM	Source for DSKTYP.EXE
FORMAT	VOL	Patch to DOS 2.0 FORMAT to always request VOL label
COLOR	PE	Passionate shades for the Personal Editor
PE-NOTAB	DOC	Fixes Personal Editor to save without those #@%& TABS
DCBA2	HOW	Modify DISKCOPY.COM (Version 2.10) for production copying

Disk No 257 — Utility 1-2-3 — v1 DS

Utility 1-2-3 is a tutorial and utility package to be used with LOTUS 1-2-3 To start type "DIR /W" and follow directions from there. Cute menu system with nice helpful hints and aids for LOTUS.

ASCII	WKS	Reference file for extended ASCII character set
ASCIIDOC	BAT	Displays ASCII character table on screen
ASCIIDOC	PRN	Prints ASCII character table
ASCIITUT	WKS	Tutorial for ASCII character generator
AUTO123	WKS	Part of printed documentation files
END	PRN	" "
HINTSTUT	WKS	Hints and techniques tutorial
INTROTUT	WKS	Introduction to tutorials
LOTUS	PRO	UTILITY 1-2-3 Prokey macros
MACROTUT	WKS	Macro samples
PRINTER	WKS	Reference file for generation of printer control characters
PRINTTUT	WKS	Tutorial for printer control generator
PROKYTUT	WKS	ProKey templates
README	BAT	Starts printout of documentation
SCREEN1	PRN	Part of printed documentation files
SCREEN2	PRN	" "
SCREEN3	PRN	" "
SCREEN4	PRN	" "
SETUP	BAT	Installs UTILITY 1-2-3 on your LOTUS 1-2-3 system disk

Disk No 258		Communications	v1 DS
HC	COM	Hex Converter, very fast	
HC	DOC	Documentation for HC.COM	
HC	ASM	Source for HC.COM	
TALK	EXE	Simple terminal emulator from December '83 Softalk	
TALK	DOC	Documentation for TALK.EXE	
TALK	ASM	Source for TALK.EXE	
RING	BAS	Turns SYSTEM control over to caller	
CTTY	DOC	Discussion of CTTY command and RING.BAS	
SCRIPT	DOC	Script files for CROSSTALK XVI	
ATO	BAS	CompuServe auto logon and message retrieval	
ATO	EXE	Compiled version of ATO.BAS	
ATO	DOC	Documentation for ATO.BAS/EXE	
QPRINT	OBJ	Link with ATO when compiled	
XAPRIN	BAS	Prints files downloaded from Compuserve database	
PCT3JR	MRG	Merge file for PC-TALK III to run on PCjr	
PCT3JR	DOC	Documentation for PCT3JR.MRG	
AT	COM	"AT hhmm" waits until hh:mm (Within 24 hours) Do "break on" if you want to interrupt it!	
AT	ASM	Source for AT.COM	
Z	COM	"Z s" sleeps for s (5 if omitted) seconds Do "break on" if you want to interrupt it!	
Z	ASM	Source for Z.COM	
SERIAL	COM	Makes BIOS serial (COM1) I/O interrupt-driven so programs using them will work at up to 9600 baud.	
SERIAL	DOC	Documents SERIAL.COM	
SERIAL	ASM	Source for SERIAL.COM	

Disk No 259	"c" Adventure	v1 DS

This is a fine D&D type adventure game that is written in "c". Not only can the game players have fun, but the hackers can get into this one and change things to suit their interests.

		ADVENTURE in "c" implementation by Jerry D. Pohl
ADVENT	EXE	Compiled adventure game ready to run
ADVENT0	EXE	Program utility to create ADVTEXT.H
CCADV	BAT	Batch file to compile ADVENT.C
CC	BAT	Batch file to compile an inserted variable program
CLADV	BAT	Batch file to link program after compiling
ADVENT	C	Initialization, save game, restore game
ENGLISH	C	Interpret game player's commands
DATABASE	C	Text file management & output
ITVERB	C	Intransitive verbs execution
VERB	C	Transitive verbs execution
TURN	C	Analysis & execution of player's command

ADVENT0	C	Utility to create "ADVTEXT.H" file
ADVENT1	TXT	Long cave description
ADVENT2	TXT	Short cave description
ADVENT3	TXT	Long & short object description
ADVENT4	TXT	Conversational descriptions & responses
ADVENT	DOC	ADVENTURE documentation file (3K)
STDIO	H	Standard I/O header
ADVENT	H	#define & structure statements
ADVWORD	H	Words & codes array
ADVCAVE	H	Cave & travel arrays
ADVTEXT	H	TXT file message indexes
ADVDEF	H	Data constants & variables definitions
ADVDEC	H	Data constants & variables declarations
*	OBJ	Object files

Disk No 260 GAMES #13 v1 DS

This is a good game disk with some neat stuff like JETSET and a couple of cribbage games. Simonsez is a fun way for the youngest of kids to get hooked on computers. Dueling Starships and the Tron game are made for two people and are both highly recommended.

DSS	EXE	Dueling Starships
DSS	DOC	Documentation for Dueling Starships
CRIB2	BAS	Game of Cribbage, enjoy
JETSET	BAS	Real Time Simulation of B747 jet flight
JETSET	DOC	Documentation for JETSET.DOC
CRIBBAGE	BAS	Game of cribbage
SCROLL1	ML	Data file for CRIBBAGE.BAS
SIMONSEZ	BAS+	Remember the sequence game for young children
SIMONSEZ	DOC	Documentation for SIMONSEZ.BAS
SLOTMACH	BAS	Nevada style—putting a coin box on your CPU is illegal!
MORSE	BAS	Morse code learning program
TRONLC	BAS+	Game of TRON
TRONLC	EXE	Compiled version of TRON

Disk No 261 Personal Datebook & Other Applications v1.1 DS

This disk contains several user-supported programs.

		Cashflow Program by Gregory N. Doudna
CASH	BAS	Data entry, file maintenance, etc.
HARDCASH	BAS	Provides printed records
CASH	DOC	Documentation for Cashflow Programs
		Personal Datebook by Lateral Programming, Inc.
MEMO	BAS	Personal Datebook: Appointments, Addresses, Memos etc.
MEMO	BAT	Runs MEMO.BAS with proper / parms

MANUAL	TXT	Reference Manual for Personal Datebook
MANUAL	EXE	Display or print the reference manual
CONVERT	BAS	Converts address list for use with wordprocessors
CONVERT	BAT	Runs CONVERT.BAS with proper / parms
		Mailing Label Package (BASRUN.EXE required)
LABELS	EXE	Menu shell for Mailing Label Package
NEWLAB	EXE	Generates new mailing label file
LABELINP	EXE	Data entry program for Mailing Label Package
SRTLAB	EXE	Sorts labels by ZIP code
LABRPT	EXE	File listing and Summary reports
LABPRT02	EXE	Label Printing program for Mailing Label Package
LABELS	DOC	Documentation for Mailing Label Package
		File Managenment System
FILEMAN	COM	File Managenment System—very neat!
MAKEMEMO	BAS	Write reminders to tickler file
SHOWMEMO	BAS	Brings up reminder notes on proper dates
		FLITEPLN 2.2
FLITEPLN	2-2	Aids in preparing flight plan (BASIC program)
FLITEPLN	DOC	Documentation for FLITEPLN.BAS
		EIGHTCRV Package
EIGHTCRV	XXX	This description of the EIGHTCRV programs
EIGHTCRV	SDA	Sample data file
EIGHTCRV	BAS	First eight curves to data
EIGHTCRV	TXT	Documentation for EIGHTCRV.BAS

Disk No 262 — PC-GOLF 1.4 — v1.1 DS

PC-GOLF is a user-supported score analysis program. By inputing your golf score and the courses you play, this program will find the problem areas in your game. The program does the work so you can sit back and enjoy your game.

		PC-GOLF Package
AMAIN	ZRO	Main program
AUTOEXEC	BAT	Used to autostart program (BASICA required)
USER	DOC	Used to print documentation—type: BASICA USER.DOC to start
*	*	Additional PC-GOLF files

Disk No 263 — Laxon & Perry FORTH—Volume 1 — v1 DS

This is a FORTH language system put together by Henry Laxen and Mike Perry. This Forth uses the files of the host operating system. Although this reduces performance, it is much more portable and more convenient for novices. Many Forth extensions such as an assembler, editor and decompiler are included in this version of Forth. Type "F83" to start, "BYE" to quit.

F83	COM	Main program—type: F83 to start

F83-FIXS	TXT	Fixes made for this version (5K)
README	PC	Notes about using L&P Forth (16K)
EXTEND86	BLK	Source code for L&P Forth extensions
CPU8086	BLK	Source code for L&P Forth extensions
UTILITY	BLK	Source code for L&P Forth extensions
HUFFMAN	BLK	Source code for L&P Forth extensions
CLOCK	BLK	Source code for L&P Forth extensions
KERNEL	COM	Source code for L&P Forth extensions

Disk No 264 — Laxon & Perry FORTH—Volume 2 — v1 DS

This disk has additional extensions to the Laxon & Perry Forth on Disk No 263.

META86	BLK	Source code for L&P Forth extensions
KERNEL86	BLK	Source code for L&P Forth extensions

Disk No 265 — Graphics & Printer Items — v1 DS

This disk contains a mixture of graphics and printer utilities.

		Graphics items
SPIRO	EXE+	Simulates a Spirograph, u enter parms, it draws
SPIRO	DOC	Documentation for SPIRO.EXE (9K)
SPIRO	BAS	Source for SPIRO.EXE
SPIRO1	EXE+	Demonstration of SPIRO
GRAF	BAS+	Plots mathematical function on graphics screen
DEFINE	BAS+	Defines graphics characters for use with PUT statements
DEFINE	INS	Instruction file for DEFINE.BAS
THING	PLT	Sample data file for DEFINE.BAS
		Printer items
SIDEWAYS	EXE	Prints text file sideways on Epson printer
SIDEWAYS	PAS	Source for SIDEWAYS.EXE
OKIMENU	BAS	Menu based program for OKIDATA printer setup
OKIMENUC	BAS	Compressed (by BetaTools BDS) version of OKIMENU.BAS
OKIMENU	DOC	Documentation for OKIDATA.BAS (17K)
OKITALIC	BAS	Downloadable italics font for OKIDATA printer
PRINT1	EXE	XON/XOFF Serial printer driver Diable 630 and ?.
PRINT2	EXE	Same as PRINT1.EXE except drives COMM2 port
PRINT	DOC	Documentation for PRINT1.EXE and PRINT2.EXE

Disk No 266 — NAEPIRS — v1 DS

This disk contains data from the National Assessment of Educational Progress Information Retrieval System (NAEPIRS) and programs to access the data. It is produced by the National Institute of Education. It has been designed so that users can ask for findings according to subject or age group; look for trends or attitudes; or compare findings between groups such as rural and urban students, males and females, students of different races, etc. Example of findings—About 10 percent of the surveyed students at each age do not read in their spare time.

SETUP	BAT	Batch file to set up working disk
AUTOEXEC	BAT	Auto start file
SPOOL	EXE	Spooler, so you don't have to wait for your printer
NAEPIRS	EXE	Main program, type "NAEPIRS" to start
JSUM	BIN	Part of NAEPIRS system
JINT	BIN	Part of NAEPIRS system
REFYR	BIN	Part of NAEPIRS system
DBFIND	DAT	NAEPIRS data file
@??	OVL	Overlay files

Disk No 267 — Data Base of Steel—Volume 3 Version 3.1 — v1 DS

Spreadsheet of Steel and Compiled Database Program

SORT	BAS	Sort source for database
SORTINT	BAS	Sort source for database
SORTSTR	BAS	Sort source for database
SS	BAS	Spreadsheet source
SSREMARK	BAS	Spreadsheet remarks
SS	EXE	Compiled spreadsheet
TAX		Sample spreadsheet
CHECK		Sample spreadsheet
MAIN	EXE	Compiled database program
REMARKST	BAS	Sort remarks
READ	ME	Description of files on this disk

Disk No 268 — Data Base of Steel—Volume 4 Version 3.1 — v1 DS

Expert System of Steel

READ	ME	Description of files on this disk
REM	BAS	Remarks for source program (33K)
EXPERT	EXE	Compiled program for expert system
EXPERT	BAS	Source code for expert system
FORM	EXE	Compiled program for database
SCAN	EXE	Compiled program for database
CLS	OBJ	Part of expert system disk
TEMP	BAS	Part of expert system disk
*		Sample programs for the expert system (27 files)

Disk No 269 BetaTool's BASIC Development System v1 DS

This disk contains completely functional versions of BetaTool's BASIC Development system except that they are limited to files of less than 6500 bytes. BetaTool's system works with the BASIC interpreter to add easy file editing, instant cross-reference lists, selective line renumber variable dump, program expand and compress. If you program in BASIC you should try this package.

BTS	DOC	Brief documentation for BASIC Development system
SAMPLE	BAS	Sample BASIC program
IBMPC	1XX	Copy to BTS.COM if you are using IBM PC BASIC Version 1.??
IBMPC	2XX	Copy to BTS.COM if you are using IBM PC BASIC Version 2.??
IBMPC	300	Copy to BTS.COM if you are using IBM PC BASIC Version 3.??
COMPAQ	113	Copy to BTS.COM if you are using COMPAQ BASIC Version 1.13
COMPAQ	114	Copy to BTS.COM if you are using COMPAQ BASIC Version 1.14
COMPAQ	200	Copy to BTS.COM if you are using COMPAQ BASIC Version 2.00
COMPAQ	210	Copy to BTS.COM if you are using COMPAQ BASIC Version 2.10
CORONA	112	Copy to BTS.COM if you are using CORONA BASIC Version 1.12

Disk No 270 PC-SIG Directory on Disk—Volume 1 v1 DS

This is the first volume of PC-SIG's Directory on disk. Directory listings are provided up to Disk No 200. For the contents of disks beyond this see Disk No 271.

README		Text file containing an introduction to this disk
1-100	UPP	Directory listing of PC-SIG Disks Nos 1 to 100
101-200	UPP	Directory listing of PC-SIG Disks Nos 101 to 200
INDEX	TXT	Index to all PC-SIG disks
DFIND	BAT	Batch file to find all occurences of a particular word
Q&A	TXT	Some questions and answers about PC-SIG and the library disks
PC-SIG	TXT	Short message about PC-SIG which could be uploaded on a BBS
ORDER	TXT	Form for ordering library disks
URESP	TXT	User response form
SUBMIT	TXT	Software submission form

Disk No 271 — PC-SIG Directory on Disk—Volume 2 — v1 DS

The second volume of PC-SIG's Directory on Disk. This volume is for listing of disks beyond No 270.

README		Text file containing an introduction to this disk
201-???	UPP	Directory listing of most PC-SIG disk Nos 201 to most current
DFIND	BAT	Batch file to find all occurences of a particular word
INDEX	TXT	Index to all PC-SIG disks
PC-SIG	TXT	Short message about PC-SIG which could be uploaded on a BBS
ORDER	TXT	Form for ordering library disks
URESP	TXT	User response form
SUBMIT	TXT	Software submission form

Disk No 272 — PC-SIG Directory on Disk—Volume 3 — v1 DS

The third volume of PC-SIG's Directory on Disk. This volume contains a complete sorted list of all files in the PC-SIG library. It will be modified as disks are updated or added to the library. Also contained on this disk is a program to compare new submissions for duplicate files.

*	MSL	Sorted list of all files in the PC-SIG library
LIB6	EXE	Compiled version of library file compare program
LIB6	BAS	Source for file compare program
LIB6	PAR	Parameter file for file compare program
LIB6	DOC	How to use library file compare program

Disk No 273 — Best Utilities — v1 DS

The programs on this disk have been taken from other library volumes. The intent was to collect on one disk all of the better utility programs. Most programs here require DOS 2.0 or above.

MEMBRAIN	EXE	Flexible RAMdisk
MEMBRAIN	DOC	Documentation for MEMBRAIN.EXE
SP	EXE	Super Spooler program—variable size
SP	DOC	Documentation for SP.EXE
BACKSCRL	COM	Retrieve what has scrolled off top of screen—very useful
BACKSCRL	DOC	Documentation for BACKSCRL.COM
VDEL	COM	Selective delete utility—prompts to delete each file
WHEREIS	COM	Find a file in any subdirectory
WHEREIS	DOC	Documentation for WHEREIS.COM
GCOPY	EXE	Selective copy—changes date to current
GCOPY	DOC	Documentation for GCOPY.EXE
GDEL	EXE	Selective delete utility
GDEL	DOC	Documentation for GDEL.EXE

SDIR24C	COM	Flexible screen directory display—many options
SDIR24C	DOC	Documentation for SDIR24C.COM
ST	COM	Super type command—2 way scrolling
ST	DOC	Documentation for ST.COM
MOVE	COM	Flexible copy, copy and erase utility with prompts
MOVE	DOC	Documentation for MOVE.COM
BROWSE	COM	Another program to allow you to look through a text file
BROWSE	DOC	Dcoumentation for BROWSE.COM
NDOSEDIT	COM	Allows you to edit the last few DOS commands
NDOSEDIT	DOC	Documentation for NDOSEDIT.DOC
FILEDUMP	COM	Dump a file in HEX and ASCII. type "FILEDUMP <FILENAME>"

Disk No 274 — Best Games — v1 DS

This disk is a collection of some of the better games in the PC-SIG library. All games run on the PCjr (though you may have to type "mode co80" first).

GAMES	TXT	Comments from the person who selected these programs
CASTLE	EXE	Find your way out of the castle and get treasures, kill monsters
CASTLE	RAN	Part of CASTLE game
SPACEVAD	EXE+	Shoot invaders before they invade earth
PACKMAN	EXE+	Gobble power pellets and eat monsters
PACKMAN	DOC	Documentation for PACKMAN.EXE
BREAKOUT	BAS+	Try to break out of a brick wall, like tennis
LANDER	BAS+	Land a space ship on a pad without crashing
LANDER	BIN	Part of LANDER
LANDER	SCR	Part of LANDER
BUGS	EXE	Shoot crawling creatures before they get you
BUGS!	SCR	Part of BUGS
LIFE2	EXE	Try to make your bacteria live
LIFE2	BAS	Source code for LIFE2
WIZARD	BAS	A role game to find the ORB of ZOT
XWING	BAS+	Try to destroy the deathstar
FILES	TXT	Files on this disk

Disk No 275 — PC-CHECK/PC-PRINT — v1 DS

There are two user-supported programs on this disk. PC-CHECK manager is a checkbook balancing program with ledger printout capabilities. PC-PRINT control changes font and page parameters from a menu.

		PC-CHECK Manager
CKBOOK	BAS	Main checkbook balancing program
CKBOOK	EXE	Compiled version
DOC	BAT	Cover page and calls CKBOOK.BAS
CK	DOC	Documentation for CKBOOK (12K)

LEDGER	DAT	List of ledger catagories used by CKBOOK
1099	EXE	1099 Tax form generation program
		PC-PRINT control
PRINTCTL	BAS	Selects various print styles and page formats
PRINTCTL	EXE	Compiled version
PRINTDOC	BAT	Runs PRINTCTL.BAS

Disk No 276 COLLIST 2.0 v1 DS

The programs on this disk work together to list column type files on your printer in a superior format. The distribution disk is coded and needs to be decoded with the "START" command before normal use.

RELSE-2	0	Displays title in directory.
COLLST	PRE	" "
INSTALL	ED	" "
DISK		" "
START	TXT	Part of COLLIST
START	EXE	This is the program to start the decoding, type "start"
*	*	Part of COLLIST (17 more files)

Disk No 277 FINDFILE v1 DS

TYPE	ME	Tells you to LISTER file COVER
BUG		Bug report form, send to author
COVER		A letter to the user about installation
DOC		The documentaion
DSKLABEL		A correct disk label
ORDER		Order form for On-Disk Software
LISTER	EXE	Used to print BUG, COVER, DOC and ORDER
MOVBAS	BAT	Moves FindFile to disk—BAS version
MOVEXE	BAT	Moves FindFile to disk—EXE version
MOVLIB	BAT	Moves FindFile to disk—for people with BASRUN.EXE
MENU	BAT	Executes the menu program
FINDFILE	BAT	Finds a file
$$DOEXBA	BAT	Setup batch file
$$NEWTRE	BAT	"
$$MENU	BAS	Gives you the menu of options
COMSEP	BAS	Makes $$TREE into $$TREE.CSV for other programs to use
FFILE	BAS	Finds any file or group of files
FFILEBIG	BAS	Use FFILE except on more than about 1,000 files
MAPTREE	BAS	Converts TREE output to something useful
SAMECHK	BAS	Checks for duplicate files
SETDRV	BAS	Resets the drive FindFile is using
COMSEP	LIB	Compiled version to be used with BASRUN.EXE
FFILE	LIB	Compiled version to be used with BASRUN.EXE

FFILEBIG	LIB	Compiled version to be used with BASRUN.EXE
MAPTREE	LIB	Compiled version to be used with BASRUN.EXE
SAMECHK	LIB	Compiled version to be used with BASRUN.EXE
SETDRV	LIB	Compiled version to be used with BASRUN.EXE
COMSEP	EXE	Faster compiled versions of BASIC programs
FFILE	EXE	Faster compiled versions of BASIC programs
FFILEBIG	EXE	Faster compiled versions of BASIC programs
MAPTREE	EXE	Faster compiled versions of BASIC programs
SETDRV	EXE	Faster compiled versions of BASIC programs
SAMECHK	EXE	Faster compiled versions of BASIC programs
FFILEMEN	DAT	The data which defines your menu

Disk No 278 — QSYS 3.0 Documentation — v1 DS

This disk contains the documentation for QSYS, a user-supported program. QSYS is a powerful operating environment, a menu system, an appointment calendar and message system, plus. The programs are on disk #118.

MAKEDOC	BAT	Batch file to print documentation
MAKEDOC	TXT	Instructions for printing documentation
Q_*	DOC	Documentation files (17)
READ	ME!	Read this first

Disk No 279 — PIANOMAN — v1 DS2

PIANOMAN is a user supported group of programs for playing, recording and editing music.

READTHIS	1ST	Important information--do read it.
READDOC	BAT	Type "READDOC" to screen the documentation
README	###	List of files on this disk
PIANOMAN	COM	Music playing, recording, and editing program
PIANOMAN	000	Overlay file for PIANOMAN
PIANOMAN	DOC	Documentation--to be screened, not printed
PLAYRPNO	COM	Utility for PIANOMAN files--turns them into programs
FUGUES	COM	Utility--combines 2 to 4 voices into one fugue
HARMNIZR	COM	Utility--combines 2 to 4 voices into chords
UTILITY	DOC	Documentation for utilities
TECHNCAL	DOC	Some technical notes
RKTYTKTY	MUS	An Irish Ballad, converted by PLAYER PIANO into:
RKTYTKTY	COM	1) a standalone program
RKTYTKTY	TRB	2) an EXTERNAL file for TURBO Pascal programs
RKTYTKTY	BSV	3) a BLOADable file for BASIC programs
TESTPLAY	PAS	TURBO Pascal driver for RKTYTKTY.TRB
TESTPLAY	BAS	BASIC driver for RKTYTKTY.BSV
CHACONNE	MUS	Showoff piece—Chaconne for unaccompanied violin

CHACONNE	COM	—Lasts about 12 minutes.
TURKISH	MUS	Turkish march.
TURKISH	COM	"
CMINOR	MUS	Fugue in C-Minor, created with help from FUGUES
CMINOR	COM	"
INVENTN4	MUS	Two-Part Invention in D-Minor, created with help
INVENTN4	COM	from FUGUES
FEST0	MUS	:
FEST1	MUS	: These are the four voices of a Chorale.
FEST2	MUS	: HARMONIZER put them together into FESTBURG, below
FEST3	MUS	:
FESTBURG	COM	Bach Chorale, showing the output of HARMONIZER
COLT45	MUS	: Shows that PLAYER PIANO can make a tune loop
COLT45	COM	: indefinitely (or until you give in and press a key)
WILLOW	MUS	For Gilbert and Sullivan lovers
WILLOW	COM	:
QNAVEE	MUS	:
QNAVEE	COM	:
WACHTAUF	COM	Wachet Auf, ruft Uns die Stimme (4-part chorale)
SYNCLOCK	MUS	The Syncopated Clock, by Leroy Anderson
SYNCLOCK	COM	:
ENTRTAN1	MUS	:
ENTRTAN2	MUS	: The FUGUES program can put together ragtime,
ENTRTAN3	MUS	: too! Here are four parts . . .
ENTRTAN4	MUS	:
ENTERTAN	COM	And here is THE ENTERTAINER

Disk No 280 — Bibliographic — v1 DS2

A5MG1084	PRN	A5 Magazine bibliography through October, 1984
BIBL	DOC	General comments on bibliography files
COM1084	LQR	Bibliographies through 10/84-PC Magazine, PC World PC Tech Journal, Softalk, Infoworld, PC Week Online Today, Capital PC Magazine Use with PC-File (use USQ2 then LU86402)
COMBIBL	LQR	Bibliographies from 10/84-Same mags as COM1084.LQR Use with PC-File (use USQ2 then LU86402)
COMDOC	PRN	Computer magazine bibliography classifications
CONFIG	TTY	Configuration file for PCRTTY.EXE
CWP	DOC	Documentation for CWP.EXE
CWP	EXE	Easy to use code practice tutor(char & word rates)
HAM1084	LQR	Bibliographies through 10/84-QST, CQ, 73, Ham Radio, QEX, RTTY Journal, and A5 magazine Use with PC-File (use USQ2 then LU86402)
HAMBIBL	LQR	Bibliographies from 10/84-Same mags as HAM1084.LQR Use with PC-File (use USQ2 then LU86402)
HAMDOC	PRN	Ham radio magazine bibliography classifications

LU86402	DOC	Documentation for LU86402.EXE
LU86402	EXE	Use to unpack library files on this disk
PCFILTER	EXE	Many feature file cleanup up program
PCFILTER	PRN	Documentation for PCFILTER.EXE
PCRTTY	EXE	Full featured ham radio RTTY baudot program
PCRTTY	PRN	Documentation for PCRTTY.EXE
SWL1084	LQR	Bibliographies through 10.84-Monitoring Times Popular Communications Use with PC-File (use USQ2 then LU86402)
SWLBIBL	LQR	Bibliographies from 10/84-Same mags as SWL1084.LQR Use with PC-File (use USQ2 then LU86402)
SWLDOC	PRN	SWL bibliography classifications
USQ2	DOC	Documentation for USQ2.EXE
USQ2	EXE	Use to unsqueeze files on this disk
WELCOME		Information on contacting Bibliography bulletin board
README	PRN	Description of files

Disk No 281 — Recipe Index — v1 DS2

RECIPES is a user supported bibliography of 1800 recipes in 1983 Family Circle and Woman's Day magazines. The version here requires PC-FILE III (Disk #5). Versions for LOTUS 1-2-3 and dBASE II cost $20.

DOC	BAT	Prints documentation (IR83PCF.DOC)
IR83PCF	DOC	Documentation (55K)
IRECIP83	DTA	Data base files
IRECIP83	HDR	"
IRECIP83	INX	"
RECIMEDS	RPT	Report formats
RECLONGP	RPT	"
RECSHORT	RPT	"
NESTMENU	DOC	List of menues
NESTMENU	BAT	Prints NESTMENU.DOC

Disk No 282 — Applications — v1 DS2

CBD, ANAYLYST AND PC-CHECK are user-supported programs. CBD The CheckBook Distribution Program, provides a quick & easy way to group check or credit card data into expense categories. ANALYST is for forecasting and allocating the costs of home ownership and in comparing ownership versus rental alternatives. It is also useful in determining if mortgage refinancing is worthwhile. PC-CHECK has been designed to efficiently and easily allow anyone to keep track of one or more home or office accounts. STKANALY.SIS was designed to calculate several measures of stock value. MERGEplan is a multiplan spreadsheet consolidator.

		MERGEPLAN V1.00 (Multiplan spreadsheet consolidator)
MERGE	EXE	Main program

		Checkbook distribution by John Stevens
CBD	BAS	Main program
CBD	DAT	Part of CBD.BAS
CBD-READ	ME	Checkbook distribution documentation (39K)
		PC-CHECK
PC-CHECK	BAS	Checkbook management program
PC-CHECK	DOC	PC-CHECK documentation
HELP	BAT	How to print PC-CHECK documentation
REGIS	DOC	User support registration
AUTOEXEC	BAT	Prints registration form
SMPLCODE	CO	Suggested two letter codes
SMPLCHK		More suggested codes
		Stock Analyst
STKANALY	SIS	Stock value analyzer
DATAST		Sample data sheet
STKANAL	DOC	STKANALY.SIS documentation (16K)
		Home Financial Analyst
ANALYST	EXE	Home ownership cost analyzer
SAMPLE	HFA	Example
ANALYST	DOC	Documentation (9K)

Disk No 283		**Utilities #7**	**v1 DS**
		KWSEARCH by Patrick Teti	
KWSEARCH	EXE	Copies text using search criteria	
KWSEARCH	DOC	Documentation for KWSEARCH (13K)	
		3 Utilities by John White	
INT	COM	Program interrupt	
INT	A	Part of INT	
INT	DOC	Documentation for INT	
INT_PORT	DOC	Additional Documentation for INT	
RAM	SYS	RAM drive installer	
RAM	A	Part of RAM	
RAM	DOC	Documentation for RAM	
SETRAM	EXE	Sets up RAM	
FFIND	EXE	Finds files by scanning for specific argument	
FFIND	C	Part of FFIND	
FFIND	DOC	Documentation for FFIND	
MAKEINT	BAT	Batch file to install INT	
MAKERAM	BAT	Batch file to install RAM	
		Directory Toolkit	
DTK	EXE	Sort directory, change attributes, etc.	
DTK	DOC	Documentation for DTK (8K)	
		Famous Sweep program from CPM	
CWEEP13	EXE	File manipulation utility	

CWEEP13	DOC	Documentation for CWEEP13 (8K)
		Docufile
AUTOEXEC	BAT	Batch file to diskcopy
KILLER	EXE	Deletes files
CATALOG	EXE	Demonstration of multiple file searcher
DOCUFILE	BAS	Creates BASIC program of text file
README	TXT	Documentation for DOCUFILE
README	BAS	BASIC version of README.TXT
HELP	BAT	DOCUFILE help screen generator
DOCUFILE	BAT	Batch file to bring up DOCUFILE in BASIC
		Letter Quality print routine
LQ	COM	Letter quality print on Epson MX printer
LQ	DOC	Documentation for LQ (9K)

Disk No 284 — Utilities #8 — v1 DS

This disk is a collection of utilities that, for the most part, are not related to one another. The labelmaker allows you to print labels for your disks, see the README.1ST. DJ (as in Disk Jockey) helps you look at specific sectors and tracks, use caution here. AUTOMENU remembers your DOS commands for you.

		Disk labelmaker
DLIB	EXE	Part of Labelmaker
DSTAT	EXE	Part of Labelmaker
LBLUT1	EXE	Part of Labelmaker
LBL	BAT	Part of Labelmaker
LABELPNT	BAS	Part of Labelmaker
INFO	DOC	Documentation info about Labelmaker
README	1ST	Startup instructions for Labelmaker
		Disk Jockey
DJ	COM	Allows you to read sectors and tracks on disk
		Automenu
AUTO	BAT	Batch file to start a menu
AUTO1	BAT	" "
AUTO2	BAT	" "
AUTOEXEC	BAT	Batch file to use at startup for AUTOMENU
AUTOMENU	COM	Main program for AUTOMENU
AUTOMENU	DOC	Documentation for AUTOMENU
AUTOTEMP	BAT	Temp batch file
AUTOCOLR	COM	Changes to color monitor
AUTOMENU	DAT	Data file used to build menu screen
AUTOMONO	COM	Changes to monochrome monitor

		Separate user-supported programs
LOAD-US	COM	Enables you to use Lotus and Symphony on hard disk
LOAD-US	DOC	Documentation for LOAD-US
NUMZAP	EXE	Removes line numbers from BASIC programs
NUMZAP	DOC	Documentation for NUMZAP
NUMZAP	BAS	BASIC source code for NUMZAP
RENUM	EXE	Renumbers a file that has been through NUMZAP
RENUM	BAS	BASIC source code for RENUM

Disk No 285 WHIZZARD Screen v1 DS

The WHIZZARD Screen I/O Routines are designed to allow maximum performance on the IBM PC. They can be called from BASIC to increase the speed at which text goes to the screen.

README	TXT	Description of programs
QPRINT	ASM	Quickly print a string at the current location
QPRINT	OBJ	Compiled version
ZPRINT	ASM	Print a string using the color/attribute given
ZPRINT	OBJ	Compiled version
CLREOL	ASM	Clear from the current position to the end of the line
CLREOL	OBJ	Compiled version
CLREOS	ASM	Clear from the current position to the end of the screen
CLREOS	OBJ	Compiled version
SCRLDN	ASM	Scroll some portion of the screen down
SCRLDN	OBJ	Compiled version
SCRLUP	ASM	Scroll some portion of the screen up
SCRLUP	ASM	Compiled version
XREP	ASM	Repeat some character along the x axis
YREP	ASM	Repeat some character down the y axis
ASMBASIC	TXT	How to call assembly routines in BASIC
ASMBASIC	ASM	Source to primary module
ASMBASIC	OBJ	Object code for ASMBASIC
ASMBASIC	EXE	Sample executable linked with the I/O subroutines
SUBDEMO	BAS	Interpreted BASIC program demonstrating ASMBASIC
SUBDEMO	EXE	Compiled program
SCRNIO	TXT	Explanation of accelerating the PRINT statement
BASPRINT	ASM	Source to primary module
BASPRINT	OBJ	Object code for BASPRINT
BASPRINT	EXE	Module to be executed after booting the system
COMPRINT	ASM	Source to primary module
COMPRINT	OBJ	Object code for COMPRINT
COMPRINT	EXE	Module to be executed after booting the system
SCRNIO	TXT	Explanation of acceleratiing the PRINT statement
PRSLASHO	ASM	Source to primary module
PRSLASHO	OBJ	Object code for PRSLASHO

PRSLASHO	EXE	Module to be executed after booting the system
EASYDEMO	BAT	BAT file demonstrating compiled routines using PRSLASHO as well as QPRINT.OBJ.
LONGDEMO	BAT	BAT file demonstrating all three modules and QPRINT from ASMBASIC.
TIMEDEMO	BAS	Source to timing program demonstrating improvement in BASIC PRINT statement
BANDDEMO	BAS	Source to graphic demonstration program showing enhancement to PRINT statement
BANDDEMO	EXE	BASIC graphic demonstration program compiled with the I/O option
DEBUGFIX	TXT	Explanation of the patch to DOS 2.0 DEBUG TRACE command
DEBUG20	FIX	PIPELINE input file which can be used to apply the patch automatically.
DETAB	BAS	Interpreted BASIC program to remove tabs
SETABS	EPS	File which can be printed to set the tab positions

Disk No 286 PC-VT v1 DS

PC-VT is a software emulator which makes the IBM PC function as a DEC VT102 or a VT100 Video Terminal. PC-VT emulates the majority of functions of the VT100/102.

PC-VT	SUM	Part of PC-VT
PC-VT	EXE	Main PC-VT program
PC-VT	CRD	Part of PC-VT
PC-VT	DOC	Documentation for PC-VT (aprox. 100 pages)
XMODVMS	LBR	XMODEM library for PC-VT
READ	ME	Authors note
PARAMS	DAT	Data file for PC-VT
DIALER	DAT	Data file for PC-VT
MACRO	DAT	Data file for PC-VT

Disk No 287 File Express—Volume 1 v1 DS

File Express is an information management program. It allows easy manipulation of small and medium sized databases using menu driven commands. File Express allows you to create and maintain files of facts, figures, names, mailing lists, patient records or what have you. See additional programs on Disk #288.

FE	EXE	Main program controls all other programs
DEFINE	EXE	Used when a new data base is defined.
SORT	EXE	This is the program used to sort the index.
REPORT	EXE	To print reports, clone databases and create mailmerge files.
LABEL	EXE	Used when printing mailing labels.
PRINT	SET	To reset printer control codes.

Disk No 288 — File Express—Volume 2 — v1 DS

FE	DOC	Users quide for the File Express package (160K)
IMPORT	EXE	To import files into File Express for use as databases
PRINT	BAT	Batch file to print documentation

Disk No 289 — Power-Worksheets — v1 DS

Power-Worksheets is a user-supported program which relieves you of the need to set up (or program) and test 1-2-3 worksheets to solve standard problems. The worksheets are fully automatic from the moment 1-2-3 is loaded. They are completely menu-driven and do not require extensive user training. Both first-time and experienced users can immediately enter data and generate useful results including graphs. The second volume contains additional worksheets and in available for $49.

README	1ST	Descriptions of worksheets on this disk
AUTO123	WKS	Lotus autostart file
AGENDA	WKS	Allows you to go from one worksheet to another.
BSTAT	WKS	Accepts data and performs two major analytical tasks.
DEPREC	WKS	A comprehensive worksheet.
NPV	WKS	Calculation program.
PROFIT	WKS	Analysis worksheet.
ROR	WKS	Another calculation program.
SREGR	WKS	Linear Regression program
TEST	WKS	Test worksheet
TV	WKS	Part of Power Worksheet
PRINTDOC	BAT	Prints 72 pages of documentation
INTRO	DOC	Introduction (6K)
BSTAT	DOC	Part of documentation (18K)
DEPREC	DOC	Part of documentation (24K)
NPV	DOC	Part of documentation (20K)
PROFIT	DOC	Part of documentation (44K)
ROR	DOC	Part of documentation (27K)
SREGR	DOC	Part of documentation (33K)

Disk No 290 — Tax 84—Lotus 1-2-3 Tax Worksheets — v1 DS

FITT, a user supported program, is a Lotus 1-2-3 worksheet (or template) intended to simplify the process of preparing a Federal Income Tax Return. It has been designed so that you do not have to be an expert user of Lotus 1-2-3 in order to take advantage of the capabilities of FITT. Forms 1040 and 2441, Schedules A, B, D, E, W, G, and C are produced.

		FITT
README	DOC	Introduction
FITT84	DOC	Documentation—20 pages
FITT84	WKS	Main worksheet file

STATES84	WKS	Optional state sales tax tables
		More Tax worksheets
TT_1040	WKS	Prints out forms
TT_HELP	WKS	Help file

Disk No 291 — Tax 84—Multiplan Templates — v1 DS

84F1040	Multiplan Worksheet
SCHC	"
SCHA	"
SCHB	"
SCHD	"
SCHE	"
SCHF	"
SCHG	"
SCHR	"
SCHSE	"
SCHW	"
TXINSTR	"
FORM2106	"
FORM2441	"
FORM3903	"
FORM3468	"
FORM2119	"
FORM4797	"
FORM5695	"
SCHD1	"
84F1041	"
SCHK1	"
F4684	"
CO104LNG	"
FORM4835	"
CO104CR	"

Disk No 292 — SPACEWAR — v1 DS

The primary program on this disk, SPACEWAR, is an excellent asteroid type arcade game. The two versions, SWC for color graphics and SWH for the Hercules graphics card, provide good detail in a fast paced game. Other games include some Turbo Pascal offerings and a large number of BASIC games and demos. The large number of small simple BASIC demos with a few Turbo programs to add spice make this an excellent package for the novice programmer.

SONGS	BAS	Menu driven tune player
MAZEMAKE	BAS	Creates mazes up to 25 x 25 on screen and printer
LMAZE	BAS	Makes larger mazes direct to printer

GUESSNUM	BAS	Out guess the computer
LIFE	BAS	The game of LIFE in basic
LLIFE	BAS	More LIFE
ROCKET	BAS	Don't blink or you will miss this mini demo
MARINE'S	BAS	A musical bit of artillary
PRODUCT	BAS	Product of two numbers
NAME	BAS	Mini demo prints your name
BAD	BAS	Bad version of above
DIVIDE	BAS	Simple division
ADD	BAS	It all adds up
SUBTRACT	BAS	And subtracts
STARS	BAS	Graphics demo that works well on Hercules
SORCERER	BAS	A nice little adventure game
MACDONAL	BAS	As in Old
STATION	BAS	Mini motion demo
DOODLE	BAS	As in Yankee
VACATION	BAS	Mini vacation demo
ANTHEM	BAS	As in Natonal
CREATURE	BAS	Tell it which way to nibble
AMERICA	BAS	The beautiful
FLOWER	BAS	With its own bee
MOVINGAL	BAS	More music
JINGLEBE	BAS	More music
OATSPEAS	BAS	More music
OLDFOLKS	BAS	More music
SWELLING	BAS	More music
TRACK	BAS	More music
SAINTS	BAS	More music
HOTCROSS	BAS	More music
LIGHTLYR	BAS	More music
MORNING	BAS	More music
SAILBOAT	BAS	A mini demo
SWIMMER	BAS	"
AVERAGE2	BAS	Averages numbers
AVERAGE#	BAS	Averages numbers
COUNTING	BAS	Sums up
PRINT	BAS	Prints a line
BIRTHDAY	BAS	Mini cake
BALL	BAS	Toss a ball
CSTLDFNS	BAS	An adventure game to defend your castle
AVERAGE	BAS	Averages numbers
GRAPHICS	BAS	Simple graphic display
CIVILWAR	BAS	Second guess the Civil War generals
EQUAT1	BAS	A simple algebra equation
EQUAT2	BAS	A simple algebra equation
EQUAT3	BAS	A simple algebra equation

EQUAT4	BAS	A simple algebra equation
TYPE	BAS	Mini typing test (may have bugs)
		Spacewars (user-supported)
SWC	EXE	For use with color graphics card
SWH	EXE	Hercules graphics version
SPACEWAR	DOC	Three pages of documentation for Spacewar
		Life game in Turbo Pascal
LIFEC	COM	Compiled for non graphics monitor
LIFECG	COM	Compiled for graphics with 99 x 99 grid
LIFEC	PAS	Source code for above
LIFECG	PAS	Source code for above
		Turbo Pascal demo
NEWSPIRO	PAS	Random character display in a curvy pattern
NEWSPIRO	COM	Compiled version of above

Disk No 293 ARCADE GAMES v1 DS

A really fine collection of colorful arcade games. If you can't find a game to suit you here perhaps your not a game player. This collection of games for the color tube will catch and hold your attention for hours. They work well on the PC jr also.

3-DEMON	EXE+	A fascinating 3-d Packman type game
BRICKS	EXE+	Another colorful breakout type game
FORTUNE	EXE	Word game like Wheel of Fortune on TV (mono)
KONG	EXE+	Jump the barrels and watch out for the gorilla
PANGO	EXE+	Use blocks to squish the bees before they get YOU
PC-GOLF	EXE+	Plays golf on your color tube
PITFALL	EXE	Diving down a long pit but don't touch the walls (mono)
PYRAMID	EXE+	Climb the pyramid and the blocks change color
BRICKS	DOC	Documentaion for BRICKS
3-DEMON	HI1	Score keeper for 3-DEMON
PANGO	HGH	Score keeper for PANGO

Disk No 294 EDIT—V1.11 v1 DS

EDIT is a general purpose text editor and word processing program. It supports a wide array of editing operations, including powerful commands that are often not available even in very expensive word processors. It supports "word wrapping", and fully automatic paragraph reformatting. Under versions 2.0 or later of DOS, EDIT even allows you to execute DOS commands, or start another program without leaving EDIT. Files are limited to about 50,000 characters (25 single spaced pages)

EDIT	EXE	Main program—type "edit" to start
EDIT	SET	Setup parameter file
EDIT	HLP	Help text
*	TXT	Documentation files (70K total)

*	SET	Print format files
PRINTDOC	BAT	Batch file to print documentation
*	PRN	Documentation files to print
READ	TXT	Brief description in EDIT text file format
READ	ME	Brief description which may be "typed" or copied to "lpt1:"

Disk No 295 — TAX-FILE v1.1 — v1 DS

The TAX-FILE is a very complete TAX RECORD KEEPING system. It enables a person with very little effort to collect records of income and expenses and to assemble them quickly in order to prepare yearly income tax forms. The TAX-FILE requires that the user have available a copy of dBASE II. At the "." prompt simply enter DO MENU. You will be taken directly into TAX-FILE. Complete documentation is available from the author. This is a user-supported program.

MENU	PRG	Main program
SETUP	PRG	Brief message on setting up system
*	PRG	Other program files (37 files)
*	DBF	Database files (8 files) Main files are TAXFILE.DBF and CHECKS.DBF
*	FRM	Form files (29 files)
TAXDATA	MEM	Tax data file—variable TRATE contains state sales tax rate
*	MEM	Other memory variable files (3 files)
READ	BAT	Types brief instruction files to screen
READ	TXT	Brief instructions
READ1	TXT	"
FILELIST	TXT	"

Disk No 296 — EAMAN Master — v1

EAMON is a computerized version of what are called "fantasy role-playing games." When you enter the universe of one of these games, you are no longer Jon (or Jane) Smith, mild-mannered computer hobbyist. Instead, you become a character in a land of adventure, doing almost anything you want to. EAMON was created by Donald Brown and converted to the PC by Jon Walker.

EAMON	BAS	Main program, type: RUN"EAMON from BASIC
NEWGUY	BAS	Part of EAMON
MAINHALL	BAS	Main hall
CAVE	BAS	Cave
*	*	Other files used by system
PRINTMAN	BAS	Allows you to read manual on screen
README	EAM	Brief notes
EAMON	DOC	Documentation (30K)

Disk No 297 — EAMAN Designer & Utilities — v1 DS

This disk is designed to be used with the EAMON master (disk #296). It allows you to create new EAMON games.

		Designer
MENU	BAS	Main program, run this program first
DUNINIT	BAS	Part of EAMON Designer
WORK	BAS	"
MLIST	BAS	"
LISTER	BAS	"
DUNGEON	BAS	"
CONFIG	BAS	"
WEAPONS	DAT	"
DESCRIPT	DAT	"
AUTOEXEC	BAT	"
DUNGEON	DOC	For those planning to create their own dungeons (6K text file)
DESIGN	DOC	Documentation (14K text file)
PRINTDOC	BAS	Prints documentation
		Utilities
UTILITY	DOC	Notes about "utility" files
WEAPINIT	BAS	Program for initializing the weapon/artifact file
NEWCAVE	BAS	Basic program with SAVE and PLAY old game commands
STARTUP	BAS	Start into a dungeon with sword, gold and you without going through main hall
FILL	BAS	Makes it easier to make a dungeon full of artifacts and monsters
DAMON	ART	Artifact file for FILL.BAS program
DAMON	MON	Monster file for FILL.BAS program
DAMON	EFF	Description file for FILL.BAS program
README	UTL	Startup notes: use BASICA /S:256

Disk No 298 — Pascal Programs/Adventure — v1 DS

PLANETS computes information relating to the position, distance, magnitude, etc. for the major planets on a specified date and time. LEYGREF'S CASTLE is a fantasy adventure game. The castle is randomly stocked for each game, thereby ensuring a different adventure each time you play.

		Planets
PLANETS	DOC	Documentation (3K)
PLANETS	COM	Main program
PLANETS	PAS	Pascal source code (28K)
		WATOR
WATORMON	PAS	Source code, Turbo Pascal, for monochrome card
WATORCOL	PAS	Source for color card
WATORMON	COM	Compiled code for mono card

WATORCOL	COM	Compiled code for color card
WATOR	DOC	List of files
READ	ME	Notes from author
		LEYGREF'S CASTLE
LEYGREF1	BAS	Main program
LEYGREF	INS	Instructions (7K text file)
LEYGREF	PIC	Part of LEYGREF
LEYGREF	DAT	"
LEYGREF	CMD	"

Disk No 299 — Mixture — v1 DS

CONTENTS	DOC	Description of files on this disk
CROSSWDS	DAT	List of BASIC keywords
MEMSET	BAS	Allows use of 640K memory in older PCs
MEMINST	DAT	Used by MEMSET.BAS
M	EXE	A user-supported version of MEMSET—fast
COMPACT	BAS	A program to compact BASIC programs
4BARLINK	BAS +	Animation program (requires color graphics)
BARS	BAS	Color graphics test pattterns
CONVERGE	BAS	"
MLTIBRST	BAS	"
TWOLINE	BAS	"
ANIMATE	BAS	"
INTLCVID	BAS	"
CHARDEFN	BAS	"
PGBRK	BAT	Produces printed listings with page breaks
PGBRK	BAS	Part of PGBRK
PGBRK	BEG	"
PGBRK	END	"
DOORS	BAS	Permits you to switch between diskplay adapters
DOORS	COM	"
PARINT	COM	Program to trap parity error interupts
PARINT	ASM	Assembly source code
PARINT	LST	Assembler listing
RED	COM	Rename files accross directories
RED	ASM	Source code
RED	LST	Assembly listing
MEGATREK	BAS	Startrek type program
NUTREK	BAS	Screen oriented startrek program
EPBENCHI	BAS	Benchmark program

REFORM	BAS	Adds spaces to BASIC program required by PC but not other BASICs
BIRD	BAS	Sound effect program
PERTCHRT	BAS	Pertchart program
DITHER	BAS	Generates 128 distinct colors on Tecmar Graphics Master board
DISKMODP	BAS	Faster, improved version of DISKMODF on #28

Disk No 300 CUBS/INV v1

There are two dBASE III programs on this disk. INV is a household goods inventory program. CUBS is a system for keeping the records of a cub scout pack. Both programs require dBASE III.

		INV—Household Goods Inventory
INV	PRG	Main program
INV	DBF	Database file
INV	NDX	Index file
INV	TXT	Sample printout
		CUBS—Cub scout record keeping
CUBS	PRG	Main program, type: "DBASE CUBS" to start
README	CUB	Brief description of CUB system
*	*	More programs in CUB system (30)

Disk No 301 1-2-3 Worksheets #1 v1 DS2

123DOC	BAS	Will document the formulas in 123
123DOC	DOC	Documentation file for 123DOC
123DOC	EXE	Will document the formulas in 123
123MAIL	TXT	Tech notes on mail labels
123PREP	DOC	Documentation file for 123PREP
123PREP	EXE	Prepares data for file import to 123
123Q&A	TXT	Questions and answers from Lotus
123RANGE	BAS	Creates a table of range names/location
123XIMAC	TXT	Tech notes of using the /XI macros
ADDLABEL	DOC	Documentation file for ADDLABL@.WKS
ADDLABL2	WKS	Address label macros on WKS
DATAFILL	TXT	Tech notes on using the /Data Fill
FOR_NEXT	WKS	123 template to use for-next loops
LOOPMAC	TXT	Tech notes on using loops in macros
LOT101	TXT	Tech notes from Lotus
LOT102	TXT	Tech notes on memory use in 123
LOT103	TXT	Tech notes on using @IF in 123
LOT105	TXT	Lotus tech notes
MACROLIB	TXT	Notes on making a library of macros
MENU	WKS	123 template to make menu macros
PICFIL	TXT	Analysis of the .pic files (graphs)

PHOTOEST	DOC	Documentation file for PHOTOEST.WKS
PHOTOEST	WKS	Photo estimation worksheet
RATIO	WKS	123 template to do financial analysis
TEXTDEMO	WKS	Example of using text in @IF functions

Disk No 302 — 1-2-3 Worksheets #2 — v1 DS2

2X2DISC	WKS	123 template-Linear statistics
ACRS	WKS	123 template-ACRS depreciation
AMORT1X	WKS	Loan amortization self study
BIORYTHM	WKS	123 template-biorythms and graph
CARCOST	WKS	123 template-auto operating expense
CASH	WKS	Demo of 123 and Cash
CASHMAN	WKS	Manual for CASH.WKS
CASHREAD	WKS	Instructions for 123 and cash
DATEWR	WKS	123 template-date value to strings
EXPENSRP	WKS	123 template-travel business expens
FLCHART	WKS	123 template-flowchart symbols
GOLF	WKS	123 template to handicap golf score
HANGROBO	WKS	Game of hangman--very slow
ICR_CALC	WKS	IRS interest calculator/underpayment
INDUST	WKS	123 template-examples of @DCOUNT
IRR	WKS	Internal rate of return calculator
LEDGER	WKS	123 template-checkbook ledger
MISTOX	WKS	Stock portfolio analysis-what-ifs
NLBE	WKS	Non-linear breakeven analysis
OPTIONZ	WKS	Options manager/stock current price
PAD	WKS	123 template-notepad,calander,phone
PRNTMENU	WKS	Menu for enhanced printer control
RENTAL	WKS	123 template-rental property analysis
TAXPLAN	WKS	123 template-1984 taxes
TREND123	DOC	Documentation file for TREND123
TREND123	WKS	123 template-macros-trend analysis

Disk No 303 — 1-2-3 Worksheets #3 — v1 DS2

AUTO123	WKS	Demo for optionware
MAGEE	DOC	Documentation file for MAGEE
MAGEE	WKS	Ledger/database date math + reports
MAIL	WKS	123 template to form letters/labels
PREVIEW	WKS	Demo for optionware goes with auto123
TAX1984	DOC	Documentation file for TAX1984
TAX1984	WKS	123 template to do 1984 taxes
WSFF1	TXT	Worksheet file format 123/symphony

WSFF2	TXT	Worksheet file format 123/symphony
WSFF3	TXT	Worksheet file format 123/symphony
WSFF4	TXT	Worksheet file format 123/symphony

Disk No 304 — 1-2-3 Macros — v1 DS2

CBB	WKS	Check Book Balancer
CDB	WKS	Cash Disbursements
CFM	WKS	Cash Flow Manager
CFP	WKS	Cash Flow Projection
LNA	WKS	Loan Amortization
LNP	WKS	Loan Payoff Calculator
LCT	WKS	Line-of-Credit Tracker
ADC	WKS	ACRS Depreciation Calc.
IRR	WKS	Internal Rate-of-Return
ARC	WKS	Accounts Receivable Tracker
EIO	WKS	EOQ Inventory Ordering
FFS	WKS	5-in-1 Financial Statement
RAR	WKS	Ratio Analyzer
IIB	WKS	Interactive Inc-Statement
STC	WKS	Statistics Calculator
GCC	WKS	Growth Capacity Calc.
QA1	WKS	Queue Analysis (single)
QAM	WKS	Queue Analysis (multi)
NVB	WKS	New Venture Budget
PVA	WKS	Price Volume Analysis
QGN	WKS	Quote Generator
MACLIB	WKS	Lotus 1-2-3 Macros
MACS	PRN	Macro set in PRN format
OLDBULL	DOC	Documentation file for macros and BBS system where they were found (19K)
MACRO_1	DOC	Macro documentation (5K)

Disk No 305 — Symphony Worksheets #1 — v1 DS2

ADDRS	WRK	Name and Address notebook uses wind
APPT	WRK	Appointment calander
BIORYM	WRK	Biorythms with graph window
CHCKWR	WRK	Converts numbers to written version
CLFORM	WRK	Example of keystroke trapping in forms
COMDOC	WRK	Documentation for comma.app
COMMA	APP	Application add-in for file import
COMPSV	CCF	Setting sheet for Compuserve
COMPSV	CTF	Translation table for Compuserve
COMTST	PRN	Test file to use with comma.app

DBSEQ	WRK	Example of forms with record #'s
DECODE	EXE	Analyzer of 123 and Symphony workst
DECODE	WRK	Can be used with decode.exe
FROMTO	TXT	Tech notes on macros 123 to Symphony
FTMAC	WRK	File transfer utilities (macros)
HAMMER	WRK	Graphics macros with trig. functions
LOTUSM	WRK	Macros to call Compuserve + download files
MENUBR	WRK	Examples of menubranch uses
NYNEW	TXT	New York Lotus SIG Newletter 10/84 (78K file)
REDIAL	WRK	Redial phone-and-login branch macro
ROULET	WRK	Roulet wheel game
SPACER	TXT	Data dependent line spacing/databas
SYM102	TXT	Tech notes-database convertsion from 123
SYMQ&A	TXT	Questions and answers from Lotus
SYNC	WRK	Synchronized windows macros
TWOCOL	WRK	Wordprocessing in two columns macro
WIDE	APP	Application-add-in for file import
WIDEDOC	WRK	Documentation for WIDE.APP
WIDTST	PRN	Test file for WIDE.APP
WNDWSY	WRK	Macro for synchronizing windows
WRDST	CTF	Translation for Wordstar files to Symphony

Disk No 306 — Symphony Worksheets #2 — v1 DS2

10_KEY	WRK	10 key calculator
1LETTER	WRK	Use with DIRECTRY.WRK
1MACROS	WRK	Use with DIRECTRY.WRK
1SHEET	WRK	Use with DIRECTRY.WRK
ADDR	WRK	Names and addresses macros
CHKBK	WRK	Macro driven checkbook
CHKBOO	DOC	Documentation file for CHKBOO
CHKBOO	WRK	Checkbook manager home or small business
CTLBRK	APP	Break menu handling add-in
DIRECTRY	WRK	Library for file names and descriptions
DISKLABL	WRK	Prints out list of disk contents
INPUT	APP	Range input 1-2-3 add-in
LABELS	WRK	Name and address labels for printer
MCA	APP	Macro conversion 1-2-3 add-in
MCA	HLP	On disk help for MCA.APP
MCARI	WRK	Documentation for MCA.APP
PHNBRS	WRK	Database using find functions
PHONE	WRK	Phone dialer sample
SYSERR	APP	DOS error retry disable
UN1	CCF	Unattended operation ccf file
UN1	WRK	Unattended operation see UN1.CCF

5.0 INDEXES

By Disk Name

By Filename

Name	Ext	Size	Disk
!	BAT	16	#9
$$COLLST	PTR	384	#276
$$COLLST	TXT	14464	#276
$$DOEXBA	BAT	394	#277
$$MENU	BAS	898	#277
$$NEWTRE	BAT	427	#277
$$TRESRT	BAT	435	#250
$JOBS	NDX	1024	#102
$SUPP	NDX	1024	#102
%-DIFF	BAS	4864	#73
(READ	ME)	1310	#184
-README-	BAT	27	#244
-README-	DOC	489	#152
0	BAS	509	#241
0	BAT	24	#159
1	BAS	5389	#241
1-2-3	TXT	10999	#159
10	BAS	6498	#241
1004-B	BAS	18048	#239
1005-A	BAS	4352	#239
1009-A	BAS	19456	#239
1099	EXE	62976	#275
10_KEY	WRK	1612	#306
11	BAS	5052	#241
12	BAS	5050	#241
123DOC	BAS	8192	#301
123DOC	DOC	3456	#301
123DOC	EXE	24704	#301
123KEY	BAT	31	#115
123KEY	BAT	31	#207
123KEY	DOC	4166	#115
123KEY	DOC	4166	#207
123KEY	PRO	602	#115
123KEY	PRO	602	#207
123MAIL	TXT	21545	#301
123PREP	DOC	8704	#141
123PREP	DOC	14317	#301
123PREP	EXE	30208	#141
123PREP	EXE	33792	#301
123Q&A	TXT	14999	#301
123RANGE	BAS	6912	#301
123STAR	UNP	1024	#184
123XIMAC	TXT	8608	#301
13	BAS	5153	#241
14	BAS	3439	#241
15	BAS	3785	#241
1500	BAS	5376	#44
15PUZZLE	BAS	3117	#83
16	BAS	15166	#241
17	BAS	4737	#241
1LETTER	WRK	4564	#306
1MACROS	WRK	4411	#306
1RD	COM	37557	#77
1RD	DOC	49719	#77
1RD	PRO	288	#77
1SHEET	WRK	4496	#306
2	BAS	3151	#241
20	BAS	13526	#241
21	BAS	5888	#44
23MATCH	BAS	1021	#35
2COLOR	COM	22	#9
2COLOR	SYS	256	#9
2MONO	COM	22	#9
2MONO	SYS	256	#9
2X2DISC	WKS	16256	#302
3	BAS	3322	#241
3-D-ROT	BAS	12672	#73
3-DEMON	EXE	59774	#293
3-DEMON	HI1	550	#293
3002-A	BAS	5632	#239
3003-A	BAS	5760	#239
3006-A	BAS	2944	#239
3012-A	BAS	11136	#239
3014-A	BAS	12672	#239
3BY5	EXE	96114	#253
3D	DOC	1792	#73
3D	EXE	25728	#73
3D	GRF	3712	#73
3DTEST1	PLT	16512	#73
3DTEST2	PLT	16512	#73
3DTT	BAS	13568	#100
4	BAS	1881	#241
4028-A	BAS	6912	#239
4BARLINK	BAS	2894	#299
5	BAS	5746	#241
5006-A	BAS	3328	#239
6	BAS	7217	#241
7	BAS	16260	#241
7013-A	BAS	6528	#239
7037-A	BAS	2304	#239
7042-A	BAS	13952	#239
78INT	BAS	896	#201
8	BAS	6810	#241
8087	ASM	8125	#134
8087	REV	8494	#159
84F1040		35502	#291
84F1041		6095	#291
9	BAS	4680	#241
@HA	OVL	3840	#266
@HB	OVL	2560	#266
@HC	OVL	512	#266
@HD	OVL	3712	#266
@HE	OVL	5120	#266
@HF	OVL	3584	#266
@HG	OVL	6656	#266
@HH	OVL	4736	#266
@HI	OVL	3328	#266
@HJ	OVL	1792	#266
@SB	OVL	6912	#266
@SD	OVL	4480	#266
_ELEM	REM	8865	#82
_EPILOG	REM	2701	#82
_FIND	BAT	1109	#82
_FIND	REM	8282	#82
_FUNKY	BAT	1533	#82
_FUNKY	REM	4556	#82
_MAIN	C	1536	#138
_PERFORM	REM	2817	#82
_QUERY	BAT	2197	#82
_QUERY	REM	2916	#82
_RUNME2	BAT	232	#82
_RUNME3	BAT	2697	#82
_SLASH	REM	1048	#82
_WHAT	BAT	1537	#82
_WHAT	REM	5575	#82

A

Name	Ext	Size	Disk
A0	BAS	2304	#105
A1	BAS	896	#105
A1	TXT	8924	#105
A2	BAS	896	#105
A2	SPC	2304	#100
A2	TXT	6260	#105
A3	BAS	896	#105
A3	TXT	6915	#105
A4	BAS	1024	#105
A4	TXT	11629	#105
A5	SPC	896	#100
A5MG1084	PRN	17024	#280
ABCFILE	DOC	60288	#119
ABCFILE	EXE	88064	#119
ABCFILE	HLP	14276	#119
ABCONVRT	BAS	1062	#119
ABSTRACT	DOC	4096	#52
ACATALOG	BAS	5120	#9
ACCOUNT	NL	4096	#200
ACCTG	PRG	1536	#102
ACCTSUM		638	#215
ACEY-DUE	BAS	2560	#175
ACOURSE	ASC	13440	#262
ACOURSE	DAT	1152	#262
ACOURSE	TXT	1536	#262
ACRS	BAS	3456	#6
ACRS	WKS	6400	#302
ACS	PIC	32776	#241
AD	COM	572	#79
ADA1	TXT	9124	#159
ADA1	TXT	16278	#160
ADA1CMP	REV	11383	#159
ADABOOK	REV	12973	#160
ADC	WKS	7936	#304
ADD	BAS	109	#292
ADD	BAT	121	#59
ADD-LF	BAS	1792	#79
ADDCHEK	PRG	1032	#295
ADDCR	BAS	512	#2
ADDCRS	BAS	858	#50

ADDEND24	DOC	3278	#78
ADDFILE	BAS	2688	#182
ADDINCO	PRG	1919	#295
ADDLABEL	DOC	865	#301
ADDLABL2	WKS	7808	#301
ADDMAIL	BAS	1024	#169
ADDMEMB	BAS	512	#169
ADDR	WRK	16000	#306
ADDR-PH	BAS	5376	#56
ADDRECD	PRG	3936	#295
ADDRESS	BAS	5010	#35
ADDRESS	DAT	1024	#218
ADDRESS	DOC	11648	#218
ADDRESS	EXE	38400	#218
ADDRESS	MEN	8192	#218
ADDRESS	NL	5120	#156
ADDRESS	NL	9216	#157
ADDRESS	NL	11264	#158
ADDRESS	NL	12288	#200
ADDRESS	SCR	10958	#158
ADDRFLCD	BAS	3200	#49
ADDRS	WRK	31104	#305
ADDSTOK	PRG	1536	#295
ADDSTR	DCL	115	#132
ADDSTR	OBJ	426	#132
ADDSUB	PRG	1024	#126
ADVANCED	BAS	256	#167
ADVANCED	DOC	1664	#167
ADVCAVE	H	8047	#259
ADVCOMP	DOC	33027	#213
ADVCOMP	EXE	38016	#213
ADVDEC	H	2000	#259
ADVDEF	H	1560	#259
ADVEN1	BAS	23424	#203
ADVENT	C	6410	#259
ADVENT	DOC	3328	#259
ADVENT	DOC	35584	#91
ADVENT	EXE	45824	#259
ADVENT	H	2567	#259
ADVENT	OBJ	25547	#259
ADVENT0	C	3523	#259
ADVENT0	EXE	11776	#259
ADVENT1	TXT	18281	#259
ADVENT2	TXT	6453	#259
ADVENT3	TXT	5559	#259
ADVENT4	TXT	18180	#259
ADVLAND	PIC	16512	#15
ADVRUN	EXE	42240	#213
ADVTEXT	H	3251	#259
ADVWORD	H	5176	#259
AELPW	NYS	3968	#40
AFT8087	MAC	3456	#142
AGCDIR	DAT	640	#262
AGE	PRG	256	#300
AGENDA	WKS	2432	#289
AGETAB		2250	#192
AID	BAS	32519	#141
AID	BAT	512	#141
AID	DOC	10752	#141
AID	EXE	53760	#141
AINIT	DAT	128	#262
AINTRO	ASC	3328	#262
AINTRO	TXT	5376	#262
AJETCRUZ	BAS	17664	#39
AJETOFF	BAS	9856	#39
ALBERT	NL	11264	#156
ALCATRAZ	BBS	9600	#103
ALDIR	BAT	105	#82
ALGEBRA	BAS	5504	#168
ALIB	INC	305	#74
ALIEN	BAS	2304	#100
ALIEN	BAS	28672	#175
ALIEN	DOC	325	#100
ALIEN	SPC	25728	#100
ALIGN	DOC	21094	#217
ALIGN	EXE	33108	#217
ALPHAHEX	BAS	6144	#66
ALPHAMAR	BAS	4735	#90
ALPHAPER	BAS	5417	#90
ALTER	COM	1024	#80
ALTER	COM	1024	#184
ALTER	DOC	2688	#184
ALTER	DOC	3840	#80
AMAIN	UNO	15104	#262
AMAIN	ZRO	8320	#262
AMERICA	BAS	416	#292
AMORT1X	WKS	27648	#302
AMPINC	NYS	3958	#40
ANALOG	BAS	4096	#18
ANALOG2	BAS	1280	#18
ANALOG3	BAS	3584	#18
ANALOG4	BAS	1920	#18
ANALOG5	BAS	1664	#18
ANALOG6	BAS	2304	#18
ANALYST	DOC	9049	#282
ANALYST	EXE	104576	#282
ANIMAL	BAS	2432	#128
ANIMAL	GME	640	#128
ANIMATE	BAS	483	#299
ANIMATE	BAS	3712	#100
ANIMATE	BAS	3712	#167
ANJAC830	PRT	468	#78
ANJAC832	PRT	539	#78
ANOVA	BAS	5376	#88
ANSI	BAT	768	#139
ANSI	SYS	2432	#95
ANSIPCH	EXE	6144	#138
ANTHEM	BAS	890	#292
ANTONYM	BAS	3840	#18
ANTONYM2	BAS	2560	#18
ANTONYMS	BAS	5248	#45
APDIR	DAT	768	#262
APERFORM	ASC	19328	#262
APERFORM	TXT	6272	#262
APLAYER	ASC	12928	#262
APLAYER	DAT	4096	#262
APLAYER	TXT	1536	#262
APLCHIP	DOC	896	#135
APPEND	PRG	34	#300
APPENDIX	BAS	31454	#90
APPENDIX	DOC	36289	#222
APPENDIX	DOC	61685	#221
APPENDIX	DOC	65205	#220
APPLECOM	BAS	768	#67
APPT	WRK	22656	#305
AQUIT	ASC	1792	#262
AQUIT	TXT	768	#262
ARC	WKS	8832	#304
ARCH	EXE	19072	#162
ARCHIE	BAS	32384	#19
ARCHIE	DOC	2048	#19
ARCHIVE	AR	11118	#132
ARCHIVE	EXE	34176	#130
ARCHIVE	MAN	2187	#130
AREACODE	BAS	8960	#182
ARKTRAV	BAS	128	#12
ARSUMARY		616	#215
ART	LSP	2560	#148
ART	TXT	2032	#211
ARTILL	BAS	7680	#28
ASCFILTR	BAS	1430	#50
ASCICHAR	BAS	2432	#9
ASCIDATA		256	#215
ASCII	BAS	640	#9
ASCII	BAS	10368	#214
ASCII	WKS	12544	#257
ASCIIDOC	BAT	17	#257
ASCIIDOC	PRN	3200	#257
ASCIITUT	WKS	81152	#257
ASDA	BAS	15616	#46
ASDADEL	BAS	896	#46
ASDARUN	BAS	3456	#46
ASK	COM	256	#80
ASK	DOC	1507	#80
ASM		71347	#114
ASM	KEY	1096	#181
ASM1	TXT	17467	#159
ASM1	TXT	21162	#160
ASM2	TXT	19749	#160
ASMBASIC	ASM	8104	#285
ASMBASIC	EXE	2432	#285
ASMBASIC	TXT	7647	#285
ASMGEN	COM	9444	#93
ASMGEN	COM	10880	#166
ASMGEN	COM	11264	#145
ASMGEN	DOC	26112	#166
ASMGEN	DOC	27904	#145
ASMGEN	DOC	29463	#93
ASMTIPS	DOC	896	#166
ASMTUTR1	DOC	23552	#166
ASMTUTR2	DOC	25088	#166
ASMTUTR3	DOC	19456	#166
ASMTUTR4	DOC	5632	#166
ASTEROID	BAS	2422	#203

ASYN-PGM	BAS	3694	#14
AT	ASM	713	#258
AT	COM	58	#258
AT&T	NYS	4352	#40
ATALLY	ASC	17664	#262
ATALLY	TXT	5248	#262
ATC	DAT	384	#229
ATC	EXE	50304	#229
ATC1	BLD	4096	#229
ATC2	BLD	4096	#229
ATEMP	DAT	128	#262
ATO	BAS	15387	#258
ATO	DOC	6872	#258
ATO	EXE	38016	#258
ATTACK	BAS	6400	#37
ATTRIB	ABS	353	#53
ATTRIB	BAS	256	#53
ATTRIB	SB	1878	#162
AUTHOR	BAS	1664	#27
AUTHOR2	BAS	1280	#27
AUTO	BAT	75	#59
AUTO	BAT	128	#284
AUTO	WKS	44928	#207
AUTO1	BAT	128	#284
AUTO123	WKS	1408	#165
AUTO123	WKS	7168	#289
AUTO123	WKS	18944	#257
AUTO123	WKS	57216	#303
AUTO2	BAT	128	#284
AUTOADD	BAT	19	#59
AUTOCOLR	COM	7168	#284
AUTOCOST	FRM	255	#295
AUTOCOST	PRG	1324	#295
AUTODEX	EXE	32000	#134
AUTODIAL	BAS	6016	#187
AUTODT	NYS	3840	#40
AUTOEXEC	BAK	30	#59
AUTOEXEC	BAT	many	
AUTOEXEC	BAT	8	#237
AUTOEXEC	BAT	10	#153
AUTOEXEC	BAT	14	#127
AUTOEXEC	BAT	14	#241
AUTOEXEC	BAT	17	#235
AUTOEXEC	BAT	17	#283
AUTOEXEC	BAT	17	#68
AUTOEXEC	BAT	19	#266
AUTOEXEC	BAT	22	#88
AUTOEXEC	BAT	36	#232
AUTOEXEC	BAT	38	#246
AUTOEXEC	BAT	40	#233
AUTOEXEC	BAT	43	#262
AUTOEXEC	BAT	128	#86
AUTOEXEC	BAT	128	#151
AUTOEXEC	BAT	128	#296
AUTOEXEC	BAT	128	#170
AUTOEXEC	BAT	128	#284
AUTOEXEC	BAT	128	#251
AUTOEXEC	BAT	384	#282
AUTOEXEC	BAT	640	#112
AUTOFILE	BAS	12050	#110
AUTOFILE	BAS	16384	#182
AUTOFILE	BAT	24	#182
AUTOFILE	BAT	512	#110
AUTOFILE	DOC	9216	#110
AUTOFILE	DOC	9216	#182
AUTOFILE	FIX	512	#182
AUTOINST	BAS	2048	#9
AUTOMENU	COM	7168	#284
AUTOMENU	DAT	381	#284
AUTOMENU	DOC	17152	#284
AUTOMONO	COM	7168	#284
AUTOPEEK	BAS	896	#9
AUTOST	BAS	6528	#9
AUTOSTRT	BAT	38	#246
AUTOTEMP	BAT	128	#284
AVERAGE	BAS	383	#292
AVERAGE	BAS	384	#105
AVERAGE#	BAS	290	#292
AVERAGE2	BAS	238	#292
AWARI	BAS	2048	#45
AWARI	BAS	4096	#178

B

B		6978	#46
B	BAS	128	#11
B-SIMPLE	BAS	17664	#20
B1	BAS	128	#27
B1	BAS	1024	#171
B10	BAS	512	#171
B11	BAS	768	#171
B12	BAS	768	#171
B13	BAS	640	#171
B14	BAS	896	#171
B15	BAS	896	#171
B16	BAS	1024	#171
B17	BAS	1024	#171
B18	BAS	768	#171
B19	BAS	1536	#171
B2	BAS	512	#171
B20	BAS	1792	#171
B3	BAS	896	#171
B4	BAS	896	#171
B5	BAS	896	#171
B6	BAS	896	#171
B7	BAS	512	#171
B8	BAS	640	#171
B9	BAS	3072	#171
BABYMATH	EXE	20352	#168
BACCRRT	BAS	3200	#45
BACH	BAS	6912	#168
BACH2	BAS	8704	#168
BACKGAM	BAS	4736	#18
BACKLOG	BAR	512	#14
BACKSCRL	COM	6395	#129
BACKSCRL	COM	6395	#273
BACKSCRL	DOC	12032	#129
BACKSCRL	DOC	12032	#273
BACKUP	BAS	512	#105
BACKUP	BAS	5888	#4
BACKUP	BAT	1889	#124
BACKUP	PRG	2048	#126
BAD	BAS	218	#292
BAGPIPES	BAS	1408	#100
BALANCE	BAS	512	#29
BALL	BAS	616	#292
BALL	BAS	2176	#44
BALL	BAS	2176	#79
BANDDEMO	BAS	12682	#285
BANDDEMO	EXE	26981	#285
BANDNOO	EXE	7965	#285
BANKER	BAS	21248	#35
BANNER	ASC	860	#193
BANNER	BAS	2432	#44
BANNER	BAS	2816	#128
BANNER	BAS	4096	#61
BARGRAPH	BAS	22016	#14
BARGRAPH	BAS	22016	#35
BARIC	BAS	2816	#128
BARS	BAS	367	#299
BAS	BAT	15	#195
BASCOM	DOC	4772	#114
BASCOM	PAT	512	#135
BASCOM	PAT	3328	#91
BASCOM	TXT	1792	#135
BASEBALL	BAS	11136	#45
BASEBALL	BAS	15616	#175
BASECONV	BAS	2048	#53
BASECONV	BAS	6528	#187
BASIC	KEY	162	#59
BASIC	KEY	162	#170
BASIC	UNP	896	#184
BASIC-KB	ASM	10075	#56
BASIC-KB	DOC	5033	#56
BASIC-KB	EXE	1280	#56
BASIC1	TXT	9178	#160
BASICAK	BAT	13	#113
BASICPRT	BAS	5248	#11
BASKEYS	BAS	359	#167
BASLIB	PAT	1024	#135
BASMENU	BAS	768	#14
BASMENU	BAS	896	#20
BASPRINT	ASM	19481	#285
BASPRINT	EXE	1920	#285
BASREF	DOC	2002	#60
BASREF	EXE	45568	#60
BASRUN	EXE	31744	#251
BASRUN	EXE	31744	#237
BASRUN	NL	2048	#157
BASRUN	PAT	1664	#135
BASSUB	BAS	2816	#142
BASSUB	OBJ	384	#142
BASTOD	BAS	50783	#238
BASTODOS	BAS	46592	#167

BASTODOS	BAS	46592	#108
BASTOFOR	BAS	18884	#167
BASTOFOR	DOC	5464	#167
BAT	COM	9533	#124
BAT	COM	9728	#205
BAT-CD	ASM	2959	#255
BAT-CD	COM	127	#255
BAT-CD	DOC	1854	#255
BAT200D	COM	9728	#139
BAT2DEMO	BAT	10241	#205
BAT2DOC	BAT	40167	#205
BATCH	DOC	5760	#192
BATCK	LIB	20608	#276
BATCK	SCR	39680	#276
BATDEMO	BAT	10183	#124
BATDOC	BAT	38490	#124
BATMAN	BAS	2032	#33
BATMAN	DOC	2506	#33
BATMENU	COM	384	#108
BATMENU	DOC	3200	#108
BATQUES	ASM	3086	#255
BATQUES	COM	36	#255
BATQUES	DOC	2256	#255
BAYES	BAS	3200	#88
BBSCOMP	BAT	118	#150
BBSLOGO	BAS	755	#150
BCAKE	BUG	1408	#94
BEAUTY	H	6542	#202
BECKLEY	NL	4096	#158
BEEP	ASM	1869	#223
BEEP	ASM	2200	#172
BEEP	COM	54	#172
BEEP	COM	89	#52
BEEP	COM	151	#113
BEEP	DOC	172	#223
BEEP	DOC	1669	#172
BEEP	EXE	768	#172
BESTLINE	BAS	896	#29
BIBL	DOC	1408	#280
BIBLE	BAS	768	#168
BIGANSI	SYS	2176	#80
BIGCAL	BAS	7431	#256
BIGCAL	DOC	4239	#256
BIGCALC	BAS	7680	#111
BIGCALC	DOC	4480	#111
BIGCHAR	BAS	1408	#67
BIGDEAL	ASM	1441	#159
BIGTYPE	BAS	1536	#28
BIGTYPE1	BAS	1152	#49
BIHEX	BAS	7808	#7
BILL		256	#215
BILLED	FRM	512	#102
BILLINGS	DBF	1024	#102
BILLINGS	NDX	1024	#102
BINOMIAL	BAS	2176	#88
BINSIX	DOC	4736	#145
BINSIX	EXE	15744	#145
BIO	BAS	3584	#45
BIO	BAS	4352	#55
BIORYM	WRK	8002	#305
BIORYTHM	BAS	4224	#44
BIORYTHM	WKS	7040	#302
BIOS	MAC	9088	#142
BIOSIO	ASM	13287	#216
BIRD	BAS	128	#299
BIRDS	BAS	2048	#14
BIRTHDAY	BAS	399	#292
BIRTHDAY	BAS	4608	#45
BKSPACE	BAS	779	#14
BLACK	BAS	16000	#18
BLACKBOX	BAS	4992	#37
BLACKBOX	BAS	8192	#72
BLACKBOX	BAS	20864	#175
BLACKJCK	BAS	8320	#1
BLACKJCK	BAS	9472	#20
BLANK	PRG	9728	#126
BLASTOFF	BAS	3200	#15
BLCKJACK	BAS	12288	#72
BLESS	BAS	640	#203
BLIMP	BAS	1408	#15
BLKFRDY	BAS	11264	#175
BLKFRI3	BAS	8192	#44
BLKLETER	BAS	512	#14
BLOB	BAS	16512	#136
BLOB	GRF	128	#136
BLOCK	EXE	5376	#175
BLUEBERY	BAS	26880	#66
BLUEBERY	DOC	1612	#66
BLUEBRY2	DOC	1386	#66
BLUEMENU	BAS	8337	#66
BLYPROGS	DOC	4224	#138
BMAC	MAC	8084	#202
BMACTST	ASM	1506	#202
BMENU	BAS	3968	#22
BMENU	DOC	4037	#22
BMENUD	BAS	3200	#22
BOARD	TST	640	#183
BOBCAT	TXT	4992	#247
BOBCAT01	DTA	282112	#247
BOBCAT01	HDR	128	#247
BOBCAT01	INX	40576	#247
BOEING	NYS	3968	#40
BOGGLE	BAS	2944	#91
BOMB	BAS	128	#53
BOMB	BAS	1920	#45
BOMB	BAS	2432	#177
BOMB	PRG	216	#300
BOND	BAS	2816	#29
BONDSTOK	PRG	736	#295
BOWLFILE	FD	1152	#23
BOWLING	BAT	36	#23
BOWLING	DOC	640	#23
BOWLPRT1	EWF	12160	#23
BOWLPRT2	EWF	12928	#23
BOXINBOX	BAS	3328	#66
BOXINPUT	BAS	13824	#66
BPR	VC	24064	#85
BPRINT	EXE	61568	#236
BREAKOUT	BAS	2176	#16
BREAKOUT	BAS	2176	#17
BREAKOUT	BAS	4864	#177
BREAKOUT	BAS	4864	#274
BREAKPT	ASM	4096	#109
BREAKPT	COM	1024	#109
BREAKPT	DOC	384	#109
BRICKS	DOC	1792	#293
BRICKS	EXE	18432	#138
BRICKS	EXE	18560	#293
BRIDGER	NL	9216	#200
BRIDGES	NL	2048	#200
BRIEFLY	BAS	2484	#241
BRKEVEN	VC	15360	#14
BROTHER1	PRT	284	#78
BROWMAIL	BAS	1152	#169
BROWSE	COM	2848	#205
BROWSE	COM	2848	#273
BROWSE	DOC	466	#205
BROWSE	DOC	466	#273
BROWSE	PRG	34	#300
BSLASH	KEY	86	#34
BSR	BAS	783	#33
BSR	DAT	409	#33
BSTAT	DOC	18268	#289
BSTAT	WKS	18432	#289
BTS	DOC	5476	#269
BUDDY		256	#251
BUDGET	BAS	7808	#29
BUDGETRK	BAS	24837	#155
BUDGETRK	DOC	8119	#155
BUDGETRK	MOD	25032	#155
BUFEXTEN	BAS	4914	#195
BUFEXTEN	COM	696	#195
BUG		1880	#250
BUG		1885	#276
BUG		1885	#277
BUG	BUG	256	#94
BUGS	EXE	24064	#177
BUGS	EXE	24064	#274
BUGS!	SCR	128	#177
BUGS!	SCR	128	#274
BUILD	EXE	29696	#26
BUILD	PAS	4170	#26
BUILDML	BAS	1664	#169
BUILFILE	BAS	1408	#182
BUILGRAF	BAS	256	#191
BUILMEMB	BAS	896	#169
BULLET1		3282	#152
BULLETIN		293	#152
BULLSEYE	BAS	256	#12
BULLSEYE	BAS	1792	#35
BUSCHECK	BAS	3328	#66
BUSICOST	FRM	245	#295
BUSIN	BAS	896	#171
BUTCHER	SNG	640	#127

BUTTRFLY	BAS	3712	#15
BUZOFF	COM	128	#33
BYE	BAS	212	#255
BYSNC	NL	4096	#158
BYTE82	DTA	2560	#121
BYTE82	HDR	128	#121
BYTE82	INX	256	#121
BYTE82	KEY	336	#121
BYTE83	DTA	18432	#123
BYTE83	HDR	128	#123
BYTE83	INX	1024	#123
BYTE83	KEY	1518	#123

C

C	ASM	3584	#138
C	BAS	256	#11
C	BUG	128	#94
C	OBJ	512	#147
C1	TXT	5087	#159
C1	TXT	15815	#160
C2	BAT	281	#193
CABLE	DOC	5317	#114
CAL	COM	1024	#111
CAL	COM	31199	#243
CAL	DOC	368	#111
CAL	PRN	51514	#243
CALENDAR	BAS	9216	#182
CALEPSON	BAS	640	#49
CALEPSON	DOC	1942	#49
CALINST	BAT	696	#243
CALLERS		128	#212
CALLERS		256	#150
CALULATE	BAS	3840	#66
CANCEL	ASM	2926	#223
CANCEL	EXE	683	#223
CANNON	BAS	2048	#11
CAPITAL	PC	6958	#152
CAPSDEF	ASM	3712	#256
CAPSDEF	COM	222	#256
CAPSDEF	DOC	4096	#256
CAPTURE	BAS	3787	#35
CARCOST	WKS	6272	#302
CASE	ASM	7936	#138
CASE	COM	256	#138
CASH	BAS	9062	#261
CASH	DOC	26667	#261
CASH	WKS	10624	#302
CASHACC	BAS	19328	#62
CASHMAN	WKS	20608	#302
CASHREAD	WKS	6912	#302
CASHREG	BAS	12416	#171
CASTLE	BAS	26230	#47
CASTLE	DOC	2688	#210
CASTLE	DOC	14976	#47
CASTLE	EXE	72832	#198
CASTLE	EXE	72832	#274
CASTLE	EXE	72960	#210

CASTLE	RAN	48384	#198
CASTLE	RAN	48384	#274
CASTLE	RAN	48512	#210
CAT	BAT	74	#216
CAT	COM	1536	#46
CAT	COM	8591	#205
CAT	DOC	14336	#205
CATALOG		0	#73
CATALOG		1348	#82
CATALOG	ASC	12288	#76
CATALOG	COM	1280	#185
CATALOG	DSK	233	#218
CATALOG	EXE	7424	#283
CATALOG	TXT	896	#128
CATCH88	BAS	6016	#4
CATEGORY	RPT	128	#247
CBB	WKS	13312	#304
CBD	BAS	20854	#282
CBD	DAT	670	#282
CBD-READ	ME	39638	#282
CC	BAT	156	#216
CC	BAT	212	#259
CC	C	3294	#149
CC	C	3544	#134
CC	DOC	466	#149
CC	EXE	12160	#149
CC	OBJ	990	#149
CCADV	BAT	1089	#259
CCIRCLE	BUG	384	#94
CD	COM	640	#28
CDB	WKS	20864	#304
CENTR351	PRT	491	#78
CENTR739	PRT	263	#78
CFILE	BAS	18944	#214
CFM	WKS	8192	#304
CFORM	BAS	18944	#214
CFP	WKS	20608	#304
CGCLOCK2	COM	1024	#205
CGCLOCK2	DOC	4096	#205
CHACONNE	COM	22597	#279
CHACONNE	MUS	18460	#279
CHANGE	BAS	9088	#23
CHANGE	BAS	29824	#214
CHANGE	EXE	30592	#130
CHANGE	EXE	32512	#57
CHANGE	MAN	756	#130
CHANGES	TXT	5494	#160
CHAP1&2	BAK	17030	#253
CHAP1&2	DOC	16963	#253
CHAP3	DOC	56184	#253
CHAP4&5	DOC	47673	#253
CHAP6	DOC	23799	#253
CHARCNT	AR	659	#132
CHARCNT	EXE	26496	#130
CHARCNT	MAN	424	#130
CHARDEFN	BAS	316	#299
CHARDISP	BAS	2944	#49
CHARDISP	BAS	3584	#167

CHARMAP	BAS	2304	#53
CHAROP	ASM	1024	#139
CHARS	BAS	2304	#6
CHARS	EXE	24704	#6
CHARS	SB	1443	#162
CHARS2	BAS	640	#62
CHART	DOC	3704	#165
CHASE	BAS	2176	#44
CHASM	BAS	32987	#10
CHASM	CFG	20	#10
CHASM	DAT	5760	#10
CHASM	DOC	128128	#10
CHCKWR	WRK	3968	#305
CHECK		4352	#267
CHECK1	DAT	128	#164
CHECK2	DAT	128	#164
CHECK3	DAT	128	#164
CHECK4	DAT	128	#164
CHECK5	DAT	128	#164
CHECKCON	BAS	1920	#46
CHECKDIR	DOC	1920	#22
CHECKDIR	EXE	36224	#22
CHECKERS	BAS	3584	#175
CHECKFIL	DBF	1024	#102
CHECKOUT	BAS	6272	#6
CHECKOUT	BAS	6272	#183
CHECKOUT	BAS	6656	#9
CHECKS		256	#215
CHECKS	DBF	1024	#295
CHECKSTU	PRG	1664	#102
CHEKFORM	BAS	2176	#66
CHEKVIEW	PRG	2354	#295
CHEMQUES	BAS	6400	#168
CHEMTEST	BAS	6912	#168
CHERTOK	NL	3072	#200
CHESS	BAS	16000	#35
CHESS	BAS	21120	#91
CHESS	EXE	9728	#178
CHESS	EXE	46464	#4
CHESS1	BAS	21473	#16
CHESS88	EXE	9472	#178
CHGMAIL	BAS	2304	#169
CHIEF	BAS	1254	#35
CHIMENE	NL	3072	#158
CHIRP	BAS	128	#53
CHISQR	BAS	3584	#88
CHKBK	WRK	6656	#306
CHKBOO	DOC	2410	#306
CHKBOO	WRK	8832	#306
CHKORDER	FRM	512	#295
CHKPAYEE	FRM	512	#295
CHMOD	BAS	1698	#184
CHMOD	C	8869	#84
CHMOD	DOC	768	#184
CHMOD	EXE	15104	#84
CHN	PAS	716	#255
CHOSIT	C	1854	#216
CHR	BAS	896	#37

CHR$PRNT	BAS	2688	#66
CHR-DEMO	BAS	6011	#220
CHR-DEMO	BAS	6014	#221
CHR-DEMO	BAS	6717	#222
CHRONSET	BAS	896	#47
CHRSET	BAS	256	#11
CHSONG	BAS	3584	#20
CIA	BAS	13824	#100
CIA	BAS	17837	#174
CIAGAME	BAS	16384	#37
CINDY	NUD	6528	#154
CINPUT	BAS	27008	#214
CIRCLE	BAS	138	#176
CIRCLE	GRA	1920	#66
CIRCLES	BAS	1024	#1
CIRCLES	BUG	384	#94
CIRCLOOP	ASC	1536	#176
CIRCLOOP	BAS	1024	#176
CISEXE	COM	3584	#80
CISEXE	DOC	1552	#80
CITOH	FNT	993	#130
CIVILWAR	BAS	7168	#45
CIVILWAR	BAS	9768	#174
CIVILWAR	BAS	10473	#292
CK	DOC	11679	#250
CK	DOC	11679	#275
CKBOOK	BAS	30976	#250
CKBOOK	BAS	30976	#275
CKBOOK	EXE	74368	#250
CKBOOK	EXE	74368	#275
CL	ASM	323	#80
CL	BAT	6	#216
CL	COM	44	#80
CL	DOC	415	#80
CLA	COM	128	#138
CLADV	BAT	76	#259
CLASROLL	BAS	9600	#168
CLASROLL	DOC	768	#168
CLEAN	COM	512	#2
CLEAN2	COM	640	#184
CLEAN2	DOC	2944	#184
CLEANUP	BAT	1134	#254
CLERK	BAS	13568	#73
CLFORM	WRK	2432	#305
CLIMATES	BAS	4608	#45
CLIMITS	BAS	13696	#214
CLINK	ASM	3471	#142
CLINK	COM	212	#142
CLKMOD	BAS	1536	#67
CLOCK	ASM	24109	#256
CLOCK	BAS	2944	#49
CLOCK	BAS	10368	#53
CLOCK	BLK	12288	#263
CLOCK	COM	384	#46
CLOCK	SYS	980	#256
CLOSE	DCL	46	#132
CLOSE	OBJ	529	#132
CLOUD-9	BAS	4736	#45
CLOWN	ART	3968	#154
CLREOL	ASM	2672	#285
CLREOL	OBJ	111	#285
CLREOS	ASM	3940	#285
CLREOS	OBJ	169	#285
CLS	ASM	644	#223
CLS	ASM	720	#172
CLS	COM	128	#113
CLS	COM	128	#2
CLS	DOC	126	#223
CLS	DOC	878	#172
CLS	INC	1185	#162
CLS	OBJ	85	#223
CLS	OBJ	98	#215
CLS	OBJ	98	#268
CLUBWARE	DSC	3757	#285
CLUSTADP	NL	2048	#156
CLUSTATT	NL	2048	#156
CLUSTKIT	NL	2048	#156
CLUSTPG	NL	9216	#156
CMD	C	21016	#147
CMD	OBJ	8073	#147
CMD185	COM	7424	#205
CMD185	DOC	11776	#205
CMD99	COM	2367	#183
CMDFILE	BAT	122	#132
CMINOR	COM	7027	#279
CMINOR	MUS	5495	#279
CMODE	DOC	1775	#84
CMP	COM	2134	#206
CMP	COM	2176	#143
CMP	DOC	7680	#143
CMP	DOC	7685	#206
CNMAR84	CCC	682	#242
CNMAY84	CCC	682	#242
CNTRLBK	BAS	512	#6
CNV2__00	BAT	609	#254
CNVPCJR	BAT	640	#254
CNVRTDC	COM	12800	#106
CO104CR		7892	#291
CO104LNG		23222	#291
COBRUN	NL	2048	#157
COENDP	ASM	289	#184
COENDP	OBJ	73	#184
COFFEE	BAS	12312	#168
COFIX	BAT	74	#184
COFREE	ASM	2017	#184
COFREE	OBJ	266	#184
COLBLNK1	COM	256	#89
COLINK		68	#184
COLLIDE	BAS	1664	#178
COLLST	LIB	17792	#276
COLLST	PRE	0	#276
COLLST	SCR	42624	#276
COLLSTD	LIB	12416	#276
COLLSTD	SCR	34816	#276
COLOR		38	#68
COLOR	BAS	128	#13
COLOR	BAS	256	#191
COLOR	BAS	1734	#195
COLOR	BAT	15	#13
COLOR	BAT	42	#195
COLOR	BAT	2048	#218
COLOR	COM	128	#50
COLOR	COM	512	#80
COLOR	DEF	87	#78
COLOR	DOC	839	#80
COLOR	EXE	640	#15
COLOR	EXE	640	#38
COLOR	PE	9452	#256
COLOR	PIC	4104	#105
COLOR	SCR	17	#195
COLOR40	COM	22	#6
COLOR80	COM	22	#6
COLORDEM	BAT	37	#15
COLORFUL	EXE	2176	#159
COLORG	COM	22	#6
COLORSEE	CLR	1792	#66
COLORSET	BAS	2176	#9
COLOUR	DOC	9088	#28
COLRFILE	BAS	256	#182
COLRGRAF	BAS	128	#191
COLSLOT	BAS	7552	#228
COLT45	COM	541	#279
COLT45	MUS	90	#279
COLTOMON	BAS	128	#27
COM	C	10299	#147
COM	OBJ	3642	#147
COM1084	LQR	62937	#280
COM2ASM	BAS	2428	#83
COM2ASM	BAS	3072	#166
COM2ASM	DOC	1664	#166
COM2ASM	DOC	2084	#83
COM2DATA	BAS	4512	#10
COM2DATA	DOC	2304	#10
COM__PKG	ASM	28415	#202
COM__PKG1	ASM	12045	#202
COMBIBL	LQR	26314	#280
COMBINE	BAT	128	#26
COMBOT	BAS	29824	#174
COMBOT	DOC	3022	#174
COMCHRON	BAS	1664	#47
COMDOC	PRN	4224	#280
COMDOC	WRK	19664	#305
COMM	BAS	4352	#60
COMM	MNU	533	#216
COMM	NL	2048	#157
COMM	SRC	5412	#60
COMMA	APP	11008	#305
COMMAND	COM	18944	#31
COMMER	DOC	6698	#42
COMMMSGS	DOC	11374	#202
COMMREAD	ME	1887	#202
COMP	BAS	3456	#145
COMPACT	BAS	12938	#299
COMPAQ	113	15744	#269

COMPAQ	114	15744	#269
COMPAQ	200	15744	#269
COMPAQ	210	15744	#269
COMPARE	COM	43638	#113
COMPARE	EXE	29440	#57
COMPARE1	DOC	1279	#113
COMPARE2	DOC	1133	#113
COMPARE3	DOC	1363	#113
COMPARE4	DOC	1094	#113
COMPARE5	DOC	1027	#113
COMPARE6	DOC	904	#113
COMPCOST	FRM	251	#295
COMPCOST	PRG	1277	#295
COMPIL	BAS	11264	#91
COMPLETE	DOC	10388	#113
COMPLEX	DOC	32161	#248
COMPLEX	LIB	43520	#248
COMPLEX1	PIC	16512	#12
COMPLEXF	FOR	3103	#248
COMPLEXP	PAS	3655	#248
COMPOUND	BAS	768	#29
COMPOUND	BAS	3200	#66
COMPRESS	BAS	4608	#47
COMPRINT	ASM	19856	#285
COMPRINT	EXE	1920	#285
COMPROM	EXE	27008	#183
COMPRS	COM	128	#33
COMPRSOF	COM	19	#186
COMPRSON	COM	19	#186
COMPSV	CCF	1536	#305
COMPSV	CTF	512	#305
COMPUTER	BAS	128	#53
COMSEP	BAS	901	#277
COMSEP	EXE	19712	#277
COMSEP	LIB	2048	#277
COMSHARE	OTC	3200	#40
COMSPEC4	ASM	5504	#183
COMSPEC4	COM	512	#183
COMSPEC4	DOC	2944	#183
COMSTRIP	PRG	512	#128
COMTST	PRN	1536	#305
CONFIDE	CRY	1600	#230
CONFIDE	EXE	35200	#230
CONFIDE	HLP	7426	#230
CONFIDE	INV	2432	#230
CONFIG	BAS	640	#296
CONFIG	BAS	29056	#152
CONFIG	BQS	33016	#212
CONFIG	EDX	512	#43
CONFIG	EXE	24576	#183
CONFIG	SYS	20	#46
CONFIG	TTY	1282	#280
CONFIG	WWW	38	#68
CONSIGLO	NL	4096	#158
CONSTANT	MEM	3072	#102
CONTENTS	BAS	1664	#105
CONTENTS	DOC	4424	#223
CONTENTS	DOC	9205	#299
CONTENTS	TXT	3957	#105
CONTENTS	TXT	3968	#36
CONTRACT	ASM	695	#223
CONTRACT	DOC	335	#223
CONTRACT	OBJ	95	#223
CONTROL	BAS	128	#20
CONTROL	BAS	128	#19
CONTROL	COM	526	#46
CONTROL	PCS	5	#19
CONTROLB	PCS	5	#19
CONTROLD	PCS	11	#19
CONTROLM	PCS	13	#19
CONV	BAS	3584	#79
CONVERGE	BAS	253	#299
CONVERT	BAS	4445	#187
CONVERT	BAS	6040	#261
CONVERT	BAT	22	#261
COPFILE	BAS	3584	#182
COPRNT	ASM	3829	#184
COPRNT	OBJ	703	#184
COPY40	COM	3584	#184
COPY40	DOC	256	#184
COPYALL	BAT	1536	#236
COPYALL	COM	3584	#184
COPYCOMP	BAT	534	#113
COPYFILE	PAS	458	#36
COPYFLD	DOC	3712	#143
COPYFLD	PRG	4480	#143
COPYINST	BAT	1152	#236
COPYIT	BAT	407	#64
COPYIT	BAT	407	#64
COPYOVER	BAT	198	#1
COPYOVER	DOC	450	#1
COPYPAD	BAT	256	#170
COPYPRTR	BAT	1152	#236
COPYRIGH	T	512	#112
COPYROM	EXE	27392	#183
COREFIX	BAS	2048	#14
CORNG	NYS	3968	#40
CORONA	112	15744	#269
CORR	EXE	51200	#232
CORR	HLP	822	#232
CORRELAT	BAS	3200	#88
CORTESI	NL	3072	#157
COSCAN	ASM	1474	#184
COSCAN	OBJ	228	#184
COSINES	VC	3328	#14
COSORT	ASM	1128	#184
COSORT	OBJ	167	#184
COSTBASE	DBF	1024	#102
COSTBILL	PRG	2688	#102
COSTMENU	PRG	4480	#102
COSTTIME	PRG	3840	#102
COSTUPDA	PRG	1664	#102
COTITL	ASM	1336	#184
COTITL	OBJ	352	#184
COUNTERS		128	#150
COUNTING	BAS	240	#292
COVER		2273	#250
COVER		3736	#277
COVER		4760	#276
COVER	ASM	2206	#184
COVER	COM	1074	#184
COVER	COM	1152	#111
COVER	DOC	13312	#184
COVER	OBJ	437	#184
COVER	PCS	1152	#19
COVERPRO	ASM	3692	#184
COVERPRO	COM	1170	#184
CPCPRO	DOC	12800	#28
CPOKEMAN	EXE	41472	#173
CPRINT	BAS	1536	#46
CPU8086	BLK	53248	#263
CPYRIGHT	TXT	1306	#160
CPYRIGHT	TXT	1311	#159
CR	BAS	1408	#2
CRAPS	BAS	3328	#16
CRASHER	BAS	4480	#27
CRAZY8	BAS	9195	#55
CRCK4	COM	1536	#9
CRE	C	4028	#147
CRE	OBJ	1493	#147
CREAL	BAS	18048	#214
CREATE	BAS	3072	#4
CREATE	BAS	4096	#23
CREATE	DCL	77	#132
CREATE	OBJ	892	#132
CREATMAR	BAS	3420	#90
CREATOR	BAS	2048	#186
CREATORD	BAS	3856	#90
CREATPER	BAS	3712	#90
CREATURE	BAS	114	#292
CREBS	NL	4096	#156
CRETURN	BAS	858	#52
CRIB2	BAS	17939	#260
CRIBBAGE	BAS	23296	#228
CRIBBAGE	BAS	23513	#260
CRIBBAGE	BLD	128	#228
CRITICAL	BAS	2176	#29
CRL	BAS	3132	#183
CRL	BAS	3200	#157
CRL	COM	102	#183
CRL	COM	128	#157
CRMAIL	EXE	34176	#8
CROSSOPT		128	#145
CROSSOPT		128	#8
CROSSREF	BAS	5248	#2
CROSSREF	DOC	15488	#8
CROSSREF	EXE	43392	#8
CROSSREF	EXE	44288	#20
CROSSREF	SCR	9728	#20
CROSSWDS	DAT	902	#8
CROSSWDS	DAT	912	#299
CRS	BAS	1460	#183
CRS	COM	10	#183
CRS	COM	128	#157

CRYPT	C	640	#163
CRYPT	DOC	1536	#163
CRYPT	EXE	5632	#163
CRYPTO	BAS	1612	#255
CS-BUS		54528	#103
CS-EDUCA		15744	#104
CS-HOME		99982	#104
CS-IBM	SIG	72576	#99
CS-INDEX		32512	#104
CS-INSTR		6656	#103
CS-NEW		10331	#125
CS-PHONE	NOS	87936	#98
CS-POST		6784	#103
CS-PRO		20864	#103
CS-TRAVL		29440	#103
CS-USERS	IBM	23040	#99
CSCREEN	BAS	19456	#214
CSPOOL	COM	1024	#2
CSPOOL	COM	1024	#27
CSTLDFNS	BAS	2345	#292
CTEMP	BAS	256	#215
CTLBRK	APP	1408	#306
CTOI	DCL	72	#132
CTOI	OBJ	582	#132
CTRANSFE	BAS	25856	#214
CTTY	DOC	2472	#258
CUB	NDX	3584	#300
CUBE		256	#73
CUBE	BAS	9536	#177
CUBE	BAS	12544	#49
CUBLDR	DBF	512	#300
CUBLDR	FMT	457	#300
CUBLDR	NDX	1536	#300
CUBPRINT	PRG	1369	#300
CUBS	DBF	560	#300
CUBS	FMT	443	#300
CUBS	NDX	1536	#300
CUBS	PRG	768	#300
CUBS1	NDX	3584	#300
CUMMING	NL	3072	#158
CURBACK	C	1425	#216
CURDOWN	C	1425	#216
CURFOR	C	1424	#216
CURSOR	C	1572	#216
CURSOR	COM	24	#205
CURUGS	PIC	2868	#158
CURUGS	PIC	2944	#157
CURUGS	PIC	2944	#200
CURUP	C	1423	#216
CURVE	ABS	1343	#239
CURVE	BAS	285	#176
CURVE	BAS	7936	#239
CURVE	NFO	11351	#239
CURVE2	BAS	790	#176
CURVE3	BAS	1210	#176
CURVEFIT	BAS	26496	#191
CURVEFIT	DOC	11264	#191
CUSTOM	BAS	3840	#190
CUSTOMER		536	#215
CV	COM	256	#184
CV	DOC	768	#184
CV2	COM	512	#205
CVTBIN	BAS	2089	#238
CVTDATE	C	2238	#216
CVTHEX	EXE	25472	#33
CWEEP13	DOC	8704	#283
CWEEP13	EXE	26368	#283
CWP	DOC	1669	#280
CWP	EXE	18432	#280
CYCLE	BAS	3584	#71

D

D	DOC	896	#143
D	EXE	2560	#143
D&CFORM	BAS	2048	#66
DAIS2000	PRT	343	#78
DAISTRS2	PRT	381	#78
DARTH	BAS	7793	#154
DATA		128	#67
DATA	DAT	128	#197
DATA	DAT	128	#105
DATA-ONE	BAS	8192	#88
DATA1	BAS	1792	#105
DATA2	BAS	2432	#105
DATABASE		150	#109
DATABASE	C	6751	#259
DATABASE	OBJ	5241	#259
DATAFILL	TXT	8067	#301
DATAFIX	BAS	7168	#48
DATAINIT	BAS	11392	#296
DATANET		17536	#180
DATAS180	PRT	282	#78
DATAS220	PRT	407	#78
DATAST		896	#282
DATE	PRG	512	#128
DATE	PRG	2048	#109
DATETEST	PRG	1536	#102
DATETIME	BAS	1792	#27
DATEWR	WKS	5120	#302
DATNOIDS	BAS	22803	#209
DAVIS	NL	4096	#200
DAY	PRG	1024	#128
DAYLOG	BAS	19584	#49
DBFIND	DAT	205824	#266
DBII-ABC	EXE	23168	#119
DBLHITOF	COM	19	#186
DBLHITON	COM	19	#186
DBLWDEOF	COM	19	#186
DBLWDEON	COM	19	#186
DBMENU	BAS	1280	#4
DBS	EXE	39808	#128
DBS	EXE	39808	#163
DBS	PRT	16312	#128
DBS	PRT	16312	#163
DBSEQ	WRK	2944	#305
DC-SORT	BAS	7040	#70
DC-SORT	EXE	27136	#70
DC4	DOC	41379	#106
DC4-CAT	EXE	56704	#106
DC4-DOC	EXE	23936	#106
DC4-FIND	EXE	19712	#106
DC4-PGM	DTA	640	#106
DC4-READ	EXE	65664	#106
DC4-SAMP	DT2	128	#106
DC4-SAMP	DTA	896	#106
DC4-SORT	EXE	48384	#106
DCATFILE	BAS	1408	#182
DCBA	HOW	1584	#6
DCBA2	HOW	2739	#256
DCOPY	COM	3199	#184
DCPATCH	DOC	472	#33
DD	BAT	26	#144
DD	BAT	26	#185
DDATE	COM	512	#28
DDATE	COM	512	#182
DEBUG	INC	8143	#162
DEBUG	PAT	94	#159
DEBUG20	FIX	555	#285
DEBUGFIX	TXT	10885	#285
DECIDE	BAS	4897	#35
DECIDE	BAS	6144	#56
DECISION	BAS	1280	#44
DECODE	EXE	34944	#305
DECODE	WRK	1280	#305
DEFAULTS	EXE	27648	#68
DEFCOPY	BAT	604	#34
DEFEND	BAS	5504	#11
DEFINE	BAS	5169	#265
DEFINE	BAS	5217	#110
DEFINE	DOC	896	#110
DEFINE	EXE	30976	#58
DEFINE	EXE	45568	#287
DEFINE	INS	896	#265
DEFKEY	BAS	9479	#113
DEFKEY	BAT	139	#113
DEFKEY	COM	4421	#34
DEFKEY	DOC	6667	#113
DEFKEY	DOC	23207	#34
DEFMAIL	EXE	30208	#34
DEFRAG	BAS	4699	#256
DEFRAG	DOC	5331	#256
DELMAIL	BAS	1408	#169
DELTAA	NYS	3968	#40
DEMO	BAS	6528	#69
DEMO	BAT	198	#75
DEMO	EXE	68864	#74
DEMO	GFL	69	#136
DEMO	PAS	37765	#74
DEMO	PIC	16512	#13
DEMO1	BAT	405	#60
DEMO1	CAL	1	#75
DEMO1	DAT	837	#75
DEMO1	FC	1536	#170

DEMO1	GRF	633	#136
DEMO1	IX	244	#75
DEMO10	GRF	256	#136
DEMO2	BAT	796	#60
DEMO2	CAL	1	#75
DEMO2	DAT	3495	#75
DEMO2	FC	7936	#170
DEMO2	GRF	1408	#136
DEMO3	BAS	8320	#12
DEMO3	BAT	721	#60
DEMO3	FC	2560	#170
DEMO3	GRF	768	#136
DEMO4	BAT	660	#60
DEMO4	GRF	896	#136
DEMO5	BAT	390	#60
DEMO5	GRF	384	#136
DEMO6	BAT	727	#60
DEMO6	GRF	768	#136
DEMO7	BAT	410	#60
DEMO7	GRF	512	#136
DEMO8	BAT	788	#60
DEMO8	GRF	512	#136
DEMO9	GRF	512	#136
DEMODFM	EXE	110080	#75
DEMOEX1	FM	5458	#75
DEMOEX2	FM	7922	#75
DEMOFED	EXE	86016	#75
DEMOG	INC	73	#74
DEMOG	PAS	16257	#74
DEMOMINI	EXE	25600	#74
DEMOMINI	OBJ	2330	#74
DEMOMINI	PAS	2085	#74
DEMOPAD		15232	#170
DEMOS	INC	197	#74
DEMOS	PAS	7583	#74
DEMOX	FM	4446	#75
DEPMENU	PRG	1280	#102
DEPOSITS	DBF	1024	#102
DEPOSITS	PRG	3456	#102
DEPPRINT	PRG	2048	#102
DEPRE---	APL	11264	#108
DEPREC	BAS	11264	#50
DEPREC	DOC	24828	#289
DEPREC	WKS	25216	#289
DEPTRANS	PRG	1408	#102
DESCEND	BAS	11312	#90
DESCRIBE		690	#158
DESCRIBE		1024	#200
DESCRIPT	DAT	1664	#297
DESCRIPT	DOC	289	#155
DESCRIPT	DOC	24091	#230
DESCRIPT	ION	27426	#54
DESCRIPT	TXT	5872	#225
DESERT	BAS	5820	#35
DESERT	BAS	7424	#55
DESIGN	BAS	13568	#79
DESIGN	EXE	52096	#208
DESIGNER	BAS	18688	#69
DESIGNER	DOC	45056	#69
DESK	DOC	15427	#65
DESKTOP	WKS	108928	#64
DESKTOP	WKS	108928	#64
DETAB	BAS	986	#285
DETAB	C	2176	#163
DETAB	C	2688	#111
DETAB	DOC	2304	#163
DETAB	DOC	2816	#93
DETAB	EXE	6656	#163
DETAB	EXE	9216	#111
DETAB	EXE	10752	#93
DETAB	EXE	15744	#162
DETAIL	BAS	2048	#23
DFM	HLP	11626	#75
DFORMAT	COM	2688	#184
DHDEMO	BAS	1859	#115
DIABLO16	PRT	535	#78
DIABLO63	PRT	834	#78
DIAL	BAT	1664	#139
DIAL	COM	384	#33
DIALER	DAT	720	#286
DIALOG11	DOC	1536	#112
DIALOG12	DOC	1280	#112
DIALOG13	DOC	3968	#112
DIALOG14	DOC	3072	#112
DIALOG15	DOC	2816	#112
DIALOG16	DOC	2816	#112
DIALOG17	DOC	7424	#112
DIALOG21	DOC	1664	#112
DIALOG22	DOC	3200	#112
DIALOG23	DOC	4608	#112
DIALOG24	DOC	1408	#112
DIALOG25	DOC	4224	#112
DIATAB		501	#192
DIGIDRAW	BAS	8064	#191
DIGIDRAW	DOC	27904	#191
DIP-MEM	COM	1536	#145
DIP-MEM	DOC	2688	#145
DIR		61	#152
DIR		61	#212
DIR		837	#34
DIR	BAS	15104	#33
DIR	DAT	384	#33
DIR	DOC	915	#33
DIR-LIST		1408	#303
DIR-LIST		2176	#306
DIR-LIST		2560	#301
DIR-LIST		2688	#302
DIR-LIST		3072	#305
DIR2	BAS	21376	#185
DIR201	BAS	21760	#139
DIR201	EXE	45568	#139
DIR99		73	#152
DIR99		73	#212
DIRCOMP	COM	1024	#196
DIRDEM	BAS	1775	#256
DIRECT	BAS	2226	#256
DIRECT	BAT	35	#172
DIRECTOR	BAS	15341	#90
DIRECTRY	BAS	2176	#111
DIRECTRY	BIN	256	#111
DIRECTRY	WRK	8648	#306
DIRLIST	DOC	2688	#195
DIRMANIP	EXE	9728	#70
DISBJRNL	WKS	53632	#165
DISBURSE	BAS	15744	#201
DISBURSE	TXT	21235	#201
DISCLAIM		1174	#193
DISK		0	#276
DISKCAT	BAS	21376	#70
DISKCAT	DOC	5373	#70
DISKCAT	EXE	44672	#70
DISKCOPY	COM	2008	#283
DISKETTE	COM	3134	#235
DISKID	REV	128	#9
DISKLABL	WRK	18944	#306
DISKMDF2	BAS	3619	#83
DISKMOD	BAS	7552	#2
DISKMOD	BAS	7552	#27
DISKMODF	BAS	3712	#28
DISKMODP	BAS	7405	#299
DISKNAME		128	#66
DISKPGM1	ABS	432	#53
DISKPGM1	BAS	3456	#53
DISKREAD	EXE	37632	#30
DISKREAD	OBJ	7154	#30
DISKREAD	PAS	7507	#30
DISKRTN	DOC	503	#38
DISKRTN	EXE	9728	#38
DISKTYPE	DOC	512	#108
DISKTYPE	EXE	1408	#108
DISNEY	NYS	4096	#40
DISPFILE	BAS	640	#182
DISPGRAF	BAS	640	#191
DISPGRDR	BAS	640	#191
DISPLAY	BAS	512	#11
DISPLAY	BAS	766	#195
DISPLAY	BAS	1420	#79
DISPLAY	BAS	21822	#90
DISPLAY	BAT	21	#195
DISPLAY	TXT	3024	#79
DISPMAIL	BAS	512	#169
DISPMEMB	BAS	1664	#169
DISPRE	ASM	8617	#256
DISPRE	COM	560	#256
DISPRE	DOC	326	#256
DISPRE	EXE	1072	#256
DISRTN	EXE	9728	#47
DISRTN	EXE	9728	#52
DISTAR	BAS	6656	#56
DITHER	BAS	1509	#299
DIVDLIST	FRM	512	#295
DIVIDE	BAS	109	#292
DIVIDEND	DBF	1024	#295
DIVILIST	PRG	1346	#295

DJ	COM	61114	#284
DKSPAT	TXT	3584	#91
DLIB	EXE	5888	#284
DLTAFILE	DTA	1120	#101
DLTAPLOT	BAS	11392	#101
DLTAPRNT	BAS	13696	#101
DM	BAS	1024	#38
DMLQ	DOC	918	#38
DN	BAT	22	#144
DN	BAT	22	#185
DNXSD	DOC	752	#144
DNXSD	DOC	752	#185
DOC		40833	#250
DOC		50930	#277
DOC		77426	#276
DOC	BAT	209	#199
DOC	BAT	246	#77
DOC	BAT	247	#129
DOC	BAT	249	#5
DOC	BAT	256	#281
DOC	BAT	1336	#250
DOC	BAT	1336	#275
DOC	TXT	640	#126
DOC41	TQT	26167	#133
DOC41	TXT	52574	#245
DOC42	TQT	11649	#133
DOC42	TXT	23210	#245
DOCTOR	BAS	8832	#72
DOCUFDOC	BAS	4692	#255
DOCUFILE	BAS	1690	#255
DOCUFILE	BAS	1792	#283
DOCUFILE	BAT	128	#283
DOCUFILE	DOC	3643	#255
DOCUMENT		9728	#153
DONA	SNG	896	#127
DONACOST	FRM	227	#295
DONATION	PRG	1335	#295
DOODLE	BAS	171	#292
DOORS	BAS	1239	#299
DOORS	COM	178	#299
DORK	FMT	1024	#300
DORK	PRG	442	#300
DOS	MAC	2056	#202
DOS	MAC	11904	#142
DOS-SIZE	DOC	1991	#255
DOS1	TXT	10141	#159
DOS1	TXT	13882	#160
DOS2	TXT	2526	#159
DOS2	TXT	6440	#160
DOS3	TXT	26984	#159
DOS_ERR	TXT	3456	#134
DOSBUG	DOC	2048	#184
DOSCOLOR	BAS	4864	#110
DOSCOLOR	BAT	896	#110
DOSDATE	ASM	1232	#216
DOSEDIT	COM	1920	#255
DOSEDIT	DOC	3280	#255
DOSFTE	PAS	2944	#135
DOSFUN	INC	2176	#135
DOSFUN	PAS	6400	#135
DOSINTS	TXT	5940	#134
DOSKEY1	DOC	1536	#181
DOSKEYS	BAS	18176	#181
DOSKEYS	DOC	3200	#181
DOSPATH	C	8320	#139
DOSTIME	ASM	1516	#216
DOTS	BAS	1408	#1
DOTS	BAS	6144	#45
DOWDIF	BAT	547	#84
DOWDIF	COM	35968	#84
DOWDIF	DOC	15416	#84
DOWN	BAS	349	#176
DOWTRY	TXT	708	#84
DRAGON	BUG	384	#94
DRAGRACE	BAS	2432	#45
DRAW	ASM	884	#15
DRAW	BAS	10752	#20
DRAW	CMT	2944	#38
DRAW	DOC	17152	#38
DRAW	EXE	640	#15
DRAW2	BAS	13184	#23
DRAWGRAF	BAS	640	#191
DRAWIT	BAS	11294	#84
DRIVE	DTA	128	#101
DRIVER	ASM	14480	#135
DRIVER	BAS	4352	#177
DRIVER	BAS	14963	#91
DRIVER	OBJ	952	#135
DRIVETST	BAS	1617	#79
DROIDS	BAS	6784	#71
DRU	NUD	7040	#154
DS	BAT	26	#144
DS	BAT	26	#185
DSKHND	BAS	1220	#115
DSKLABEL		166	#276
DSKLABEL		171	#277
DSKLABEL		171	#250
DSKPGM2	BAS	2031	#52
DSKTEST	BAS	2742	#172
DSKTEST	DOC	1618	#172
DSKTST	BAS	2586	#79
DSKTYP	ASM	6883	#256
DSKTYP	EXE	1408	#256
DSNAME	P	681	#36
DSS	DOC	46976	#260
DSS	EXE	70528	#260
DSTAT	EXE	1152	#284
DTCOPY	BAT	431	#64
DTCOPY	BAT	431	#64
DTEXFILE	BAS	2560	#182
DTK	DOC	8832	#283
DTK	EXE	56832	#283
DUMP	ASM	9365	#256
DUMP	BAS	2304	#4
DUMP	EXE	1408	#256
DUMPFILE	PAS	1710	#36
DUMPSCRN	BAS	256	#217
DUMPSCRN	DOC	1408	#217
DUMPSCRN	MRG	512	#217
DUOPOLY	BUG	325	#94
DUP	BAT	57	#87
DUPONT	NYS	3968	#40
DVED	COM	44855	#191
DVORAK		815	#46
DVORAK	BAT	14	#46
DVORAK	COM	2235	#46
DVORAK	DOC	4594	#46
DVORAK	KEY	1126	#181
DW1	NL	6144	#158
DW2	NL	7168	#158
DWLEGAL	NL	4096	#158
DWNLOAD	BAS	893	#14
DX	BAT	25	#144
DX	BAT	25	#185
DXSAVE	BAT	34	#144
DXSAVE	BAT	34	#185
DYNA	BUG	512	#94

E

E1	BAS	896	#27
E2	BAS	896	#27
E3	BAS	896	#27
EAMON	ART	896	#296
EAMON	DES	6630	#296
EAMON	EFF	10200	#296
EAMON	MON	768	#296
EAMON	NAM	128	#296
EAMON	ROM	1728	#296
EASEL	ASC	1920	#191
EASEL	BAS	1536	#191
EASYDEMO	BAT	1524	#285
EASYFILE	BAS	1536	#182
EASYGRAF	ASC	2048	#191
EASYGRAF	BAS	1664	#191
EASYMAIL	ASC	2176	#169
EASYMAIL	BAS	1408	#169
EASYRITE	BAS	30592	#66
EASYRITE	BAS	42795	#146
EASYWORD	BAS	4992	#66
EASYWR11	UNP	4480	#184
ECHOARG	AR	769	#132
ECHOARG	EXE	26368	#130
ECHOARG	MAN	556	#130
ED	DOC	4608	#137
ED	DOC	26803	#162
ED	EXE	36992	#162
ED	EXE	44608	#78
ED0	C	384	#137
ED1	CCC	1792	#137
ED10	C	6656	#137
ED11	A	11136	#137
ED2	C	11776	#137
ED3	C	17792	#137

ED4	C	11264	#137
ED5	C	2432	#137
ED6	C	640	#137
ED7	C	2816	#137
ED8	C	4864	#137
ED9	C	2944	#137
EDIPAGE	BAS	1920	#48
EDIT	BAS	7040	#46
EDIT	BAT	76	#20
EDIT	BAT	884	#124
EDIT	BAT	896	#139
EDIT	EXE	31232	#137
EDIT	EXE	38528	#58
EDIT	EXE	44032	#294
EDIT	HLP	5562	#294
EDIT	SET	23	#294
EDIT-MOD	PAS	21192	#172
EDITCHEK	PRG	2364	#295
EDITDOC0	PRN	3296	#294
EDITDOC0	SET	85	#294
EDITDOC0	TXT	2063	#294
EDITDOC1	PRN	6748	#294
EDITDOC1	SET	112	#294
EDITDOC1	TXT	4574	#294
EDITDOC2	PRN	19111	#294
EDITDOC2	SET	116	#294
EDITDOC2	TXT	13008	#294
EDITDOC3	PRN	87266	#294
EDITDOC3	SET	104	#294
EDITDOC3	TXT	43400	#294
EDITDOCA	PRN	20729	#294
EDITDOCA	SET	121	#294
EDITDOCA	TXT	7211	#294
EDITINCO	PRG	3193	#295
EDITNO	BAS	3790	#80
EDITNO	DOC	2111	#80
EDITOR	DOC	11813	#172
EDITOR	PIC	3091	#158
EDITOR	PIC	3200	#157
EDITOR	PIC	3200	#200
EDITOR	TXT	4183	#160
EDITRECD	PRG	5283	#295
EDIX	EXE	67691	#43
EDLIN	BAS	2048	#205
EDT		361	#192
EDT-MAIN	PAS	24882	#172
EDTORIAL	NL	2048	#158
EDTORIAL	NL	2048	#157
EDTORIAL	NL	3072	#156
EDTORIAL	NL	3072	#200
EFS	BAS	20418	#46
EGGS	BAS	384	#100
EGGS	DOC	590	#100
EGGS	PIC	16512	#12
EIGHT	DAT	4480	#76
EIGHTCRV	BAS	17536	#261
EIGHTCRV	SDA	100	#261
EIGHTCRV	TXT	2533	#261
EIGHTCRV	XXX	149	#261
EIO	WKS	3840	#304
EJLUTIL	DOC	7040	#140
EJLUTIL	LBR	5504	#140
ELECTRIC	BAS	6656	#47
ELEPH	DAT	8960	#15
ELEPH	EXE	18048	#15
ELEPHANT	BAS	3584	#15
ELINE	C	1764	#216
ELIZA	BAS	6656	#4
ELIZA	BAS	10752	#72
ELLEN	NUD	10240	#154
EMBEDDED	BAS	1024	#49
EMC80	BBS	13184	#103
EMPHASOF	COM	19	#186
EMPHASON	COM	19	#186
EMPTY		1	#26
ENCRYPT	DOC	7040	#129
ENCRYPT	EXE	24576	#129
END	PRN	245	#257
ENGINE	BAS	128	#53
ENGLISH	C	3181	#259
ENGLISH	OBJ	2619	#259
ENTAB	C	2816	#111
ENTAB	EXE	9344	#111
ENTAB	EXE	15872	#162
ENTEP	BAS	3072	#44
ENTEP	BAS	3072	#154
ENTER	BAT	128	#26
ENTER	PRG	1920	#126
ENTERTAN	COM	28813	#279
ENTRTAN1	MUS	6070	#279
ENTRTAN2	MUS	6070	#279
ENTRTAN3	MUS	6070	#279
ENTRTAN4	MUS	6070	#279
ENVIRON	DOC	2560	#138
EPBENCHI	BAS	718	#299
EPIMRG	BAS	3456	#88
EPISETUP	BAK	128	#88
EPISETUP	DAT	128	#88
EPISTAT	BAS	11264	#88
EPLQ1500	PRT	581	#78
EPSONCHR	ASM	30848	#186
EPSONCHR	DOC	1024	#186
EPSONCHR	EXE	3072	#186
EPSONSET	BAS	4736	#66
EPSONUTL	BAS	2304	#61
EQ	EXE	22272	#249
EQNSOLVE	BAS	3584	#37
EQUAL	DCL	65	#132
EQUAL	OBJ	442	#132
EQUAT1	BAS	337	#292
EQUAT2	BAS	337	#292
EQUAT3	BAS	337	#292
EQUAT4	BAS	329	#292
EQUATOR	TXT	21760	#249
EQUIP102	COM	1792	#196
EQUIP102	DOC	7808	#196
ER	EXE	74624	#146
ERR	C	256	#163
ERR	C	1708	#147
ERR	OBJ	1153	#147
ERRATA		2843	#124
ERROR	DCL	49	#132
ERROR	OBJ	496	#132
ERRS	C	256	#163
ESC	DCL	73	#132
ESC	OBJ	499	#132
ESCKEY	BAS	1792	#66
ESCREEN	C	1767	#216
ESCT	C	512	#163
ESKOD	NYS	3968	#40
ESP	DOC	9198	#173
ESP	EXE	29824	#173
ESSXFADE	BAS	1152	#15
ET4	BAS	16761	#80
ET4	EXE	37248	#80
EUCHRE	BAS	22784	#229
EUCHRE	DOC	3645	#229
EUCHRE	INS	4794	#229
EUCHRE	SRC	36352	#229
EVRONWRD	BAS	3328	#24
EW	KEY	245	#59
EW	KEY	245	#170
EXAMPLE		640	#88
EXAMPLE		768	#199
EXAMPLE	ASM	640	#10
EXAMPLE	MSS	1664	#231
EXDIR	BAT	111	#82
EXECSOL	NL	4096	#200
EXELOAD	EXE	1676	#43
EXIO	ASM	8003	#202
EXIT	PCS	256	#19
EXMEM	ASM	7054	#202
EXMEM	H	338	#202
EXNOTES	FNT	1024	#127
EXPAND	ASM	721	#223
EXPAND	BAS	640	#256
EXPAND	DOC	321	#223
EXPAND	DOC	1632	#256
EXPAND	OBJ	89	#223
EXPENSRP	WKS	5248	#302
EXPERT	BAS	29184	#268
EXPERT	EXE	72960	#268
EXPLIST	DOC	34176	#7
EXPLIST	EXE	48000	#7
EXPLISTR	EXE	19584	#7
EXPMAIL	EXE	34176	#7
EXPNDTAB	ASM	3986	#158
EXPOPT		128	#7
EXTCODES	REM	1546	#82
EXTEND86	BLK	30720	#263
EXTRA		6784	#215
EXTRACT	BAS	4864	#233
EYE	TXT	2919	#211
EZFDOCM	BAS	7296	#182

EZGDOCM	BAS	10496	#191
EZSIG3	HLP	17664	#187

F

F1040	VC	19968	#85
F104064K	VC	16384	#85
F1040A	VC	5504	#85
F1040B	VC	4864	#85
F1040D	VC	25856	#85
F1040DOC	VC	20736	#85
F1040INS	VC	8832	#85
F1040SIM	VC	256	#85
F4684		4914	#291
F83	COM	26368	#263
F83-FIXS	TXT	5120	#263
FACT	LSP	128	#148
FACTOR	BAS	896	#206
FACTS		4096	#146
FAMILY	BAS	21621	#90
FAMILYDA	Y	4864	#15
FASTPRT	COM	366	#59
FASTPRT	DOC	5834	#59
FC	DOC	73600	#170
FC	EXE	111360	#170
FC	HLP	1280	#170
FCBCRT	BAS	1794	#80
FCBEXM	BAS	2341	#80
FCBREAD	BSV	292	#80
FCMAGIC	ASM	4992	#204
FCMAGIC	OBJ	366	#204
FCOPY	DCL	52	#132
FCOPY	EXE	26820	#204
FCOPY	LNK	128	#204
FCOPY	OBJ	418	#132
FCOPY	OBJ	4963	#204
FCOPY	PAS	7552	#204
FCST	BAR	384	#14
FE	DOC	159974	#288
FE	EXE	79488	#287
FEDTAX	VC	12032	#14
FEDTAX83	WKS	37888	#109
FEDTAX83	WKS	38400	#207
FENCE	BAS	4352	#12
FENCE	BAS	4352	#17
FEST0	MUS	355	#279
FEST1	MUS	380	#279
FEST2	MUS	420	#279
FEST3	MUS	410	#279
FESTBURG	COM	16195	#279
FF	BAT	20	#48
FF	DOC	290	#48
FF	TXT	2	#48
FFILE		1536	#268
FFILE		3328	#215
FFILE	BAS	2290	#277
FFILE	EXE	22016	#277
FFILE	EXE	22784	#250
FFILE	LIB	3456	#277
FFILE	LIB	4096	#250
FFILEBIG	BAS	2133	#277
FFILEBIG	EXE	21760	#277
FFILEBIG	LIB	3200	#277
FFILEMEN	DAT	722	#277
FFIND	C	2098	#283
FFIND	DOC	826	#283
FFIND	EXE	7680	#283
FFS	WKS	11008	#304
FIFTEEN	BAS	4352	#72
FILE	COM	10097	#235
FILE	PAS	19239	#223
FILECATA	LOG	207	#231
FILECMD	BAS	7726	#84
FILECMD2	BAS	8482	#84
FILECOPY	BAS	8064	#204
FILEDATE	BAS	2944	#66
FILEDUMP	COM	1408	#109
FILEDUMP	COM	1408	#273
FILEFILE	BAS	768	#182
FILEIO	C	235	#50
FILELIST		1515	#82
FILELIST	BAS	3712	#205
FILELIST	TXT	1024	#295
FILEMAN	COM	937	#78
FILEMAN	COM	11776	#261
FILEMENU	BAS	1536	#182
FILEMOD	ASC	8633	#52
FILEOUT	BAS	5632	#204
FILEREFS	EXE	18944	#231
FILES	DOC	3072	#112
FILES	LST	692	#113
FILES	TXT	975	#274
FILES	TXT	1291	#273
FILESEC		1	#212
FILESORT	BAS	5248	#53
FILETRAN	BAS	3968	#88
FILING	NL	4096	#200
FILKQQ	INC	5376	#135
FILP	C	768	#163
FILPS	C	512	#163
FILTER	BAS	1280	#38
FILTER	BAS	1430	#52
FILTER	DOC	528	#38
FILUQQ	INC	1536	#135
FINAL	BAS	4608	#23
FINANCE	BAS	17920	#107
FINANCE	BAS	17920	#171
FINANCE	BAS	22016	#25
FINANCE	BAS	22016	#14
FINANCE	DOC	20394	#227
FINANCE	EXE	42880	#249
FINANCE	EXE	77312	#227
FINANCE1	BAS	6400	#25
FINANCE4	DOC	56419	#164
FINANCE4	EXE	92800	#164
FIND	COM	896	#9
FIND	EXE	31488	#57
FIND	PAT	1024	#134
FINDBILL	PRG	5248	#102
FINDFILE	ASM	13951	#82
FINDFILE	BAT	125	#250
FINDFILE	BAT	1120	#277
FINDFILE	COM	209	#82
FINDP	AR	2055	#132
FINDP	EXE	30976	#130
FINDP	MAN	1822	#130
FINISH	BAS	6144	#15
FINISH	BAS	16512	#49
FINISHTX	BAS	24064	#49
FINPAK	BAS	16565	#47
FIREFIRE	BAS	3072	#228
FISHERS	BAS	1792	#88
FITT84	DOC	48384	#290
FITT84	WKS	89344	#290
FIVE	DAT	4352	#76
FIX-2A-1	DOC	2304	#212
FIX-2A-1	MRG	3200	#212
FIX-TEST	BAS	3968	#190
FIXDEL	EXE	9728	#52
FIXFILES	BAS	2176	#152
FIXFILES	BAS	2176	#212
FIXIT	BAS	896	#52
FIXTEXT	BAS	4608	#111
FIXUSERS	BAS	4352	#212
FIXWS	COM	1536	#201
FIXWS	DOC	1536	#201
FK	COM	2432	#28
FK	DOC	8806	#28
FK203	ASM	6177	#33
FK203	EXE	1152	#33
FKREST	ASM	4100	#80
FKREST	COM	327	#80
FKSET	ASM	7155	#80
FKSET	COM	693	#80
FLA-CENT		193	#219
FLA-INC		193	#219
FLA-POP		193	#219
FLAG	BAS	384	#27
FLAPAN		2929	#219
FLASH		115	#150
FLASHCRD		896	#93
FLASHCRD	BAS	11008	#93
FLASHCRD	LST	128	#93
FLASHDAN	BAS	1636	#208
FLCHART	WKS	8192	#140
FLCHART	WKS	8192	#302
FLIER		4864	#189
FLIGHT	NEW	1967	#80
FLIGTSF	NYS	3840	#40
FLIP	MEM	256	#27
FLIPD	MEM	128	#27
FLIPPER	BAS	6016	#93
FLITEPLN	2-2	35165	#261

FLITEPLN	DOC	3967	#261
FLOWER	BAS	672	#292
FLOWERS	PIC	16512	#12
FLTSIM	UNP	1024	#184
FLUSH	BAT	128	#36
FLUSH	DCL	44	#132
FLUSH	OBJ	796	#132
FLY	BAS	4608	#203
FLYBY	BAS	2688	#15
FM	CNF	128	#151
FM	DEF	6528	#151
FM	DOC	55680	#151
FM	EXE	105311	#151
FMT	AR	36267	#132
FMT	EXE	44160	#130
FMT	FNT	1020	#130
FMT	MAN	6448	#130
FMUTIL	EXE	30719	#151
FOILS	BAS	3584	#27
FONH	PIC	896	#158
FONH	PIC	896	#200
FONS	PIC	2680	#158
FONS	PIC	2688	#157
FONS	PIC	2688	#200
FOOTBAL	BAS	7424	#174
FOOTBALL	BAS	6400	#45
FOOTBALL	BAS	9472	#174
FOR_NEXT	WKS	2560	#301
FORECAST	APL	12672	#108
FOREPSON	PRT	754	#78
FORM	BAS	13824	#214
FORM	EXE	53504	#268
FORM2106		6775	#291
FORM2119		5738	#291
FORM2441		6817	#291
FORM3468		13053	#291
FORM3903		4025	#291
FORM4797		6990	#291
FORM4835		6202	#291
FORM5695		8208	#291
FORMAT	BAT	3712	#139
FORMAT	EXE	33024	#58
FORMAT	VOL	609	#256
FORMDISP	BAS	896	#46
FORMGEN	BAS	12160	#201
FORMGEN	TXT	2432	#201
FORMLIST		128	#215
FORMLIST		128	#268
FORT1	TXT	6687	#159
FORT1	TXT	7980	#160
FORTH	BAS	4096	#48
FORTH	BAT	38	#161
FORTH	MSG	282	#161
FORTH	OBJ	26368	#161
FORTH1	TXT	15235	#160
FORTH2	TXT	16422	#160
FORTH3	TXT	3366	#160
FORTRAN	NL	4096	#157
FORTRANS	BAS	2816	#88
FORTUNE	EXE	31616	#293
FORWARD	BAS	512	#105
FOS	BAS	24576	#107
FOS-DESC		7684	#107
FOS2	BAS	17792	#107
FOUR	DAT	4608	#76
FOUR	EXE	24704	#51
FPLOT	BAS	7231	#114
FPLOT	DOC	1406	#114
FPR	C	5577	#84
FPRINT	DOC	571	#236
FPRINT	EXE	52096	#236
FPRINT	HLP	2790	#236
FPRINT	TRY	2646	#236
FRAME	C	2363	#216
FRANK	BAS	6144	#18
FRED	DOC	10490	#83
FRED	EXE	37504	#83
FRED	SUM	1152	#83
FREDDIE	EXE	15488	#83
FREE	ASM	6325	#256
FREE	COM	1024	#140
FREE	COM	1034	#256
FREE	DOC	1595	#256
FREE	DOC	25694	#115
FREE1	BIN	8264	#6
FREE1	DOC	4951	#6
FREE1	EXE	2944	#6
FREE3	COM	1536	#6
FREE3	DOC	2896	#6
FREE4	COM	6024	#52
FREE4	DOC	2892	#52
FREE5	COM	1792	#52
FREE5	DOC	3033	#52
FREECOPY	ASM	92160	#226
FREECOPY	COM	5172	#226
FREECOPY	DOC	28544	#226
FREECOPY	LST	192998	#226
FREECOPY	MAP	190	#226
FREECOPY	REF	30321	#226
FREEWILL	ASC	79032	#193
FREEWILL	DOC	1176	#193
FRM001	DAT	202	#190
FROG	EXE	37632	#174
FROMTO	TXT	5376	#305
FSKEL	BAT	2048	#139
FT-ETC	EXE	26112	#240
FT-ETC	PCS	128	#240
FT-ETC	TXT	39328	#240
FT-ETC-C	EXE	47488	#240
FT-ETC-M	EXE	43264	#240
FT-ETC-R	EXE	27520	#240
FTMAC	WRK	1664	#305
FUGUES	COM	15856	#279
FUL001	DAT	449	#190
FULLEDIT	BAS	10880	#46
FULLSCRN	BAS	7269	#190
FULLSCRN	BSC	15467	#190
FULLSCRN	BSN	983	#190
FUNC1	BAS	1152	#67
FUNC2	BAS	1024	#67
FUNCTION	DOC	1323	#248
FUNCTION	PAS	3442	#248
FUNKY	ASM	6370	#82
FUNKY	COM	261	#82
FUNNELS	DOC	14713	#229
FUNNELS	EXE	59904	#229
FUNNELS	INV	2432	#229
FUPGRADE	NL	2048	#157
FUTRDATE	BAS	3584	#51
FUTRDATE	DOC	3571	#51
FUTURE	BAS	896	#29

G

G1	BAS	768	#27
G2	BAS	768	#27
G3	BAS	768	#27
G4	BAS	768	#27
G5	BAS	768	#27
GALAXY	BAS	512	#45
GALAXY2	BAS	1664	#45
GALLERY	BAS	2944	#37
GAMES	TXT	4125	#274
GANNETT	NYS	3712	#40
GASFORM	BAS	2944	#66
GASTON	NL	5120	#200
GC	EXE	38272	#87
GC	EXE	38272	#161
GCC	WKS	5888	#304
GCOPY	DOC	1024	#204
GCOPY	DOC	1024	#273
GCOPY	DOC	1024	#140
GCOPY	EXE	14336	#204
GCOPY	EXE	14336	#273
GCOPY	EXE	14336	#140
GDATE	DCL	47	#132
GDATE	OBJ	438	#132
GDEL	DOC	1024	#140
GDEL	DOC	1024	#204
GDEL	DOC	1024	#273
GDEL	EXE	13312	#140
GDEL	EXE	13312	#204
GDEL	EXE	13312	#273
GDUMP	BAS	3200	#6
GDUMP	EXE	23040	#6
GDUMP1	BAS	640	#47
GDUMP2	BAS	640	#47
GEMAR70	OPT	3185	#40
GEMINI	ABS	1152	#128
GEMINI	DBF	1536	#295
GENEL	NYS	3927	#40
GENERAL	BAS	18874	#90
GENLEDGR	WKS	40576	#165
GENLJRNL	WKS	38528	#165

GERTRUD	NL	2048	#156
GERTRUDE	NL	2048	#158
GETARG	DCL	89	#132
GETARG	OBJ	682	#132
GETBILLS	DBF	0	#102
GETC	DCL	59	#132
GETC	OBJ	672	#132
GETCF	DCL	74	#132
GETCF	OBJ	710	#132
GETDATE	C	1514	#216
GETDATE	PRG	2048	#102
GETDIR	EXE	28928	#36
GETDIR	OBJ	2337	#36
GETDIR	PAS	2304	#36
GETFCB	ASM	1533	#132
GETFCB	OBJ	117	#132
GETINSER	DBF	1024	#102
GETLINE	C	1384	#216
GETLINE	DCL	95	#132
GETLINE	OBJ	525	#132
GETMEM	ASM	3072	#111
GETMEM	COM	384	#111
GETSEC	ASM	2560	#36
GETSEC	OBJ	111	#36
GETTIME	C	1539	#216
GIRL	NUD	17920	#154
GLASSTTY	PAS	2079	#202
GLCHART	EXE	21760	#237
GLCHECKS	EXE	6400	#237
GLCTRL	FIL	512	#237
GLENTRY	EXE	23040	#237
GLIB	INC	919	#74
GLMENU	EXE	24832	#237
GLOBCONS	INC	1999	#132
GLOBE	BAS	3147	#91
GLOBE	DAT	13691	#91
GLOBE	REF	0	#92
GLOBTYPS	INC	734	#132
GLOBVARS	INC	120	#132
GLSTATE	EXE	12160	#237
GLTRIAL	EXE	17024	#237
GMOT	NYS	4119	#40
GMUS64	EXE	28160	#127
GNV		3304	#219
GNV-65		205	#219
GNV-POP		101	#219
GO	BAT	14	#78
GOBBLE	BAS	2944	#24
GODFATHR	BAS	768	#168
GOLF	BAS	6197	#35
GOLF	WKS	2816	#302
GOLF2	BAS	7296	#91
GOMOKU	DOC	1979	#51
GOMOKU	EXE	32128	#51
GOMOKU	PAS	10731	#51
GOURMET	DBF	90880	#117
GOURMET	HI	40448	#116
GOURMET	LOW	32512	#116
GPRINT	BAS	4864	#46
GRABBAG	ASM	21189	#159
GRABBAG	C	10321	#160
GRABBAG	EXE	1664	#159
GRABBAG	EXE	16162	#161
GRADE-1	LST	2163	#241
GRADE-2	LST	3150	#241
GRADE-3	LST	5149	#241
GRADE-4	LST	6348	#241
GRADE-5	LST	8000	#241
GRADUATE	BAT	287	#43
GRAF	BAS	4483	#265
GRAF2	COM	1280	#2
GRAFGE	BAS	8335	#28
GRAFGE	DOC	1920	#28
GRAFHAT	BAS	1408	#6
GRAFHAT	EXE	22272	#6
GRAFTRAX	ASM	32465	#33
GRAFTRAX	BAS	2180	#33
GRAFTRAX	COM	1120	#33
GRAFTRAX	DOC	1903	#33
GRAPH	BAS	5632	#191
GRAPH1	BAS	12160	#11
GRAPH2	BAS	6144	#191
GRAPH2	BAS	24581	#195
GRAPH2	DOC	13440	#195
GRAPHICS	BAS	179	#292
GRAPHICS	BAS	12928	#12
GRAPHICS	COM	789	#27
GRAPHII	BAS	2432	#191
GRAPHING	NL	4096	#200
GRAPHIT	BAS	2432	#191
GRAPHS	VC	15360	#14
GRD1		256	#95
GRD2		256	#95
GRD3		256	#95
GRD4		256	#95
GRD5		256	#95
GRD6		256	#95
GRDRAW	LF	4864	#142
GREATCIR	BAS	2304	#49
GREATRHM	BAS	4608	#49
GREEKRTS	BAS	1536	#45
GREP	C	16726	#149
GREP	DOC	3467	#149
GREP	EXE	18432	#149
GRINCH	BAS	8320	#174
GROUP1	DAT	128	#164
GROUP2	DAT	128	#164
GROUP3	DAT	128	#164
GROUP4	DAT	128	#164
GROUP5	DAT	128	#164
GROWTH	BAS	1792	#25
GROWTH	BAS	4352	#73
GROWTH	BAS	5376	#67
GROWTH1	BAS	1536	#25
GROWTH2	BAS	5376	#48
GRPH64K	BAS	853	#83
GRPH64K	DOC	4180	#83
GSDUMP	BAS	512	#28
GTEST	BAS	512	#11
GTIME	DCL	47	#132
GTIME	OBJ	438	#132
GTOJ	C	2037	#216
GUESS_1	BAS	640	#105
GUESS_2	BAS	1024	#105
GUESSNUM	BAS	387	#292
GUIDE	BAT	91	#59
GUIDE	PRG	2560	#126
GUIDE1	REF	1779	#6
GUIDE2	REF	4175	#6
GUMUP1	DOC	6089	#28
GUNIT	INC	897	#74
GYNN	NL	6144	#156

H

H1	BAS	768	#27
H2	BAS	768	#27
HAL-PC	TXT	15616	#107
HALS	DOC	1320	#28
HAM1084	LQR	59308	#280
HAMBIBL	LQR	8462	#280
HAMDOC	PRN	7680	#280
HAMMER	WRK	6144	#305
HAMMOND	NL	3072	#156
HAMURABI	BAS	3328	#128
HAMURABI	BAS	4736	#178
HANG	COM	384	#33
HANGADV1	WRD	19456	#153
HANGBAS1	WRD	12544	#153
HANGCMT	REF	222	#153
HANGED1	WRD	28928	#153
HANGMAN	BAS	3840	#20
HANGMAN	BAS	3968	#4
HANGMAN	EXE	43052	#153
HANGMAN	REF	40	#153
HANGMUSE	MSC	4864	#153
HANGROBO	WKS	16384	#302
HANOI	BAS	4862	#83
HANOI	BAS	4864	#44
HANOI	DOC	145	#44
HAPPYB	BAS	256	#11
HARDBO	DOC	3819	#238
HARDCASH	BAS	5914	#261
HARDWARE		59	#150
HARMNIZR	COM	17083	#279
HARRINGT	NL	2048	#158
HARRIS	NL	2048	#156
HAT	BAS	588	#195
HAT	DMP	16392	#195
HATDANCE	BAS	1664	#1
HAYSMODM	BAS	2944	#187
HC	ASM	42645	#258
HC	COM	3456	#110
HC	COM	3693	#258

HC	DOC	2768	#258
HC	DOC	3200	#110
HCONFIG	EXE	4724	#254
HDATA		256	#192
HDATA	BAK	256	#192
HDD512	EXE	1152	#51
HDRAW	BAS	7168	#38
HDS320	EXE	1152	#51
HEADCLN	BAS	2432	#66
HEAPSORT	BAS	1536	#11
HEARING	BAS	1280	#49
HEBREW	ASM	5632	#62
HEBREW	COM	1045	#62
HELP	BAT	128	#283
HELP	BAT	896	#282
HELP	BBS	1095	#150
HELP	BUG	643	#94
HELP	DOC	9660	#254
HELP	EDX	14848	#43
HELP	EXE	4772	#254
HELP	TXT	1180	#68
HELP01		1024	#212
HELP01		1125	#152
HELP02		844	#152
HELP02		896	#212
HELP03		528	#152
HELP03		640	#212
HELP04		476	#152
HELP04		512	#212
HELP05		381	#152
HELP05		512	#212
HELP06		8832	#212
HELP06		8832	#152
HELP07		1880	#152
HELP07		1920	#212
HELP08		512	#212
HELP1	BUG	690	#94
HELP1	PIC	16512	#38
HELP1	PIC	16512	#13
HELP1	PIK	16512	#38
HELP2	BUG	605	#94
HELP2	PIC	16512	#13
HELP2	PIC	16512	#38
HELP2	PIK	16512	#38
HELP3	BUG	307	#94
HELP4	BUG	666	#94
HELP5	BUG	540	#94
HELP6	BUG	399	#94
HELP7	BUG	1003	#94
HELP8	BUG	571	#94
HELPCOM	BAS	15744	#46
HELPE	DEF	12084	#78
HELPME	BAT	1536	#86
HELPREG	DOC	2494	#254
HERMREAD	ME	7121	#255
HERZFELD	NL	4096	#157
HEX	BAS	9344	#52
HEXCONV	BAS	7680	#2

HEXPRINT	BAS	4096	#66
HEXSAY	BAS	2304	#66
HGRI	EXE	2048	#2
HIDEFILE	BAS	10240	#52
HIDEFILE	BAS	11288	#46
HIDESEEK	BAS	1920	#45
HILBERT	BUG	384	#94
HINT1	DOC	384	#203
HINT2	DOC	384	#203
HINT3	DOC	512	#203
HINTSTUT	WKS	10880	#257
HIQUE	BAS	5258	#80
HIQUE2	BAS	5504	#91
HISCORE	PC	384	#17
HISTGRAM	BAS	1024	#191
HISTOGRM	BAS	4480	#88
HISTORY	BAS	19712	#76
HISTORY	COM	9115	#235
HO	NL	3072	#200
HOBBIT	BAS	12032	#44
HOLD81	DBF	1024	#102
HOLDLIST	DTA	472	#101
HOME	CRT	2816	#151
HOME	NAM	128	#151
HOME	TRN	5888	#151
HOMEBDGT	VC	4736	#14
HOMESOL	NL	4096	#200
HONEY	NUD	6528	#154
HORSE	BAS	4352	#44
HOSKINS	NL	9216	#156
HOST	BAS	12160	#33
HOST	DOC	379	#33
HOST-III	DOC	32503	#125
HOST-III	EXE	51840	#125
HOST2	BAS	12544	#81
HOST2	DOC	848	#81
HOSTCALL	BAT	11	#125
HOSTCALL	DOC	78631	#125
HOSTCALX	EXE	44032	#125
HOSTCL2X	EXE	63104	#125
HOTCROSS	BAS	87	#292
HP	C	1536	#142
HPLASERJ	PRT	888	#78
HPTHINKJ	PRT	477	#78
HRA1	EXE	63744	#192
HRADATA		12160	#192
HRADOC	TXT	11070	#192
HRAINP1	EXE	52992	#192
HRAPRINT	EXE	25088	#192
HRSERACE	BAS	4608	#55
HS	DAT	128	#177
HS	DAT	128	#209
HUFFMAN	BLK	49152	#263
HUSTLE	BAS	7168	#175
HUSTLE	DAT	82	#175
HUSTLE	DOC	1728	#175
HYPERDRV	DOC	12032	#51

I

I-8087	DOC	640	#112
I_WILL	SNG	604	#127
IBBS	BAS	44628	#150
IBBS	DOC	11813	#150
IBBS	EXE	81408	#150
IBM		38	#68
IBM	CNF	128	#151
IBMCMPCT	PRO	496	#158
IBMCOLOR	PRO	563	#158
IBMCOLOR	PRT	887	#78
IBMCS	BAS	13184	#11
IBMDIY	BAS	20992	#11
IBMEPSON	PRT	952	#78
IBMGRAPH	PRO	570	#158
IBMLABEL	BAS	7424	#66
IBMMATRX	PRO	519	#158
IBMMC	BAS	21760	#11
IBMMINI	EXE	30208	#188
IBMMINI	EXE	30336	#197
IBMPC	1XX	15744	#269
IBMPC	2XX	15744	#269
IBMPC	300	15744	#269
IBMPCTIP	DOC	4736	#135
IBMSONG	BAS	5120	#13
IBMTTY	C	16064	#216
IBMW5216	PRT	579	#78
ICICLE	BAS	384	#35
ICR_CALC	WKS	9472	#302
IDEX		384	#215
IDEX		384	#268
IDSPR132	PRT	948	#78
IDSPR460	PRT	456	#78
IEX	C	7006	#147
IEX	OBJ	2721	#147
IFTHEN	BAS	2048	#105
IIB	WKS	11264	#304
IMAX	DCL	54	#132
IMAX	OBJ	378	#132
IMIN	DCL	54	#132
IMIN	OBJ	378	#132
IMPORT	EXE	27904	#288
IN12	FMT	384	#236
IN12HS	FMT	384	#236
IN12INDT	FMT	384	#236
IN12TITL	FMT	384	#236
INCOFILE	MEM	512	#295
INCOME	BAS	8832	#29
INCOME	DBF	1536	#295
INCOME	FRM	512	#295
INCOND	FMT	384	#236
IND	NDX	25088	#300
INDE	C	640	#163
INDEX	BAK	116	#300
INDEX	BAS	1664	#105
INDEX	BAT	128	#26

INDEX	C	384	#163
INDEX	DCL	71	#132
INDEX	DOC	6144	#9
INDEX	OBJ	440	#132
INDEX	P	279	#36
INDEX	PRG	138	#300
INDEX	TXT	4917	#105
INDEXFIL	SMX	7168	#246
INDEXMAR	BAS	4923	#90
INDEXPC	BAS	5059	#90
INDUST	DJA	4992	#40
INDUST	WKS	21504	#302
INFO	BAT	434	#223
INFO	BAT	5760	#26
INFO	BIN	16512	#191
INFO	DOC	703	#284
INFO	DOC	3747	#190
INFO1	BAT	1408	#183
INIT	LSP	2048	#148
INITIO	DCL	61	#132
INITIO	OBJ	5142	#132
INPORT	ASM	936	#172
INPORT	DOC	606	#172
INPUT	APP	5120	#306
INPUT	EXE	29696	#26
INPUT	INC	2229	#162
INPUT	PAS	6912	#26
INSERT	BAS	8448	#4
INSERTS	DBF	1024	#102
INSERTS	NDX	1024	#102
INSPI	BUG	218	#94
INSTALL	BAT	128	#151
INSTALL	BAT	146	#59
INSTALL	BAT	384	#86
INSTALL	BAT	896	#242
INSTALL	ED	0	#276
INSTALL	EXE	31744	#68
INSTALL	TXT	6765	#68
INSTR	BAS	7680	#95
INSTRUCT	ION	752	#244
INSTRUCT	WKS	116480	#65
INSTVXPT	RCE	18560	#236
INT	A	3080	#283
INT	C	4612	#147
INT	COM	512	#283
INT	DOC	1561	#283
INT	OBJ	2361	#147
INT_PKG	ASM	12893	#202
INT_PORT	DOC	1854	#283
INTEGRAL	DCL	235	#194
INTEGRAL	PAS	3364	#194
INTEREST	BAS	3200	#171
INTEREST	DBF	1024	#295
INTEREST	PRG	1333	#295
INTERUPT	MAC	3865	#51
INTLCVID	BAS	296	#299
INTOOLS	PAS	3968	#140
INTRCOST	FRM	244	#295
INTRCOST	PRG	661	#295
INTRLIST	FRM	512	#295
INTRLIST	PRG	1351	#295
INTRO	BAS	3072	#105
INTRO	DOC	6194	#289
INTRO	TXT	11118	#159
INTRODUC	BAS	12896	#90
INTROTUT	WKS	41472	#257
INTRPAID	FRM	512	#295
INTRPAID	PRG	1333	#295
INTRPT	ASM	1685	#30
INTRPT	OBJ	234	#30
INV	BAK	1152	#300
INV	DBF	512	#300
INV	NDX	1536	#300
INV	PRG	1152	#300
INV	TXT	16650	#300
INVCAT	DAT	128	#164
INVEN	BAS	11008	#37
INVENPRC	BAS	12032	#171
INVENRPT	BAS	7070	#171
INVENT	COM	3225	#235
INVENT	DOC	161664	#235
INVENTN4	COM	3955	#279
INVENTN4	MUS	3310	#279
INVENTRY	BAS	10112	#62
INVENTRY	DAT	505	#62
INVENTRY	DOC	301	#62
INVENTRY	DOC	13568	#171
INVEST	DAT	128	#164
INVMENU	PRG	3328	#102
INVOICE		1302	#113
INVOICE		1504	#215
INVOICE	DC4	1976	#106
INVOICES	DBF	1536	#102
INVOICES	NDX	1024	#102
INVOICES	PRG	4992	#102
INVPRINT	BAK	1251	#300
INVPRINT	PRG	1243	#300
IO	C	10853	#147
IO	OBJ	2906	#147
IOMENU	PRG	2560	#102
IOPOST	PRG	4096	#102
IOREVIEW	PRG	2048	#102
IOS1_20	ASM	7680	#138
IOSTUFF	DOC	5203	#30
IOSTUFF	INC	5142	#30
IOSTUFF	OBJ	7105	#30
IOSTUFF	PAS	7340	#30
IPCOGOLF	BAS	7808	#55
IPPOKER	BAS	33792	#55
IPPOKER	DOC	5804	#55
IPUTD		128	#215
IPUTD1		256	#268
IPUTD1		512	#215
IPUTD10		128	#268
IPUTD10		256	#215
IPUTD11		128	#268
IPUTD11		640	#215
IPUTD12		128	#268
IPUTD12		384	#215
IPUTD13		128	#268
IPUTD13		256	#215
IPUTD14		128	#268
IPUTD14		512	#215
IPUTD15		128	#215
IPUTD2		384	#215
IPUTD2		1152	#268
IPUTD3		384	#215
IPUTD3		512	#268
IPUTD4		128	#268
IPUTD4		896	#215
IPUTD5		128	#268
IPUTD5		384	#215
IPUTD6		128	#268
IPUTD6		384	#215
IPUTD7		128	#268
IPUTD7		384	#215
IPUTD8		128	#268
IPUTD8		256	#215
IPUTD9		128	#268
IPUTD9		384	#215
IQBUILD	BAS	4608	#18
IQUEEN	BAS	4224	#45
IR83PCF	DOC	55936	#281
IRECIP83	DTA	248704	#281
IRECIP83	HDR	256	#281
IRECIP83	INX	43264	#281
IRR	WKS	6656	#304
IRR	WKS	7552	#302
ISALPHAN	DCL	59	#132
ISALPHAN	OBJ	453	#132
ISDIGIT	DCL	56	#132
ISDIGIT	OBJ	423	#132
ISLETTER	DCL	57	#132
ISLETTER	OBJ	486	#132
ISLOWER	DCL	46	#132
ISLOWER	OBJ	431	#132
ISUPPER	DCL	56	#132
ISUPPER	OBJ	427	#132
ITALICOF	COM	19	#186
ITALICON	COM	19	#186
ITALICS	BAS	6528	#61
ITEM	DBF	6656	#116
ITEM	NDX	10240	#116
ITOC	DCL	84	#132
ITOC	OBJ	519	#132
ITOP	LSP	3740	#160
ITVERB	C	4219	#259
ITVERB	OBJ	3727	#259

J

JACK		896	#268
JAIME	BAS	299	#176
JAMMER	BAS	7808	#24

JANE	NUD	8448	#154
JBREAK	BAS	2176	#17
JESUSLOV	BAS	640	#168
JET		512	#73
JETPILOT	BAS	14080	#55
JETPILOT	DOC	3456	#55
JETSET	BAS	25856	#260
JETSET	BAS	25984	#39
JETSET	DOC	1452	#39
JETSET	DOC	46080	#260
JETSET	EXE	36736	#39
JEWELL	NL	3072	#157
JHBAND	MUS	6767	#175
JHORCH	MUS	2144	#175
JINGLEBE	BAS	173	#292
JINT	BIN	4832	#266
JNGLEBLS	SNG	420	#127
JOBCOSTS		168	#215
JOBCOSTS	FRM	512	#102
JOBCOSTS	PRG	6016	#102
JOBINDX	PRG	1152	#102
JOBSINDX	PRG	1024	#102
JOGLOG	WKS	100992	#207
JORDAN	NL	8192	#157
JOURNAL		924	#215
JOYSTEST	BAS	1536	#49
JOYSTICK	BAS	640	#49
JOYSTICK	DOC	165	#21
JOYSTICK	EXE	23424	#21
JR-DIAL	COM	41590	#129
JSB	BAS	6144	#208
JSUM	BIN	84	#266
JTOG	C	2603	#216
JTOJ	C	1813	#216
JUKEBOX	BAS	2944	#100
JUKECARA	MUS	896	#100
JUKEDOWN	MUS	896	#100
JUKEGARO	MUS	1024	#100
JUKEIMPO	MUS	896	#100
JUKESATI	MUS	1024	#100
JUKESECO	MUS	1280	#100
JUKESOUN	MUS	768	#100
JUKESUNR	MUS	640	#100
JUKETAKE	MUS	1152	#100
JUKETHIR	MUS	10880	#100
JUKI	CNF	128	#151
JUMBLE	BAS	768	#28
JUMPJOE	EXE	61696	#177
JUMPJOE	SOL	14464	#177
JUMPJOE2	DOC	14427	#209
JUMPJOE2	EXE	62720	#209
JUNK	OBJ	503	#147
JUSTIFY	ASM	72229	#211
JUSTIFY	EXE	17792	#211

K

K0	BAS	11136	#105
K1	BAS	768	#27
K1	BAS	7808	#105
K2	BAS	768	#27
K2	BAS	2816	#105
K3	BAS	768	#27
K4	BAS	768	#27
K5	BAS	768	#27
KALCOL	BAS	896	#25
KALEID	BAS	2560	#1
KB_FLAG	BAS	3200	#6
KBBUFF	BAS	3072	#181
KBBUFF	DOC	1024	#181
KBD_FIX	ASM	12594	#255
KBD_FIX	BAS	2432	#128
KBD_FIX	COM	689	#255
KBD_FIX	COM	768	#128
KBDDFM	TXT	12066	#75
KBDFED	TXT	9849	#75
KBDFIX	BAS	1350	#114
KBFIX	ASM	32991	#255
KBFIX	COM	1360	#255
KBFIX	DOC	413	#255
KBUFF	COM	50	#224
KBUFF	DOC	3015	#224
KEDIT	TXT	22062	#160
KELLYSER	OTC	2944	#40
KENO	BAS	5530	#35
KERNEL86	BLK	190592	#264
KEY	BAS	2684	#205
KEYBOARD	ASM	7589	#56
KEYBOARD	DOC	2802	#56
KEYBOARD	EXE	1280	#56
KEYCODES	EDX	3072	#43
KEYDEF	BAS	5192	#195
KEYFLAGS	ASM	7008	#83
KEYFLAGS	COM	330	#83
KEYLISTS		578	#215
KEYLISTS		578	#268
KEYLK	DOC	2952	#80
KEYLK3	ASM	13634	#80
KEYLK3	EXE	1536	#80
KEYLOC	ASM	7424	#79
KEYLOC	DOC	1792	#79
KEYLOC	EXE	1536	#79
KEYMOVE	BAS	1280	#46
KEYPUNCH	BAS	2688	#206
KEYS	BAS	690	#113
KEYSBAS	BAS	2944	#9
KEYSET	BAS	2048	#66
KEYSMP	BAS	2560	#9
KILL	BAS	6579	#84
KILLER	EXE	1920	#283
KILLNULL	BAS	384	#47
KILLNULL	BAS	384	#187
KING	BAS	6144	#44
KINGDOM	BAS	5644	#35
KNOCK	ASC	1664	#175
KNOCK	BAS	640	#175
KONG	EXE	44800	#293
KRUGGEL	NL	2048	#156
KVSET	COM	4096	#142
KVUTIL	COM	896	#142
KVUTIL	DOC	3584	#142
KWIC	AR	1387	#132
KWIC	EXE	27392	#130
KWIC	MAN	712	#130
KWSEARCH	DOC	13135	#283
KWSEARCH	EXE	39424	#283
KYBD	BAS	1664	#2
KYBD	BAS	1664	#186
KYBDSET	SUB	512	#53
KYLIST		128	#215
KYLIST		128	#268

L

L	BAT	19	#216
L4	ASM	19409	#255
L4	ASM	21888	#198
L4	COM	2668	#255
L4	DOC	2688	#198
L4	DOC	4195	#255
L4	EXE	2688	#198
LABEL	ASM	7595	#256
LABEL	C	2531	#255
LABEL	DOC	1730	#255
LABEL	EXE	1232	#255
LABEL	EXE	1232	#256
LABEL	EXE	55040	#287
LABELEPS	BAS	2816	#67
LABELINP	EXE	18688	#261
LABELPNT	BAS	5098	#284
LABELPRT	BAS	2816	#111
LABELS	BAS	1280	#67
LABELS	DOC	8022	#261
LABELS	EXE	4345	#261
LABELS	WRK	10752	#306
LABLFILE	BAS	23069	#66
LABLFILE	BAS	32190	#146
LABMAIL	BAS	896	#169
LABPRINT	BAS	4480	#169
LABPRT02	EXE	6784	#261
LABRPT	EXE	5504	#261
LABSELEC	BAS	2432	#169
LADYBUG	EXE	84096	#94
LADYBUG	GET	4909	#94
LADYBUG	LST	151752	#94
LANDER	BAS	1536	#83
LANDER	BAS	3200	#27
LANDER	BAS	3456	#35
LANDER	BAS	17920	#55
LANDER	BAS	17920	#274
LANDER	BIN	5760	#55
LANDER	BIN	5760	#274
LANDER	SCR	128	#55
LANDER	SCR	128	#274

LANDSEQ	BAS	3584	#15
LAR	DOC	1792	#111
LAR	DOC	1792	#135
LAR	EXE	26112	#111
LAR	EXE	26752	#135
LAURINOL	NL	3072	#200
LAYOUT	UNP	1152	#238
LBANNER	BAS	2816	#128
LBL	BAT	195	#284
LBLUT1	EXE	29440	#284
LC	SB	609	#162
LCAPR84	CCC	902	#242
LCATE	OBJ	86	#215
LCFEB84	CCC	902	#242
LCT	WKS	9088	#304
LD	BAT	72	#216
LDIR	BAS	4480	#22
LDIR	C	10240	#142
LDIR	DOC	384	#142
LDIR	EXE	14080	#142
LDIRC	BAS	4382	#22
LDRPRINT	PRG	1147	#300
LEARN	HLP	11036	#232
LEASE	BAS	2176	#29
LEDGER	DAT	1664	#250
LEDGER	DAT	1664	#275
LEDGER	DOC	2822	#165
LEDGER	WKS	9728	#302
LEHRMAN	NL	4096	#200
LEM	BAS	6016	#35
LENGTH	DCL	57	#132
LENGTH	OBJ	418	#132
LET	BAS	4864	#105
LETTER		3584	#217
LETTER	TXT	2322	#232
LETUS	BAT	45	#121
LETUS	BAT	45	#122
LETUS	BAT	45	#123
LETUS	DOC	28194	#121
LEYGREF	CMD	1408	#298
LEYGREF	DAT	1280	#298
LEYGREF	INS	7424	#298
LEYGREF	PIC	1024	#298
LEYGREF1	BAS	15377	#298
LF	COM	512	#28
LF	COM	896	#7
LF	EXE	67200	#146
LIBRIAN	DOC	1536	#138
LIBRIAN	MRG	1024	#138
LICENSE		3176	#276
LIFE	ASM	9202	#79
LIFE	BAS	1664	#12
LIFE	BAS	2183	#292
LIFE	EXE	1152	#79
LIFE2	BAS	9059	#79
LIFE2	BAS	9059	#274
LIFE2	EXE	26415	#79
LIFE2	EXE	26415	#274
LIFEC	COM	11356	#292
LIFEC	PAS	5696	#292
LIFECG	COM	11248	#292
LIFECG	PAS	5464	#292
LIGHTLYR	BAS	183	#292
LINEBUG	BAS	849	#211
LINECNT	AR	680	#132
LINECNT	EXE	26496	#131
LINECNT	MAN	235	#130
LINES	BAS	1920	#44
LINK	BAT	128	#137
LINREGRS	BAS	11136	#62
LISP	PAS	25600	#142
LISP1	TXT	9141	#160
LISP1	TXT	15377	#159
LIST	BAT	256	#137
LIST	COM	2371	#255
LIST	DOC	2176	#255
LIST	EXE	640	#38
LIST1	ADA	2295	#160
LIST1	ADA	4596	#159
LIST1	ASM	6301	#159
LIST1	ASM	16092	#160
LIST1	BAS	3351	#160
LIST1	C	881	#160
LIST1	C	6037	#159
LIST1	FOR	5561	#160
LIST1	PAS	1250	#159
LISTER	BAS	951	#276
LISTER	BAS	10112	#2
LISTER	EXE	20352	#250
LISTER	EXE	20608	#277
LISTFILE	BAS	2304	#182
LISTING	COM	22210	#248
LISTING	DOC	1699	#248
LISTING	PAS	21175	#248
LISTMAIL	BAS	2176	#169
LISTMAR	BAS	4720	#90
LISTMATE	ABS	2990	#252
LISTMATE	DOC	66560	#252
LISTMATE	EXE	89036	#252
LISTMATE	HLP	41245	#252
LISTMATE	SYS	4573	#252
LISTMATE	TXT	26346	#252
LISTPCI	BAS	3955	#90
LISTPER	BAS	3944	#90
LISTSKIP	10P	2688	#66
LISTSKIP	17P	2688	#66
LITUPLIF	BAS	2048	#24
LKTOOL	BAT	24	#132
LLIFE	BAS	2183	#292
LLIST	EXE	16896	#162
LMAZE	BAS	3135	#292
LNA	WKS	12288	#304
LNP	WKS	3072	#304
LNREGRES	BAS	4608	#88
LOAD	ASM	4637	#134
LOAD	COM	291	#134
LOAD-US	ABS	2299	#252
LOAD-US	COM	8897	#252
LOAD-US	DOC	2463	#252
LOADNEW	BAT	128	#181
LOAN	BAS	2304	#35
LOAN2	BAS	4992	#48
LOAN3	BAS	7680	#49
LOANANAL	BAS	39936	#93
LOANSVGS	BAS	39936	#155
LOCAL	H	384	#163
LOCATE	ASM	688	#172
LOCATE	ASM	688	#223
LOCATE	DOC	187	#223
LOCATE	DOC	936	#172
LOCATE	OBJ	95	#223
LOCMAIL	BAS	1280	#169
LODEMO	BAS	16384	#139
LOGMENU	LOG	2942	#239
LOGO	BIN	16512	#191
LOGO40	BAS	1280	#12
LOGO82	COM	2132	#121
LOGO83A	COM	2132	#122
LOGO83B	COM	2132	#123
LOGOC	BAS	1536	#11
LOGOFF	LOG	5248	#239
LOGON	LOG	1024	#239
LOGREV	LOG	10368	#239
LONGDEMO	BAT	2081	#285
LONGLEYR	DAT	1010	#232
LONGLEYS	DAT	834	#232
LONGTERM	BAS	17611	#54
LONGZONE	BAS	2944	#9
LOOK	ASM	14554	#256
LOOK	COM	752	#256
LOOK	COM	1024	#9
LOOK	DOC	296	#256
LOOK	PRG	640	#300
LOOKCUB	FMT	633	#300
LOOKLDR	FMT	628	#300
LOOKLDR	PRG	375	#300
LOOKUP	BAS	3072	#233
LOOKUP	BAS	5376	#4
LOOPMAC	TXT	8015	#301
LORES	ASM	30208	#139
LORES	BAS	16384	#139
LORES	DOC	20864	#139
LORES	EXE	7552	#139
LORES	OBJ	3456	#139
LORES	USR	2432	#139
LOSTGOLD	BAS	19584	#71
LOT101	TXT	8489	#301
LOT102	TXT	11136	#301
LOT103	TXT	15744	#301
LOT105	TXT	13058	#301
LOTUS	PRO	4224	#257
LOTUS1A	UNP	256	#184
LOTUSM	WRK	9344	#305
LPCTALK	BAS	896	#16

LPT12SET	BAS	2688	#66
LPT_PKG	ASM	15875	#202
LQ	BAS	1024	#38
LQ	COM	5760	#283
LQ	DOC	9216	#283
LRS	BAS	128	#53
LS	BAT	83	#216
LSN	EDX	17920	#43
LSNCFG	EDX	455	#43
LTYPE	C	3200	#142
LTYPE	EXE	12800	#142
LU	DOC	6144	#140
LU	EXE	22528	#140
LU86402	DOC	12403	#280
LU86402	EXE	24320	#280
LUDWIG	BUG	1792	#94
LUMP	C	1099	#149
LUMP	DOC	489	#149
LUMP	EXE	11904	#149
LUNAR	BAS	1792	#11
LUNAR	BAS	2176	#79

M

M	EXE	16128	#299
M1		1920	#192
M1	BAS	384	#180
M10	BAS	1664	#180
M11	BAS	1152	#180
M12	BAS	512	#180
M13	BAS	640	#180
M14	BAS	896	#180
M15	BAS	1024	#180
M16	BAS	512	#180
M17	BAS	384	#180
M18	BAS	512	#180
M19	BAS	1024	#180
M2	BAS	384	#180
M20	BAS	1024	#180
M21	BAS	512	#180
M22	BAS	896	#180
M23	BAS	1920	#180
M24	BAS	896	#180
M25	BAS	768	#180
M26	BAS	1024	#180
M3	BAS	512	#180
M4	BAS	896	#180
M5	BAS	1792	#180
M6	BAS	512	#180
M7	BAS	1024	#180
M8	BAS	2176	#180
M8087	MAC	7296	#140
M9	BAS	640	#180
M_PCWRIT	COM	1433	#78
MA	BAS	41896	#179
MA	BAT	14	#46
MA	DOC	25882	#179
MACDONAL	BAS	1051	#292

MACK	NL	6144	#156
MACLIB	WKS	12800	#304
MACOPY	BAT	370	#179
MACRO	AR	20766	#132
MACRO	DAT	720	#286
MACRO	EXE	32640	#58
MACRO	EXE	33920	#131
MACRO	MAN	2983	#130
MACRO_1	DOC	5120	#304
MACROLIB	TXT	23984	#301
MACROTUT	WKS	11136	#257
MACTEST	ASM	1024	#109
MADOC	BAT	667	#179
MAG	DTA	7936	#247
MAG	HDR	128	#247
MAG	INX	3328	#247
MAG	RPT	128	#247
MAGDALEN	BAS	1402	#81
MAGEE	DOC	15488	#303
MAGEE	WKS	44160	#303
MAIL	BAS	2560	#89
MAIL	DBF	2048	#126
MAIL	PRG	1536	#126
MAIL	TXT	1242	#89
MAIL	WKS	8320	#303
MAIL1	BAS	20480	#79
MAIL1	DOC	2816	#79
MAILENTR	PRG	1024	#126
MAILFMT	FMT	640	#126
MAILINFO	PRG	1152	#126
MAILIST1	BAS	40832	#169
MAILIST1	DOC	26752	#169
MAILIST2	BAS	16000	#62
MAILLAB	PRG	896	#126
MAILLIST	BAS	7936	#47
MAILLIST	BAS	7936	#169
MAILLTTR	PRG	1664	#126
MAILMEMB	BAS	1024	#169
MAILMENU	BAS	1408	#169
MAILMRG	BAS	7168	#233
MAILSORT	BAS	2688	#169
MAIN	BAS	50304	#214
MAIN	EXE	89728	#267
MAIN	PRG	9856	#300
MAKE	COM	3371	#60
MAKE-REF	DOC	3546	#60
MAKEBKUP	BAT	2042	#254
MAKECONV	DOC	4284	#60
MAKECOPY	BAT	13	#127
MAKEDATA	BAS	5120	#145
MAKEDOC1	DOC	8745	#60
MAKEDOC2	DOC	12186	#60
MAKEG64	BAT	93	#127
MAKEINT	BAT	126	#283
MAKEM64	BAT	93	#127
MAKEMEMO	BAS	6781	#261
MAKEMONO	BAT	62	#127
MAKERAM	BAT	445	#283

MAKSTKFL	BAS	23808	#40
MAKSTKFL	DOC	16206	#40
MAN	IM	618	#130
MANOR	BAS	14208	#100
MANUAL		41798	#219
MANUAL		44288	#237
MANUAL	BAT	256	#237
MANUAL	BAT	576	#87
MANUAL	BAT	576	#161
MANUAL	DOC	41840	#87
MANUAL	DOC	41840	#161
MANUAL	DOC	48721	#222
MANUAL	DOC	50245	#116
MANUAL	DOC	124953	#221
MANUAL	DOC	125065	#220
MANUAL	EXE	23040	#261
MANUAL	PRG	2208	#295
MANUAL	TXT	512	#295
MANUAL	TXT	36116	#261
MANUAL	TXT	50304	#117
MANUAL	TXT	115251	#74
MANUAL1	CRN	31609	#78
MANUAL1	TXT	18874	#68
MANUAL2	CRN	29486	#78
MANUAL2	TXT	19648	#68
MANUAL3	CRN	34981	#78
MANUAL3	TXT	19691	#68
MANUAL4	CRN	36766	#78
MANYCOPY	BAT	35	#78
MAPMAKER	EXE	81280	#219
MAPTREE	BAS	1207	#277
MAPTREE	BAS	1896	#250
MAPTREE	EXE	20096	#277
MAPTREE	LIB	2432	#277
MARINE° S	BAS	667	#292
MARKS	NL	4096	#200
MARS-ESC	BAS	12800	#174
MASTER	BAS	5120	#18
MASTER	TXT	153216	#215
MASTER2	BAS	3910	#208
MASTFILE		5760	#231
MASTHEAD		1457	#158
MASTHEAD		1536	#156
MASTHEAD		1536	#157
MASTHEAD		1664	#200
MASTHEAD	TXT	5240	#160
MASTMIND	BAS	3712	#252
MATH	BAS	1152	#180
MATH	BAS	2304	#37
MATH	BAS	6400	#18
MATH	BAS	17664	#95
MATH	EXE	38784	#249
MATH----	APL	6912	#108
MATHFUNC	BAS	15872	#67
MATRIX	BAS	2688	#180
MAXIT	BAS	4608	#1
MAXMIN1		128	#215
MAXMIN8		128	#215

MAXWELLS	SNG	444	#127
MAZE	BAS	3328	#228
MAZE	BAS	16512	#69
MAZE	RES	128	#69
MAZEMAKE	BAS	3118	#292
MCA	APP	53248	#306
MCA	HLP	768	#306
MCARI	WRK	44800	#306
MCNEMAR	BAS	1920	#88
MCODE	%%%	128	#15
MDM7	DOC	12288	#9
MDM7I	COM	7552	#9
MDMIBM	ASM	4724	#9
MDRAW	BAS	7424	#38
MEAN	BAS	640	#29
MEDBULL	BAS	256	#12
MEDIA	FRM	512	#102
MEDICAL	PRG	1322	#295
MEDICOST	FRM	241	#295
MEDIPAY	FRM	512	#295
MEDLEY	BAS	9271	#175
MEGATREK	BAS	40468	#299
MEM640	DOC	7040	#183
MEM640	DOC	7312	#80
MEM640	ZAP	813	#80
MEM640	ZAP	896	#183
MEMBER	ASC	1664	#169
MEMBERS	BAS	896	#169
MEMBRAIN	BAS	5632	#45
MEMBRAIN	DOC	4096	#198
MEMBRAIN	DOC	4096	#273
MEMBRAIN	EXE	3584	#198
MEMBRAIN	EXE	3584	#273
MEMDRV	ASM	13824	#111
MEMDRV	SYS	640	#111
MEMDUMP	BAS	1930	#46
MEMINST	DAT	6	#299
MEMO	BAS	3453	#195
MEMO	BAS	17152	#190
MEMO	BAS	26731	#261
MEMO	BAT	24	#261
MEMO	FIL	448	#195
MEMORY	BAS	10496	#71
MEMORY	BAS	10496	#72
MEMORY	COM	1466	#79
MEMORY	DOC	3122	#79
MEMORY	TXT	18734	#159
MEMPEEK	BAS	3840	#28
MEMSET	BAS	648	#299
MEMSHIFT	UNP	512	#184
MEMSIZE	BAS	3712	#61
MENCON	C	7494	#216
MENU	BAK	1490	#300
MENU	BAS	128	#9
MENU	BAS	640	#297
MENU	BAS	896	#37
MENU	BAS	1171	#195
MENU	BAS	1739	#241
MENU	BAS	1792	#19
MENU	BAS	3072	#233
MENU	BAS	4096	#18
MENU	BAS	4096	#1
MENU	BAS	4352	#17
MENU	BAS	4992	#23
MENU	BAS	5760	#11
MENU	BAS	7706	#90
MENU	BAT	49	#277
MENU	BAT	6528	#139
MENU	DAT	896	#76
MENU	PCS	2304	#19
MENU	PGM	1280	#100
MENU	PRG	1390	#300
MENU	PRG	2361	#295
MENU	WKS	8832	#301
MENU1		384	#152
MENU1		384	#212
MENU1G		640	#152
MENU1G		640	#212
MENU2		512	#152
MENU2		512	#212
MENU2	BAS	774	#83
MENU2G		768	#212
MENU2G		896	#152
MENU3		384	#152
MENU3		384	#212
MENU3G		640	#152
MENU3G		768	#212
MENU4		512	#212
MENU4G		896	#212
MENU5		1536	#212
MENU5G		1536	#212
MENUBR	WRK	6656	#305
MENUCHEK	PRG	798	#295
MENUINCO	PRG	1024	#295
MENUMAKR	BAS	3796	#134
MENUMILE	PRG	3523	#295
MENUPRNT	BAS	4992	#66
MENUREPT	PRG	1861	#295
MERGE	EXE	30464	#26
MERGE	EXE	39680	#282
MERGE	PAS	4096	#26
MESSAGE	DCL	51	#132
MESSAGE	OBJ	468	#132
MESSAGES		128	#212
MESSAGES		896	#150
META86	BLK	49280	#264
METABAS	TXT	13638	#159
METEOR	BAS	3456	#4
METEOR	BAS	3584	#17
METEOR	BAS	3968	#14
METZGER	NL	6144	#157
MHCHIMLT	BAS	2944	#88
MHCHISQR	BAS	2048	#88
MICHELLE	SNG	672	#127
MIDWEST	BBS	13824	#103
MILEGONE	FRM	512	#295
MINASI	NL	4096	#158
MINGLE	BAS	18176	#233
MINI	INC	758	#74
MINI	OBJ	744	#74
MINI-WP	BAS	18048	#56
MINICALC	DOC	12166	#89
MINICALC	DOC	12166	#170
MINICALC	EXE	52864	#89
MINICALC	EXE	52864	#170
MINIMATH	BAS	2816	#45
MINIPROG	BAS	1280	#9
MINIPRT	DOC	2048	#184
MINITEL	ABS	384	#188
MINITEL	DOC	42624	#188
MINITEL	DQC	21888	#188
MINITEL	LBR	52736	#188
MINUET	BAS	1085	#168
MINUET2	BAS	1093	#168
MIS		128	#95
MIS	DBF	1024	#126
MISC	BUG	1005	#94
MISC	FRM	233	#295
MISCCOST	FRM	258	#295
MISCCOST	PRG	1324	#295
MISCLIST	FRM	193	#295
MISSLE	BAS	1942	#35
MISTOX	WKS	37504	#302
MKFLOP1	BAT	646	#132
MKFLOP2	BAT	245	#132
MKFLOP3	BAT	2349	#132
MKOBJ	BAT	22	#132
MKPR	BAT	31	#132
MKPRIMS	BAT	715	#132
MKTOOL	BAT	45	#132
MKUT	BAT	31	#132
MKUTILS	BAT	772	#132
ML2	DBF	1024	#126
ML2	DOC	1152	#126
ML2	PRG	1152	#126
ML2A	PRG	256	#126
ML2EDIT	PRG	896	#126
ML2ENTR	PRG	768	#126
ML2INFO	PRG	384	#126
ML2LAB	PRG	3584	#126
ML2LAB1	PRG	256	#126
ML2LAB2	PRG	256	#126
ML2LAB4	PRG	384	#126
ML2LIST	PRG	1920	#126
ML2LST1	PRG	256	#126
ML2LTTR	PRG	896	#126
ML2MULTI	PRG	1792	#126
ML2REC	PRG	256	#126
ML2SORT	PRG	896	#126
ML2ZIPCT	PRG	768	#126
MLABEL5	PRG	1536	#126
MLTIBRST	BAS	501	#299
MMOUSE	BAT	384	#86
MOD100IN	BAS	2304	#113

MOD100IN	DOC	5031	#113
MODEM	ASM	56560	#81
MODEM	COM	9623	#81
MODEM7	COM	7552	#4
MODEM7	DOC	12288	#4
MODROW	TXT	2564	#38
MODULE	OBJ	11569	#223
MODULE	PAS	8768	#223
MODULO	BAS	512	#9
MOLY-PAY	BAS	8704	#73
MONBLNK1	COM	200	#89
MONBLNK1	DOC	1536	#89
MONEYMKT	INT	7	#40
MONITOR		640	#2
MONITOR	BAS	7296	#8
MONITOR	DOC	55168	#8
MONO	BAS	128	#13
MONO	BAT	14	#13
MONO	COM	22	#6
MONO	COM	128	#50
MONO	EXE	640	#15
MONO	EXE	640	#38
MONO	PIC	4104	#105
MONOCHR		38	#68
MONOCLKF	COM	257	#182
MONOCLKF	DOC	384	#182
MONOCLOK	COM	384	#256
MONOFILE	BAS	256	#182
MONOGRAF	BAS	128	#191
MONOGRPH	BAS	23014	#195
MONOKEYD	BAS	5192	#195
MONOMEMO	BAS	3273	#195
MONOMENU	BAS	1189	#195
MONOSET	BAS	1664	#9
MONSW	BAS	2304	#15
MONTHS	HBW	640	#62
MONTOCOL	BAS	256	#27
MOON	BAS	4352	#203
MOON	BAS	18816	#17
MOON	BAS	23428	#24
MORE	COM	384	#279
MORE	COM	384	#223
MORNING	BAS	262	#292
MORSE	BAS	6784	#255
MORSE	BAS	6784	#260
MORSECOD	BAS	2944	#93
MOUNTAIN	BAS	5248	#23
MOUNTX	PIC	16128	#12
MOUSE	SPR	256	#69
MOVBAS	BAT	278	#277
MOVE	COM	384	#80
MOVE	COM	2138	#183
MOVE	COM	2138	#273
MOVE	DOC	795	#80
MOVE	DOC	1664	#183
MOVE	DOC	1664	#273
MOVEBUG	BUG	238	#94
MOVEFF	BAT	812	#250
MOVEXE	BAT	276	#277
MOVINGAL	BAS	154	#292
MOVLIB	BAT	341	#277
MPG-CAL	BAS	1408	#73
MS2	UNP	1024	#184
MSBEDIT	EXE	54784	#172
MSBFILE	EXE	51840	#223
MSBUILD	HLP	903	#41
MSCMD	ASM	32746	#41
MSCOMM	ASM	17923	#41
MSDEFS	H	9065	#41
MSFILE	ASM	30846	#41
MSKERM	ASM	36007	#41
MSKERMIT	DOC	104652	#42
MSKERMIT	EXE	84224	#42
MSKERMIT	HLP	9371	#42
MSKERMIT	INI	266	#41
MSPOOL	COM	768	#2
MSPOOL	COM	768	#27
MSPOOL	COM	896	#89
MSPOOL	DOC	556	#27
MSPOOL	DOC	5058	#89
MSPOOL2	COM	1020	#204
MSPOOL2	DOC	7914	#204
MSQUARE	BAS	4096	#44
MSRECV	ASM	19278	#41
MSSEND	ASM	32419	#41
MSSERV	ASM	24057	#41
MSSET	ASM	40202	#41
MSTERM	ASM	12354	#41
MSXDMB	ASM	121	#41
MSXDMB	HLP	179	#41
MSXGEN	ASM	12267	#42
MSXHP150	ASM	10248	#42
MSXIBM	ASM	21776	#41
MSXRB	ASM	39824	#42
MSXSYS	DOC	13731	#42
MSXWNG	ASM	13646	#42
MSYIBM	ASM	30720	#41
MTH	C	8005	#147
MTH	OBJ	2120	#147
MUGGER	ADV	6784	#213
MUGGER	DAT	7168	#213
MUGGER	DAT	7296	#91
MUGGER	HDR	256	#213
MUGGER	REF	4992	#213
MULREG	EXE	76288	#232
MULREG	HLP	1934	#232
MULTREG	EXE	49664	#206
MUSIC	BAS	4096	#107
MUSIC	BAS	14399	#92
MUSIC	BAS	14464	#108
MUSIC	DAT	1664	#92
MUSIC	DOC	1664	#108
MUSICBOX	BAS	17920	#50
MUSICFIL	BAS	14438	#175
MUSICIAN	DOC	29217	#127
MUSICIAN	EXE	30208	#127
MUSTCREA	DCL	84	#132
MUSTCREA	OBJ	543	#132
MUSTOPEN	DCL	82	#132
MUSTOPEN	OBJ	523	#132
MV	BAT	15	#216
MV	DOC	1408	#196
MV	EXE	14592	#196
MVPFORTH	ASM	57643	#31
MVPFORTH	DOC	11790	#31
MVPFORTH	EXE	10496	#31
MX80	BAS	1408	#11
MX80	FNT	1020	#130
MY-DATE	BAT	128	#183
N			
NADIA	BAS	384	#55
NAEPIRS	EXE	43392	#266
NAMCNV	TXT	4596	#92
NAME	BAS	149	#292
NAMEBRK	PRG	2688	#126
NAMETEST	PRG	1408	#102
NARGS	DCL	38	#132
NARGS	OBJ	387	#132
NB	B1	256	#233
NB	B2	256	#233
NB	BAS	1920	#233
NB	BAT	28	#233
NB	CFG	128	#233
NB	H1	3968	#233
NB	H2	3968	#233
NB	H3	3968	#233
NB	H4	3968	#233
NB	H5	3968	#233
NB	H6	3968	#233
NB	X	3968	#233
NB1	BAS	15360	#233
NB10	BAS	7808	#233
NB12	BAS	11776	#233
NB13	BAS	6912	#233
NB14	BAS	7168	#233
NB16	BAS	7040	#233
NB17	BAS	3072	#233
NB18	BAS	2048	#233
NB19	BAS	10496	#233
NB2	BAS	10240	#233
NB20	BAS	9472	#233
NB21	BAS	6656	#233
NB23	BAS	5632	#233
NB24	BAS	8832	#233
NB3	BAS	8064	#233
NB5	BAS	6144	#233
NB6	BAS	3712	#233
NB7	BAS	768	#233
NBZ	COM	1143	#233
NCCLSPRE	BAS	1920	#49
NCCLSPRE	BAS	1920	#180
NDATETST	PRG	128	#102

NDOSEDIT	COM	2560	#205
NDOSEDIT	COM	2560	#273
NDOSEDIT	DOC	5632	#205
NDOSEDIT	DOC	5632	#273
NECLABEL	BAS	5632	#66
NEINST	COM	15620	#217
NEINST	PAS	10519	#217
NELIST	COM	19488	#217
NELIST	DOC	10624	#217
NELIST	PAS	21248	#217
NEPRN	DAT	36	#217
NESTMENU	BAT	256	#281
NESTMENU	DOC	5248	#281
NETPREST	BAS	896	#29
NEW	PRG	2304	#102
NEW1	KEY	512	#112
NEW123	UNP	1152	#184
NEW2	KEY	512	#112
NEW_IN_2	54	3940	#68
NEWBELL	ASM	1499	#255
NEWBELL	COM	92	#255
NEWCHESS	BAS	21504	#203
NEWCLOCK	DOC	1271	#114
NEWCLOCK	SYS	384	#114
NEWCOM		1020	#150
NEWFONT	BAS	6935	#228
NEWKEY	BAS	256	#2
NEWKEY	DOC	42730	#181
NEWKEY	EXE	4608	#181
NEWKEY1	EXE	9216	#181
NEWLAB	EXE	2048	#261
NEWS	EXE	55296	#156
NEWS	EXE	74880	#157
NEWS	EXE	76416	#200
NEWS	EXE	78080	#158
NEWSLOGO	PIC	16512	#158
NEWSLOGO	PIC	16512	#156
NEWSLOGO	PIC	16512	#157
NEWSLOGO	PIC	16512	#200
NEWSPIRO	COM	14103	#292
NEWSPIRO	PAS	9526	#292
NEWTREK	BAS	25088	#24
NEWTREK	HOW	3625	#24
NEWUSER		68	#152
NEWUSER		768	#212
NEWYEAR	DOC	10042	#176
NEWYEAR	EXE	43648	#176
NEWYEAR	PAS	11227	#176
NEXTSHOW	BAS	3456	#15
NFL-PK	BAS	6912	#61
NICELIST	BAS	2816	#66
NIEHOFF	NL	8192	#157
NIM	BAS	8832	#11
NIM	BAS	8832	#18
NISLEY	NL	2048	#156
NKYPKY	TXT	5304	#238
NLBE	WKS	30592	#302
NOCOLOR	ASM	3370	#115
NOCOLOR	COM	256	#115
NOCOLOR	COM	1024	#186
NOCOLOR	DOC	506	#115
NOCOLOR	DOC	1024	#186
NOECHO	DOC	512	#108
NOISE	BAS	640	#27
NONLIN	BAS	29184	#67
NORMAL	BAS	3200	#88
NORMAL-Z	BAS	7424	#47
NORMAL-Z	BAS	7424	#180
NORTPAT2	DOC	1024	#138
NOSLASHO	BAT	580	#285
NOTICE		1295	#222
NOTICE		1341	#220
NOTICE		1341	#221
NOTICE	DOC	2624	#235
NPANN	PIC	4352	#157
NPANN	PIC	4533	#158
NPANN	PIC	4608	#200
NPV	DOC	20848	#289
NPV	WKS	12288	#289
NUDE	BAS	5632	#208
NUDE	BAS	5901	#176
NUDE84	TXT	7688	#208
NUKE-NY	BAS	15360	#209
NUKE-SF	BAS	11058	#228
NUM-WORD	BAS	3200	#6
NUM2	BAS	3584	#18
NUM3	BAS	1024	#18
NUMBER	NDX	2560	#116
NUMBERS	BAS	3712	#18
NUMERIC	BAS	1280	#29
NUMSAM	CFG	128	#119
NUMSAM	DAT	896	#119
NUMSAM	NUM	128	#119
NUMSAM1	NDX	256	#119
NUMVERT	BAS	1152	#9
NUSQ	COM	2176	#256
NUSQ	COM	3584	#139
NUSQ	DOC	11077	#256
NUTREK	BAS	50909	#299
NVB	WKS	10624	#304
NWCLOCK	BAS	10932	#83
NYNEW	TXT	78592	#305
NYTEST	BAT	76	#176
NYTEST1	BAT	76	#176

O

OATSPEAS	BAS	181	#292
ODDS	TXT	11768	#159
OFF-YRS		105	#219
OFFICES		2751	#219
OJETCRUZ	EXE	49408	#39
OKI8283A	PRT	205	#78
OKI84A92	PRT	474	#78
OKIBMSON	PRT	505	#78
OKIMENU	BAS	19807	#265
OKIMENU	DOC	17656	#265
OKIMENUC	BAS	8801	#265
OKIMOD	DOC	1201	#80
OKIP2350	PRT	411	#78
OKIP2410	PRT	422	#78
OKITALIC	BAS	8689	#265
OKIWRITE	PRT	486	#78
OLD-NEW	BAT	128	#183
OLDBULL	DOC	19456	#304
OLDEPSON	PRT	989	#78
OLDER	ASM	2928	#255
OLDER	COM	124	#255
OLDFOLKS	BAS	343	#292
OLDWOMAN	SNG	512	#127
OLY2CRX1	PRT	303	#78
ONE	DAT	4608	#76
OPEN	DCL	75	#132
OPEN	OBJ	879	#132
OPERATOR	BAS	12416	#24
OPKEYS	BAS	512	#9
OPT123	VC	6272	#85
OPTCASH	VC	6272	#85
OPTIONZ	WKS	21376	#302
OPTMAR	DOC	3456	#85
OPTMAR	GIN	6272	#85
OPTTEST	VC	6144	#85
ORDER		4139	#277
ORDER		4139	#250
ORDER		4139	#276
ORDER	FM	5774	#75
ORDERFRM	TXT	1792	#247
ORGANIZE	PRG	23834	#295
ORIGINAL	KEY	86	#34
OTHDEMO	BAS	6144	#15
OTHELLO	BAS	6912	#1
OTHELLO	BAS	8320	#20
OTHELLO	BAS	8832	#72
OTHRCOST	PRG	1326	#295
OUTPUTS	PRF	6528	#201
OWTAB		947	#192

P

P87_INT		5760	#140
PAC-GAL	EXE	39296	#228
PACGIRLA	EXE	48896	#21
PACKMAN	DOC	4736	#24
PACKMAN	DOC	4736	#274
PACKMAN	EXE	37120	#24
PACKMAN	EXE	37120	#274
PACMANGL	EXE	42752	#173
PAD	WKS	29312	#135
PAD	WKS	29312	#207
PAD	WKS	29312	#302
PAGE	BAT	68	#70
PAGE	COM	206	#113
PAGEII	ASC	568	#193
PAGEIII	ASC	769	#193

PAGEIV	ASC	816	#193
PAGEIX	ASC	887	#193
PAGES	KIP	4	#70
PAGESKIP	DOC	564	#70
PAGEV	ASC	1019	#193
PAGEVI	ASC	852	#193
PAGEVII	ASC	555	#193
PAGEVIII	ASC	757	#193
PAINT	BAS	384	#12
PALLETTE	BAS	768	#28
PANGO	EXE	29696	#293
PANGO	HGH	640	#293
PANTHR	PIC	3456	#154
PAPER	OUT	128	#218
PARAMS	DAT	367	#286
PARCHK	ASM	23533	#256
PARCHK	COM	1806	#256
PARCHK	DOC	4111	#256
PARINT	ASM	5313	#299
PARINT	COM	451	#299
PARINT	LST	11043	#299
PARSE	P	1531	#36
PARSER	INC	10249	#82
PARTA	PAS	14803	#36
PARTB	PAS	17091	#36
PARTC	PAS	10520	#36
PARTCOPY	EXE	20480	#52
PAS-BEEP	DOC	422	#172
PAS1	TXT	6994	#159
PAS1	TXT	14621	#160
PAS87	ASM	5120	#140
PASC	BAT	256	#36
PASCAL	NL	3072	#157
PASCL	BAT	256	#36
PASCLG	BAT	256	#36
PASSWRDS		1	#212
PATCH2	BAT	633	#159
PATCH256	ASC	2422	#52
PATCHER	BAS	2595	#135
PATHMAN	BAS	9344	#15
PATTERNS	BAS	2206	#92
PATTERNS	BAS	3200	#11
PATTERNS	BAS	4096	#1
PAUSE	C	1660	#216
PAYBILLS	PRG	8576	#102
PAYCHECK		1504	#215
PAYCHKS		2898	#215
PAYEMPS	PRG	2816	#102
PAYFIND	PRG	4096	#102
PAYMENT	BAS	3200	#9
PAYMENU	PRG	1536	#102
PAYROLL	PRG	11776	#102
PAYSUM		1505	#215
PC	EXE	50176	#87
PC	EXE	50176	#161
PC-BW	COM	1107	#113
PC-BW	D11	1039	#113
PC-CALC	BAS	32085	#224
PC-CALC	DOC	65280	#224
PC-CALC	EXE	2048	#199
PC-CALC	EXE	50944	#224
PC-CHECK	BAS	44928	#282
PC-CHECK	DOC	16896	#282
PC-CODE1	153	21219	#112
PC-CODE1	DOC	9486	#112
PC-CODE1	EXE	38016	#112
PC-CODE2	153	20263	#112
PC-CODE2	DOC	6331	#112
PC-CODE2	EXE	38528	#112
PC-COLOR	BAS	7424	#66
PC-DEF	EXE	12288	#5
PC-DIAL	COM	41242	#129
PC-DIAL	DOC	49985	#129
PC-DIAL	PRO	286	#129
PC-EXPOR	EXE	16512	#5
PC-FILE	DOC	108505	#5
PC-FILE	EXE	33408	#5
PC-FILE	PRO	128	#5
PC-FIX	EXE	14080	#5
PC-FONT2	EXE	40320	#225
PC-FONT2	PRN	70786	#225
PC-FONT2	TST	2599	#225
PC-FORM	EXE	51840	#190
PC-GOLF	EXE	51200	#293
PC-HELP	EXE	19328	#112
PC-IMPOR	EXE	15104	#5
PC-LABEL	EXE	8960	#5
PC-LIB	BAS	16897	#89
PC-LIB	DOC	5848	#89
PC-MAP	BAS	10880	#22
PC-MENU	153	2307	#112
PC-MENU	EXE	19712	#112
PC-OVL	EXE	21376	#5
PC-PAD	ABS	896	#170
PC-PAD	BAS	8704	#61
PC-PAD	BAS	8704	#170
PC-PAD	BAT	21	#170
PC-PAD	DOC	20992	#170
PC-PAD	LST	15744	#61
PC-PAD	LST	15744	#170
PC-PAGE	COM	1337	#113
PC-PAGE	D11	1269	#113
PC-PAGE	DOC	7357	#113
PC-PRINT	DOC	11816	#238
PC-PRINT	EXE	28672	#5
PC-PRINT	EXE	41507	#238
PC-READ	COM	18652	#194
PC-READ	DOC	14882	#194
PC-SETUP	EXE	10368	#5
PC-SIG	DOC	1500	#236
PC-SORT	EXE	18432	#5
PC-SPEAK	BAS	10752	#187
PC-STAT2	LOG	3968	#112
PC-TALK	BAS	35200	#16
PC-TALK	DEF	640	#114
PC-TALK	DIR	0	#16
PC-TALK	DIR	512	#114
PC-TALK	DOC	41472	#16
PC-TALK	KEY	0	#16
PC-TALK	KEY	5248	#114
PC-TAMP1	153	2588	#112
PC-TAMP1	DOC	767	#112
PC-TAMP1	EXE	21632	#112
PC-TAMP2	153	1881	#112
PC-TAMP2	EXE	20864	#112
PC-TOUCH	BAS	12160	#249
PC-TOUCH	DOC	3977	#249
PC-TOUCH	EXE	33664	#249
PC-TOUCH	FIL	3993	#249
PC-TTY	COM	1355	#113
PC-TTY	D11	1287	#113
PC-TTY	DOC	7179	#113
PC-UTIL	EXE	18816	#5
PC-VT	CRD	7154	#286
PC-VT	DOC	230656	#286
PC-VT	EXE	31698	#286
PC-VT	SUM	5632	#286
PC-ZAP	DOC	153728	#143
PC-ZAP	EXE	42112	#143
PC-ZERO	153	689	#112
PC-ZERO	DOC	710	#112
PC-ZERO	EXE	19584	#112
PC3SC	DOC	399	#34
PC3SC	MRG	1222	#34
PCADD	GRA	4480	#66
PCAGE82	DTA	39680	#121
PCAGE82	HDR	128	#121
PCAGE82	INX	2176	#121
PCAGE82	KEY	2540	#121
PCAGE83	DTA	80896	#122
PCAGE83	HDR	128	#122
PCAGE83	INX	4352	#122
PCAGE83	KEY	5789	#122
PCCALC	DOC	86758	#199
PCCALC	EXE	48128	#199
PCCALC	MSG	34816	#199
PCCALC2	EXE	48768	#199
PCCALC3	EXE	46464	#199
PCCH1	EQE	45406	#120
PCCH2	EQE	41992	#120
PCCHESS	EXE	23680	#120
PCCHESS	PQT	27850	#120
PCFILECH	BAS	10880	#73
PCFILTER	EXE	14848	#280
PCFILTER	PRN	4864	#280
PCFL	EXE	7552	#159
PCFL	EXE	8576	#160
PCFORM	BAS	3840	#48
PCGLOBE	BAS	4842	#83
PCGLOBE	BAS	5376	#51
PCHALLEN	BAS	1536	#49
PCHEERS	BAS	11776	#21
PCINIT	BAS	512	#17
PCJUNK	C	1438	#147

PCJUNK	OBJ	1137	#147
PCKEY	BAS	4224	#156
PCMAG82	DTA	91392	#121
PCMAG82	HDR	128	#121
PCMAG82	INX	4992	#121
PCMAG82	KEY	5724	#121
PCMAG83A	DTA	80384	#122
PCMAG83A	HDR	128	#122
PCMAG83A	INX	4352	#122
PCMAG83A	KEY	6713	#122
PCMAG83B	DTA	117120	#123
PCMAG83B	HDR	128	#123
PCMAG83B	INX	6400	#123
PCMAG83B	KEY	8162	#123
PCMAN	BAS	7552	#15
PCMAN	BAS	10112	#17
PCMAN	BAS	13056	#173
PCMAN	EXE	48384	#21
PCMANHI	FIL	128	#21
PCOVL	EXE	22656	#199
PCPG	EXE	71680	#136
PCPG	FT1	1919	#136
PCPG	FT2	4034	#136
PCPG	FT3	6383	#136
PCPG	FT4	11936	#136
PCPG	FT5	9790	#136
PCPG	HLP	4217	#136
PCPG	PIC	16512	#136
PCPG	SYM	73472	#136
PCRTTY	EXE	27136	#280
PCRTTY	PRN	10624	#280
PCS	DOC	21632	#19
PCT3JR	DOC	2459	#258
PCT3JR	MRG	2868	#258
PCT3VT	BAS	7696	#114
PCTEC83	DTA	22528	#123
PCTEC83	HDR	128	#123
PCTEC83	INX	1280	#123
PCTEC83	KEY	1997	#123
PCUGINTR	TXT	2863	#160
PCUGINTR	TXT	4992	#159
PCUGNEWS	TOC	1480	#158
PCUGNEWS	TOC	1664	#157
PCUGNEWS	TOC	1664	#200
PCUGNEWS	TOC	1792	#156
PCUTIL	COM	3584	#142
PCUTIL	DOC	5632	#142
PCW83	DTA	95104	#123
PCW83	HDR	128	#123
PCW83	INX	5120	#123
PCW83	KEY	6830	#123
PCWRITE	NL	6144	#158
PDRAW	BAS	7168	#13
PDRAW	DOC	15170	#13
PDSOFTWR	DOC	4224	#14
PE	TXT	13346	#159
PE-NOTAB	DOC	1233	#256
PEDIGREE	BAS	23692	#90
PEEK	BAS	896	#9
PEEKPOKE	TXT	3072	#79
PEEKPRNT	BAS	3840	#66
PELTO	NL	3072	#158
PENCIL	BAS	2632	#177
PENCIRC	BAS	512	#191
PENCLEAR	BAS	256	#191
PENDRAW	BAS	256	#191
PENLINE	BAS	384	#191
PENPAINT	BAS	768	#191
PENSAVE	BAS	256	#191
PEOPLE	BAS	2944	#11
PEPATCH	DOC	684	#33
PEPATCHS	DOC	14976	#108
PEPCON	DOC	1476	#59
PEPSON	BAS	13225	#59
PEPSON	EXE	29312	#59
PERMUTE	BAS	512	#37
PERSONNE	DBF	1024	#102
PERT	BAS	3072	#29
PERT	DAT	640	#206
PERTCHRT	BAS	10496	#299
PERTCHT	BAS	13184	#206
PFSFILE	UNP	1408	#184
PGBRK	BAS	384	#299
PGBRK	BAT	317	#299
PGBRK	BEG	128	#299
PGBRK	END	128	#299
PGMCVRT	BAS	5145	#190
PHANT	PIC	4480	#154
PHASER	BAS	128	#53
PHASERB	BAS	128	#53
PHNBRS	WRK	5504	#306
PHOENIX	BAS	384	#55
PHONE	WRK	1413	#306
PHOTOEST	DOC	1408	#301
PHOTOEST	WKS	9984	#301
PI-COMP	COM	6656	#111
PI-COMP	DOC	5760	#111
PIANO1	BAS	9027	#168
PIANO2	BAS	9316	#168
PIANOMAN	000	26496	#279
PIANOMAN	COM	36311	#279
PIANOMAN	DOC	12795	#279
PICFIL	TXT	4108	#301
PICKER	BAS	3456	#171
PICKTRAN	BAS	13056	#171
PICTURE	BAS	384	#128
PIE2	BAS	2432	#191
PIECHART	BAS	2432	#191
PIL	LSP	4608	#134
PINTE	NL	5120	#158
PINUP1	NUD	10752	#154
PINUP1	PIC	6464	#115
PINUP2	PIC	10489	#115
PINUP3	PIC	7171	#115
PINUP4	PIC	8285	#115
PINWHEEL	BAS	384	#128
PINWRITE	PRT	464	#78
PITFALL	EXE	28160	#293
PIZZA	EXE	28800	#179
PKXP1091	PRT	562	#78
PLACGONE	FRM	512	#295
PLAN		2176	#251
PLANACT	BAR	512	#14
PLANETS	COM	25705	#298
PLANETS	DOC	3622	#298
PLANETS	PAS	28897	#298
PLANNER	NL	3072	#157
PLANNING	NL	4096	#200
PLAYRPNO	COM	26502	#279
PLIB	INC	2674	#74
PLOGO82	COM	2132	#121
PLOGO83	COM	2132	#122
PLOGO83	COM	2132	#123
PLOT	BAS	1152	#47
PLOT	BAS	1152	#191
PLOT	BAT	30	#195
PLOTTER	BAS	3584	#11
PLTSEQFL	ALL	266	#40
PLTSEQFL	DAT	266	#40
PLTSTKFL	BAS	18560	#40
PLTSTKFL	DOC	12211	#40
PMODE	ASM	3200	#108
PMODE	COM	384	#108
POISSON	BAS	1792	#88
POKEPEEK	DOC	4352	#52
POLICOST	FRM	512	#295
POLICOST	PRG	701	#295
POLY	BUG	256	#94
POLYMAZE	EXE	28672	#161
POLYSPI	BUG	256	#94
PONGPONG	BAS	4992	#1
PORTABLE	NL	3072	#156
PORTCOST	BAS	9088	#101
PORTMRKT	BAS	11008	#101
PORTPACK	BAT	194	#101
PORTPACK	DOC	65716	#101
PORTS	DOC	1840	#172
PORTS	EXE	26112	#172
PORTS	PAS	2634	#172
POSTER	BAS	3173	#33
POSTFILE	DBF	2560	#102
POW	COM	3165	#201
POW	DOC	25771	#201
PR	EXE	19680	#78
PR	VC	23936	#85
PR1	LET	1073	#89
PR256	ASM	26752	#52
PRACTICE		445	#276
PRDEMO	BAS	2048	#11
PRETTY	PAS	384	#36
PRETTY1	COM	223	#159
PRETTY1	COM	223	#160
PREVIEW	EXE	29696	#223
PREVIEW	PAS	3102	#223

PREVIEW	WKS	60544	#303
PRF	PRF	313	#208
PRIME	PAS	723	#30
PRIMER	DOC	49280	#10
PRIMS	AR	20840	#132
PRINGRAF	BAS	1024	#191
PRINT	BAS	201	#292
PRINT	BAS	2304	#11
PRINT	BAS	3584	#23
PRINT	BAS	5504	#7
PRINT	BAT	398	#288
PRINT	C	6272	#111
PRINT	COM	11358	#235
PRINT	DOC	1578	#265
PRINT	DOC	7955	#59
PRINT	EXE	10880	#111
PRINT	SET	24	#287
PRINT	TST	1181	#78
PRINT	TXT	7168	#126
PRINT1	EXE	12288	#265
PRINT2	EXE	12288	#265
PRINT20	DOC	657	#186
PRINTALL	BAT	61	#253
PRINTCTL	BAS	11520	#250
PRINTCTL	BAS	11520	#275
PRINTCTL	EXE	37120	#250
PRINTCTL	EXE	37120	#275
PRINTDOC		25173	#88
PRINTDOC	BAT	24	#127
PRINTDOC	BAT	115	#294
PRINTDOC	BAT	292	#113
PRINTDOC	BAT	768	#289
PRINTDOC	BAT	1024	#53
PRINTDOC	BAT	1424	#250
PRINTDOC	BAT	1424	#275
PRINTDOC	EXE	13952	#181
PRINTER	ASM	25964	#110
PRINTER	BAS	495	#14
PRINTER	BAS	4992	#67
PRINTER	COM	1152	#110
PRINTER	COM	12663	#248
PRINTER	DAT	384	#110
PRINTER	DOC	1753	#78
PRINTER	DOC	10240	#110
PRINTER	PAS	2077	#248
PRINTER	PAS	10410	#36
PRINTER	WKS	9600	#257
PRINTER2	BAS	4736	#49
PRINTERS	BAS	2631	#90
PRINTF	AR	2959	#132
PRINTF	EXE	29568	#131
PRINTF	MAN	704	#130
PRINTFIX	COM	128	#46
PRINTGR	ASM	2558	#61
PRINTGR	DOC	1681	#61
PRINTGR1	EXE	1024	#61
PRINTGR2	EXE	896	#61
PRINTING	DOC	407	#193
PRINTMAN	BAS	684	#296
PRINTMAN	BAS	896	#215
PRINTMAN	COM	1033	#78
PRINTMAR	BAS	4755	#90
PRINTNEC	BAS	5504	#7
PRINTOUT	PRG	2048	#102
PRINTPER	BAS	6988	#90
PRINTQUE	BAS	16000	#195
PRINTQUE	DOC	12416	#195
PRINTSET		28	#49
PRINTSET		28	#186
PRINTSET	DOC	769	#49
PRINTSET	DOC	769	#186
PRINTSTY		128	#192
PRINTTUT	WKS	38272	#257
PRINTXT1	CMD	6016	#139
PRINTXT1	DOC	9344	#139
PRINTXT1	INC	3584	#139
PRLIST	BAS	3584	#25
PRN-APX	BAT	158	#222
PRN-APX	BAT	256	#220
PRN-APX	BAT	256	#221
PRN-MAN	BAT	169	#222
PRN-MAN	BAT	256	#220
PRN-MAN	BAT	256	#221
PRN2GRAF	BAS	768	#191
PRNSTATS	BAS	3770	#172
PRNSTATS	DOC	1717	#172
PRNT-CHR	COM	3200	#220
PRNT-CHR	COM	3200	#221
PRNT-CHR	COM	3328	#222
PRNT-SCN	COM	704	#220
PRNT-SCN	COM	704	#221
PRNT-SCN	COM	1408	#222
PRNT-SET	COM	5120	#220
PRNT-SET	COM	5120	#221
PRNT2	BAS	5760	#89
PRNT3	BAS	5608	#89
PRNTCALL	BAS	3072	#66
PRNTGRAF	BAS	640	#191
PRNTIT	PRG	2501	#295
PRNTMENU	WKS	4352	#302
PRNTSAVE	BAS	512	#191
PRNTSCRN	NL	4096	#156
PROB	EXE	51712	#232
PROB	HLP	4180	#232
PROBLEM		1511	#94
PROBLEMS		5160	#268
PRODUCT	BAS	109	#292
PROFEEL		2499	#54
PROFEEL	DOC	4022	#114
PROFILE	BAS	640	#6
PROFILE	BUG	64	#94
PROFILE	MEM	256	#206
PROFILE	MEM	256	#6
PROFILER	BAS	1792	#6
PROFIT	DOC	44909	#289
PROFIT	WKS	18944	#289
PROGHEAD	BAS	1920	#66
PROGRAM	DOC	901	#113
PROGRAM	DOC	5953	#2
PROGRAMN	OTE	27934	#54
PROJECTS	BAS	7808	#143
PROJECTS	DAT	2944	#143
PROKEY	UNP	1536	#238
PROKYTUT	WKS	24576	#257
PROLOG	LSP	4392	#148
PROTECT	BAS	2944	#233
PROTECT	BAT	28	#233
PROTOTYP	AAA	256	#231
PROTOTYP	ASM	256	#231
PROTOTYP	CCC	256	#231
PROTOTYP	FFF	128	#231
PROTOTYP	NCI	256	#231
PROVERB1	BAS	5376	#56
PROWRITE	PRT	565	#78
PRSLASHO	ASM	23440	#285
PRSLASHO	EXE	2176	#285
PRT	BAT	256	#249
PRTCOM1	BAT	128	#86
PRTCOM2	BAT	128	#86
PRTEK912	PRT	559	#78
PRTEXTRA	BAS	640	#215
PRTFIX	COM	128	#33
PRTFIX	DOC	123	#33
PRTGRAF	BAS	1152	#15
PRTLPT1	BAT	128	#86
PRTLPT2	BAT	128	#86
PRTSC_1	ASM	4696	#61
PRTSC_2	ASM	3445	#61
PRTSCFX	ASM	8576	#108
PRTSCFX	COM	4096	#186
PRTSCFX	COM	4096	#108
PRTSCFX	DOC	2944	#186
PRTSCFX	DOC	2944	#108
PRTSCRN	ASM	8448	#135
PRTSCRN	COM	175	#135
PRTSET	BAS	1664	#6
PRTSETUP	VC	2560	#14
PSCREEN	BAS	12597	#59
PSCREEN	EXE	27904	#59
PSQUISH	BAS	4736	#167
PSTYLES	BAS	2816	#11
PT	LSP	4019	#148
PTURTLE	LSP	4096	#134
PUFF	BAS	384	#24
PUNYCALC	BAS	13568	#206
PUNYCALC	DOC	384	#206
PUPGRADE	NL	2048	#157
PURGE	COM	1152	#184
PURGE	DOC	3712	#184
PURGEDUP	COM	10313	#255
PURGEDUP	DOC	1160	#255
PUTC	DCL	44	#132
PUTC	OBJ	582	#132
PUTCF	DCL	60	#132

PUTCF	OBJ	623	#132
PUTDEC	DCL	47	#132
PUTDEC	OBJ	536	#132
PUTNAMHL	MUT	3200	#40
PUTSTR	DCL	62	#132
PUTSTR	OBJ	436	#132
PV------	APL	6016	#109
PVA	WKS	3840	#304
PVTAX	BAS	640	#29
PX	COM	22912	#255
PX	DOC	14588	#255
PYRAMID		256	#73
PYRAMID	EXE	34176	#293

Q

Q	BAS	384	#9
Q_CMDS	INC	3154	#82
QA1	WKS	3200	#304
QAM	WKS	5888	#304
QD	COM	2176	#33
QD	DOC	4992	#33
QD	EXE	2816	#79
QDCOPY	DOC	896	#92
QDISPLAY	INC	1422	#82
QDXT	EXE	2688	#79
QGETKEY	INC	2972	#82
QGN	WKS	20736	#304
QM	EXE	2816	#79
QMXT	EXE	2816	#79
QNAVEE	COM	1093	#279
QNAVEE	MUS	535	#279
QPRINT	ASM	4933	#84
QPRINT	ASM	6555	#285
QPRINT	BAS	994	#84
QPRINT	BIN	105	#84
QPRINT	OBJ	256	#258
QPRINT	OBJ	304	#285
QR	KEY	241	#59
QS	RIO	270	#256
QS	TXT	3403	#256
QSORT	BAS	2560	#11
QSPOOL	COM	846	#79
QSWAP	COM	281	#79
QTR2G	BAR	384	#14
QUADRAM	DOC	1609	#79
QUADRIVE	DOC	5868	#48
QUERY	ASM	674	#195
QUERY	ASM	7084	#82
QUERY	BAS	1927	#195
QUERY	COM	138	#195
QUERY	COM	360	#82
QUEST	BAS	13440	#76
QUEST	NL	2048	#200
QUESTION		5600	#268
QUICKBOX	CLR	3712	#66
QUICKREF	BAS	13568	#59
QUICKREF	DOC	13765	#59
QUICKS	ME	960	#78
QUICKSRT	BAS	1152	#53
QUIET	DOC	2515	#238
QUILT	PIC	16512	#12
QUMESP20	PRT	546	#78
QWERTY		804	#46
QWERTY	BAT	14	#46
QWERTY	COM	24	#46

R

R1	BAS	768	#27
R2	BAS	768	#27
R3	BAS	768	#27
R4	BAS	768	#27
R5	BAS	768	#27
RACE	BAS	3712	#92
RACECAR	BAS	15104	#174
RACJAM	SCO	268	#24
RACKET	BBS	14431	#125
RAIL	BUG	2826	#94
RAM	A	4492	#283
RAM	DOC	1438	#283
RAM	SYS	512	#283
RAMDISK	ASM	10368	#51
RAMDISK	COM	672	#172
RAMDISK	DOC	716	#172
RAMDISK	DOC	759	#110
RAMDISK	SYS	768	#110
RAMDSK16	COM	672	#184
RAMDSK18	COM	672	#184
RAMDSK32	COM	672	#184
RAMDSK36	COM	672	#184
RANDOMIZ	BAS	3456	#88
RANDSEED	BAS	1792	#66
RANGERD	BAS	1280	#24
RANKTEST	BAS	6528	#88
RAR	WKS	7424	#304
RATBAS	TXT	30080	#3
RATBAS	UM	9856	#3
RATEADJ	BAS	3072	#88
RATIO	WKS	24064	#301
RBASE	UNP	2688	#238
RBBS-PC	BAS	51755	#152
RBBS-PC	BQS	45719	#212
RBBS-PC	DEF	1152	#212
RBBS-PC	DOC	74313	#152
RBBS-PC	DQC	67519	#212
RBBS-PC	EXE	108928	#212
RBBS-PC	EXE	109952	#152
RBBS-PC	REM	5877	#152
RBBS-PC	REM	5877	#212
RBBSUTIL	BAS	9166	#150
RBBSUTIL	EXE	33920	#150
RDTH		14848	#192
RE-VIEW	COM	1280	#138
RE-VIEW	DOC	12160	#138
READ	BAT	90	#295
READ	ME	many	
READ	ME	256	#250
READ	ME	679	#267
READ	ME	768	#112
READ	ME	768	#170
READ	ME	849	#109
READ	ME	959	#232
READ	ME	983	#78
READ	ME	1029	#127
READ	ME	1098	#129
READ	ME	1243	#214
READ	ME	1296	#298
READ	ME	2213	#268
READ	ME	2578	#294
READ	ME	2678	#113
READ	ME	2988	#215
READ	ME	4381	#162
READ	ME	7106	#194
READ	ME	9149	#286
READ	ME!	4291	#278
READ	TXT	1277	#295
READ	TXT	2203	#294
READ-ME	DOC	768	#218
READ1	TXT	1168	#295
READ_ME		1294	#68
READ_ME	DOC	917	#233
READC	C	785	#216
READCHAR	ASM	1994	#223
READCHAR	DOC	901	#223
READCHAR	OBJ	130	#223
READDOC	BAT	60	#279
READING	BAS	1536	#18
READISCO	PE	13126	#160
README		many	
README		330	#153
README		503	#146
README		720	#253
README		1408	#151
README		3200	#236
README	###	2792	#279
README	056	5621	#202
README	1ST	647	#119
README	1ST	2372	#284
README	1ST	15115	#289
README	BAK	220	#98
README	BAS	4736	#283
README	BAT	157	#257
README	BAT	186	#232
README	CUB	1024	#300
README	DOC	786	#228
README	DOC	961	#290
README	DOC	1544	#120
README	DOC	2069	#241
README	DOC	2231	#235
README	DOC	2338	#216
README	INV	1024	#300
README	NOW	2669	#133
README	PRN	3584	#280

README	TXT	680	#101
README	TXT	1152	#251
README	TXT	1785	#148
README	TXT	3712	#283
README	TXT	5109	#285
README1		710	#130
README2		166	#131
README2	004	2697	#4
README3		317	#132
READS	C	1978	#216
READTHIS	1ST	3273	#279
READTHIS	NOW	2669	#133
REAL$	BAS	1664	#9
REAL1		128	#215
REAL3		128	#215
REALTIME		128	#215
REALTIME		128	#268
REBOOT	ASM	384	#50
REBOOT	COM	19	#50
REBOOT	EXE	640	#50
RECAP	BAS	9344	#23
RECIEABL		248	#215
RECIMEDS	RPT	128	#281
RECLONGP	RPT	128	#281
RECORD	COM	8938	#235
RECORDD	BAS	3968	#23
RECORDP	BAS	4224	#23
RECSHORT	RPT	128	#281
RECTJRNL	WKS	21248	#165
RED	ASM	9750	#299
RED	COM	1071	#299
RED	LST	24115	#299
REDIAL	WRK	2176	#305
REFCARD	DOC	4098	#230
REFCD	DOC	11266	#256
REFDEX	NDX	1024	#126
REFER	DOC	59903	#230
REFERALS	DBF	1024	#126
REFERENC	BAS	18104	#90
REFLIST	DOC	32421	#231
REFLIST	EXE	24064	#231
REFORM	BAS	7217	#299
REFS	PRG	512	#126
REFYR	BIN	56	#266
REGDISP	ASM	5376	#109
REGFORM	DOC	985	#78
REGIS	DOC	1280	#282
REGRESS	BAS	768	#29
REGRESS	BAS	1536	#67
REGRESS	BAS	4736	#180
REL1_5		3	#246
RELSE-2	0	40	#276
REM	BAS	33920	#268
REMARKS1	BAS	19200	#215
REMARKS2	BAS	28672	#215
REMARKS3	BAS	11392	#215
REMARKS4	BAS	28288	#215
REMARKST	BAS	10368	#267
REMCACC	BAS	8192	#62
REMOVE	BAS	1280	#16
REMOVE	DCL	51	#132
REMOVE	OBJ	628	#132
REMREM	BAS	517	#167
RENTAL	WKS	4736	#302
RENUMEMB	BAS	2048	#169
REORMAIL	BAS	1536	#169
REPEAT	BAS	512	#105
REPLY	ASM	1902	#223
REPLY	COM	54	#223
REPLY	EXE	640	#223
REPORT	EXE	79104	#287
REPORT	NL	4096	#200
REPORTME	PRG	2304	#102
REPORTS	BAS	10496	#25
RESCMD	BAS	2688	#28
RESCMD	BAS	3072	#183
RESCMD	DOC	4386	#28
RESCMD	DOC	5120	#183
RESCMDCK	BAS	5504	#28
RESET	BAT	408	#276
RESET	COM	19	#186
RESPOND	ASM	2170	#223
RESPOND	DOC	404	#223
RESPOND	OBJ	129	#223
RESPONSE		5632	#199
RESTATTR	BAS	1024	#46
RESWORDS	TXT	285	#217
REVERSE	BAS	1920	#45
REVHDR	PRG	1152	#102
REVIEW	PRG	8704	#102
REVMRGN	PRG	512	#102
REVUMEMB	BAS	1408	#169
RHMLINE	BAS	3712	#49
RICE	NL	5120	#200
RICHTER	NL	5120	#156
RING	BAS	2056	#258
RINGBACK	MRG	512	#212
RKF45	C	8070	#194
RKF45	DCL	1537	#194
RKF45	H	388	#194
RKF45	PAS	10484	#194
RKTYTKTY	BSV	484	#279
RKTYTKTY	COM	835	#279
RKTYTKTY	MUS	325	#279
RKTYTKTY	TRB	477	#279
RM	BAT	72	#216
RM18	ASM	17152	#184
RM2		3200	#192
RMSPC	ASM	26880	#138
RMSPC	COM	1458	#138
ROADRALY	BAS	6272	#72
ROCKET	BAS	202	#292
ROCKET	BAS	2688	#44
ROD	BAS	768	#79
ROFF	DOC	7176	#50
ROFF	EXE	18688	#50
ROFF	EXE	21882	#194
ROFF	H	3134	#50
ROFF	HE	3456	#50
ROFF1	C	11192	#50
ROFF2	C	9422	#50
ROFF3	C	302	#50
ROFF3	C	1144	#194
ROHDE	NL	5120	#157
ROMBIOS	ASM	9856	#110
ROMCHAR	BAS	1024	#37
ROMREAD	BAS	856	#183
ROMREAD	DOC	512	#183
ROOM	NAM	832	#296
ROR	DOC	27055	#289
ROR	WKS	14976	#289
ROSE	NL	3072	#200
ROSTERS	PRG	3328	#300
ROULET	WRK	3072	#305
ROULETTE	BAS	1792	#55
ROULETTE	BAS	5504	#44
ROUNDER	BAS	519	#176
ROUNDER1	BAS	666	#176
ROUNDER2	BAS	936	#176
ROUNDER3	BAS	1867	#176
ROUNDER4	BAS	1149	#176
ROWCOL	BAS	640	#170
ROXANN	NUD	7808	#154
RPNC	HLP	522	#232
RPRTHED		5376	#192
RRSKFCT		384	#192
RSMOHED		1280	#192
RSVD	COM	19328	#145
RT	EXE	35456	#3
RT	UM	3328	#3
RTOP12		7424	#192
RUBIC	BAS	8960	#48
RUBIC3	BAS	8960	#92
RUBIK	BAS	28928	#72
RULER	DEF	83	#78
RUN	BAT	128	#19
RUN	BAT	1797	#113
RUNCOLOR	BAT	53	#13
RUNFIRST	BAS	1291	#90
RUNME	BAT	2333	#82
RUNOFF	BAS	14336	#48
RUNOFF	RNO	15616	#48
RUSQ	EXE	16512	#143
RV-EDIT	BAS	8960	#19
RV-EDIT	BAS	12416	#190
RV-EDIT	DOC	10335	#190
RV-EDIT	DOC	10368	#19
RWTTAB		1152	#192

S

S	BAR	256	#14
S-AIRLIN		4224	#97
S-BARTER		3712	#97

S-BBS		49024	#99	SAMP1	TXT	1931	#113	SCHD1		6710	#291
S-CHAT		2560	#96	SAMP2	TXT	1931	#113	SCHE		13900	#291
S-DADATE		6784	#97	SAMPDRAW	BAS	384	#191	SCHEDULE	BAS	2304	#23
S-INFO	SIG	13696	#96	SAMPLE		384	#233	SCHF		13223	#291
S-INFOX		6016	#97	SAMPLE	BAS	384	#269	SCHG		20585	#291
S-INTRO	ED	27648	#96	SAMPLE	BAS	2873	#5	SCHIEVE	NL	6144	#158
S-LAWYER		2944	#97	SAMPLE	CFG	137	#119	SCHK1		5931	#291
S-LBRARY		6656	#96	SAMPLE	DAT	7040	#119	SCHNELL	NL	7168	#157
S-MAIL		13312	#96	SAMPLE	HFA	384	#282	SCHNELL1	NL	6144	#157
S-MGRAM		11520	#96	SAMPLE	KEY	472	#112	SCHR		14675	#291
S-MOBIL		3200	#97	SAMPLE	MSG	1792	#112	SCHROE	DER	3328	#92
S-MODEL1		7296	#97	SAMPLE	NUM	128	#119	SCHROE	DER	3328	#154
S-MUSES		5120	#97	SAMPLE	PAS	4822	#30	SCHSE		5613	#291
S-PHONE	NOS	65408	#98	SAMPLE	TPN	300	#155	SCHW		2879	#291
S-POST		10752	#96	SAMPLE	TWD	3187	#66	SCHWABCM	BAS	3072	#40
S-PUBLIC	CAT	1536	#97	SAMPLE	TXT	1408	#86	SCIENCE	EXE	39808	#249
S-PUBLSH		8704	#96	SAMPLE	WKS	114048	#64	SCISUBV1	BAS	35840	#67
S-STOCK		10368	#97	SAMPLE	WKS	114048	#64	SCN	C	14991	#147
S-STORE		7168	#97	SAMPLE1	3X5	19456	#253	SCN	OBJ	5993	#147
S-TRAVEL		2944	#97	SAMPLE1	COD	2048	#112	SCN-DEMO	BAS	4430	#221
S-USERS	IBM	27392	#96	SAMPLE1	MAP	3072	#253	SCN-DEMO	BAS	4444	#222
S-WINE		7296	#97	SAMPLE1	NDX	640	#119	SCN-DEMO	BAS	4480	#220
S-XWORDS		20096	#97	SAMPLE2	3X5	5888	#253	SCNMAP	BAS	5888	#81
S1	BAS	640	#180	SAMPLE2	COD	1792	#112	SCNMAP	DOC	6315	#81
S1	BAS	1024	#27	SAMPLE2	MAP	1024	#253	SCONTROL	H	1930	#216
S10	BAS	1280	#180	SAMPLE3	COD	2560	#112	SCOPE	BAS	4736	#20
S11	BAS	768	#180	SAMPLE3	MAP	2048	#253	SCOPY	DCL	98	#132
S12	BAS	512	#180	SAMPLE3	WP	8369	#253	SCOPY	OBJ	431	#132
S13	BAS	1664	#180	SAMPLE4	MAP	1024	#253	SCORES	BAS	8704	#23
S14	BAS	896	#180	SAMPLE4	WS	2048	#253	SCR10	DOC	1920	#179
S15	BAS	1536	#180	SAMPLEA		512	#233	SCR11	DOC	1920	#179
S16	BAS	896	#180	SAMPLES	BAS	128	#1	SCR12	DOC	1920	#179
S17	BAS	896	#180	SAMPLEX		1408	#233	SCR13	DOC	1920	#179
S18	BAS	768	#180	SAMPLEY		2048	#233	SCR14	DOC	1920	#179
S2	BAS	1024	#27	SAMPLSIZ	BAS	3456	#88	SCR15	DOC	1920	#179
S2	BAS	1664	#180	SANTA	BAS	6400	#154	SCR16	DOC	1920	#179
S3	BAS	640	#180	SATURN	BAS	512	#11	SCR17	DOC	1920	#179
S3	BAS	1024	#27	SATURN	BAS	768	#4	SCR18	DOC	1920	#179
S4	BAS	640	#180	SAV1		128	#95	SCR19	DOC	1920	#179
S4	BAS	1152	#27	SAV2		128	#95	SCR2	DOC	1920	#179
S5	BAS	384	#180	SAV3		128	#95	SCR20	DOC	1920	#179
S5	BAS	1280	#27	SAV4		128	#95	SCR21	DOC	1920	#179
S6	BAS	640	#180	SAV5		128	#95	SCR22	DOC	1920	#179
S6	BAS	1024	#27	SAV6		128	#95	SCR23	DOC	1920	#179
S7	BAS	640	#180	SAVE	COM	512	#256	SCR24	DOC	1920	#179
S7	BAS	896	#27	SAVEGRAF	BAS	1280	#191	SCR25	DOC	1920	#179
S8	BAS	1408	#180	SAVINGS	BAS	3200	#66	SCR26	DOC	1920	#179
S9	BAS	768	#180	SB	DOC	30189	#162	SCR27	DOC	1920	#179
SAILBOAT	BAS	306	#292	SB	EXE	28416	#162	SCR3	DOC	1920	#179
SAINTS	BAS	175	#292	SCAN	BAS	31232	#214	SCR4	DOC	1920	#179
SALECOST	PRG	1330	#295	SCAN	EXE	80768	#268	SCR5	DOC	1920	#179
SALESTAX	MEM	512	#295	SCATRGRM	BAS	5632	#88	SCR6	DOC	1920	#179
SALESTAX	PRG	4992	#102	SCAV2XX	ASM	8192	#135	SCR7	DOC	1920	#179
SALETAX	PRG	1083	#295	SCAV2XX	COM	17557	#135	SCR8	DOC	1920	#179
SAMECHK	BAS	774	#277	SCHA		4974	#291	SCR9	DOC	1920	#179
SAMECHK	EXE	19456	#277	SCHB		4677	#291	SCRAMBLE	BAS	3968	#37
SAMECHK	LIB	1920	#277	SCHC		7254	#291	SCRATT	C	2520	#216
SAMENAME	BAS	448	#250	SCHD		13810	#291	SCREEN	ASM	2636	#15

SCREEN	ASM	8810	#218	SCROLL	BAS	2464	#115	SEC8	PIC	4608	#156
SCREEN	BAS	1920	#4	SCROLL	BLD	128	#33	SEC9	PIC	2944	#156
SCREEN	BAS	3669	#255	SCROLL	DOC	4752	#33	SECOND		256	#215
SCREEN	BAS	3712	#156	SCROLL	SUB	1536	#53	SECRETNO	BAS	2071	#35
SCREEN	COM	1658	#218	SCROLL1	BAS	1284	#33	SECURITY	FRM	512	#295
SCREEN	DOC	3628	#255	SCROLL1	ML	128	#260	SEESWTCH	BAS	4096	#53
SCREEN	EXE	1280	#15	SCROLL2	BAS	1673	#33	SEIV	DOC	11302	#238
SCREEN	EXE	2432	#218	SCROLLK	BAS	2860	#38	SEL	C	21233	#147
SCREEN	EXE	75264	#86	SCROLLK	COM	251	#144	SEL	OBJ	5438	#147
SCREEN	INC	2233	#162	SCROLLK	COM	251	#186	SELECT	BAS	6656	#88
SCREEN	LST	28826	#218	SCROLLK	COM	251	#38	SELLERS		81	#173
SCREEN	PAS	1152	#36	SCROLLK	DOC	372	#144	SERIAL	ASM	4563	#258
SCREEN	TXT	124544	#86	SCROLLK	DOC	372	#186	SERIAL	BAS	3328	#48
SCREEN1		384	#215	SCTEST		128	#215	SERIAL	COM	1113	#258
SCREEN1	BAS	16512	#219	SCTEST		128	#268	SERIAL	DOC	2193	#258
SCREEN1	PRN	1625	#257	SD	COM	1505	#28	SERIALNO	BAS	7552	#73
SCREEN14		512	#215	SD20	COM	1408	#80	SERPENT	BAS	2944	#37
SCREEN2		1024	#268	SD20	DOC	419	#80	SESAME	BAS	4096	#55
SCREEN2	BAS	16392	#219	SDB	C	390	#147	SET-PRTR	C	5504	#186
SCREEN2	PRN	1625	#257	SDB	EXE	38528	#147	SET-PRTR	EXE	7296	#186
SCREEN3	BAS	16512	#219	SDB	HLP	1343	#147	SET51LNS	COM	19	#186
SCREEN3	PRN	1625	#257	SDB	MEM	25395	#147	SETANSI	ASM	1818	#223
SCREEN4		256	#215	SDB	OBJ	468	#147	SETANSI	COM	203	#223
SCREEN4	BAS	16512	#219	SDBGEN	ARF	94	#147	SETANSI	EXE	971	#223
SCREEN4	PRN	1570	#257	SDBGEN	BAT	34	#147	SETCOLOR	ASM	3388	#27
SCREEN5	BAS	16512	#219	SDBGREP	BAT	125	#147	SETCOLOR	BAT	49	#13
SCREEN6		128	#215	SDBIO	H	7988	#147	SETCOLOR	COM	112	#27
SCREEN8		256	#215	SDBLUMP	BAT	220	#147	SETCW132	COM	19	#186
SCREENIN	BAS	3712	#141	SDBXC	BAT	103	#147	SETDISK	ASM	14952	#82
SCREENIN	DOC	3772	#141	SDIR	ASM	15872	#50	SETDISK	COM	216	#82
SCREENS		512	#11	SDIR	COM	1280	#2	SETDRIVE	BAS	1408	#101
SCRINIT	C	934	#216	SDIR	COM	1292	#50	SETDRV	BAS	578	#277
SCRIPT	DOC	12397	#258	SDIR	COM	1408	#185	SETDRV	EXE	19072	#277
SCRIPT	DOC	12672	#143	SDIR	COM	3221	#255	SETDRV	LIB	1792	#277
SCRIPT	NL	3072	#156	SDIR	DOC	896	#185	SETKEY	BAS	3911	#172
SCRLDN	ASM	1989	#285	SDIR	DOC	1280	#255	SETKEY	DOC	1707	#172
SCRLDN	OBJ	108	#285	SDIR	EXE	1792	#28	SETP	ASM	3264	#223
SCRLKY	ASM	8192	#186	SDIR1	COM	1555	#224	SETP	EXE	789	#223
SCRLKY	COM	251	#186	SDIR1	DOC	1004	#224	SETP	OBJ	435	#223
SCRLUP	ASM	1981	#285	SDIR22	ASM	23429	#34	SETPRF19	COM	19	#186
SCRLUP	OBJ	108	#285	SDIR22	COM	1312	#34	SETPRINT	PRG	2501	#295
SCRN		49719	#77	SDIR24C	ASM	46848	#185	SETPRN	ASM	4480	#138
SCRN	ASM	4224	#110	SDIR24C	COM	2304	#185	SETPRN	COM	256	#138
SCRN	DOC	3078	#110	SDIR24C	COM	2304	#273	SETPRN	DOC	2816	#138
SCRN	OVL	16384	#243	SDIR24C	DOC	1536	#185	SETPRTR	C	5504	#79
SCRNCOLR	ASM	6945	#255	SDIR24C	DOC	1536	#273	SETPRTR	EXE	7296	#79
SCRNCOLR	COM	236	#255	SEARCH	BAK	570	#300	SETRAM	C	2034	#283
SCRNCOLR	DOC	1056	#255	SEARCH	PRG	376	#300	SETRAM	EXE	2048	#283
SCRNIO	TXT	10938	#285	SEARCH	PRG	1408	#126	SETS	C	1664	#163
SCRNSAVE	ASM	13312	#224	SEAWOLF	BAS	7296	#174	SETUP	BAS	415	#195
SCRNSAVE	BAS	4188	#195	SEC&BYTE	BAS	640	#49	SETUP	BAS	12288	#95
SCRNSAVE	COM	310	#195	SEC0	PIC	3200	#156	SETUP	BAT	33	#266
SCRNSAVE	COM	310	#107	SEC1	PIC	3072	#156	SETUP	BAT	54	#107
SCRNSAVE	COM	384	#144	SEC3	PIC	3584	#156	SETUP	BAT	556	#120
SCRNSAVE	COM	688	#224	SEC4	PIC	2304	#156	SETUP	BAT	559	#257
SCRNSAVE	DOC	1119	#107	SEC5	PIC	2688	#156	SETUP	PRG	520	#295
SCRNSAVE	DOC	2397	#224	SEC6	PIC	2432	#156	SHARP	NL	6144	#200
SCROLL	ASM	3038	#33	SEC7	PIC	2944	#156	SHEEPMAY	SNG	476	#127

SHELL	BAT	509	#33
SHELL	COM	256	#111
SHELL	DOC	4224	#111
SHELLSRT	BAS	640	#14
SHELLSRT	BAS	1408	#53
SHEWALKS	SNG	640	#127
SHIELDS	BAS	128	#53
SHIFT	DEF	507	#78
SHIFTBS	COM	96	#52
SHIFTIBM	COM	16	#52
SHIFTS	BAS	1280	#73
SHIP		1408	#73
SHOP	BAS	7680	#45
SHOP	DBF	1024	#116
SHORCH	MUS	1474	#175
SHORTERM	BAS	16342	#54
SHOW	ASM	38912	#196
SHOW	EXE	21744	#196
SHOWBOX	BAS	1792	#66
SHOWFIL	PRG	384	#126
SHOWMEMO	BAS	4378	#261
SHUTTL	PIC	5504	#154
SIDEWAYS	EXE	30720	#265
SIDEWAYS	PAS	3673	#265
SIDIR	BAT	114	#82
SIMONSEZ	BAS	2963	#260
SIMONSEZ	DOC	1431	#260
SIMPLE	PRT	385	#78
SIREN	BAS	128	#12
SIREN	BAS	256	#53
SIX	DAT	4096	#76
SIXBOXES	BAS	4096	#66
SIZER	ASM	9287	#110
SIZER	COM	257	#110
SIZER	DOC	3200	#110
SK	UNP	2048	#238
SKELETON	BAS	23809	#245
SKELETON	BQS	13907	#133
SKETCH	BAS	3072	#191
SKETCH	BAS	7387	#195
SKETCH	DOC	9088	#195
SKP6PERF	COM	19	#186
SKP8PERF	COM	19	#186
SLASH	ASM	4653	#82
SLASH	COM	171	#82
SLASHO	BAT	580	#285
SLIB	INC	1372	#74
SLIDE	ASM	34816	#196
SLIDE	COM	19067	#196
SLIDE	CTR	128	#244
SLIDE	EXE	42624	#244
SLIDE	MAN	13638	#244
SLIDE	SDE	73472	#244
SLIDEDOC	EXE	24320	#244
SLIMLINE	NL	2048	#156
SLINKY	BUG	768	#94
SLOT	BAS	4811	#228
SLOT	BAS	6016	#44
SLOTCOLR	BAS	9511	#203
SLOTMACH	BAS	4864	#37
SLOTMACH	BAS	9508	#260
SLOTMACH	BAS	12288	#61
SLRYJRNL	WKS	12032	#165
SMADDEL1	BAS	17920	#246
SMADDEL1	HS1	5636	#246
SMALLPR	INT	11	#70
SMALLPRT	BAT	80	#70
SMALLPRT	DOC	664	#70
SMCONFG1	BAS	3712	#246
SMCONFG1	HS1	5728	#246
SMCOVER	DOC	2816	#246
SMENTRY1	BAS	21888	#246
SMENTRY1	HS1	2756	#246
SMENTRY1	HS2	4727	#246
SMGRAPH1	BAS	20608	#246
SMGRAPH1	HS1	2745	#246
SMGRAPH1	HS2	3143	#246
SMGRAPH1	HS3	3836	#246
SMITD100	PRT	535	#78
SMOKE		5120	#192
SMOKWHY2	EXE	54272	#192
SMPLCHK		512	#282
SMPLCODE	CO	384	#282
SMURF	BAS	8830	#208
SMUSERG	DOC	19328	#246
SNOOPY	BAS	2816	#45
SNOOPY	BAS	2816	#154
SNOOPY3	BAS	8832	#154
SNOW1	BAS	128	#11
SNOW2	BAS	128	#11
SNOW3	BAS	128	#11
SNOWFLAK	BUG	384	#94
SOFT82	DTA	22784	#121
SOFT82	HDR	128	#121
SOFT82	INX	1280	#121
SOFT82	KEY	1450	#121
SOFT83	DTA	94208	#122
SOFT83	HDR	128	#122
SOFT83	INX	5120	#122
SOFT83	KEY	5738	#122
SOFTWARE		44	#150
SOLFE	BAS	3869	#80
SOLITAIR	BAS	13312	#203
SOLITARE	BAS	12032	#174
SOLUTION		1280	#268
SOME	DBF	1024	#126
SONGS	BAS	7424	#24
SONGS	BAS	8918	#292
SORCERER	BAS	14723	#292
SORRY	BAS	128	#53
SORT	BAS	1152	#14
SORT	BAS	12032	#267
SORT	BAS	12288	#214
SORT	BLD	512	#206
SORT	DOC	5888	#206
SORT	EXE	29824	#57
SORT	EXE	36096	#26
SORT	EXE	38656	#287
SORT	INC	896	#3
SORT	NL	2048	#157
SORT	PAS	5248	#26
SORT-BLK	BAS	9856	#47
SORTDIF	BAS	7040	#85
SORTED	DBF	1024	#126
SORTEST	BAS	6962	#206
SORTF	AR	13380	#132
SORTF	EXE	32384	#131
SORTF	MAN	678	#130
SORTFILE	BAS	2944	#23
SORTINT	BAS	11648	#267
SORTREDI	NL	2048	#157
SORTS	BAS	4864	#81
SORTS	DOC	1512	#81
SORTSTR	BAS	11392	#267
SORTTREE	BAT	605	#250
SOUND1	BAS	128	#53
SOUNDEMO	BAS	4028	#92
SOUNDS	BAS	4736	#33
SOUNDS	BUG	1982	#94
SP	DOC	8966	#186
SP	DOC	8966	#273
SP	EXE	2304	#186
SP	EXE	2304	#273
SP	SHR	2864	#232
SPACER	TXT	4480	#305
SPACEVAD	EXE	9216	#176
SPACEVAD	EXE	9216	#274
SPACEWAR	DOC	4808	#292
SPC	EXE	2304	#186
SPEC-OCC	BAS	10881	#182
SPEC-OCC	DOC	915	#182
SPECCOPY	BAT	413	#246
SPECIAL	DOC	2042	#78
SPEECH	BAS	3968	#56
SPEED	ASM	1480	#255
SPEED	COM	23	#255
SPEED411	COM	15	#28
SPEEDUP	BAS	512	#11
SPEEDUP	COM	128	#11
SPEEDUP2	DOC	2816	#184
SPELL	BAS	7978	#168
SPELL1	DAT	4253	#168
SPELL2	DAT	2299	#168
SPELL3	DAT	6168	#168
SPELL4	DAT	7811	#168
SPELLBEE	BAS	3968	#168
SPELLDAT	BAS	384	#168
SPELLER	BAS	3328	#71
SPELLER	BAS	3328	#72
SPIN3510	PRT	477	#78
SPIN3550	PRT	503	#78
SPIN5530	PRT	486	#78
SPINOUT	BAS	3968	#37
SPINOUT	BAS	4864	#49

SPINSQ	BUG	256	#94
SPIRO	BAS	1505	#265
SPIRO	BUG	384	#94
SPIRO	DOC	9216	#265
SPIRO	EXE	22548	#265
SPIRO1	EXE	23680	#265
SPLITA	BAT	1165	#160
SPLITB	BAT	848	#161
SPONSORS	TXT	1695	#159
SPONSORS	TXT	2220	#160
SPOOL	EXE	2176	#266
SPOOLBAS	BAS	1536	#38
SPOOLER	DOC	958	#38
SPOOLER1	COM	768	#38
SPOOLER2	COM	896	#38
SPPC	EXE	34304	#232
SPPC	HLP	8807	#232
SPRITE	BAS	2868	#238
SPRITE	COM	21142	#238
SPRITE	DOC	3064	#238
SPRITE	SAV	16128	#238
SPSCN	C	1280	#163
SPSCN	DOC	1280	#163
SPSCN	EXE	6144	#163
SPSHIPS	BAS	768	#14
SQ	C	28246	#161
SQ	EXE	17024	#161
SQ-USQ	DOC	5504	#140
SQIBM	COM	14336	#144
SQIBM	COM	14336	#145
SQIBM	COM	14336	#185
SQIBM	DOC	768	#144
SQIBM	DOC	768	#145
SQIBM	DOC	768	#185
SQPC161	EXE	21376	#140
SQUARE	BAS	132	#176
SQUARE	BAS	6400	#45
SQUARE	BAS	17664	#92
SQUARE	BUG	332	#94
SQUARE	DOC	12672	#92
SQUARE	SUM	4608	#92
SQUEEZE	EXE	18432	#115
SQUISH	BAS	6400	#9
SQUISH	DOC	5541	#28
SQUISH	DOC	5566	#9
SQUISH	EXE	28416	#28
SQUISH	SRC	7175	#28
SQUSQ	DOC	3162	#115
SR	BAS	44416	#211
SREED550	PRT	531	#78
SREGR	DOC	33180	#289
SREGR	WKS	12032	#289
SRS	BAS	128	#53
SRT	C	8623	#147
SRT	OBJ	2654	#147
SRTLAB	EXE	2944	#261
SS	BAR	384	#14
SS	BAS	28672	#267
SS	EXE	64384	#267
SSREMARK	BAS	32640	#267
SSS	BAR	384	#14
SSSSS	BAR	256	#14
SSSSSS	BAR	256	#14
ST	ARF	36	#242
ST	COM	14336	#111
ST	COM	14336	#273
ST	DOC	1152	#111
ST	DOC	1152	#273
ST	EXE	98048	#242
ST	HLP	18432	#242
ST	SPC	151	#242
STAR1015	PRT	508	#78
STAR3D	DOC	1024	#178
STAR3D	EXE	2560	#178
STARLANE	BAS	15104	#6
STARMAP	BAS	5865	#83
STARS	BAS	201	#292
STARS	BAS	2663	#35
START	BAS	256	#15
START	BAS	384	#11
START	BAS	2048	#171
START	BAT	32	#250
START	BAT	87	#68
START	BAT	128	#26
START	EXE	32896	#276
START	TXT	1548	#276
START	TXT	1783	#250
STARTREK	BAS	14208	#13
STARTREK	BAS	14208	#16
STARTREK	BAS	14208	#17
STARTREK	BAS	23040	#71
STARTREK	BAS	25600	#2
STARTREK	BAS	25728	#178
STARTREK	BAS	45312	#44
STARTREK	DOC	2400	#71
STARTREK	DUM	128	#13
STARTREK	DUM	128	#16
STARTREK	DUM	6144	#17
STARTREK	EXE	61824	#178
STARTREK	HOW	6144	#13
STARTREK	HOW	6144	#16
STARTRK2	BAS	6144	#17
STARTUP	BAS	384	#27
STARTUP	BAS	6237	#66
STARTUP	BAT	62	#9
STARTUP	BAT	1669	#152
STARTUP	CLR	6332	#66
STARWARS	BAS	512	#55
STARWARS	BAS	4224	#23
STARWRIT	PRT	541	#78
STAT	BAS	896	#180
STATCAPS	BAS	17664	#61
STATES84	WKS	112000	#290
STATEX	NDX	1024	#126
STATEZIP	DBF	1024	#126
STATEZIP	PRG	3328	#126
STATFILE	BAS	768	#182
STATION	BAS	310	#292
STATMAIL	BAS	768	#169
STATMEMB	BAS	384	#169
STATS		0	#61
STATS	BAK	2689	#300
STATS	PRG	2688	#300
STATUS	LST	5470	#94
STC	WKS	9728	#304
STDIO	H	896	#259
STEEPDES	APL	9856	#110
STEEPDES	APL	9856	#134
STERILE	PRG	268	#300
STICK	BAS	384	#6
STKANAL	DOC	3200	#282
STKANALY	SIS	12160	#282
STL-BBS1		12969	#97
STL-BBS1	INS	12544	#97
STL-BBS1	NOS	6784	#97
STL-BBS2		3968	#97
STLOUIS	BBS	23808	#92
STOCK		312	#215
STOCKS	DBF	1024	#295
STOKLIST	FRM	442	#295
STOPGAP	BAS	8064	#167
STORY	BAS	5666	#35
STORY	BAS	5666	#168
STRIKE9	BAS	2100	#35
STRINGS	BAS	512	#1
STRINGS	DBF	1024	#126
STRUCT	MAC	3072	#109
STUDENT	BAT	15	#43
SUBDEMO	BAS	21504	#285
SUBDEMO	EXE	37402	#285
SUBDEX	NDX	1024	#126
SUBGRAPH	BAS	10373	#195
SUBJECTS	DBF	1024	#126
SUBMIT	DOC	1166	#244
SUBS	PRG	384	#126
SUBTRACT	BAS	177	#292
SUMMARY		256	#150
SUMSTAT	EXE	50176	#232
SUMSTAT	HLP	700	#232
SUPERBAK	PRG	2944	#126
SUPERDIR	BAS	5376	#217
SUPERDIR	DOC	3712	#217
SUPPLIER	DBF	1024	#102
SUPPLIER	NDX	1024	#102
SUPPORT	NL	8192	#156
SUPRTREK	BAS	25600	#16
SURF87	DOC	4358	#115
SURF87	EXE	8576	#115
SURFPR	BAS	10615	#115
SURROUND	BAS	4864	#37
SURVIVAL	BAS	12672	#203
SURVIVAL	BAS	19200	#17
SURVIVAL	BAS	19328	#4
SUSAN	NUD	9216	#154

SW-PEG	BAS	6784	#92
SWARMS	BAS	13056	#45
SWC	EXE	22528	#292
SWELLING	BAS	155	#292
SWH	EXE	25088	#292
SWIMMER	BAS	1125	#292
SWIRL	BAS	300	#176
SWL1084	LQR	12878	#280
SWLBIBL	LQR	2916	#280
SWLDOC	PRN	2304	#280
SYM102	TXT	7424	#305
SYMQ&A	TXT	12514	#305
SYNC	WRK	1280	#305
SYNCLOCK	COM	1045	#279
SYNCLOCK	MUS	505	#279
SYNONYM	BAS	3840	#18
SYNONYM2	BAS	2048	#18
SYNONYMS	BAS	6400	#45
SYS	BAS	384	#9
SYSCOM	INC	2048	#135
SYSERR	APP	2048	#306
SYSINFO	SYS	512	#192
SYSMENU	COM	11631	#250
SYSMENU	DOC	6912	#250
SYSMENU	PAS	6404	#250
SYSTAB		501	#192
SYSTAT	COM	1408	#2
SYSTAT	COM	1408	#28
SYSTAT	DOC	1050	#28
SYSTEM	BAT	128	#19

T

T-ROAD	BAS	17481	#228
T-TEST	BAS	3712	#88
T86	BAT	109	#161
T86D	EXE	52736	#161
T86TXT1	TXT	1094	#161
T86TXT2	TXT	1153	#161
TABLE	BAS	5504	#233
TABLEOFC	BAS	11779	#90
TABLET	BAS	7424	#50
TABLET	BAS	9216	#110
TABS	ASM	11307	#256
TABS	BAS	3840	#145
TABS	DOC	1158	#256
TABS	EXE	2048	#256
TABSET1	PAS	2560	#36
TABSET2	PAS	2944	#36
TADAA	BAS	128	#53
TADADADA	BAS	128	#53
TAG	COM	30365	#243
TAG	HLP	16896	#243
TAG	PRN	46192	#243
TAGINST	BAT	690	#243
TAINCOST	FRM	261	#295
TAINCOST	PRG	705	#295
TALK	ASM	11219	#258
TALK	DOC	224	#258
TALK	EXE	896	#258
TALK450	DOC	7424	#144
TALK450	DOC	7424	#187
TALK450	MRG	1024	#144
TALK450	MRG	1024	#187
TALLY160	PRT	611	#78
TAMCHN0	EXE	4864	#251
TAMCHN1	EXE	37248	#251
TAMCHN2	EXE	20224	#251
TAMCHN3	EXE	19456	#251
TAMCHN4	EXE	24192	#251
TAMCHN5	EXE	36992	#251
TAMCHN6	EXE	11776	#251
TAMCHN7	EXE	30080	#251
TAMCHN8	EXE	32640	#251
TAMSTART	EXE	6784	#251
TANDT	PIC	2048	#157
TANDT	PIC	2198	#158
TANDT	PIC	2304	#200
TANK	BAS	7808	#93
TARGET	BAS	4434	#83
TARGET	DOC	272	#83
TARGET	PIC	1024	#83
TASKLIST	BAS	4224	#66
TASKPLAN	BAS	22057	#155
TAX		3328	#267
TAX1982	VC	42624	#107
TAX1984	DOC	3983	#303
TAX1984	WKS	37888	#303
TAXCOST	PRG	1536	#295
TAXDATA	MEM	512	#295
TAXES	PRG	1324	#295
TAXFILE	DBF	1024	#295
TAXLIST	FRM	512	#295
TAXMAN	BAS	3584	#45
TAXPAID	FRM	512	#295
TAXPLAN	WKS	13952	#302
TAXRETRN	VC	24320	#23
TAXSCH		1312	#215
TBBS-NOS		6784	#99
TBL	C	2670	#147
TBL	OBJ	1283	#147
TCLOCK	BAS	25221	#182
TDATA		128	#95
TECH	CLR	128	#189
TECH	EXE	64000	#189
TECH	KEY	1133	#189
TECH	MNL	40960	#189
TECHNCAL	DOC	1720	#279
TED	AR	35948	#132
TED	EXE	41088	#131
TED	MAN	3856	#130
TELE	BAT	785	#124
TELE	BAT	896	#139
TELLTIME	BAS	2304	#168
TEMP	BAS	512	#215
TEMP	BAS	512	#268
TEMP	SPC	109	#195
TEMPCONV	BAS	2176	#73
TEMPGRAF	BAS	16512	#191
TEMPLE	KEY	290	#59
TEMPLE	KEY	290	#170
TERM	BAS	5686	#114
TERM	DOC	2140	#114
TEST		812	#215
TEST		896	#268
TEST	ATR	1653	#133
TEST	BAS	128	#15
TEST	BAS	5632	#3
TEST	HDR	128	#133
TEST	KEY	1726	#181
TEST	PRN	1122	#280
TEST	RAT	2304	#3
TEST	SUB	128	#102
TEST	WKS	10112	#289
TESTASCI	BAS	128	#214
TESTDATA	ACC	1280	#62
TESTDATA	DTA	242	#195
TESTERR	BAT	710	#82
TESTF	BAT	1179	#82
TESTFILE		256	#90
TESTFIND	BAT	444	#82
TESTIPUT		168	#215
TESTPLAY	BAS	1158	#279
TESTPLAY	PAS	1658	#279
TESTPRNT	BAS	256	#191
TESTQ	BAT	286	#82
TESTSCRN	BAS	16512	#11
TESTSET	BAT	453	#82
TESTTAB	PAS	1004	#158
TESTTWO		176	#215
TESTWRIT	DOC	1347	#66
TEXT	ONE	1280	#146
TEXT	TWO	1152	#146
TEXTCHAR		2304	#69
TEXTDEMO	WKS	6016	#301
TEXTTOOL	DOC	1845	#89
TF1		144	#60
TF2		116	#60
TFER		256	#215
THING	PLT	3624	#265
THINKING	TXT	5426	#159
THOMAS	NL	2048	#200
THREE	DAT	4608	#76
TICCLOCK	BAS	11008	#50
TICKTOCK	BAS	128	#14
TICTACTO	BAS	3200	#24
TICTACTO	BAS	22528	#72
TIME	BAS	640	#9
TIME	BAS	640	#182
TIME	PRG	512	#128
TIMECALC	PRG	3200	#102
TIMED	TXT	2218	#211
TIMEDEMO	BAS	14295	#285
TIMEPRIN	FIL	896	#285

TIMER		3969	#238
TIMER	EXE	1408	#255
TIMESHOW	BAS	2304	#66
TIMI	PAS	512	#36
TIMING	BAS	384	#28
TIMM	PAS	1152	#36
TIMU	PAS	1792	#36
TINST855	PRT	648	#78
TITLE	BAS	309	#241
TITLE	MAC	699	#202
TITLE2	BAS	85	#241
TITLES		1148	#192
TKSOLVER	UNP	5632	#238
TM-BREAK	BAS	768	#67
TM-DIAL2	BAS	1536	#67
TM-LDIR1	BAS	1408	#67
TM-TIME1	BAS	1152	#67
TMDAY	BAS	6400	#51
TMUS64	EXE	26112	#127
TOC	TXT	7581	#160
TODD	NL	3072	#156
TOOLS	BUG	628	#94
TOOLS	MAN	5383	#130
TOPOFORM	COM	19	#186
TORPEDOB	BAS	128	#53
TOSH1350	PRT	662	#78
TPNCALC	EXE	84608	#234
TPNDOC		14181	#234
TRACE	LSP	768	#148
TRACK	BAS	1808	#292
TRADE	BAS	12800	#45
TRADENET		31104	#180
TRADER	BAS	13056	#100
TRADER	PRN	112174	#242
TRAILER	BAS	384	#203
TRAN	C	1024	#142
TRANDUMP	BAS	1280	#11
TRANDUMP	BAS	1408	#167
TRANFILE	MEM	512	#295
TRANS		6144	#251
TRANS315	PRT	757	#78
TRANSFER	BAS	384	#19
TRANSFER	BAS	17536	#214
TRANSFER	BAT	87	#68
TRANSFER	BAT	689	#40
TRANSIT	BAS	5120	#233
TRANSLIT	AR	3498	#132
TRANSLIT	C	1536	#163
TRANSLIT	DOC	3456	#163
TRANSLIT	EXE	7168	#163
TRANSLIT	EXE	28416	#131
TRANSLIT	EXE	30208	#57
TRANSLIT	MAN	1721	#130
TRAP	BAS	1152	#35
TRAVEL	DBF	1536	#295
TREASURY	BAS	1536	#29
TREES	BUG	479	#94
TREK	BAS	17152	#27
TREKINFO	DOC	7168	#44
TREKPIK	EXE	50048	#197
TREKRUN	EXE	70784	#197
TREND123	DOC	3250	#114
TREND123	DOC	3250	#207
TREND123	DOC	3328	#302
TREND123	MAC	4224	#114
TREND123	MAC	4224	#207
TREND123	WKS	4224	#302
TRIANGLE	BAS	272	#176
TRONLC	BAS	4480	#260
TRONLC	EXE	26864	#260
TRS2PC	BAS	9728	#167
TRUCKER	BAS	17024	#18
TRUMPET	BAS	1536	#203
TRUST		13707	#193
TRUTH	H	305	#202
TSTCOM	C	3519	#202
TSTCOM2	C	3731	#202
TSTEXMEM	C	1361	#202
TSTINT	C	2426	#202
TSTINTEG	C	3107	#194
TSTINTEG	PAS	1216	#194
TSTLPT	C	2185	#202
TSTRKF45	C	4696	#194
TSTRKF45	PAS	4523	#194
TT_1040	WKS	80128	#290
TT_HELP	WKS	16640	#290
TTXC1014	PRT	329	#78
TUNE	COM	384	#52
TURKISH	COM	5167	#279
TURKISH	MUS	3950	#279
TURN	C	15605	#259
TURN	OBJ	12397	#259
TURTLE	LSP	3584	#134
TUTOR	BAS	896	#95
TUTOR1	TXT	8659	#68
TUTOR2		1632	#211
TUTOR2	TXT	7702	#68
TUTOR3	TXT	5598	#68
TUTOR4	TXT	3885	#68
TUTOR5	TXT	7393	#68
TUTORIAL		3978	#211
TUTORIAL		15293	#54
TUTORIAL	DOC	11968	#78
TUTORIAL	DOC	69139	#230
TV	WKS	2816	#289
TWINKLE	BAS	1663	#92
TWO	BAT	245	#59
TWO	DAT	4352	#76
TWOCOL	WRK	4096	#305
TWOLINE	BAS	102	#299
TWOSIDE	BAS	2176	#11
TWOSIDE	COM	256	#11
TXINSTR		12355	#291
TXT	ADS	23109	#159
TXTMUSIC	EXE	28672	#127
TXTPRO	DOC	1256	#84
TXTPRO	EXE	2560	#84
TXTSCAN	BAS	1024	#190
TYPE	BAS	716	#292
TYPE	ME	743	#277
TYPE	ME	882	#230
TYPE	NDX	2560	#116
TYPEMAN	COM	1065	#78

U

U-FILE	EXE	62592	#133
U-FORMAT	EXE	38656	#133
U-MIND	BAS	15233	#245
U-MIND	BQS	12259	#133
U-MIND	DOC	51120	#245
U-MIND	DQC	26518	#133
U-OPT	DOC	2124	#245
U-OPT	DQC	1434	#133
U-OPT	EQE	23034	#133
U-OPT	EXE	25601	#245
U-ZAP	EXE	62720	#133
UASMLS	DOC	3158	#114
UASMLS	EXE	22656	#114
UGASK	PIC	2362	#158
UGASK	PIC	2432	#157
UGASK	PIC	2432	#200
UGCOURSE	TXT	20608	#262
UGINTRO	TXT	8448	#262
UGLESSON	TXT	8192	#262
UGOS	PIC	2816	#157
UGOS	PIC	3038	#158
UGOS	PIC	3072	#200
UGPERFOR	TXT	8832	#262
UGPLAYER	TXT	17664	#262
UGQUIT	TXT	8576	#262
UGTALLY	TXT	14720	#262
UN	P	128	#67
UN1	CCF	1536	#306
UN1	WRK	4992	#306
UNDERLOF	COM	19	#186
UNDERLON	COM	19	#186
UNDOC	DOC	11212	#108
UNDOWS	DOC	2620	#201
UNDOWS	EXE	12800	#201
UNIQUE	AR	795	#132
UNIQUE	EXE	27392	#131
UNIQUE	MAN	463	#130
UNLUMP	C	1437	#149
UNLUMP	EXE	14336	#149
UNPROT	DOC	460	#67
UNPROT	TXT	423	#2
UNPROT2	TXT	1117	#28
UNROTATE	AR	1290	#132
UNROTATE	EXE	27648	#131
UNROTATE	MAN	1017	#130
UNSMALLP	BAT	124	#70
UNSMALLP	DOC	602	#70
UNSMALLP	RNT	11	#70

UNSQ	EXE	15744	#120
UNSQ	EXE	15744	#212
UNSQ	PAS	4603	#36
UNSQUEEZ	EXE	15744	#115
UNWS	ASM	8463	#81
UNWS	ASM	8576	#53
UNWS	BAS	768	#117
UNWS	COM	2944	#53
UNWS	EXE	2816	#81
UP	COM	128	#138
UPBEAT	BAS	128	#53
UPDATE	BAT	18	#9
UPDATMAR	BAS	9555	#90
UPDATORD	BAS	13793	#90
UPDATPER	BAS	11541	#90
UPDLOAD	BAS	4224	#48
UPDMEMB	BAS	768	#169
UPDSTKFL	ALL	266	#40
UPDSTKFL	DAT	266	#40
UPNUM	COM	256	#145
UPNUM	DOC	512	#145
UPPER	ASM	1792	#110
UPPER	COM	625	#110
UPPER	DOC	384	#110
UPVC	DOC	2552	#84
UPVC	DOC	2688	#92
USA		10641	#219
USA	PIC	16512	#13
USA-CENT		673	#219
USA-FUND		195	#219
USA-SUN		193	#219
USALIST	BAS	4608	#44
USASTATE	PIC	16512	#13
USATEMP	PIC	16512	#13
USER	DOC	3200	#262
USERS		256	#150
USETAX	PRG	3968	#102
USINGTHE	BAS	27066	#90
USMAP	PIC	16392	#220
USMAP	PIC	16392	#221
USMAP	PIC	16392	#222
USQ	COM	22016	#133
USQ2	DOC	1024	#280
USQ2	EXE	16512	#280
USQIBM	COM	22016	#144
USQIBM	COM	22016	#145
USQIBM	COM	22016	#185
USQIBM	DOC	637	#144
USQIBM	DOC	637	#145
USQIBM	DOC	637	#185
USQLC10	COM	12288	#140
USRINIT1	BAS	768	#152
USRINIT1	BAS	768	#212
USRINIT2	BAS	1664	#152
USRINIT2	BAS	1664	#212
UTIL	DAT	15062	#60
UTIL	DOC	17234	#162
UTIL	DOC	49152	#109
UTIL	EXE	22016	#60
UTIL	EXE	46080	#109
UTIL	HLP	15062	#60
UTIL102	COM	4352	#196
UTIL102	DOC	8576	#196
UTILITES	MAC	12160	#142
UTILITY	123	2	#257
UTILITY	AR	7001	#132
UTILITY	BAT	10112	#139
UTILITY	BLK	112640	#263
UTILITY	COM	8831	#235
UTILITY	DOC	7079	#279
UTILITY_	APL	8832	#108
UTILREAD	ME	1241	#109
UTMP	BAS	3840	#249
UTSCAN	BAS	1024	#52
UTSPACE	OBJ	128	#212
UTSPACE	OBJ	128	#152

V

VACATION	BAS	334	#292
VALIDATE	BAS	3968	#233
VAMPIRE	BAS	768	#228
VANDR	PIC	3328	#157
VANDR	PIC	3491	#158
VANDR	PIC	3584	#200
VARIABLE	BAS	1408	#105
VBARCHRT	VC	1152	#85
VBREAKEV	VC	5248	#85
VCCOM	DOC	2432	#92
VCHKBK1	VC	2176	#85
VCOPY	BAT	2637	#124
VCOPY	BAT	2688	#139
VDEL	COM	768	#28
VDEL	COM	768	#273
VDISK	ASM	8724	#34
VDISK	COM	672	#34
VDISK	COM	768	#145
VDISK2	ASM	8726	#34
VDISK2	COM	672	#34
VDL	COM	1024	#204
VDL	DOC	2048	#204
VECTS	EXE	12288	#138
VERB	C	13035	#259
VERB	OBJ	10553	#259
VERBIAGE		49792	#69
VERS_1	60	1357	#68
VERSION	C	384	#163
VI	BAT	11	#216
VIDEO	ASM	1351	#36
VIRTUAL	PRN	512	#70
VISICALC	UNP	2432	#184
VISICOM	DOC	2432	#206
VISIPROT	DOC	2688	#204
VOLKSWTR	KEY	256	#59
VOLKSWTR	KEY	256	#170
VOLSER	COM	1152	#34
VOLSER	COM	1152	#89
VOLSER	DOC	1295	#89
VPRINT	ASM	8065	#70
VPRINT	COM	1408	#70
VPRINT	DOC	1742	#70
VSPREAD	VC	3072	#85
VSPREAD1	VC	1536	#85
VTYPE	C	3968	#138
VTYPE	DOC	2688	#183
VTYPE	DOC	2688	#138
VTYPE	EXE	11776	#183
VTYPE	EXE	11776	#138
VUE	BAS	5504	#190
VUE	EXE	11776	#142
VW128FIX	BAT	2165	#93
VW128FIX	INS	31	#93
VXPRINTP	TBL	512	#236
VXPRINTQ	TBL	512	#236
VXPRINTR	TBL	512	#236
VXPRINTS	TBL	512	#236
VXPRINTT	TBL	512	#236
VXPRINTU	TBL	512	#236
VXPRINTV	TBL	512	#236

W

W2		384	#215
W20	COM	3456	#141
WA-TOR	000	16896	#217
WA-TOR	COM	23921	#217
WA-TOR	DOC	9600	#217
WA-TOR	PAS	34497	#217
WACHTAUF	COM	21379	#279
WAHP	SMP	1792	#246
WAIT	COM	128	#28
WAITIN	BAS	128	#11
WALLS	BAS	227	#176
WASH	COM	3328	#9
WASH	DOC	15872	#9
WATKINS	NL	3072	#157
WATOR	BAK	386	#298
WATOR	DOC	382	#298
WATORCOL	COM	15435	#298
WATORCOL	PAS	10857	#298
WATORMON	COM	15435	#298
WATORMON	PAS	10857	#298
WB-UPTLE	BAS	2432	#62
WC	C	1664	#163
WC	DOC	1920	#163
WC	EXE	10240	#163
WDJ20B	SMP	1792	#246
WDOW	SMP	1792	#246
WEAPINIT	BAS	896	#297
WEAPONS	DAT	1152	#297
WEATHER	BAS	6656	#45
WEBER	NL	4096	#158
WEBER	NL	4096	#157
WEBER	SCR	3537	#158

WEEKDAY	C	1850	#216
WEIGHTFM	BAS	3968	#66
WELCOME		308	#150
WELCOME		640	#212
WELCOME		808	#280
WELCOME	BAS	4224	#15
WELCOMEG		1280	#212
WELLTEMP	BAS	8485	#203
WESTENDP	NL	4096	#158
WHAT	ASM	14491	#82
WHAT	COM	266	#82
WHEEL	BAS	2048	#203
WHEREIS	ASM	7242	#255
WHEREIS	ASM	7242	#256
WHEREIS	BAS	3817	#256
WHEREIS	COM	451	#255
WHEREIS	COM	451	#256
WHEREIS	COM	512	#110
WHEREIS	COM	512	#273
WHEREIS	DOC	1024	#110
WHEREIS	DOC	1024	#273
WHITE	NL	19456	#158
WHITHEAD	NL	3072	#156
WIBM	SMP	1792	#246
WIDE	APP	10880	#305
WIDEDOC	WRK	16767	#305
WIDTST	PRN	256	#305
WILL		12648	#193
WILLOW	COM	1033	#279
WILLOW	MUS	485	#279
WILLTELL	BAS	384	#37
WILLTELL	DAT	4096	#37
WINDCHIL	BAS	2048	#73
WIZARD	BAS	27520	#71
WIZARD	BAS	27520	#274
WMD	SMP	1792	#246
WMTELL	BAS	5444	#80
WNDWSY	WRK	3840	#305
WOLPERT	NL	7168	#158
WOMBAT	BAS	15232	#1
WORD	UNP	2304	#184
WORDCNT	AR	829	#132
WORDCNT	EXE	26624	#131
WORDCNT	MAN	381	#130
WORDNEW	UNP	2688	#184
WORDPLAY	BAS	2571	#203
WORDS	BAS	2560	#18
WORK	CRT	2304	#151
WORK	NAM	128	#151
WORK	TRN	3712	#151
WORKCOST	FRM	233	#295
WORKCOST	PRG	1269	#295
WORKFILE	BAS	13952	#66
WORKFILE	DAT	384	#66
WORLDMAP	BAS	9472	#93
WORM	PIC	16512	#12
WORM1	BAS	1408	#20
WORM2	PIC	16512	#12
WORMCITY	BAS	10880	#83
WRAP	COM	133	#113
WRDST	CTF	512	#305
WRITEC	C	818	#216
WRITECOM	BAS	1152	#145
WRITERS	GDE	2518	#160
WRITERS	GDE	2840	#159
WRITES	C	944	#216
WRITEUS	TXT	5783	#159
WRITING	NL	3072	#200
WRT	DOC	1152	#145
WRT	DOC	1536	#204
WRTE	COM	512	#204
WRTE	COM	512	#145
WRTP	COM	512	#204
WRTP	COM	512	#145
WS	KEY	1254	#181
WS-ASCII	BAS	896	#46
WS-DOS	BAS	4354	#38
WS-DOS	BAS	4739	#201
WSFF1	TXT	14464	#303
WSFF2	TXT	79872	#303
WSFF3	TXT	3712	#303
WSFF4	TXT	19968	#303
WSFIX2	TXT	2688	#53
WSMOD	DOC	4096	#53
WSPATCH2	TXT	10752	#53
WTE	SMP	2944	#246
WUMPUS	BAS	10368	#24
WX	EXE	73618	#68
WXO	EXE	82976	#68

X

X2COLOR	COM	128	#140
XAPRIN	BAS	1536	#258
XC	C	24797	#149
XC	DOC	2237	#149
XC	EXE	19072	#149
XDIR	COM	1920	#80
XDIR	DOC	1844	#80
XENIX	ASM	7296	#142
XFER	HLP	2519	#150
XFERLIST		159	#150
XLBFUN	C	9216	#148
XLBIND	C	1664	#148
XLCONT	C	17664	#148
XLDBUG	C	4224	#148
XLDMEM	C	6912	#148
XLEVAL	C	8064	#148
XLFIO	C	9472	#148
XLFTAB	C	5760	#148
XLGLOB	C	2304	#148
XLINIT	C	3456	#148
XLIO	C	3072	#148
XLISP	C	1792	#148
XLISP	DOC	27049	#134
XLISP	EXE	43776	#134
XLISP	EXE	45674	#148
XLISP	H	7078	#148
XLISP	MEM	54784	#148
XLJUMP	C	2432	#148
XLLIST	C	19072	#148
XLMATH	C	6272	#148
XLOBJ	C	16896	#148
XLPRIN	C	3072	#148
XLREAD	C	8832	#148
XLSETF	C	2048	#148
XLSTR	C	4480	#148
XLSTUB	C	256	#148
XLSUBR	C	4480	#148
XLSYM	C	4736	#148
XLSYS	C	3328	#148
XMAS	BAS	10496	#47
XMASCARD	BAS	2944	#56
XMODEM	ASM	52521	#54
XMODEM	COM	9728	#54
XMODEM	DOC	7621	#54
XMODVMS	LBR	30208	#286
XOFF	DOC	1353	#34
XOFF	MRG	4448	#34
XREF	BAS	5504	#145
XREF	EXE	26624	#162
XREF	PAS	22043	#36
XREFMOD	BAS	5888	#49
XREP	ASM	6818	#285
XREP	OBJ	303	#285
XT370	DOC	14534	#110
XTAB	BAS	4224	#88
XUP	BAS	2048	#89
XWING	BAS	34688	#174
XWING	BAS	34688	#274
XX	HED	128	#48
XXX		many	
XXX		582	#155
XXX		1408	#170
XXX		2457	#184
XXX	BAK	1176	#179
XXX	BAK	3072	#126
XXX	BOT	13	#174
XXXAUTOF	DAT	4	#75
XXXPAD	FM	5066	#75
XXXX	DAT	1	#190
XXXXXXXX	XX1	3	#161
XXXXXXXX	XX2	3	#161
XXXXXXXX	XX3	3	#161
XXXXXXXX	XX4	3	#161
XXXXXXXX	XX5	3	#161
XYZ	FM	4986	#75

Y

YAHTZEE	BAS	9728	#14
YAHTZEE	BAS	15104	#1
YAHTZEE	BAS	16000	#20
YAHTZEE	BAS	20608	#61

YESORNO	BAS	2560	#66
YESTER	BAS	512	#24
YESTRDAY	SNG	520	#127
YNKEDODL	SNG	244	#127
YOUNG	NL	3072	#157
YOURMENU	BAS	9344	#66
YR17	BAR	384	#14
YR20	BAR	512	#14
YREP	ASM	6960	#285
YREP	OBJ	310	#285

Z

Z	ASM	1419	#258
Z	COM	126	#258
ZAP'EM	BAS	4224	#37
ZAP'EM	BAS	5888	#71
ZAP-EM	BAS	4431	#35
ZAPDEB	BAS	3105	#256
ZAPDEB	DOC	408	#256
ZAPTRE	BAS	3025	#256
ZAPTRE	DOC	397	#256
ZELLER	BAS	640	#6
ZIPCLEAR	BAS	3584	#66
ZOOSORT	BAS	33920	#27
ZOOTIME	BAS	34048	#27
ZORK3	UNP	768	#184
ZPRINT	ASM	7060	#285
ZPRINT	OBJ	307	#285
ZSQ	EXE	19840	#185
ZSQ-ZUSQ	DOC	1792	#185
ZUSQ	EXE	13696	#185

By Subject

6.0 MISCELLANEOUS

Glossary

AI	Artificial Intelligence; a program that appears to give a computer thinking ability.
algorithm	a series of instructions designed to solve a specific problem.
alphanumeric	letters and numbers.
application program	a program designed to solve a specific problem. See program
ASCII "ass-key"	American Standard Code for Information Interchange; the standard codes for a character set understood by all computers.
BASIC	Beginner's All purpose Symbolic Instruction Code. A programming language.
baud	transmission rate of information (bits per second). 300 or 1200 baud communication over phone lines is most common.
binary	the binary number system using 2 as its base and using only the digits 0 and 1.
bit	BInary digiT; primary unit of information used by computers, either on or off, 1 or 0.
boot	initially loading the operating system into the computer, starting or restarting.
buffer	a temporary storage of data; e.g. between computer and printer. see data
bug	a program error.
bus	a standardized circuit interface which usually allows the addition of plug-in PC boards. See PCB
byte	eight bits = one byte the basic unit of information used by a computer. 1 ASCII character requires 1 byte of storage. See bit
CAD/CAM	Computer Aided Design/Computer Aided Manufacturing.
chip	a small piece of silicon containing integrated circuits.
code	instructions of a program. Usually in human readable form.
communications program	a program used to transmit information over a telephone line through a modem. See modem

compiler	a program that translates a "high-level" language to machine code understood by the computer. See language; computer language
computer	an electronic machine that manipulates information to provide desired, useful results.
computer language	language a computer can understand.
console	a keyboard and display device for communicating with the computer. See CRT; monitor; screen
CP/M	a popular operating system used on 8-bit microcomputers. See DOS
CPU	Central Processing Unit; the primary functioning unit, the 'brains' of the computer.
CRT	Cathode Ray Tube; television-like display tube. See monitor; screen
cursor	a position indicator, usually a dash or rectangle where the next character will be typed on the CRT. See CRT; input
daisy wheel printer	a typewriter-quality slow speed printer. See dot matrix printer
data	information stored in a computer.
data base	an organized body of information stored in a computer such as a mailing list.
disk	magnetic media which spins to allow input or retrieval of information. See floppy disk; hard disk; input
diskette	small disk used in microcomputers.
disk drive	reads and writes information to and from a disk or diskette.
DOS	Disk Operating System; a program which controls the flow of information to or from a disk.
documentation	the printed instructions that come with a computer, software, program or peripheral equipment. See program; peripheral; software
dot matrix printer	a fast printer whose characters are composed of dots, widely used to print data but required for graphics. See daisy wheel printer
editor	a program that manipulates text files.
electronic mail	messages exchanged by linked computers, through bulletin boards or through commercial services.
emulate	to use a computer to operate on data and instructions prepared for a computer of a different type.
execute	to perform a computer instruction or series of instructions.
file	organized collection of related information.

filename	the character string used to refer to a disk file. A PC DOS example is "NAME.EXT"
firmware	a program stored permanently in PROM or ROM. See PROM; ROM; RAM
floppy Disk	a flexible magnetic disk for storage of data. See data
flowchart	a diagrammatic representation of the sequence of events involved in solution of a problem.
format	to prepare a new disk to receive information; a specific arrangement of data.
graphics	a pictorial representation of data such as a graph, bar-column or drawing.
hard copy	printed output.
hardware	physical components of a computer. See software
hexadecimal	a numbering system based on 16 as compared to the decimal system based on 10.
input	information entered into a computer.
interactive	two-way immediate communication between computer and human.
interface	a connection to complete an operation; a physical connection between two systems or devices.
interpreter	program which allows a computer to perform instructions written in a language such as BASIC.
I/O	Input/Output; information exchanged between computer and peripheral equipment.
joystick	a device that inputs positional information to the computer. See mouse; input
K	computer shorthand for 1024. e.g. K=1024, 64K=65,536. Used to designate the number of bytes in RAM. See Kilobyte; RAM
Kilobyte	1024 bytes, same as "K".
keyboard	a typewriter-like set of keys used for input of data. See terminal; input; data
language	a set of characters and/or symbols combined under specific rules to form a "high-level" language understood by the computer through a compiler or interpreter. See compiler.
loop	a set of instructions which are repeated by a computer.
machine code	the internal language used by the computer.
machine readable	information stored in a way that can be retrieved by a computer.

mainframe	large capacity computer usually of large physical size.
Megabyte	one million bytes.
menu	the options listed on the CRT for selection by operator. See CRT
merge	combine sets of sorted information or files.
microprocessor	a CPU on a silicon chip. See CPU
modem	MOdulator/DEModulator; a device for transmitting computer information over telephone lines.
monitor	a television-like display device. See CRT
motherboard	the primary computer circuit board.
mouse	a device that inputs positional information to the computer. See joystick
multi-user	a computer that can simultaneously support more than one terminal. See terminal; network
network	a number of computers capable of transmitting to each other. See multi-user
off-line	Not under control of central processor; not in operation. See on-line
on-line	under the control of the central processor; turned on. See off-line
operating system	fundamental instructions on which a computer operates. DOS is the PC's operating system. See DOS; CP/M
output	information generated by the computer to the CRT, printer or other peripheral device. See CRT; peripheral device
PCB or PC Board	Printed Circuit Board; integrated circuit board.
peripheral	an auxiliary device that is connected to the computer. e.g. printer, plotter, modem.
plotter	a peripheral device that produces hardcopy graphics. See peripheral; graphics; hardcopy
program	a series of instructions designed to perform a task or solve a specific problem on a computer. See software
programmer	One who writes programs. See program
PROM	Programmable Read Only Memory; changeable ROM. See ROM; RAM
protocol	rules or conventions for communicating between devices. See syntax
RAM	Random Access Memory; memory that is lost when power is off. See ROM

RAMdisk	a simulated disk drive using a computer's RAM memory, faster than a magnetic disk but lost when the power is turned off. See RAM
ROM	Read Only Memory; memory that is retained when power is off. See RAM; PROM
run	start the operation of a program.
screen	a television-like display device. See CRT; monitor
serial	a way of sending data sequentially on a single wire. Modems and some printers communicate serially.
software	a system of instructions that directs the computer operation, usually on a disk; a program. See program; hardware
sort	to rearrange information into a prescribed order. See data
source code	the program as written by the programmer.
spooler	a buffer between the computer and a printer to allow the computer to continue processing while the printer is printing. See buffer
storage device	equipment for storing information such as on a disk or tape. See disk drive; hard disk
syntax	the grammar rules of a computer language.
terminal	a keyboard and monitor connected to a computer. See keyboard; monitor
word processor	a program for processing or editing text.

How to get copies of disks

You may order copies of disks from us or contact your local computer club. Check a current issue of a PC related magazine for a club near you. In some cases you may also contact the authors of programs directly for the latest versions of programs.

Adding to the library

We are always looking for new and interesting programs to include in the library. If you have any we would like to hear from you. Corrected and later versions of programs already in the library would also be appreciated. It is the policy of PC Software Interest Group to compensate authors/contributors of programs which become part of the library with complimentary selections from the library. An insertion form is printed on one of the following pages.

ORDER FORM #41

PC Software Interest Group
1030 E Duane Suite J
Sunnyvale, CA 94086
(408) 730-9291

ship to: ______________________
____
____
____

Circle disk numbers desired

1	2	3	4	5	6	7	8	9	10	11	12	13	14	15	16	17	18	19	20
21	22	23	24	25	26	27	28	29	30	31	32	33	34	35	36	37	38	39	40
41	42	43	44	45	46	47	48	49	50	51	52	53	54	55	56	57	58	59	60
61	62	63	64	65	66	67	68	69	70	71	72	73	74	75	76	77	78	79	80
81	82	83	84	85	86	87	88	89	90	91	92	93	94	95	96	97	98	99	100
101	102	103	104	105	106	107	108	109	110	111	112	113	114	115	116	117	118	119	120
121	122	123	124	125	126	127	128	129	130	131	132	133	134	135	136	137	138	139	140
141	142	143	144	145	146	147	148	149	150	151	152	153	154	155	156	157	158	159	160
161	162	163	164	165	166	167	168	169	170	171	172	173	174	175	176	177	178	179	180
181	182	183	184	185	186	187	188	189	190	191	192	193	194	195	196	197	198	199	200
201	202	203	204	205	206	207	208	209	210	211	212	213	214	215	216	217	218	219	220
221	222	223	224	225	226	227	228	229	230	231	232	233	234	235	236	237	238	239	240
241	242	243	244	245	246	247	248	249	250	251	252	253	254	255	256	257	258	259	260
261	262	263	264	265	266	267	268	269	270	271	272	273	274	275	276	277	278	279	280
281	282	283	284	285	286	287	288	289	290	291	292	293	294	295	296	297	298	299	300
301	302	303	304	305	306														

Total # __________ x $6.00 = __________

( ) Copy of this Directory $8.95 __________

Sub-total __________

California residents add 6.5/7% state tax __________

$4.00 Shipping and handling ($10 foreign) __________

( ) 1 year PC-SIG membership $15 ($25 foreign) __________

Total __________

Method of payment: ( ) check enclosed ( ) Visa ( ) M/C

Card No.__________________ exp date__________ sig______________________

Foreign orders should include payment in US dollars by credit card, International money order or check drawn on US bank.

PC-SIG SOFTWARE LIBRARY SUBMISSION FORM

PC Software Interest Group (PC-SIG)
1030 E Duane Suite J
Sunnyvale, CA 94086

name/
address ______________________________
____
____
____

phone # ( )______________________

SOFTWARE SUBMISSION:

Type: ( ) new public domain program(s)
( ) new user-supported program—suggested donation $ ________
( ) corrected versions of programs already in library

[disk #]/filename(s) ______________________________

Source language: ( ) BASIC ( ) Pascal ( ) Assembly ( ) c ( ) other ________

Are you the author ? ( ) Yes ( ) No—who is? ______________________

Special requirements: ( ) color ( ) monochrome DOS version No ________

other ______________________________

Please describe each file enclosed. A disk file containing a one line file description in a format similiar to what is presented in this book would be helpful.

These programs are to the best of my knowledge in the public domain or if I wrote them I hereby place in the public domain or release them as user-supported programs. They may be freely distributed.

Signed ______________________________ date ________

What library disk(s) would you like in return? ______________________

ORDER FORM **#41**

PC Software Interest Group
1030 E Duane Suite J
Sunnyvale, CA 94086
(408) 730-9291

ship to: ____________________
____
____
____

Circle disk numbers desired

1	2	3	4	5	6	7	8	9	10	11	12	13	14	15	16	17	18	19	20
21	22	23	24	25	26	27	28	29	30	31	32	33	34	35	36	37	38	39	40
41	42	43	44	45	46	47	48	49	50	51	52	53	54	55	56	57	58	59	60
61	62	63	64	65	66	67	68	69	70	71	72	73	74	75	76	77	78	79	80
81	82	83	84	85	86	87	88	89	90	91	92	93	94	95	96	97	98	99	100
101	102	103	104	105	106	107	108	109	110	111	112	113	114	115	116	117	118	119	120
121	122	123	124	125	126	127	128	129	130	131	132	133	134	135	136	137	138	139	140
141	142	143	144	145	146	147	148	149	150	151	152	153	154	155	156	157	158	159	160
161	162	163	164	165	166	167	168	169	170	171	172	173	174	175	176	177	178	179	180
181	182	183	184	185	186	187	188	189	190	191	192	193	194	195	196	197	198	199	200
201	202	203	204	205	206	207	208	209	210	211	212	213	214	215	216	217	218	219	220
221	222	223	224	225	226	227	228	229	230	231	232	233	234	235	236	237	238	239	240
241	242	243	244	245	246	247	248	249	250	251	252	253	254	255	256	257	258	259	260
261	262	263	264	265	266	267	268	269	270	271	272	273	274	275	276	277	278	279	280
281	282	283	284	285	286	287	288	289	290	291	292	293	294	295	296	297	298	299	300
301	302	303	304	305	306														

Total # __________ x $6.00 = __________

( ) Copy of this Directory $8.95 __________

Sub-total __________

California residents add 6.5/7% state tax __________

$4.00 Shipping and handling ($10 foreign) __________

( ) 1 year PC-SIG membership $15 ($25 foreign) __________

Total __________

Method of payment: ( ) check enclosed ( ) Visa ( ) M/C

Card No.__________________ exp date__________ sig____________________

Foreign orders should include payment in US dollars by credit card, International money order or check drawn on US bank.

PC-SIG SOFTWARE LIBRARY SUBMISSION FORM

PC Software Interest Group (PC-SIG)
1030 E Duane Suite J
Sunnyvale, CA 94086

name/
address ______________________________

____

____

phone # ( )______________________

SOFTWARE SUBMISSION:

Type: ( ) new public domain program(s)
( ) new user-supported program—suggested donation $ ________
( ) corrected versions of programs already in library

[disk #]/filename(s) ______________________________

Source language: ( ) BASIC ( ) Pascal ( ) Assembly ( ) c ( ) other ________

Are you the author ? ( ) Yes ( ) No—who is? ______________________

Special requirements: ( ) color ( ) monochrome DOS version No ________

other ______________________________

Please describe each file enclosed. A disk file containing a one line file description in a format similiar to what is presented in this book would be helpful.

These programs are to the best of my knowledge in the public domain or if I wrote them I hereby place in the public domain or release them as user-supported programs. They may be freely distributed.

Signed ______________________________ date ____________

What library disk(s) would you like in return? ______________________